CLASSICAL READINGS
IN CHRISTIAN APOLOGETICS

A.D. 100-1800

CLASSICAL READINGS
IN CHRISTIAN APOLOGETICS

A.D. 100-1800

L. Russ Bush

Academie
Books

1415 Lake Drive, S.E., Grand Rapids, Michigan 49506

from Zondervan Publishing House

CLASSICAL READINGS IN CHRISTIAN APOLOGETICS, A.D. 100-1800
Copyright © 1983 by The Zondervan Corporation
Grand Rapids, Michigan

Library of Congress Cataloging in Publication Data
Main entry under title:

Classical readings in Christian apologetics, A.D. 100–
1800.

  Includes bibliographies.
  1. Apologetics—Addresses, essays, lectures.
I. Bush, L. Russ, 1944–
BT1105.C63 1983   239   83-12372
ISBN 0-310-45641-X

Edited by Norma Camp
Designed by Louise Bauer

Printed in the United States of America
83 84 85 86 87 88/9 8 7 6 5 4 3 2 1

To

John P. Newport
and
Milton Ferguson

my teachers,
colleagues,
and friends

CONTENTS

PREFACE

Apologetics is a confusing term to many younger theological students, because the English word *apology* has been applied as a synonym for excuses, especially those where one is sorrowfully admitting guilt and asking for forgiveness. The term is used by the writers of the Bible, however, to describe a reasonable and forceful defense. In New Testament Greek, the noun form *apologia* means primarily "a speech made in defense," though nothing forbids including the idea of a written defense. In the King James Version it is translated "answer" in Acts 25:16; 1 Corinthians 9:3; 2 Timothy 4:16; and, of course, the famous "answer" all Christians are to be ready to give for the hope that is within them is an *apologia* (1 Peter 3:15).

In a sense the Bible itself serves as an apology for true religion. John tells us that he writes for the express purpose of winning converts to Christ, and Luke undoubtedly put together his two-volume work as a substantial apologetic to or for Theophilus. Matthew clearly uses the promise-fulfillment argument to speak to his Jewish brethren and persuade them that Jesus is the Christ. Mark, no less than the others, has an apologetic approach to evangelism, and Paul's famous 1 Corinthians 15 is only one place out of many where Paul clearly uses a persuasive argument to confirm the faith of his readers. Thus apology as a theological term means a stated defense of Christian faith.

Link gives this definition of apology:

> Whereas the word apology denotes a particular defence of the Christian faith, apologetics is the working out and presentation of intellectual, scientific and philosophical arguments which may underlie such an apology. In the early church Apologists like Aristides, Justin Martyr, Tertullian and Origen raised the apology to the status of a distinct genre of theological literature.[1]

Apologetic works are primarily intellectual in their orientation. No rule says that an appeal to emotion cannot serve to persuade many to accept the truthfulness of Christianity, but the thrust of the word apologetics seems to put it more at home in the courtroom than at a musical concert. In both settings Christ may be honored, but the method of presentation would be different.

Studies in Christian apologetics are certainly not new. However, there does seem to be a renewed interest in apologetic studies in recent years. Several excellent secondary-source textbooks on the views of many contemporary and histor-

---

[1]Hans-Georg Link, "Apology" in *The New International Dictionary of New Testament Theology*, 3 vols., Engl. ed., ed. Colin Brown (Grand Rapids: Zondervan, 1975), 1:51.

ical apologists are currently available. Nevertheless, a person's education is not complete if only secondary sources have been read—no matter how fine those sources may be. This observation is true in many areas of study but especially in apologetics.

The collection of apologetic writings reprinted in this book is only a sample of the vast literature available to the scholar. Though these selections are readily available in large theological libraries, their relevance is by no means limited to academicians. Pastors, denominational leaders, students, vocational church workers, and dedicated lay people can strengthen their faith and continue their spiritual growth by contact with some of these great thinkers in Christian history. As the dear Lord has blessed these essays through the centuries, may He continue to use them for His purposes.

Special note: In some of the writings reprinted in this book the Scripture references had originally been added as editorial footnotes. These have been incorporated into the text in this volume in modern form and enclosed in brackets.

ACKNOWLEDGMENTS

Mary Anne Barroz may have spent as many hours working on this book as I have. She surely served as an efficient and pleasant secretary, putting up with my frequent instances of inefficiency and unpleasantness. Debra Permenter also added her secretarial skills, which are considerable and for which I am grateful. My faculty colleagues at Southwestern Seminary are among the finest theological educators to be found, and many of them have contributed ideas and suggestions, some of which related to this book! The administration and trustees of Southwestern generously allowed me to spend my sabbatical year in Cambridge, England, and much of my final editing was done at the Tyndale House Library there. The new version of Augustine was prepared at the suggestion and the encouragement of Professor Henry Chadwick, and the Cambridge University Library (a magnificent storehouse of information) provided the resources necessary for completing the newly translated material in the manuscript. Mary Zengeni, our English neighbor and gracious friend, typed the chapter on Augustine as well as the final chapter. Authors' wives are generally mentioned in paragraphs such as these, but my wife, Cindy, deserves more than a mention. She gave up many hours that rightfully belonged to her in order to let me "do my work." Cindy, Barbara Walker, and Kay Courtade contributed their proofreading skills in the final stages of this project. To all of the above I want to express my deepest appreciation.

INTRODUCTION

Truth in a sinful world is always controversial. God Himself is Truth Itself. To believe that God exists is to believe that Truth exists (though historically the reverse has not always been the case). God's Word is truth revealed to humans in a sinful world, and what it says has been challenged by the world's spokesmen from the beginning. Yet whenever God's truth has been opposed, defenders of that truth have raised their banner, and the battles have raged through the centuries.

The term *Christian apologetics* is, like many terms, twofold in its meaning. It can refer to the defense of the faith, or it can name that secondary discipline of the academic study of the methods and arguments of the outstanding historical defenders of Christian truth. In the academic context it is common to label things in order to get a rational hold on them. Two useful apologetic categories are "popular" and "systematic." Popular works are written for those people who have had no previous formal study in an area. Systematic works are written for professional scholars who want a more technical presentation.

A general defense of certain key elements of Christian truth in light of perennial objections and recurring, standard alternatives would be likely to be written in a popular style. A modern popular approach can be found in Josh McDowell's *Evidence That Demands a Verdict*.[1]

Systematic apologetic works are more comprehensive and philosophically relevant. A systematic apologetic is a defense of Christian truth in light of significant historical and contemporary objections both to the epistemological method used and to the content of Christian truth. Modern examples of the systematic approach include Norman Geisler's excellent introductory study *Christian Apologetics*[2] and E. J. Carnell's important volume *An Introduction to Christian Apologetics*.[3]

This contemporary academic division into systematic and popular styles does not apply with equal precision, however, to the

---

[1]Arrowhead Springs, Colo.: Campus Crusade for Christ International, 1972.
[2]Grand Rapids: Baker, 1976.
[3]Grand Rapids: Eerdmans, 1948.

major apologetic writings throughout the history of Christianity. Many times the styles are mixed. The selections in this present volume are taken from among the most significant apologetic writings the Christian community produced in the first eighteen hundred years of its history. Both popular and systematic elements may be found.

Selections from the Bible are not included in this volume; nevertheless an excellent summary of biblical apologetics has been given by Bernard Ramm.[4] Ramm discusses passages dealing with the knowledge of God, the veracity of the system of biblical faith, or the criteria for establishing elements of biblical truth.

In the early postbiblical days of the church the most serious intellectual opposition to Christian doctrine came from the world of Greek philosophy. Several of the classical apologetic essays in this book come from this time period.

Justin Martyr (c100–167), born in Samaria at Flavius Neopolis (Ancient Shechem), set himself to defend Christianity from ridicule and misrepresentation by the pagans. He argued that Christianity fulfilled the highest goals of all pagan philosophers and that it should be seen as the most worthy of all philosophies to be believed. Justin contended that divine reason (logos) resided in Jesus Christ. Justin is the first writer after Paul who fully seems to have understood the concept of a Christian world view where all truth is interrelated horizontally to all other truths as well as vertically to God.

Athenagoras, the Christian philosopher of Athens, Greece, was one of the most articulate believers of the second century A.D. His defense of the faith before Marcus Aurelius was clear and decisive. Incest, cannibalism, and atheism were the standard charges leveled at the Christians in that day, and Athenagoras thoroughly destroyed each objection and then offered positive reasons for Christian beliefs. He was an effective popular apologist.

Iranaeus almost qualifies as one of the apostolic Fathers. He was closely related to John through Polycarp, and he emphasized his faithfulness to the apostolic tradition. Iranaeus expounded a rather fully developed ecclesiastical tradition, however. His

---

[4]*International Standard Bible Encyclopedia*, rev. ed., 5 vols. (Grand Rapids: Eerdmans, 1979—), 1:189–92.

staunch written opposition to the Gnostics has turned out to be one of our few available sources for discovering who and what Gnostics were. In addition, he vigorously defended the divine authority of the New Testament canon and of orthodox doctrine. Iranaeus was the major Christian spokesman in the late second century.

Tertullian, the African apologist, was one of the greatest of the early Latin Fathers. He argued for Christianity by appealing to the absurdity of persecution, to the true authority of Scripture, and to the factual evidence that supports orthodox faith. His brilliance and his versatility made him a powerful apologist for Christianity in the days of the late second century.

Few works from the early Christian church compare in importance with Origen's apologetic masterpiece *Contra Celsum* (*Against Celsus*). Many see this as the culmination of the whole apologetic movement of the second and third centuries. Between A.D. 177–80 Celsus (an unknown eclectic Platonist) had written a comprehensive attack on Christian faith and against the church as an organized society. Ambrose, a wealthy Gnostic converted to Christ by Origen, came across this book some seventy years later and asked Origen, the successor to Clement at the Catechetical School in Alexandria, to formulate a reply. Origen reluctantly wrote the reply in A.D. 248. His keen, logical, penetrating mind so completely demolished the arguments that even today his work is considered the most significant intellectual defense of the faith to come from the Ante-Nicene period.

Athanasius was the fourth-century champion of orthodoxy. Though he was not officially a part of the Council of Nicea (325), his writings defending orthodox christology supported the position of Bishop Alexander whose view was finally recognized to be the correct position. Athanasius was appointed to be the new bishop when Alexander died and thus became the focal point of attack by the Arians during the next generation. His defense of the Christian faith was, however, comprehensive and sound. His intellectual skill perhaps saved the church from the curse of a pagan intellectualism that had begun to make inroads in his day.

Augustine was the most outstanding theologian the church had seen since Paul. In his early life he was drawn toward skepticism, but his dramatic conversion changed all that and his intellectual skills were turned toward the defense of the faith against the

pagan critics and skeptics. Although he had previously been drawn
to the optimistic humanism of Neoplatonism, his biblical studies
convinced him that a more radical diagnosis of man's condition
was necessary and that salvation must be purely by God's grace.
Augustine's apologetic skills were directed primarily at those
pagans who blamed Christians for the calamities that befell Rome.
However, his message of truth transcends the controversies of his
own historical moment.

Augustinian thought dominated European Christianity in the
Middle Ages. One of the most interesting representatives of this
Augustinian age was Anselm of Canterbury. His contribution to
Christian apologetics is an early example of what would later be
seen as a distinct Scholasticism. He defends his faith by defending
the existence of God. What makes his theistic reasoning more interesting is that he was not writing a proof for unbelievers, but for
believers. Anselm is clearly a systematic apologist; however, his
works are not as comprehensive as those of either Augustine or
Aquinas.

Thomas Aquinas was the greatest philosophical theologian of
the medieval church. The literary output of this man was enormous. His *Summa contra Gentiles* was a lengthy apologetic manual for Christian missionaries. His *Summa Theologica* is the best-
known theological document of the period. Aquinas is famous for
his acceptance of Aristotelian philosophical categories as opposed
to the Platonism of most earlier writing theologians. He clearly
separates philosophy and theology (e.g., the universe might be
eternal if philosophy were ultimate, but by divine revelation we
learn and believe in creation); nevertheless, he does argue that
God's existence can be established philosophically as well as by
revelation. When kept in context, however, the "five ways"[5] of
philosophically showing God's existence do not destroy the value,
even the necessity, of divine revelation for Aquinas. But this was a
clear shift in apologetic method from that used by Anselm.

John Calvin, the outstanding French Reformer, is known primarily for his distinct return to the older Augustinian theology.
Calvinism is a term that applies most directly, not to the writings
of Calvin alone, but to the theological stance taken at the Synod of

---

[5]*Summa Theologica*, Q 2, Art. 3.

Dort (1618) in its response to the teachings of Jacobus Arminius. Of course, that stance and Calvin's writings are closely related. Calvin, as a young man, wrote the *Institutes* (1536) in an attempt to summarize all Bible doctrine. Because he was such a good thinker, his theological system was methodologically consistent. This consistency is at the heart of apologetic concerns, and for that reason Calvin is included in this volume even though he is not generally considered to be an apologist as such.

Joseph Butler, English bishop and scholar, wrote the *Analogy of Religion*, which proved to be the greatest theological book of the early eighteenth century. He did more to discredit the deistic liberalism that was sweeping English church life than any other Christian writer. Butler's method was empirically based in factual evidences. Difficulties found in Christianity are analogous to the difficulties found in nature, he argued. We do not give up our belief in the truthfulness of our knowledge of nature; so we can with equal justification maintain our faith in Christianity. This simple appeal to the probability argument for truth has been enormously popular with many Christian writers since Butler.

William Paley was not an original thinker, but he had a marvelous ability to explain plain arguments. He believed that anyone should be able to see that the order of the world leads clearly to a belief in the existence and the goodness of God. On both internal and external grounds Paley argued that Christianity was the true religion revealed by God. His books became textbooks at Cambridge and had a profound and lasting influence. In fact, Paley's evidentialist arguments were never refuted, though their persuasive power did decline in the light of nineteenth-century science and evolutionary philosophy.

These twelve writers characteristically represent the developments in apologetic studies prior to the nineteenth century. The selections reprinted here are by no means exhaustive, but they are a fair sampling, and they do illustrate the various methods, styles, and issues that have faced Christian thinkers in the past. The rather radical apologetic changes of the nineteenth century were rooted in the philosophy of Kant as it was translated by the work of Hegel. This Kantian shift was at the epistemological level, and the implications of this shift are only now being fully understood. Modern apologists must contend for the faith in the face of a philosophical naturalism and a cleverly selective skepticism that earlier apologists did not confront. Nevertheless, there should be more than antiquarian interest in these classical works, for our lives can be enriched by studying the writers included in this volume. Truth is still truth despite the Kantian impasse.

∽ 1 ∽

JUSTIN MARTYR
(A.D. c100–c167)

Justin's pupil Tatian referred to him as "the most admirable Justin." Tertullian spoke of him as a "philosopher and martyr." Hippolytus called him simply "the martyr." The consensus of scholarly opinion is that Justin is one of the greatest of the early Christian apologists.

Justin was born in Flavia Neapolis, a city in Samaria about twenty-five miles (40 km.) inland from the Mediterranean Sea. Though scholars cannot be certain, they generally believed that he was born around A.D. 100.

Clearly Justin was a dedicated student, for his writings demonstrate a familiarity with a wide range of Greek literature and pagan thought. In his *Dialogue with Trypho* Justin describes how he had studied one after the other of the philosophical systems— Stoicism, Aristotelianism, Pythagoreanism, and Platonism and then came to Christianity.

Justin describes his conversion in *Dialogue with Trypho* (chaps. 7–8). One day as he stood near the Aegean Sea just outside the city of Ephesus, an old man approached him.

"Does philosophy produce happiness?" asked the old man.

"Absolutely," Justin replied, "and it alone."

In an extended conversation the old man suggested to Justin that there were many questions Plato could not answer, but there is a true philosophy with an explanation for all questions. That philosophy is Christianity. The old man said:

A long time ago, . . . long before the time of those reputed philosophers, there lived blessed men who were just and loved by God, men who spoke through the inspiration of the Holy Spirit and predicted events that would take place in the future, which events are now taking place. We call these men the prophets. They alone knew the truth and communicated it to men, whom they neither deferred to nor feared. With no desire for personal glory, they reiterated only what they heard and saw when inspired by the Holy Spirit. Their writings are still extant, and whoever reads them with the proper faith will profit greatly in his knowledge of the origin and end of things, and of any matter that a philosopher should know. In their writings they gave no proof at that time of their statements, for, as reliable witness of the truth, they were beyond proof; but the happenings that have taken place and are now taking place force you to believe their words. They also are worthy of belief because of the miracles which they performed, for they exalted God, the Father and creator of all things, and made known Christ, His son, who was sent by Him. This the false prophets, who are filled with an erring and unclean spirit, have never done nor even do now, but they undertake to perform certain wonders to astound men and they glorify the demons and spirits of error. Above all beseech God to open to you the gates of light, for no one can perceive or understand these truths unless he has been enlightened by God and His Christ.

Justin then describes his response:

When he had said these and many other things which it is not now fitting time to tell, he went his way, after admonishing me to meditate on what he had told me, and I never saw him again. But my spirit was immediately set on fire, and affection for the prophets, and for those who are friends of Christ, took hold of me; while pondering on his words, I discovered that his was the only sure and useful philosophy. Thus it is that I am now a [true] philosopher. Furthermore, it is my wish that everyone would be of the same sentiments as I, and never spurn the Saviour's words; for they have in themselves such tremendous majesty that they can instill fear into those who have wandered from the path of righteousness, whereas they ever remain a great solace to those who heed them.

Many scholars have treated this narrative of Justin's conversion as a fictional account. However, it is difficult to establish adequate grounds on which one could totally reject the historical credibility of the story. It may well be that his conversion was not as sudden as his description seems to imply. Perhaps there were other factors involved in addition to the simple reasoning of the old man by the sea. For example, Justin's writings indicate that he had made a thorough study of the Old and the New Testament Scriptures.

After his conversion Justin became a professor of philosophical Christianity in his own private school in Rome. Since he was a layman, he probably operated the school in his home. He also seems to have traveled considerably throughout the Roman Empire, spending his time in a ministry of teaching and evangelism.

In the year A.D. 167 Justin and six others were brought to trial, charged with the crime of being Christians. All of them admitted to the charge. They were scourged and then beheaded. Eusebius writes that the Cynic Crescens connived to bring about Justin's death. Apparently Justin had at one time disputed with Crescens about the truth of the gospel.

Because Justin says in his works that Christ was born "one-hundred fifty years ago," scholars believe that Justin's first apology must have been written in the middle of the second century. The work was addressed to Antoninus Pius who reigned from 138 to 161. Justin also refers to Felix as the Prefect of Alexandria. Felix was the prefect from 148 to 154.

Justin's *Apology* can be quite naturally divided into three parts. First, he tries to show that Christians are innocent of the crimes for which they have been accused, and they should not be punished without fair trials. If Christians are guilty of actual crimes, he says, they should be punished, but it is not right to accuse Christians of being atheists. They do worship God, but they do not worship false images. There are no better citizens of the Roman Empire than Christians, he argues. He asks his readers to consider the high moral character of Christian converts and to remember the Christian doctrine of a final judgment.

In the second part (chaps. xxii–lx) Justin tries to prove (chaps. xxiv–xxix) that Christianity teaches truth. But Christianity is not to be believed simply because of similarities with other philosophical writings. Biblical truth is older and of more intrinsic value than any of the philosophers. Next Justin argues that Jesus is uniquely the Son of God. Finally, Justin contends (chaps. liv–lx) that the demons had at least partial knowledge prior to the coming of Christ of what was to be. Thus they inspired evil men to write myths and legends that anticipated the coming of Christ, and these have been used to reduce His influence and keep people away from Christ. The demons had not known of the Cross, however, and thus could not imitate it.

The third part of the *Apology* (chaps. lxi–lxviii) is not directly apologetical. Its significance is primarily for those who are interested in the life and theology of the early church.

BIBLIOGRAPHY

Barnard, L. W. *Justin Martyr: His Life and Thought.* Cambridge: At the University Press, 1967.

_____. "Justin Martyr in Recent Study." *Scottish Journal of Theology* 22 (June 1969):152–64.

Blunt, A. W. F. *The Apologies of Justin Martyr.* Cambridge: At the University Press, 1911.

Gildersleeve, Basil L. *The Apologies of Justin Martyr.* New York: Harper & Brothers, 1877.

Goodenough, Erwin R. *The Theology of Justin Martyr.* Amsterdam: Philo, 1968.

Keresztes, Paul. "The Emperor Antoninus Pius and the Christians." *Journal of Ecclesiastical History* 22 (January 1971):1–18.

Osborn, Eric Francis. *Justin Martyr.* Tübingen: Mohr, 1973.

THE FIRST APOLOGY
OF JUSTIN

CHAPTER I.

Address

TO the Emperor Titus Ælius Adrianus Antoninus Pius Augustus Cæsar, and to his son Verissimus the philosopher, and to Lucius the philosopher, the natural son of Cæsar, and the adopted son of Pius, a lover of learning, and to the sacred senate, with the whole people of the Romans, I, Justin, the son of Priscus and grandson of Bacchius, natives of Flavia Neopolis in Palestine, present this address and petition in behalf of those of all nations who are unjustly hated and wantonly abused, myself being one of them.

CHAPTER II.

Justice demanded

REASON directs those who are truly pious and philosophical to honour and love only what is true, declining to follow traditional opinions,[1] if these be worthless. For not only does sound reason direct us to refuse the guidance of those who did or taught anything wrong, but it is incumbent on the lover of truth, by all means, and if death be threatened, even before his own life, to choose to do and say what is right. Do you, then, since ye are called pious and philosophers,

---

From Alexander Roberts and James Donaldson, eds., *Ante-Nicene Christian Library*, trans. Marcus Dods (Edinburgh: T. & T. Clark, 1867), 2:7–8, 10–11, 13–17, 22–30, 31, 32–40, 43–45, 46–47, 50–55.
[1]Literally, "the opinions of the ancients."

guardians of justice and lovers of learning, give good heed, and hearken to my address; and if ye are indeed such, it will be manifested. For we have come, not to flatter you by this writing, nor please you by our address, but to beg that you pass judgment, after an accurate and searching investigation, not flattered by prejudice or by a desire of pleasing superstitious men, nor induced by irrational impulse or evil rumours which have long been prevalent, to give a decision which will prove to be against yourselves. For as for us, we reckon that no evil can be done us, unless we be convicted as evil-doers, or be proved to be wicked men; and you, you can kill, but not hurt us.

.   .   .

CHAPTER V.

Christians charged with atheism

SINCE of old these evil demons, effecting apparitions of themselves, both defiled women and corrupted boys, and showed such fearful sights to men, that those who did not use their reason in judging of the actions that were done, were struck with terror; and being carried away by fear, and not knowing that these were demons, they called them gods, and gave to each the name which each of the demons chose for himself. And when Socrates endeavoured, by true reason and examination, to bring these things to light, and deliver men from the demons, then the demons themselves, by means of men who rejoiced in iniquity, compassed his death, as an athiest and a profane person, on the charge that "he was introducing new divinities;" and in our case they display a similar activity. For not only among the Greeks did reason (Logos) prevail to condemn these things through Socrates, but also among the Barbarians were they condemned by Reason (or the Word, the Logos) Himself, who took shape, and became man, and was called Jesus Christ; and in obedience to Him, we not only deny that they who did such things as these are gods,[2] but assert that they are wicked and impious demons,[3] whose actions will not bear comparison with those even of men desirous of virtue.

---

[2]The word δαίμων means in Greek a god, but the Christians used the word to signify an evil spirit. Justin uses the same word here for god and demon. The connection which Justin and other Christian writers supposed to exist between evil spirits and the gods of the heathens will be apparent from Justin's own statements. The word διάβολος, devil, is not applied to these demons. There is but one devil, but many demons.

[3]idem.

CHAPTER VI.

Charge of atheism refuted

HENCE are we called atheists. And we confess that we are atheists, so far as gods of this sort are concerned, but not with respect to the most true God, the Father of righteousness and temperance and the other virtues, who is free from all impurity. But both Him, and the Son who came forth from Him and taught us these things, and the host of the other good angels who follow and are made like to Him,[4] and the prophetic Spirit, we worship and adore, knowing them in reason and truth, and declaring without grudging to every one who wishes to learn, as we have been taught.

·   ·   ·

CHAPTER IX.

Folly of idol worship

AND neither do we honour with many sacrifices and garlands of flowers such deities as men have formed and set in shrines and called gods; since we see that these are soulless and dead, and have not the form of God (for we do not consider that God has such a form as some say that they imitate to His honour), but have the names and forms of those wicked demons which have appeared. For why need we tell you who already know, into what forms the craftsmen, carving and cutting, casting and hammering, fashion the materials? And often out of vessels of dishonour, by merely changing the form, and making an image of the requisite shape, they make what they call a god; which we consider not only senseless, but to be even insulting to God, who, having ineffable glory and form, thus gets His name attached to things that are corruptible, and require constant service. And that the artificers of these are both intemperate, and, not to enter into particulars, are practised in every vice, you very well know; even their own

---

[4]This is the literal and obvious translation of Justin's words. But from c. 13, 16, and 61, it is evident that he did not desire to inculcate the worship of angels. We are therefore driven to adopt another translation of this passage, even though it be somewhat harsh. Two such translations have been proposed: the first connecting "us" and "the host of the other good angels" as the common object of the verb "taught;" the second connecting "these things" with "the host of," etc., and making these two together the subject taught. In the first case the translation would stand, "taught these things to us and to the host," etc.; in the second case the translation would be, "taught us about these things, and about the host of the others who follow Him, viz. the good angels."

girls who work along with them they corrupt. What infatuation! that dissolute men should be said to fashion and make gods for your worship, and that you should appoint such men the guardians of the temples where they are enshrined; not recognising that it is unlawful even to think or say that men are the guardians of gods.

CHAPTER X.

How God is to be served

BUT we have received by tradition that God does not need the material offerings which men can give, seeing, indeed, that He Himself is the provider of all things. And we have been taught, and are convinced, and do believe, that He accepts those only who imitate the excellences which reside in Him, temperance, and justice, and philanthropy, and as many virtues as are peculiar to a God who is called by no proper name. And we have been taught that He in the beginning did of His goodness, for man's sake, create all things out of unformed matter; and if men by their works show themselves worthy of this His design, they are deemed worthy, and so we have received—of reigning in company with Him, being delivered from corruption and suffering. For as in the beginning He created us when we were not, so do we consider that, in like manner, those who choose what is pleasing to Him are, on account of their choice, deemed worthy of incorruption and of fellowship with Him. . . .

CHAPTER XI.

What kingdom Christians look for

AND when you hear that we look for a kingdom, you suppose, without making any inquiry, that we speak of a human kingdom; whereas we speak of that which is with God, as appears also from the confession of their faith made by those who are charged with being Christians, though they know that death is the punishment awarded to him who so confesses. For if we looked for a human kingdom, we should also deny our Christ, that we might not be slain; and we should strive to escape detection, that we might obtain what we expect. But since our thoughts are not fixed on the present, we are not concerned when men cut us off; since also death is a debt which must at all events be paid.

CHAPTER XII.

Christians live as under God's eye

AND more than all other men are we your helpers and allies in promoting peace, seeing that we hold this view, that it is alike impossible for the wicked, the covetous, the conspirator, and for the virtuous, to escape the notice of God, and that each man goes to everlasting punishment or salvation according to the value of his actions. For if all men knew this, no one would choose wickedness even for a little, knowing that he goes to the everlasting punishment of fire; but would by all means restrain himself, and adorn himself with virtue, that he might obtain the good gifts of God, and escape the punishments. For those who, on account of the laws and punishments you impose, endeavour to escape detection when they offend (and they offend, too, under the impression that it is quite possible to escape your detection, since you are but men), those persons, if they learned and were convinced that nothing, whether actually done or only intended, can escape the knowledge of God, would by all means live decently on account of the penalties threatened, as even you yourselves will admit. But you seem to fear lest all men become righteous, and you no longer have any to punish. Such would be the concern of public executioners, but not of good princes. . . .

CHAPTER XIII.

Christians serve God rationally

WHAT sober-minded man, then, will not acknowledge that we are not atheists, worshipping as we do the Maker of this universe, and declaring, as we have been taught, that He has no need of streams of blood and libations and incense; whom we praise to the utmost of our power by the exercise of prayer and thanksgiving for all things wherewith we are supplied, as we have been taught that the only honour that is worthy of Him is not to consume by fire what He has brought into being for our sustenance, but to use it for ourselves and those who need, and with gratitude to Him to offer thanks by invocations and hymns[5] for our creation, and for all the means of health, and for the various qualities of the different kinds of things, and for the changes of the seasons; and to present before Him petitions for our existing again in incorruption through faith in Him. Our teacher of these things is Jesus Christ, who also was born for this purpose, and was crucified under Pontius Pilate, procurator of Judæa, in the times of Tiberius Cæsar; and that we reasonably worship Him, having learned that He is the Son of the true God Himself, and holding Him in the second place, and the prophetic Spirit in the third, we will prove. For they proclaim our madness to consist in this, that we give to a crucified man a place second to the unchangeable and

---

[5]πομπὰς καὶ ὕμνους. "Grabe, and it should seem correctly, understands πομπὰς to be *solemn prayers.* . . . He also remarks, that the ὕμνοι were either psalms of David, or some of those psalms and songs made by the primitive Christians, which are mentioned in Eusebius, *H. E.* v. 28."—TROLLOPE.

eternal God, the Creator of all; for they do not discern the mystery that is herein. . . .

.   .   .

CHAPTER XVIII.

Proof of immortality and the resurrection

FOR reflect upon the end of each of the preceding kings, how they died the death common to all, which, if it issued in insensibility, would be a godsend[6] to all the wicked. But since sensation remains to all who have ever lived, and eternal punishment is laid up (*i.e.* for the wicked), see that ye neglect not to be convinced, and to hold as your belief, that these things are true. For let even necromancy, and the divinations you practise by immaculate children,[7] and the evoking of departed human souls,[8] and those who are called among the magi, Dream-senders and Assistant-spirits (Familiars),[9] and all that is done by those who are skilled in such matters—let these persuade you that even after death souls are in a state of sensation; and those who are seized and cast about by the spirits of the dead, whom all call dæmoniacs or madmen;[10] and what you repute as oracles, both of Amphilochus, Dodona, Pytho, and as many other such as exist; and the opinions of your authors, Empedocles and Pythagoras, Plato and

---

[6]ἕρμαιον, a piece of unlooked-for luck, Hermes being the reputed giver of such gifts: vid. Liddell and Scott's *Lex.*; see also the Scholiast, quoted by Stallbaum in Plato's *Phaed.* p. 107, on a passage singularly analogous to this.

[7]Boys and girls, or even children, prematurely taken from the womb, were slaughtered, and their entrails inspected, in the belief that the souls of the victims (being still conscious, as Justin is arguing) would reveal things hidden and future. Instances are abundantly cited by Otto and Trollope.

[8]This form of spirit-rapping was familiar to the ancients, and Justin again (*Dial. c. Tryph.* c. 105) uses the invocation of Samuel by the witch of Endor as a proof of the immortality of the soul.

[9]Valesius (on Euseb. *H. E.* iv. 7) states that the magi had two kinds of familiars: the first, who were sent to inspire men with dreams which might give them intimations of things future; and the second, who were sent to watch over men, and protect them from diseases and misfortunes. The first, he says, they called (as here) ὀνειροπομπούς, and the second παρέδρους.

[10]Justin is not the only author in ancient or recent times who has classed dæmoniacs and maniacs together; neither does he stand alone among the ancients in the opinion that dæmoniacs were possessed by the spirits of departed men. References will be found in Trollope's note.

Socrates, and the pit of Homer,[11] and the descent of Ulysses to inspect these things, and all that has been uttered of a like kind. Such favour as you grant to these, grant also to us, who not less but more firmly than they believe in God; since we expect to receive again our own bodies, though they be dead and cast into the earth, for we maintain that wth God nothing is impossible.

CHAPTER XIX.

The resurrection possible

AND to any thoughtful person would anything appear more incredible, than, if we were not in the body, and some one were to say that it was possible that from a small drop of human seed bones and sinews and flesh be formed into a shape such as we see? For let this now be said hypothetically: if you yourselves were not such as you now are, and born of such parents [and causes], and one were to show you human seed and a picture of a man, and were to say with confidence that from such a substance such a being could be produced, would you believe before you saw the actual production? No one will dare to deny [that such a statement would surpass belief]. In the same way, then, you are now incredulous because you have never seen a dead man rise again. But as at first you would not have believed it possible that such persons could be produced from the small drop, and yet now you see them thus produced, so also judge ye that it is not impossible that the bodies of men, after they have been dissolved, and like seeds resolved into earth, should in God's appointed time rise again and put on incorruption. For what power worthy of God those imagine who say, that each thing returns to that from which it was produced, and that beyond this not even God Himself can do anything, we are unable to conceive; but this we see clearly, that they would not have believed it possible that they could have become such and produced from such materials, as they now see both themselves and the whole world to be. And that it is better to believe even what is impossible to our own nature and to men, than to be unbelieving like the rest of the world, we have learned; for we know that our master Jesus Christ said, that "what is impossible with men is possible with God" [Matt. 19:26], and, "Fear not them that kill you, and after that can do no more; but fear Him who after death is able to cast both soul and body into hell" [Matt. 10:28]. And hell is a place where those are to be punished who have lived wickedly, and who do not believe that those things which God has taught us by Christ will come to pass.

---

[11]See the *Odyssey*, Book xi. line 25, where Ulysses is described as digging a pit or trench with his sword, and pouring libations, in order to collect around him the souls of the dead.

CHAPTER XX.

Heathen analogies to Christian doctrine

AND the Sibyl[12] and Hystaspes said that there should be a dissolution by God of things corruptible. And the philosophers called Stoics teach that even God Himself shall be resolved into fire, and they say that the world is to be formed anew by this revolution; but we understand that God, the creator of all things, is superior to the things that are to be changed. If, therefore, on some points we teach the same things as the poets and philosophers whom you honour, and on other points are fuller and more divine in our teaching, and if we alone afford proof of what we assert, why are we unjustly hated more than all others? For while we say that all things have been produced and arranged into a world by God, we shall seem to utter the doctrine of Plato; and while we say that there will be a burning up of all, we shall seem to utter the doctrine of the Stoics; and while we affirm that the souls of the wicked, being endowed with sensation even after death, are punished, and that those of the good being delivered from punishment spend a blessed existence, we shall seem to say the same things as the poets and philosophers; and while we maintain that men ought not to worship the works of their hands, we say the very things which have been said by the comic poet Menander, and other similar writers, for they have declared that the workman is greater than the work.

CHAPTER XXI.

Analogies to the history of Christ

AND when we say also that the Word, who is the first-birth[13] of God, was produced without sexual union, and that He, Jesus Christ, our teacher, was crucified and died, and rose again, and ascended into heaven, we propound nothing different from what you believe regarding those whom you esteem sons of Jupiter. For you know how many sons your esteemed writers ascribe to Jupiter: Mercury, the interpreting word and teacher of all; Aesculapius, who, though he was a great physician, was struck by a thunderbolt, and so ascended to heaven; and Bacchus too, after he had been torn limb from limb; and Hercules, when he had committed himself to the flames to escape his toils; and the sons of Leda, the Dioscuri; and Perseus, son of Danae; and Bellerophon, who, though sprung from mortals,

---

[12]The Sibylline Oracles are now generally regarded as heathen fragments largely interpolated by unscrupulous men during the early ages of the church. For an interesting account of these somewhat perplexing documents, see Burton's *Lectures on the Ecclesiastical History of the First Three Centuries*, Lect. xvii. The prophecies of Hystaspes were also commonly appealed to as genuine by the early Christians.

[13]*i.e.* first-born.

rose to heaven on the horse Pegasus. For what shall I say of Ariadne, and those who, like her, have been declared to be set among the stars? And what of the emperors who die among yourselves, whom you deem worthy of deification, and in whose behalf you produce some one who swears he has seen the burning Caesar rise to heaven from the funeral pyre? And what kind of deeds are recorded of each of these reputed sons of Jupiter, it is needless to tell to those who already know. This only shall be said, that they are written for the advantage and encouragement[14] of youthful scholars; for all reckon it an honourable thing to imitate the gods. But far be such a thought concerning the gods from every well-conditioned soul, as to believe that Jupiter himself, the governor and creator of all things, was both a parricide and the son of a parricide, and that being overcome by the love of base and shameful pleasures, he came in to Ganymede and those many women whom he violated, and that his sons did like actions. But, as we said above, wicked devils perpetrated these things. And we have learned that those only are deified who have lived near to God in holiness and virtue; and we believe that those who live wickedly and do not repent are punished in everlasting fire.

CHAPTER XXII.

Analogies to the Sonship of Christ

MOREOVER, the Son of God called Jesus, even if only a man by ordinary generation, yet, on account of His wisdom, is worthy to be called the Son of God; for all writers call God the Father of men and gods. And if we assert that the Word of God was born of God in a peculiar manner, different from ordinary generation, let this, as said above, be no extraordinary thing to you, who say that Mercury is the angelic word of God. But if any one objects that He was crucified, in this also He is on a par with those reputed sons of Jupiter of yours, who suffered as we have now enumerated. For their sufferings at death are recorded to have been not all alike, but diverse; so that not even by the peculiarity of His suffering does He seem to be inferior to them; but, on the contrary, as we promised in the preceding part of this discourse, we will now prove Him superior—or rather have already proved Him to be so—for the superior is revealed by His actions. And if we even affirm that He was born of a virgin, accept this in common with what you accept of Perseus. And in that we say that He made whole

---

[14]διαφορὰν καὶ προτροπὴν. The irony here is so obvious as to make the proposed reading (διαφθορὰν καὶ παρατροπὴν, corruption and depravation) unnecessary. Otto prefers the reading adopted above. Trollope, on the other hand, inclines to the latter reading, mainly on the score of the former expressions being unusual. See his very sensible note *in loc.*

the lame, the paralytic, and those born blind, we seem to say what is very similar to the deeds said to have been done by Aesculapius.

CHAPTER XXIII.

The argument

AND that this may now become evident to you—(firstly[15]) that whatever we assert in conformity with what has been taught us by Christ, and by the prophets who preceded Him, are alone true, and are older than all the writers who have existed; that we claim to be acknowledged, not because we say the same things as these writers said, but because we say true things: and (secondly) that Jesus Christ is the only proper Son who has been begotten by God, being His Word and first-begotten, and power; and, becoming man according to His will, He taught us these things for the conversion and restoration of the human race: and (thirdly) that before He became a man among men, some, influenced by the devils before mentioned, related beforehand, through the instrumentality of the poets, those circumstances as having really happened, which, having fictitiously devised, they narrated, in the same manner as they have caused to be fabricated the scandalous reports against us of infamous and impious actions,[16] of which there is neither witness nor proof—we shall bring forward the following proof.

CHAPTER XXIV.

Varieties of heathen worship

IN the first place [we furnish proof], because, though we say things similar to what the Greeks say, we only are hated on account of the name of Christ, and though we do no wrong, are put to death as sinners; other men in other places worshipping trees and rivers, and mice and cats and crocodiles, and many irrational animals. Nor are the same animals esteemed by all; but in one place one is worshipped, and another in another, so that all are profane in the judgment of one another, on account of their not worshipping the same objects. And this is the sole accusation you bring against us, that we do not reverence the same gods as you do, nor offer to the dead libations and the savour of fat, and crowns for

---

[15]The Benedictine editor, Maranus, Otto, and Trollope, here note that Justin in this chapter promises to make good three distinct positions: 1*st*, That Christian doctrines alone are true, and are to be received, not on account of their resemblance to the sentiments of poets or philosophers, but on their own account; 2*d*, that Jesus Christ is the incarnate Son of God, and our teacher; 3*d*, that before His incarnation, the devils, having some knowledge of what He would accomplish, enabled the heathen poets and priests in some points to anticipate, though in a distorted form, the facts of the incarnation. The first he establishes in chap. xxiv.–xxix.; the second in chap. xxx.–liii.; and the third in chap. liv. et sq.

[16]We have here followed the reading and rendering of Trollope.

their statues,[17] and sacrifices. For you very well know that the same animals are with some esteemed gods, with others wild beasts, and with others sacrificial victims.

CHAPTER XXV.

False gods abandoned by Christians

AND, secondly, because we—who, out of every race of men, used to worship Bacchus the son of Semele, and Apollo the son of Latona (who in their loves with men did such things as it is shameful even to mention), and Proserpine and Venus (who were maddened with love of Adonis, and whose mysteries also you celebrate), or Aesculapius, or some one or other of those who are called gods—have now, through Jesus Christ, learned to despise these, though we be threatened with death for it, and have dedicated ourselves to the unbegotten and impassible God; of whom we are persuaded that never was he goaded by lust of Antiope, or such other women, or of Ganymede, nor was rescued by that hundred-handed giant whose aid was obtained through Thetis, nor was anxious on this account[18] that her son Achilles should destroy many of the Greeks because of his concubine Briseis. Those who believe these things we pity, and those who invented them we know to be devils.

CHAPTER XXVI.

Magicians not trusted by Christians

AND, thirdly, because after Christ's ascension into heaven the devils put forward certain men who said that they themselves were gods; and they were not only persecuted by you, but even deemed worthy of honours. There was a Samaritan, Simon, a native of the village called Gitto, who in the reign of Claudius Caesar, and in your royal city of Rome, did mighty acts of magic, by virtue of the art of the devils operating in him. He was considered a god, and as a god was honoured by you with a statue, which statue was erected on the river Tiber, between the two bridges, and bore this inscription, in the language of Rome:

"Simoni Deo Sancto,"[19]
"To Simon the holy God."

---

[17]ἐν γραφαῖς στεφάνους. The only conjecture which seems at all probable is that of the Benedictine editor followed here.

[18]*i.e.* on account of the assistance gained for him by Thetis, and in return for it.

[19]It is very generally supposed that Justin was mistaken in understanding this to have been a statue erected to Simon Magus. This supposition rests on the fact that in the year 1574 there was dug up in the island of the Tiber a fragment of marble, with the inscription "Semoni Sanco Deo," etc., being probably the base of a statue erected to the Sabine deity

And almost all the Samaritans, and a few even of other nations, worship him, and acknowledge him as the first god; and a woman, Helena, who went about with him at that time, and had formerly been a prostitute, they say is the first idea generated by him. And a man, Menander, also a Samaritan, of the town Capparetaea, a disciple of Simon, and inspired by devils, we know to have deceived many while he was in Antioch by his magical art. He persuaded those who adhered to him that they should never die, and even now there are some living who hold this opinion of his. And there is Marcion, a man of Pontus, who is even at this day alive, and teaching his disciples to believe in some other god greater than the Creator. And he, by the aid of the devils, has caused many of every nation to speak blasphemies, and to deny that God is the maker of this universe, and to assert that some other, being greater than He, has done greater works. All who take their opinions from these men, are, as we before said, called Christians; just as also those who do not agree with the philosophers in their doctrines, have yet in common with them the name of philosophers given to them. And whether they perpetrate those fabulous and shameful deeds[20]—the upsetting of the lamp, and promiscuous intercourse, and eating human flesh—we know not; but we do know that they are neither persecuted nor put to death by you, at least on account of their opinions. But I have a treatise against all the heresies that have existed already composed, which, if you wish to read it, I will give you.

·   ·   ·

CHAPTER XXVIII.

God's care for men

FOR among us the prince of the wicked spirits is called the serpent, and Satan, and the devil, as you can learn by looking into our writings. And that he would be sent into the fire with his host, and the men who follow him, and would be punished for an endless duration, Christ foretold. For the reason why God has delayed to do this, is His regard for the human race. For He foreknows

---

Semo Sancus. This inscription Justin is supposed to have mistaken for the one he gives above. This has always seemed to us very slight evidence on which to reject so precise a statement as Justin here makes; a statement which he would scarcely have hazarded in an apology addressed to Rome, where every person had the means of ascertaining its accuracy. If, as is supposed, he made a mistake, it must have been at once exposed, and other writers would not have so frequently repeated the story as they have done. See *Burton's Bampton Lectures*, p. 374.

[20]Which were commonly charged against the Christians.

that some are to be saved by repentance, some even that are perhaps not yet born.[21] In the beginning He made the human race with the power of thought and of choosing the truth and doing right, so that all men are without excuse before God; for they have been born rational and contemplative. And if any one disbelieves that God cares for these things,[22] he will thereby either insinuate that God does not exist, or he will assert that though He exists He delights in vice, or exists like a stone, and that neither virtue nor vice are anything, but only in the opinion of men these things are reckoned good or evil. And this is the greatest profanity and wickedness.

.   .   .

CHAPTER XXX.
Was Christ not a magician?

BUT lest any one should meet us with the question, What should prevent that He whom we call Christ, being a man born of men, performed what we call His mighty works by magical art, and by this appeared to be the Son of God? we will now offer proof, not trusting mere assertions, but being of necessity persuaded by those who prophesied [of Him] before these things came to pass, for with our own eyes we behold things that have happened and are happening just as they were predicted; and this will, we think, appear even to you the strongest and truest evidence.

CHAPTER XXXI.
Of the Hebrew prophets

THERE were, then, among the Jews certain men who were prophets of God, through whom the prophetic Spirit published beforehand things that were to come to pass, ere ever they happened. And their prophecies, as they were spoken and when they were uttered, the kings who happened to be reigning among the Jews at the several times carefully preserved in their possession, when they had been arranged in books by the prophets themselves in their own Hebrew language. And when Ptolemy king of Egypt formed a library, and endeavoured to collect the writings of all men, he heard also of these prophets, and sent to

---

[21]Literally, "For He foreknows some about to be saved by repentance, and some not yet perhaps born."

[22]Those things which concern the salvation of man; so Trollope and the other interpreters, except Otto, who reads τούτων masculine, and understands it of the men first spoken of.

Herod, who was at that time king of the Jews,[23] requesting that the books of the prophets be sent to him. And Herod the king did indeed send them, written, as they were, in the foresaid Hebrew language. And when their contents were found to be unintelligible to the Egyptians, he again sent and requested that men be commissioned to translate them into the Greek language. And when this was done, the books remained with the Egyptians, where they are until now. They are also in the possession of all Jews throughout the world; but they, though they read, do not understand what is said, but count us foes and enemies; and, like yourselves, they kill and punish us whenever they have the power, as you can well believe. For in the Jewish war which lately raged, Barchochebas, the leader of the revolt of the Jews, gave orders that Christians alone should be led to cruel punishments, unless they would deny Jesus Christ and utter blasphemy. In these books, then, of the prophets we found Jesus our Christ foretold as coming, born of a virgin, growing up to man's estate, and healing every disease and every sickness, and raising the dead, and being hated, and unrecognised, and crucified, and dying, and rising again, and ascending into heaven, and being, and being called, the Son of God. We find it also predicted that certain persons should be sent by Him into every nation to publish these things, and that rather among the Gentiles [than among the Jews] men should believe on Him. And He was predicted before He appeared, first 5000 years before, and again 3000, then 2000, then 1000, and yet again 800; for in the succession of generations prophets after prophets arose.

CHAPTER XXXII.

Christ predicted by Moses

MOSES then, who was the first of the prophets, spoke in these very words: "The sceptre shall not depart from Judah, nor a lawgiver from between his feet, until He come for whom it is reserved; and He shall be the desire of the nations, binding His foal to the vine, washing His robe in the blood of the grape" [Gen. 49:11]. It is yours to make accurate inquiry, and ascertain up to whose time the Jews had a lawgiver and king of their own. Up to the time of Jesus Christ, who taught us, and interpreted the prophecies which were not yet understood, [they had a lawgiver] as was foretold by the holy and divine Spirit of prophecy through Moses, "that a ruler would not fail the Jews until He should come for whom the kingdom was reserved" (for Judah was the forefather of the Jews, from whom also they have their name of Jews); and after He (*i.e.* Christ) appeared, you began to rule the Jews, and gained possession of all their territory. And the prophecy, "He shall be the expectation of the nations," signified that there would be some of all

---

[23]Some attribute this blunder in chronology to Justin, others to his transcribers: it was Eleazar the high priest to whom Ptolemy applied.

nations who should look for Him to come again. And this indeed you can see for yourselves, and be convinced of by fact. For of all races of men there are some who look for Him who was crucified in Judea, and after whose crucifixion the land was straightway surrendered to you as spoil of war. And the prophecy, "binding His foal to the vine, and washing His robe in the blood of the grape," was a significant symbol of the things that were to happen to Christ, and of what He was to do. For the foal of an ass stood bound to a vine at the entrance of a village, and He ordered His acquaintances to bring it to Him then; and when it was brought, He mounted and sat upon it, and entered Jerusalem, where was the vast temple of the Jews which was afterwards destroyed by you. And after this He was crucified, that the rest of the prophecy might be fulfilled. For this "washing His robe in the blood of the grape" was predictive of the passion He was to endure, cleansing by His blood those who believe on Him. For what is called by the Divine Spirit through the prophet "His robe," are those men who believe in Him in whom abideth the seed[24] of God, the Word. And what is spoken of as "the blood of the grape," signifies that He who should appear would have blood, though not of the seed of man, but of the power of God. And the first power after God the Father and Lord of all is the Word, who is also the Son; and of Him we will, in what follows, relate how He took flesh and became man. For as man did not make the blood of the vine, but God, so it was hereby intimated that the blood should not be of human seed, but of divine power, as we have said above. And Isaiah, another prophet, foretelling the same things in other words, spoke thus: "A star shall rise out of Jacob, and a flower shall spring from the root of Jesse; and in His arm shall the nations trust" [Isa. 11:1]. And a star of light has arisen, and a flower has sprung from the root of Jesse—this Christ. For by the power of God He was conceived by a virgin of the seed of Jacob, who was the father of Judah, who, as we have shown, was the father of the Jews; and Jesse was His forefather according to the oracle, and He was the son of Jacob and Judah according to lineal descent.

CHAPTER XXXIII.

Manner of Christ's birth predicted

AND hear again how Isaiah in express words foretold that He should be born of a virgin; for he spoke thus: "Behold, a virgin shall conceive, and bring forth a son, and they shall say for His name, 'God with us'" [Isa. 7:14]. For things which were incredible and seemed impossible with men, these God predicted by the Spirit of prophecy as about to come to pass, in order that, when they came to pass, there might be no unbelief, but faith, because of their predic-

---

[24]Grabe would here read, not σπέρμα, but πνεῦμα, the spirit; but the Benedictine, Otto, and Trollope all think that no change should be made.

tion. But lest some, not understanding the prophecy now cited, should charge us with the very things we have been laying to the charge of the poets who say that Jupiter went in to women through lust, let us try to explain the words. This, then, "Behold, a virgin shall conceive," signifies that a virgin should conceive without intercourse. For if she had had intercourse with any one whatever, she was no longer a virgin; but the power of God having come upon the virgin, overshadowed her, and caused her while yet a virgin to conceive. And the angel of God who was sent to the same virgin at that time brought her good news, saying, "Behold, thou shalt conceive of the Holy Ghost, and shalt bear a Son, and He shall be called the Son of the Highest, and thou shalt call His name Jesus; for He shall save His people from their sins" [Luke 1:32; Matt. 1:21]—as they who have recorded all that concerns our Saviour Jesus Christ have taught, whom we believed, since by Isaiah also, whom we have now adduced, the Spirit of prophecy declared that He should be born as we intimated before. It is wrong, therefore, to understand the Spirit and the power of God as anything else than the Word, who is also the first-born of God, as the foresaid prophet Moses declared; and it was this which, when it came upon the virgin and overshadowed her, caused her to conceive, not by intercourse, but by power. And the name Jesus in the Hebrew language means Σωτήρ (Saviour) in the Greek tongue. Wherefore, too, the angel said to the virgin, "Thou shalt call His name Jesus, for He shall save His people from their sins." And that the prophets are inspired[25] by no other than the Divine Word, even you, as I fancy, will grant.

CHAPTER XXXIV.
Place of Christ's birth foretold

AND hear what part of earth He was to be born in, as another prophet, Micah, foretold. He spoke thus: "And thou, Bethlehem, the land of Judah, art not the least among the princes of Judah; for out of thee shall come forth a Governor, who shall feed my people" [Micah 5:2]. Now there is a village in the land of the Jews, thirty-five stadia from Jerusalem, in which Jesus Christ was born, as you can ascertain also from the registers of the taxing made under Cyrenius, your first procurator in Judea.

CHAPTER XXXV.
Other fulfilled prophecies

AND how Christ after He was born was to escape the notice of other men until He grew to man's estate, which also came to pass, hear what was foretold

---

[25]θεοφοροῦνται, lit. are borne by a god—a word used of those who were supposed to be wholly under the influence of a deity.

regarding this. There are the following predictions:[26]—"Unto us a child is born, and unto us a young man is given, and the government shall be upon His shoulders;" [Isa. 9:6] which is significant of the power of the cross, for to it, when He was crucified, He applied His shoulders, as shall be more clearly made out in the ensuing discourse. And again the same prophet Isaiah, being inspired by the prophetic Spirit, said, "I have spread out my hands to a disobedient and gainsaying people, to those who walk in a way that is not good. They now ask of me judgment, and dare to draw near to God" [Isa. 65:2; 58:2]. And again in other words, through another prophet, He says, "They pierced my hands and my feet, and for my vesture they cast lots" [Ps. 22:16]. And indeed David, the king and prophet, who uttered these things, suffered none of them; but Jesus Christ stretched forth His hands, being crucified by the Jews speaking against Him, and denying that He was the Christ. And as the prophet spoke, they tormented Him, and set Him on the judgment-seat, and said, Judge us. And the expression, "They pierced my hands and my feet," was used in reference to the nails of the cross which were fixed in His hands and feet. And after He was crucified they cast lots upon His vesture, and they that crucified Him parted it among them. And that these things did happen, you can ascertain from the Acts of Pontius Pilate.[27] And we will cite the prophetic utterances of another prophet, Zephaniah,[28] to the effect that He was foretold expressly as to sit upon the foal of an ass and to enter Jerusalem. The words are these: "Rejoice greatly, O daughter of Zion; shout, O daughter of Jerusalem: behold, thy King cometh unto thee; lowly, and riding upon an ass, and upon a colt the foal of an ass" [Zech. 9:9].

CHAPTER XXXVI.

Different modes of prophecy

BUT when you hear the utterances of the prophets spoken as it were personally, you must not suppose that they are spoken by the inspired themselves, but by the Divine Word who moves them. For sometimes He declares things that are to come to pass, in the manner of one who foretells the future; sometimes He speaks as from the person of God the Lord and Father of all; sometimes as from the person of Christ; sometimes as from the person of the people answering the

---

[26]These predictions have so little reference to the point Justin intends to make out, that some editors have supposed that a passage has here been lost. Others think the irrelevancy an insufficient ground for such a supposition.

[27]ἄκτων. These Acts of Pontius Pilate, or regular accounts of his procedure sent by Pilate to the Emperor Tiberius, are supposed to have been destroyed at an early period, possibly in consequence of the unanswerable appeals which the Christians constantly made to them. There exists a forgery in imitation of these Acts. See Trollope.

[28]The reader will notice that these are not the words of Zephaniah, but of Zechariah (ix. 9), to whom also Justin himself refers them in the *Dial. Tryph. c. 53.*

Lord or His Father, just as you can see even in your own writers, one man being the writer of the whole, but introducing the persons who converse. And this the Jews who possessed the books of the prophets did not understand, and therefore did not recognise Christ even when He came, but even hate us who say that He has come, and who prove that, as was predicted, He was crucified by them.

CHAPTER XXXVII.

Utterances of the Father

AND that this too may be clear to you, there were spoken from the person of the Father, through Isaiah the prophet, the following words: "The ox knoweth his owner, and the ass his master's crib; but Israel doth not know, and my people hath not understood. Woe, sinful nation, a people full of sins, a wicked seed, children that are transgressors, ye have forsaken the Lord" [Isa. 1:3].[29] And again elsewhere, when the same prophet speaks in like manner from the person of the Father, "What is the house that ye will build for me? saith the Lord. The heaven is my throne, and the earth is my footstool" [Isa. 66:1]. And again, in another place, "Your new moons and your sabbaths my soul hateth; and the great day of the fast and of ceasing from labour I cannot away with; nor, if ye come to be seen of me, will I hear you: your hands are full of blood; and if ye bring fine flour, incense, it is abomination unto me: the fat of lambs and the blood of bulls I do not desire. For who hath required this at your hands? But loose every bond of wickedness, tear asunder the tight knots of violent contracts, cover the houseless and naked, deal thy bread to the hungry" [Isa. 1:13–15; 18:6]. What kind of things are taught through the prophets from [the person of] God, you can now perceive.

CHAPTER XXXVIII.

Utterances of the Son

AND when the Spirit of prophecy speaks from the person of Christ, the utterances are of this sort: "I have spread out my hands to a disobedient and gainsaying people, to those who walk in a way that is not good" [Isa. 65:2]. And again: "I gave my back to the scourges, and my cheeks to the buffetings; I turned not away my face from the shame of spittings; and the Lord was my helper: therefore was I not confounded: but I set my face as a firm rock; and I knew that I should not be ashamed, for He is near that justifieth me" [Isa. 50:6–8]. And again, when he says, "They cast lots upon my vesture, and pierced my hands and my feet" [Ps. 22:18]; "And I lay down and slept, and rose again, because the Lord

---

[29]Isa. 1:3. This quotation varies only in one word from that of the Septuagint.

sustained me" [Ps. 3:5]. And again, when he says, "They spake with their lips, they wagged the head, saying, Let him deliver himself"]Ps. 22:7]. And that all these things happened to Christ at the hand of the Jews, you can ascertain. For when He was crucified, they did shoot out the lip, and wagged their heads, saying, "Let him who raised the dead save himself."[30]

CHAPTER XXXIX.

Direct predictions by the Spirit

AND when the Spirit of prophecy speaks as predicting things that are to come to pass, He speaks in this way: "For out of Zion shall go forth the law, and the word of the Lord from Jerusalem. And He shall judge among the nations, and shall rebuke many people; and they shall beat their swords into ploughshares, and their spears into pruning-hooks: nation shall not lift up sword against nation, neither shall they learn war any more" [Isa. 2:4]. And that it did so come to pass, we can convince you. For from Jerusalem there went out into the world, men, twelve in number, and these illiterate, of no ability in speaking: but by the power of God they proclaimed to every race of men that they were sent by Christ to teach to all the word of God; and we who formerly used to murder one another do not only now refrain from making war upon our enemies, but also, that we may not lie nor deceive our examiners, willingly die confessing Christ. For that saying, "The tongue has sworn, but the mind is unsworn,"[31] might be imitated by us in this matter. But if the soldiers enrolled by you, and who have taken the military oath, prefer their allegiance to their own life, and parents, and country, and all kindred, though you can offer them nothing incorruptible, it were verily ridiculous if we, who earnestly long for incorruption, should not endure all things, in order to obtain what we desire from Him who is able to grant it.

.   .   .

CHAPTER XLIII.

Responsibility asserted

BUT lest some suppose, from what has been said by us, that we say that whatever happens, happens by a fatal necessity, because it is foretold as known beforehand, this too we explain. We have learned from the prophets, and we hold it to be true, that punishments, and chastisements, and good rewards, are

---

[30]Comp. Matt. 27:39.
[31]Eurip. *Hipp.* 608.

rendered according to the merit of each man's actions. Since if it be not so, but all things happen by fate, neither is anything at all in our own power. For if it be fated that this man, *e.g.*, be good, and this other evil, neither is the former meritorious nor the latter to be blamed. And again, unless the human race have the power of avoiding evil and choosing good by free choice, they are not accountable for their actions, of whatever kind they be. But that it is by free choice they both walk uprightly and stumble, we thus demonstrate. We see the same man making a transition to opposite things. Now, if it had been fated that he were to be either good or bad, he could never have been capable of both the opposites, nor of so many transitions. But not even would some be good and others bad, since we thus make fate the cause of evil, and exhibit her as acting in opposition to herself; or that which has been already stated would seem to be true, that neither virtue nor vice is anything, but that things are only reckoned good or evil by opinion; which, as the true word shows, is the greatest impiety and wickedness. But this we assert is inevitable fate, that they who choose the good have worthy rewards, and they who choose the opposite have their merited awards. For not like other things, as trees and quadrupeds, which cannot act by choice, did God make man: for neither would he be worthy of reward or praise did he not of himself choose the good, but were created for this end;[32] nor, if he were evil, would he be worthy of punishment, not being evil of himself, but being able to be nothing else than what he was made.

CHAPTER XLIV.

Not nullified by prophecy

AND the holy Spirit of prophecy taught us this, telling us by Moses that God spoke thus to the man first created: "Behold, before thy face are good and evil: choose the good" [Deut. 30:15, 19]. . . . Plato, when he says, "The blame is his who chooses, and God is blameless,"[33] took this from the prophet Moses and uttered it. For Moses is more ancient than all the Greek writers. And whatever both philosophers and poets have said concerning the immortality of the soul, or punishments after death, or contemplation of things heavenly, or doctrines of the like kind, they have received such suggestions from the prophets as have enabled them to understand and interpret these things. And hence there seem to be seeds of truth among all men; but they are charged with not accurately understanding [the truth] when they assert contradictories. So that what we say

---

[32]Or, "but were made so." The words are, ἀλλὰ τοῦτο γενόμενος, and the meaning of Justin is sufficiently clear.
[33]Plato, *Rep.* x.

about future events being foretold, we do not say it as if they came about by a fatal necessity; but God foreknowing all that shall be done by all men, and it being His decree that the future actions of men shall all be recompensed according to their several value, He foretells by the Spirit of prophecy that He will bestow meet rewards according to the merit of the actions done, always urging the human race to effort and recollection, showing that He cares and provides for men. . . .

CHAPTER XLVI.
The Word in the world before Christ

BUT lest some should, without reason, and for the perversion of what we teach, maintain that we say that Christ was born one hundred and fifty years ago under Cyrenius, and subsequently, in the time of Pontius Pilate, taught what we say He taught; and should cry out against us as though all men who were born before Him were irresponsible—let us anticipate and solve the difficulty. We have been taught that Christ is the first-born of God, and we have declared above that He is the Word of whom every race of men were partakers; and those who lived reasonably[34] are Christians, even though they have been thought atheists; as, among the Greeks, Socrates and Heraclitus, and men like them; and among the barbarians, Abraham, and Ananias, and Azarias, and Misael, and Elias, and many others whose actions and names we now decline to recount, because we know it would be tedious. So that even they who lived before Christ, and lived without reason, were wicked and hostile to Christ, and slew those who lived reasonably. But why, through the power of the Word, according to the will of God the Father and Lord of all, He was born of a virgin as a man, and was named Jesus, and was crucified, and died, and rose again, and ascended into heaven, an intelligent man will be able to comprehend from what has been already so largely said. . . .

---

[34]μετὰ λόγου, "with reason," or "the Word."

CHAPTER LII.

Certain fulfilment of prophecy

SINCE, then, we prove that all things which have already happened had been predicted by the prophets before they came to pass, we must necessarily believe also that those things which are in like manner predicted, but are yet to come to pass, shall certainly happen. For as the things which have already taken place came to pass when foretold, and even though unknown, so shall the things that remain, even though they be unknown and disbelieved, yet come to pass. For the prophets have proclaimed two advents of His: the one, that which is already past, when He came as a dishonoured and suffering man; but the second, when, according to prophecy, He shall come from heaven with glory, accompanied by His angelic host, when also He shall raise the bodies of all men who have lived, and shall clothe those of the worthy with immortality, and shall send those of the wicked, endued with eternal sensibility, into everlasting fire with the wicked devils. And that these things also have been foretold as yet to be, we will prove. By Ezekiel the prophet it was said: "Joint shall be joined to joint, and bone to bone, and flesh shall grow again [Ezek. 37:7–8]; and "every knee shall bow to the Lord, and every tongue shall confess Him" [Isa. 45:23]. And in what kind of sensation and punishment the wicked are to be, hear from what was said in like manner with reference to this; it is as follows: "Their worm shall not rest, and their fire shall not be quenched;" [Isa. 66:24] and then shall they repent, when it profits them not. And what the people of the Jews shall say and do, when they see Him coming in glory, has been thus predicted by Zechariah the prophet: "I will command the four winds to gather the scattered children; I will command the north wind to bring them, and the south wind, that it keep not back. And then in Jerusalem there shall be great lamentation, not the lamentation of mouths or of lips, but the lamentation of the heart; and they shall rend not their garments, but their hearts. Tribe by tribe they shall mourn, and then they shall look on Him whom they have pierced; and they shall say, Why, O Lord, hast Thou made us to err from Thy way? The glory which our fathers blessed, has for us been turned into shame" [Zech. 2:6; 12:3–14; Isa. 63:17; 64:11].

CHAPTER LIII.

Summary of the prophecies

THOUGH we could bring forward many other prophecies, we forbear, judging these sufficient for the persuasion of those who have ears to hear and understand; and considering also that those persons are able to see that we do not make mere assertions without being able to produce proof, like those fables that are told of the so-called sons of Jupiter. For with what reason should we believe of a crucified man that He is the first-born of the Unbegotten God, and Himself will pass judgment on the whole human race, unless we had found testimonies concerning Him, published before He came and was born as man, and unless we saw that things had happened accordingly—the devastation of the land of the Jews, and men of every race persuaded by His teaching through the apostles, and rejecting their old habits, in which, being deceived, they had had their conversation; yea, seeing ourselves too, and knowing that the Christians from among the Gentiles are both more numerous and more true than those from among the Jews and Samaritans? For all the other human races are called Gentiles by the Spirit of prophecy; but the Jewish and Samaritan races are called the tribe of Israel, and the house of Jacob. And the prophecy in which it was predicted that there should be more believers from the Gentiles than from the Jews and Samaritans, we will produce: it ran thus: "Rejoice, O barren, thou that dost not bear; break forth and shout, thou that dost not travail, because many more are the children of the desolate than of her that hath an husband"]Isa. 54:1]. For all the Gentiles were "desolate" of the true God, serving the works of their hands; but the Jews and Samaritans, having the word of God delivered to them by the prophets, and always expecting the Christ, did not recognise Him when He came, except some few, of whom the Spirit of prophecy by Isaiah had predicted that they should be saved. He spoke as from their person: "Except the Lord had left us a seed, we should have been as Sodom and Gomorrah" [Isa. 1:9]. For Sodom and Gomorrah are related by Moses to have been cities of ungodly men, which God burned with fire and brimstone, and overthrew, no one of their inhabitants being saved except a certain stranger, a Chaldean by birth, whose name was Lot; with whom also his daughters were rescued. And those who care may yet see their whole country desolate and burned, and remaining barren. And to show how those from among the Gentiles were foretold as more true and more believing, we will cite what was said by Isaiah[35] the prophet; for he spoke as follows: "Israel is uncircumcised in heart, but the Gentiles are uncircumcised in the flesh." So many things, therefore, as these, when they are seen with the eye, are enough to produce conviction and belief in those who embrace the truth, and are not bigoted in their opinions, nor are governed by their passions.

CHAPTER LIV.

Origin of heathen mythology

BUT those who hand down the myths which the poets have made, adduce no proof to the youths who learn them; and we proceed to demonstrate that they

---

[35]The following words are found, not in Isaiah, but in Jer. 9:26.

have been uttered by the influence of the wicked demons, to deceive and lead astray the human race. For having heard it proclaimed through the prophets that the Christ was to come, and that the ungodly among men were to be punished by fire, they put forward many to be called sons of Jupiter, under the impression that they would be able to produce in men the idea that the things which were said with regard to Christ were mere marvelous tales, like the things which were said by the poets. And these things were said both among the Greeks and among all nations where they [the demons] heard the prophets foretelling that Christ would specially be believed in; but that in hearing what was said by the prophets they did not accurately understand it, but imitated what was said of our Christ, like men who are in error, we will make plain. The prophet Moses, then, was, as we have already said, older than all writers; and by him, as we have also said before, it was thus predicted: "There shall not fail a prince from Judah, nor a lawgiver from between his feet, until He come for whom it is reserved; and He shall be the desire of the Gentiles, binding His foal to the vine, washing His robe in the blood of the grape" [Gen. 49:10–11]. The devils, accordingly, when they heard these prophetic words, said that Bacchus was the son of Jupiter, and gave out that he was the discoverer of the vine, and they number wine[36] [or, the ass] among his mysteries; and they taught that, having been torn in pieces, he ascended into heaven. And because in the prophecy of Moses it had not been expressly intimated whether He who was to come was the Son of God, and whether He would, riding on the foal, remain on earth or ascend into heaven, and because the name of "foal" could mean either the foal of an ass or the foal of a horse, they, not knowing whether He who was foretold would bring the foal of an ass or of a horse as the sign of His coming, nor whether He was the Son of God, as we said above, or of man, gave out that Bellerophon, a man born of man, himself ascended to heaven on his horse Pegasus. And when they heard it said by the other prophet Isaiah, that He should be born of a virgin, and by his own means ascend into heaven, they pretended that Perseus was spoken of. And when they knew what was said, as has been cited above, in the prophecies written aforetime, "Strong as a giant to run his course" [Ps. 19:5], they said that Hercules was strong, and had journeyed over the whole earth. And when, again, they learned that it had been foretold that He should heal every sickness, and raise the dead, they produced Aesculapius.

---

[36]In the MSS. the reading is οἶνον (wine); but as Justin's argument seems to require ὄνον (an ass), Sylburg inserted this latter word in his edition; and this reading is approved by Grabe and Thirlby, and adopted by Otto and Trollope. It may be added, that ἀναγράφουσι is much more suitable to ὄνον than to οἶνον.

CHAPTER LV.

Symbols of the cross

BUT in no instance, not even in any of those called sons of Jupiter, did they imitate the being crucified; for it was not understood by them, all the things said of it having been put symbolically. And this, as the prophet foretold, is the greatest symbol of His power and rule; as is also proved by the things which fall under our observation. For consider all the things in the world, whether without this form they could be administered or have any community. For the sea is not traversed except that trophy which is called a sail abide safe in the ship; and the earth is not ploughed without it: diggers and mechanics do not their work, except with tools which have this shape. And the human form differs from that of the irrational animals in nothing else than in its being erect and having the hands extended, and having on the face extending from the forehead what is called the nose, through which there is respiration for the living creature; and this shows no other form than that of the cross. And so it was said by the prophet, "The breath before our face is the Lord Christ."[37] And the power of this form is shown by your own symbols on what are called "vexilla" [banners] and trophies, with which all your state processions are made, using these as the insignia of your power and government, even though you do so unwittingly. And with this form you consecrate the images of your emperors when they die, and you name them gods by inscriptions. Since, therefore, we have urged you both by reason and by an evident form, and to the utmost of our ability, we know that now we are blameless even though you disbelieve; for our part is done and finished.

---

[37]From Lam. 4:20 (Sept.).

✑ 2 ✑

ATHENAGORAS
(A.D. Second Century)

According to Philip of Side (a deacon of Chrysostom), Athenagoras was the first head of the school of Alexandria. He was a philosopher who originally intended to write against the Christians. Being a true scholar, he decided that he must study the divine Scriptures in order to write more effectively against those who believed them. However, according to Philip, he was caught by the "all-holy Spirit" and, like Paul, changed from a persecutor to a teacher of the faith. Athenagoras became a brilliant Christian apologist. He was well acquainted with the dominant Platonic philosophy as well as Christian theology in his day.

Philip also tells us that Clement was a student of Athenagoras. Several scholars have questioned this, because strong evidence indicates that Clement was a student of Pantaenus. Philip reverses the order, however, making Pantaenus a student of Clement. Eusebius clearly makes the succession of the heads of the Alexandrian school (after Athenagoras) go from Pantaenus through Clement to Origen. There are several facts in favor of Philip's reference, however. The most important one is that Philip himself was a student at the school after it had been moved from Alexandria and relocated in Pamphylia. Philip studied under Rhodon, the head of the school at that time. Thus, he likely had some factual basis for his statements.

The internal evidence of the writings of Athenagoras tells us only that he was an Athenian and a philosopher. It is not necessarily surprising that an Athenian would be the first head of the school in Alexandria. Most scholars think that Pantaenus was a Sicilian.

Clement does appear to be indebted to the writings of Athenagoras. However, there is no instance where Clement has reproduced verbatim a passage from Athenagoras.

Nothing is known positively about the death of Athenagoras. Some sources seem to indicate that he may have been martyred. However, this idea of martyrdom apparently arose from a confusion between Athenagoras and Athenogenes.

The apologetic writing reproduced here is literally entitled the *Embassy*, as the first footnote indicates. Although the Greek term could have the meaning of "plea" or "apology," section 11 seems to indicate that this essay was addressed to the emperor face to face. This cannot be set aside as mere rhetoric, especially in view of the historic basis, which is now quite generally allowed for the many pagan embassies sent to the emperors from Alexandria between A.D. 35 and 180.

The *Embassy* is addressed to the emperors Marcus Aurelius Antoninus and his son Lucius Aurelius Commodus. History tells us that Commodus became associated with his father as emperor on November 27, 176. Marcus Aurelius died on March 17, 180. Since Athenagoras refers to them both as emperor, the work must be dated somewhere between 176 and 180.

The *Embassy* of Athenagoras is probably the finest single apologetic work from the period of the early church. He appears to be well acquainted with the leading ideas of the current philosophies, and he may be properly characterized as sharing the essential and pervading spirit of the age—eclecticism (not following any one system exclusively but selecting good elements from more than one system).

From Plato Athenagoras derives his ideas of God's essential goodness and the primacy of the immaterial. That he was on the whole a Platonist is clearly seen from his continual references to Plato and from the thoroughly Platonic view that pervades much of his work. His Platonism was modified by his eclecticism, however, and one can detect a Stoic emphasis in his contrasts between human life and the natural life of animals and in his emphasis on the harmony and order of the world as a proof of God's existence. From the Neo-Pythagoreans he seems to have adopted a view of the cosmos as an enclosed sphere moving in rhythm. His analysis of the contradictory nature of the cults and his belief that the conflicting doctrines of philosophy indicated that *reason* has its limits seem to have been ideas that were prominent among the Skeptics. Athenagoras regarded the Gentile philosophers as possessing some measure of divine knowledge, but he firmly believed that they would forever be unable to come to the full knowledge of God through reason alone because this could be obtained only through revelation.

Athenagoras had that unusual ability to tie everything together, express himself clearly, and use language that catches the imagination of the reader. He was a scholar in every sense of the word and at the same time had a profound faith in Christ. He had the ability to penetrate to the heart of a matter in a way that would touch the mind (and then the heart) of the pagan world around him. Modern Christian apologists need to sit for a while at the feet of Athenagoras and learn how to speak to a non-Christian world.

We must recognize the proper context in order to interpret the early apologists correctly. They were not writing to Christians, but to pagans. Thus they emphasized the elements of Christian thought that could be most easily commended to the pagan world. Specifically, they tried to defend Christianity against charges of atheism, incest, and cannibalism.

Athenagoras was a skillful apologist. He not only answers these stock charges but he also shows that Christian worship is more reasonable than the worship and the morals of those leveling the accusations against the Christians. His frequent and authoritative appeal to the Greek philosophers for support should not be taken as a sign of a weak commitment to Scripture on his part, for Athenagoras was simply seeking common ground with the pagans. His goal is to emphasize those aspects of Christianity that sound like the very best in Greek religion in order to get the rulers to stop the persecution against the Christians. It seems to be quite clear that if Athenagoras had written a doctrinal treatise, there would be no equal in his historical time frame.

An edited version of the *Embassy* (*A Plea for the Christians*) by Athenagoras is reprinted in this chapter. His speech is outlined in chapter iii. Chapters iv to xii reply to the charge of atheism. In chapters xiii–xvii, xviii–xxii, and xxiii–xxx Athenagoras responds to three objections. His reply to the second charge of cannibalism is in chapter xxxi. Chapters xxxii–xxxvi respond to charges of promiscuity. The last section is a final prayer for the rulers.

BIBLIOGRAPHY

Barnard, L. W. "The Embassy of Athenagoras." *Vigiliae Christianae* 21 (1967): 88–92.

Bethune-Baker, J. F. *An Introduction to the Early History of Christian Doctrine.* 9th ed. London: Methuen, 1951 (1903).

Carrington, Philip. *The Early Christian Church.* Vol. 2. The Second Christian Century. Cambridge: At the University Press, 1957.

Quasten, Johannes. *Patrology.* 3 vols. Westminster, Maryland: Newman, 1953.

Quasten, Johannes, and Plumpe, Joseph C., eds. *Ancient Christian Writers.* Vol. 23: *Athenagoras.* Translated and annotated by Joseph Hugh Creehan. Westminster, Maryland: Newman, 1956.

Smith, William, and Wace, Henry, eds. "Athenagoras." In A *Dictionary of Christian Biography.* London: John Murry, 1877.

A PLEA[1] FOR THE CHRISTIANS

BY ATHENAGORAS THE ATHENIAN: PHILOSOPHER AND CHRISTIAN

TO the Emperors Marcus Aurelius Antoninus and Lucius Aurelius Commodus, conquerors of Armenia and Sarmatia, and more than all, philosophers.

CHAPTER I.

Injustice shown towards the Christians

IN your empire, greatest of sovereigns, different nations have different customs and laws; and no one is hindered by law or fear of punishment from following his ancestral usages, however ridiculous these may be. A citizen of Ilium calls Hector a god, and pays divine honours to Helen, taking her for Adrasteia. The Lacedaemonian venerates Agamemnon as Zeus, and Phylonoë the daughter of Tyndarus; and the man of Tenedos worships Tennes.[2] The Athenian sacrifices to Erechtheus as Poseidon. The Athenians also perform religious rites and celebrate mysteries in honour of Agraulus and Pandrosus, women who were deemed guilty of impiety for opening the box. In short, among every nation and people, men offer whatever sacrifices and celebrate whatever mysteries they please. The Egyptians reckon among their gods even cats, and crocodiles, and serpents, and asps, and dogs. And to all these both you and the laws give permission so to act, deeming, on the one hand, that to believe in no god at all is

---

From Alexander Roberts and James Donaldson, eds., *Ante-Nicene Christian Library*, trans. B. P. Pratten (Edinburgh: T. & T. Clark, 1867), 2:375–96, 401–4, 405–12, 413–21.

[1]Literally, "embassy."

[2]There are here many varieties of reading: we have followed the text suggested by Gesner.

impious and wicked, and on the other, that it is necessary for each man to worship the gods he prefers, in order that, through fear of the deity, men may be kept
from wrong-doing. But why—for do not, like the multitude, be led astray by
hearsay—why is a mere name odious to you?[3] Names are not deserving of hatred:
it is the unjust act that calls for penalty and punishment. And accordingly, with
admiration of your mildness and gentleness, and your peaceful and benevolent
disposition towards every man, individuals live in the possession of equal rights;
and the cities, according to their rank, share in equal honour; and the whole
empire, under your intelligent sway, enjoys profound peace. But for us who are
called Christians you have not in like manner cared; but although we commit no
wrong—nay, as will appear in the sequel of this discourse, are of all men most
piously and righteously disposed towards the Deity and towards your government—you allow us to be harassed, plundered, and persecuted, the multitude
making war upon us for our name alone. We venture, therefore, to lay a statement of our case before you—and you will learn from this discourse that we
suffer unjustly, and contrary to all law and reason—and we beseech you to bestow some consideration upon us also, that we may cease at length to be slaughtered at the instigation of false accusers. For the fine imposed by our persecutors
does not aim merely at our property, nor their insults at our reputation, nor the
damage they do us at any other of our greater interests. These we hold in contempt, though to the generality they appear matters of great importance; for we
have learned, not only not to return blow for blow, nor to go to law with those
who plunder and rob us, but to those who smite us on one side of the face to
offer the other side also, and to those who take away our coat to give likewise our
cloak. But, when we have surrendered our property, they plot against our very
bodies and souls, pouring upon us wholesale charges of crimes of which we are
guiltless even in thought, but which belong to these idle praters themselves, and
to the whole tribe of those who are like them.

CHAPTER II.

Claim to be treated as others are when accused

IF, indeed, any one can convict us of a crime, be it small or great, we do
not ask to be excused from punishment, but are prepared to undergo the sharpest
and most merciless inflictions. But if the accusation relates merely to our name—
and it is undeniable, that up to the present time the stories told about us rest on
nothing better than the common undiscriminating popular talk, nor has any
Christian been convicted of crime—it will devolve on you, illustrious and benev-

---

[3]We here follow the text of Otto: others read ἡμῖν.

olent and most learned sovereigns, to remove by law this despiteful treatment, so that, as throughout the world both individuals and cities partake of your beneficence, we also may feel grateful to you, exulting that we are no longer the victims of false accusation. . . . I must at the outset of my defence entreat you, illustrious emperors, to listen to me impartially: not to be carried away by the common irrational talk and prejudge the case, but to apply your desire of knowledge and love of truth to the examination of our doctrine also. Thus, while you on your part will not err through ignorance, we also, by disproving the charges arising out of the undiscerning rumour of the multitude, shall cease to be assailed.

CHAPTER III.

Charges brought against the Christians

THREE things are alleged against us: atheism, Thyestean feasts, Oedipodean intercourse. But if these charges are true, spare no class: proceed at once against our crimes; destroy us root and branch, with our wives and children, if any Christian[4] is found to live like the brutes. And yet even the brutes do not touch the flesh of their own kind; and they pair by a law of nature, and only at the regular season, not from simple wantonness; they also recognise those from whom they receive benefits. If any one, therefore, is more savage than the brutes, what punishment that he can endure shall be deemed adequate to such offences? But, if these things are only idle tales and empty slanders, originating in the fact that virtue is opposed by its very nature to vice, and that contraries war against one another by a divine law (and you are yourselves witnesses that no such iniquities are committed by us, for you forbid informations to be laid against us), it remains for you to make inquiry concerning our life, our opinions, our loyalty and obedience to you and your house and government, and thus at length to grant to us the same rights (we ask nothing more) as to those who persecute us. For we shall then conquer them, unhesitatingly surrendering, as we now do, our very lives for the truth's sake.

CHAPTER IV.

The Christians are not atheists, but acknowledge one only God

AS regards, first of all, the allegation that we are atheists—for I will meet the charges one by one, that we may not be ridiculed for having no answer to give to those who make them—with reason did the Athenians adjudge Diagoras guilty of atheism, in that he not only divulged the Orphic doctrine, and published the mysteries of Eleusis and of the Cabiri, and chopped up the wooden statue of

---

[4]Thus Otto; others read, "if any one of men."

Hercules to boil his turnips, but openly declared that there was no God at all. But to us, who distinguish God from matter, and teach that matter is one thing and God another, and that they are separated by a wide interval (for that the Deity is uncreated and eternal, to be beheld by the understanding and reason alone, while matter is created and perishable), is it not absurd to apply the name of atheism? If our sentiments were like those of Diagoras, while we have such incentives to piety—in the established order, the universal harmony, the magnitude, the colour, the form, the arrangement of the world—with reason might our reputation for impiety, as well as the cause of our being thus harassed, be charged on ourselves. But, since our doctrine acknowledges one God, the Maker of this universe, who is Himself uncreated (for that which is does not come to be, but that which is not) but has made all things by the Logos which is from Him, we are treated unreasonably in both respects, in that we are both defamed and persecuted.

CHAPTER V.

Testimony of the poets to the unity of God

POETS and philosophers have not been voted atheists for inquiring concerning God. Euripides, speaking of those who, according to popular preconception, are ignorantly called gods, says doubtingly:

> "If Zeus indeed does reign in heaven above,
> He ought not on the righteous ills to send."[5]

But speaking of Him who is apprehended by the understanding as matter of certain knowledge, he gives his opinion decidedly, and with intelligence; thus:

> "Seest thou on high him who, with humid arms,
> Clasps both the boundless ether and the earth?
> Him reckon Zeus, and him regard as God."[6]

For, as to these so-called gods, he neither saw any real existences, to which a name is usually assigned, underlying them ("Zeus," for instance: "who Zeus is I know not, but by report"), nor that any names were given to realities which actually do exist (for of what use are names to those who have no real existences underlying them?); but Him he did see by means of His works, considering with an eye to things unseen the things which are manifest in air, in ether, on earth.

---

[5]From an unknown play.
[6]From an unknown play; the original is ambiguous; comp. Cic. *De nat. Deorum*, ii. c. 25, where the words are translated—"Seest thou this boundless ether on high which embraces the earth in its moist arms? Reckon this Zeus." Athenagoras cannot so have understood Euripides.

Him therefore, from whom proceed all created things, and by whose Spirit they are governed, he concluded to be God; and Sophocles agrees with him, when he says:

> "There is one God, in truth there is but one,
> Who made the heavens, and the broad earth beneath."[7]

[Euripides is speaking] of the nature of God, which fills His works with beauty, and teaching both where God must be, and that He must be One.

CHAPTER VI.

Opinions of the philosophers as to the one God

PHILOLAUS, too, when he says that all things are included in God as in a stronghold, teaches that He is one, and that He is superior to matter. Lysis and Opsimus[8] thus define God: the one says that He is an ineffable number, the other that He is the excess of the greatest number beyond that which comes nearest to it. So that since ten is the greatest number according to the Pythagoreans, being the Tetractys[9] and containing all the arithmetic and harmonic principles, and the Nine stands next to it, God is a unit—that is, one. For the greatest number exceeds the next least by one. Then there are Plato and Aristotle—not that I am about to go through all that the philosophers have said about God, as if I wished to exhibit a complete summary of their opinions; for I know that, as you excel all men in intelligence and in the power of your rule, in the same proportion do you surpass them all in an accurate acquaintance with all learning, cultivating as you do each several branch with more success than even those who have devoted themselves exclusively to any one. But, inasmuch as it is impossible to demonstrate without the citation of names that we are not alone in confining the notion of God to unity, I have ventured on an enumeration of opinions. Plato, then, says, "To find out the Maker and Father of this universe is difficult; and, when found, it is impossible to declare Him to all,"[10] conceiving of one uncreated and eternal God. And if he recognises others as well, such as the sun, moon, and stars, yet he recognises them as created: "gods, offspring of gods, of whom I am the Maker, and the Father of works which are indissoluble apart from my will; but whatever is compounded can be dissolved."[11] If, therefore, Plato is not an atheist for conceiving of one uncreated God, the Framer of the universe, neither

---

[7]Not found in his extant works.
[8]Thus Otto; common text has ἄψει.
[9]One, two, three, and four together forming *ten*.
[10]*Timaeus*, p. 28, C.
[11]*Timaeus*, p. 41, A.

are we atheists who acknowledge and firmly hold that He is God who has framed all things by the Logos, and holds them in being by His Spirit. Aristotle, again, and his followers, recognising the existence of one whom they regard as a sort of compound living creature (ζωον), speak of God as consisting of soul and body, thinking His body to be the etherial space and the planetary stars and the sphere of the fixed stars, moving in circles; but His soul, the reason which presides over the motion of the body, itself not subject to motion, but becoming the cause of motion to the other. The Stoics also, although by the appellations they employ to suit the changes of matter, which they say is permeated by the Spirit of God, they multiply the Deity in name, yet in reality they consider God to be one. For, if God is an artistic fire advancing methodically to the production of the several things in the world, embracing in Himself all the seminal principles by which each thing is produced in accordance with fate, and if His Spirit pervades the whole world, then God is one according to them, being named Zeus in respect of the fervid part (τὸ ζέον) of matter, and Hera in respect of the air (ὁ ἀήρ), and called by other names in respect of that particular part of matter which He pervades.

CHAPTER VII.

Superiority of the Christian doctrine respecting God

SINCE, therefore, the unity of the Deity is confessed by almost all, even against their will, when they come to treat of the first principles of the universe, and we in our turn likewise assert that He who arranged this universe is God,— why is it that they can say and write with impunity what they please concerning the Deity, but that against us a law lies in force, though we are able to demonstrate what we apprehend and justly believe, namely that there is one God, with proofs and reasons accordant with truth? For poets and philosophers, as to other subjects so also to this, have applied themselves in the way of conjecture, moved, by reason of their affinity with the afflatus from God, each one by his own soul, to try whether he could find out and apprehend the truth; but they have not been found competent fully to apprehend it, because they thought fit to learn, not from God concerning God, but each one from himself; hence they came each to his own conclusion respecting God, and matter, and forms, and the world. But we have for witnesses of the things we apprehend and believe, prophets, men who have pronounced concerning God and the things of God, guided by the Spirit of God. And you too will admit, excelling all others as you do in intelligence and in piety towards the true God (τὸ ὄντως θεῖον), that it would be irrational for us to cease to believe in the Spirit from God, who moved the mouths of the prophets like musical instruments, and to give heed to mere human opinions.

CHAPTER VIII.

Absurdities of polytheism

AS regards, then, the doctrine that there was from the beginning one God, the Maker of this universe, consider it in this wise, that you may be acquainted with the argumentative grounds also of our faith. If there were from the beginning two or more gods, they were either in one and the same place, or each of them separately in his own. In one and the same place they could not be. For, if they are gods, they are not alike; but because they are uncreated they are unlike: for created things are like their patterns; but the uncreated are unlike, being neither produced from any one, nor formed after the pattern of any one. Hand and eye and foot are parts of one body, making up together one man: is God in this sense one?[12] And indeed Socrates was compounded and divided into parts, just because he was created and perishable; but God is uncreated, and impassible, and indivisible—does not, therefore, consist of parts. But if, on the contrary, each of them exists separately, since He that made the world is above the things created, and about the things He has made and set in order, where can the other or the rest be? For if the world, being made spherical, is confined within the circles of heaven, and the Creator of the world is above the things created, managing that[13] by His providential care of these, what place is there for the second god, or for the other gods? For he is not in the world, because it belongs to the other; nor about the world, for God the Maker of the world is above it. But if he is neither in the world nor about the world (for all that surrounds it is occupied by this one[14]), where is he? Is he above the world and [the first] God? In another world, or about another? But if he is in another or about another, then he is not about us, for he does not govern the world; nor is his power great, for he exists in a circumscribed space. But if he is neither in another world (for all things are filled by the other), nor about another (for all things are occupied by the other), he clearly does not exist at all, for there is no place in which he can be. Or what does he do, seeing that there is another to whom the world belongs, and he is above the Maker of the world, and yet is neither in the world nor about the world? Is there, then, some other place where he can stand? But God, and what belongs to God, are above him. And what, too, shall be the place, seeing that the other fills the regions which are above the world? Perhaps he exerts a providential care? [By no means.] And yet, unless he does so, he has done nothing. If, then,

---

[12]*i.e.* Do several gods make up one God?—*Otto.* Others read affirmatively, "God is one."

[13]*i.e.* the world.

[14]*i.e.* the Creator, or first God.

he neither does anything nor exercises providential care, and if there is not another place in which he is, then this Being of whom we speak is the one God
from the beginning, and the sole Maker of the world.

CHAPTER IX.

The testimonies of the prophets

IF we satisfied ourselves with advancing such considerations as these, our
doctrines might by some be looked upon as human. But, since the voices of the
prophets confirm our arguments—for I think that you also, with your great zeal
for knowledge, and your great attainments in learning, cannot be ignorant of the
writings either of Moses or of Isaiah and Jeremiah, and the other prophets, who,
lifted in ecstasy above the natural operations of their minds by the impulses of the
Divine Spirit, uttered the things with which they were inspired, the Spirit making
use of them as a flute-player breathes into a flute;—what, then, do these men
say? "The Lord is our God; no other can be compared with Him."[15] And again:
"I am God, the first and the last, and besides me there is no God" [Isa. 44:6]. In
like manner: "Before me there was no other God, and after me there shall be
none; I am God, and there is none besides me" [Isa. 43:10–11]. And as to His
greatness: "Heaven is my throne, and the earth is the footstool of my feet: what
house will ye build for me, or what is the place of my rest?" [Isa. 66:1]. But I
leave it to you, when you meet with the books themselves, to examine carefully
the prophecies contained in them, that you may on fitting grounds defend us
from the abuse cast upon us.

CHAPTER X.

The Christians worship the Father, Son, and Holy Ghost

THAT we are not atheists, therefore, seeing that we acknowledge one God,
uncreated, eternal, invisible, impassible, incomprehensible, illimitable, who is
apprehended by the understanding only and the reason, who is encompassed by
light, and beauty, and spirit, and power ineffable, by whom the universe has
been created through His Logos, and set in order, and is kept in being—I have
sufficiently demonstrated. [I say "His Logos"], for we acknowledge also a Son of
God. Nor let any one think it ridiculous that God should have a Son. For though
the poets, in their fictions, represent the gods as no better than men, our mode of
thinking is not the same as theirs, concerning either God the Father or the Son.
But the Son of God is the Logos of the Father, in idea and in operation; for after

---

[15]Isa. xli. 4; Ex. xx. 2, 3 (as to sense).

the pattern of Him and by Him[16] were all things made, the Father and the Son being one. And, the Son being in the Father and the Father in the Son, in oneness and power of spirit, the understanding and reason (νοῦς καὶ λόγος) of the Father is the Son of God. But if, in your surpassing intelligence, it occurs to you to inquire what is meant by the Son, I will state briefly that He is the first product of the Father, not as having been brought into existence (for from the beginning, God, who is the eternal mind [νοῦς], had the Logos in Himself, being from eternity instinct with Logos [λογικός]); but inasmuch as He came forth to be the idea and energizing power of all material things, which lay like a nature without attributes, and an inactive earth, the grosser particles being mixed up with the lighter. The prophetic Spirit also agrees with our statements. "The Lord," it says, "made me, the beginning of His ways to His works" [Prov. 8:22]. The Holy Spirit Himself also, which operates in the prophets, we assert to be an effluence of God, flowing from Him, and returning back again like a beam of the sun. Who, then, would not be astonished to hear men who speak of God the Father, and of God the Son, and of the Holy Spirit, and who declare both their power in union and their distinction in order, called atheists? Nor is our teaching in what relates to the divine nature confined to these points; but we recognise also a multitude of angels and ministers, whom God the Maker and Framer of the world distributed and appointed to their several posts by His Logos, to occupy themselves about the elements, and the heavens, and the world, and the things in it, and the goodly ordering of them all.

CHAPTER XI.

The moral teaching of the Christians repels the charge brought against them

IF I go minutely into the particulars of our doctrine, let it not surprise you. It is that you may not be carried away by the popular and irrational opinion, but may have the truth clearly before you. For presenting the opinions themselves to which we adhere, as being not human, but uttered and taught by God, we shall be able to persuade you not to think of us as atheists. What, then, are those teachings in which we are brought up? "I say unto you, Love your enemies; bless them that curse you; pray for them that persecute you" [Luke 6:27–28]; "that ye may be the sons of your Father who is in heaven, who causes His sun to rise on the evil and the good, and sends rain on the just and the unjust" [Matt. 5:44–45]. Allow me here to lift up my voice boldly in loud and audible outcry, pleading as I do before philosophic princes. For who of those that reduce syllogisms, and clear up ambiguities, and explain etymologies, or of those who teach homonyms

---

[16]Or, "by Him and through Him."

and synonyms, and predicaments and axioms, and what is the subject and what the predicate, and who promise their disciples by these and such like instructions to make them happy: who of them have so purged their souls as, instead of hating their enemies, to love them; and, instead of speaking ill of those who have reviled them (to abstain from which is of itself an evidence of no mean forbearance), to bless them; and to pray for those who plot against their lives? On the contrary, they never cease with evil intent to search out skilfully the secrets of their art,[17] and are ever bent on working some ill, making the art of words and not the exhibition of deeds their business and profession. But among us you will find uneducated persons, and artisans, and old women, who, if they are unable in words to prove the benefit of our doctrine, yet by their deeds exhibit the benefit arising from their persuasion of its truth: they do not rehearse speeches, but exhibit good works; when struck, they do not strike again; when robbed, they do not go to law; they give to those that ask of them, and love their neighbours as themselves.

CHAPTER XII.
Consequent absurdity of the charge of atheism

SHOULD we, then, unless we believed that a God presides over the human race, thus purge ourselves from evil? Most certainly not. But, because we are persuaded that we shall give an account of everything in the present life to God, who made us and the world, we adopt a temperate and benevolent and generally despised method of life, believing that we shall suffer no such great evil here, even should our lives be taken from us, compared with what we shall there receive for our meek and benevolent and moderate life from the great Judge. . . . [Shall] men who reckon on the present life of very small worth indeed . . . and who know that the life for which we look is far better than can be described in words, provided we arrive at it pure from all wrong-doing; who, moreover, carry our benevolence to such an extent, that we not only love our friends ("for if ye love them," He says, "that love you, and lend to them that lend to you, what reward will ye have?" [Luke 6:32, 34; Matt. 5:46]),—shall we, I say, when such is our character, and when we live such a life as this, that we may escape condemnation at last, not be accounted pious? These, however, are only small matters taken from great, and a few things from many, that we may not further trespass on your patience; for those who test honey and whey, judge by a small quantity whether the whole is good.

---

[17]The meaning is here doubtful; but the probable reference is to the practices of the Sophists.

CHAPTER XIII.

Why the Christians do not offer sacrifices

BUT, as most of those who charge us with atheism, and that because they have not even the dreamiest conception of what God is, and are doltish and utterly unacquainted with natural and divine things, and such as measure piety by the rule of sacrifices, charge us with not acknowledging the same gods as the cities, be pleased to attend to the following considerations, O emperors, on both points. And first, as to our not sacrificing: the Framer and Father of this universe does not need blood, nor the odour of burnt-offerings, nor the fragrance of flowers and incense, forasmuch as He is Himself perfect fragrance, needing nothing either within or without; but the noblest sacrifice to Him is for us to know who stretched out and vaulted the heavens, and fixed the earth in its place like a centre, who gathered the water into seas and divided the light from the darkness, who adorned the sky with stars and made the earth to bring forth seed of every kind, who made animals and fashioned man. When, holding God to be this Framer of all things, who preserves them in being and superintends them all by knowledge and administrative skill, we "lift up holy hands" to Him, what need has He further of a hecatomb?

> "For they, when mortals have transgress'd or fail'd
> To do aright, by sacrifice and pray'r,
> Libations and burnt-offerings, may be soothed."[18]

And what have I to do with holocausts, which God does not stand in need of?— though indeed it does behove us to offer a bloodless sacrifice and "the service of our reason."[19]

CHAPTER XIV.

Inconsistency of those who accuse the Christians

THEN, as to the other complaint, that we do not pray to and believe in the same gods as the cities, it is an exceedingly silly one. Why, the very men who charge us with atheism for not admitting the same gods as they acknowledge, are not agreed among themselves concerning the gods. The Athenians have set up as gods Celeus and Metanira: the Lacedaemonians Menelaus; and they offer sacrifices and hold festivals to him, while the men of Ilium cannot endure the very sound of his name, and pay their adoration to Hector. The Ceans worship

---

[18]Hom. *Il.* ix. 499 sq., Lord Derby's translation, which version the translator has for the most part used.
[19]Comp. Rom. 12:1.

Aristaeus, considering him to be the same as Zeus and Apollo; the Thasians Theagenes, a man who committed murder at the Olympic games; the Samians Lysander, notwithstanding all the slaughters and all the crimes perpetrated by him; Alcman and Hesiod Medea, and the Cilicians Niobe; the Sicilians Philip the son of Butacides; the Amathusians Onesilus; the Carthaginians Hamilcar. Time would fail me to enumerate the whole. When, therefore, they differ among themselves concerning their gods, why do they bring the charge against us of not agreeing with them? Then look at the practices prevailing among the Egyptians: are they not perfectly ridiculous? For in the temples at their solemn festivals they beat their breasts as for the dead, and sacrifice to the same beings as gods; and no wonder, when they look upon the brutes as gods, and shave themselves when they die, and bury them in temples, and make public lamentation. If, then, we are guilty of impiety because we do not practise a piety corresponding with theirs, then all cities and all nations are guilty of impiety, for they do not all acknowledge the same gods.

CHAPTER XV.

The Christians distinguish God from matter

BUT grant that they acknowledge the same. What then? Because the multitude, who cannot distinguish between matter and God, or see how great is the interval which lies between them, pray to idols made of matter, are we therefore, who do distinguish and separate the uncreated and the created, that which is and that which is not, that which is apprehended by the understanding and that which is perceived by the senses, and who give the fitting name to each of them,—are we to come and worship images? If, indeed, matter and God are the same, two names for one thing, then certainly, in not regarding stocks and stones, gold and silver, as gods, we are guilty of impiety. But if they are at the greatest possible remove from one another—as far asunder as the artist and the materials of his art—why are we called to account? For as is the potter and the clay (matter being the clay, and the artist the potter), so is God, the Framer of the world, and matter, which is subservient to Him for the purposes of His art. But as the clay cannot become vessels of itself without art, so neither did matter, which is capable of taking all forms, receive, apart from God the Framer, distinction and shape and order. And as we do not hold the pottery of more worth than him who made it, nor the vessels of glass and gold than him who wrought them; but if there is anything about them elegant in art we praise the artificer, and it is he who reaps the glory of the vessels: even so with matter and God—the glory and honour of the orderly arrangement of the world belongs of right not to matter, but to God, the Framer of matter. . . .

CHAPTER XVI.

The Christians do not worship the universe

BEAUTIFUL without doubt is the world . . . yet it is not this, but its Artificer, that we must worship. The world was not created because God needed it; for God is Himself everything to Himself,—light unapproachable, a perfect world, spirit, power, reason. If, therefore, the world is an instrument in tune, and moving in well-measured time, I adore the Being who gave its harmony, and strikes its notes and sings the accordant strain, and not the instrument. . . . I do not ask of matter what it has not to give, nor passing God by do I pay homage to the elements, which can do nothing more than what they were bidden; for, although they are beautiful to look upon, by reason of the art of their Framer, yet they still have the nature of matter. And to this view Plato also bears testimony; "for," says he, "that which is called heaven and earth has received many blessings from the Father, but yet partakes of body; hence it cannot possibly be free from change."[20] If, therefore, while I admire the heavens and the elements in respect of their art, I do not worship them as gods, knowing that the law of dissolution is upon them, how can I call those objects gods of which I know the makers to be men? Attend, I beg, to a few words on this subject.

CHAPTER XVII.

The names of the gods and their images are but of recent date

AN apologist must adduce more precise arguments than I have yet given, both concerning the names of the gods, to show that they are of recent origin, and concerning their images, to show that they are, so to say, but of yesterday. You yourselves, however, are thoroughly acquainted with these matters, since you are versed in all departments of knowledge, and are beyond all other men familiar with the ancients. I assert, then, that it was Orpheus, and Homer, and Hesiod who[21] gave both genealogies and names to those whom they call gods. Such, too, is the testimony of Herodotus.[22] "My opinion," he says, "is that Hesiod and Homer preceded me by four hundred years, and no more; and it was they who framed a theogony for the Greeks, and gave the gods their names, and assigned them their several honours and functions, and described their forms." Representations of the gods, again, were not in use at all, so long as statuary, and painting, and sculpture were unknown. . . . You perceive, then, that the time

---

[20]*Polit.* p. 269, D.
[21]We here follow the text of Otto; others place the clause in the following sentence.
[22]ii. 53.

since representations of form and the making of images began is so short, that we can name the artist of each particular god. The image of Artemis at Ephesus, for example, and that of Athenâ (or rather of Athelâ, for so is she named by those who speak more in the style of the mysteries; for thus was the ancient image made of the olive tree called), and the sitting figure of the same goddess, were made by Endoeus, a pupil of Daedalus; the Pythian god was the work of Theodorus and Telecles; and the Delian god and Artemis are due to the art of Tectaeus and Angelio; Hera in Samos and in Argos came from the hands of Smilis, and the other statues[23] were by Phidias; Aphrodité the courtezan in Cnidus is the production of Praxiteles; Aesclepius in Epidaurus is the work of Phidias. In a word, of not one of these statues can it be said that it was not made by man. If, then, these are gods, why did they not exist from the beginning? Why, in sooth, are they younger than those who made them? Why, in sooth, in order to their coming into existence, did they need the aid of men and art? They are nothing but earth, and stones, and matter, and curious art.

CHAPTER XVIII.

The gods themselves have been created, as the poets confess

BUT, since it is affirmed by some that, although these are only images, yet there exist gods in honour of whom they are made; and that the supplications and sacrifices presented to the images are to be referred to the gods, and are in fact made to the gods; and that there is not any other way of coming to them, for

" 'Tis hard for man
To meet in presence visible a God;"[24]

and whereas, in proof that such is the fact, they adduce the energies possessed by certain images, let us examine into the power attached to their names. . . This then especially I beg you carefully to consider. The gods, as they affirm, were not from the beginning, but every one of them has come into existence just like ourselves. And in this opinion they all agree. Homer speaks of

"Old Oceanus,
The sire of gods, and Tethys;"[25]

and Orpheus (who, moreover, was the first to invent their names, and recounted their births, and narrated the exploits of each, and is believed by them to treat

---

[23]The reading is here doubtful.
[24]Hom. *Il.* xx. 131.
[25]Hom. *Il.* xiv. 301, 302.

with greater truth than others of divine things, whom Homer himself follows in most matters, especially in reference to the gods)—he, too, has fixed their first origin to be from water:

"Oceanus, the origin of all."

For, according to him, water was the beginning of all things, and from water mud was formed, and from both was produced an animal, a dragon with the head of a lion growing to it, and between the two heads there was the face of a god, named Heracles and Kronos. This Heracles generated an egg of enormous size, which, on becoming full, was, by the powerful friction of its generator, burst into two, the part at the top receiving the form of heaven (οὐρανός), and the lower part that of earth (γῆ). The goddess Gê, moreover, came forth with a body; and Ouranos, by his union with Gê, begat females, Clotho, Lachesis, and Atropos; and males, the hundred-handed Cottys, Gyges, Briareus, and the Cyclopes Brontes, and Steropes, and Argos, whom also he bound and hurled down to Tartarus, having learnt that he was to be ejected from his government by his children; whereupon Gê, being enraged, brought forth the Titans.[26]

> "The godlike Gaia bore to Ouranos
> Sons who are by the name of Titans known,
> Because they vengeance[27] took on Ouranos,
> Majestic, glitt'ring with his starry crown."[28]

CHAPTER XIX.

The philosophers agree with the poets respecting the gods

SUCH was the beginning of the existence both of their gods and of the universe. Now what are we to make of this? For each of those things to which divinity is ascribed is conceived of as having existed from the first. For, if they have come into being, having previously had no existence, as those say who treat of the gods, they do not exist. For, a thing is either uncreated and eternal, or created and perishable. . . . And in what are the gods superior to matter, since they derive their constitution from water? But not even water, according to them, is the beginning of all things. From simple and homogeneous elements what could be constituted? Moreover, matter requires an artificer, and the artificer requires matter. For how could figures be made without matter or an artificer?

---

[26]Hom. *Il.* xiv. 246.
[27]τισάσθην.
[28]Orpheus, *Fragments.*

Neither, again, is it reasonable that matter should be older than God; for the efficient cause must of necessity exist before the things that are made.

.   .   .

CHAPTER XXII.

Pretended symbolical explanations

. . . ZEUS is, according to the Stoics, the fervid part of nature; Hera is the air (ἀήρ)—the very name, if it be joined to itself, signifying this;[29] Poseidon is what is drunk (water, πόσις). But these things are by different persons explained of natural objects in different ways. Some call Zeus twofold masculine-feminine air; others the season which brings about mild weather, on which account it was that he alone escaped from Kronos. But to the Stoics it may be said, If you acknowledge one God, the supreme and uncreated and eternal One, and as many compound bodies as there are changes of matter, and say that the Spirit of God, which pervades matter, obtains according to its variations a diversity of names, the forms of matter will become the body of God; but when the elements are destroyed in the conflagration, the names will necessarily perish along with the forms, the Spirit of God alone remaining. Who, then, can believe that those bodies, of which the variation according to matter is allied to corruption, are gods? . . . But why should I trespass on your patience by saying more, when you know so well what has been said by each of those who have resolved these things into nature, or what various writers have thought concerning nature. . . . For whilst they wander up and down about the forms of matter, they miss to find the God who can only be beheld by the reason, while they deify the elements and their several parts, applying different names to them at different times: calling the sowing of the corn, for instance, Osiris (hence they say, that in the mysteries, on the finding of the members of his body, or the fruits, Isis is thus addressed: We have found, we wish thee joy), the fruit of the vine Dionysus, the vine itself Semelé, the heat of the sun the thunderbolt. And yet, in fact, they who refer the fables to actual gods, do anything rather than add to their divine character; for they do not perceive, that by the very defence they make for the gods, they confirm the things which are alleged concerning them. What have Europa, and the bull, and the swan, and Leda, to do with the earth and air, that the abominable intercourse of Zeus with them should be taken for the intercourse of the earth and air? But missing to discover the greatness of God, and not being able to rise

---

[29]*Perhaps* ἠρ(αηρ)α.

on high with their reason (for they have no affinity for the heavenly place), they pine away among the forms of matter, and rooted to the earth, deify the changes of the elements: just as if any one should put the ship he sailed in in the place of the steersman. But as the ship, although equipped with everything, is of no use if it have not a steersman, so neither are the elements, though arranged in perfect order, of any service apart from the providence of God. For the ship will not sail of itself; and the elements without their Framer will not move.

CHAPTER XXIII.

Opinions of Thales and Plato

YOU may say, however, since you excel all men in understanding, How comes it to pass, then, that some of the idols manifest power, if those to whom we erect the statues are not gods? For it is not likely that images destitute of life and motion can of themselves do anything without a mover. That in various places, cities, and nations, certain effects are brought about in the name of idols, we are far from denying. None the more, however, if some have received benefit, and others, on the contrary, suffered harm, shall we deem those to be gods who have produced the effects in either case. But I have made careful inquiry, both why it is that you think the idols to have this power, and who they are that, usurping their names, produce the effects. It is necessary for me, however, in attempting to show who they are that produce the effects ascribed to the idols, and that they are not gods, to have recourse to some witnesses from among the philosophers. First Thales, as those who have accurately examined his opinions report, divides [superior beings] into God, demons, and heroes. God he recognises as the Intelligence (νοῦς) of the world; by demons he understands beings possessed of soul (ψυχικαί); and by heroes the separated souls of men, the good being the good souls, and the bad the worthless. Plato again, while withholding his assent on other points, also divides [superior beings] into the uncreated God and those produced by the uncreated One for the adornment of heaven, the planets, and the fixed stars, and into demons. . . .

CHAPTER XXIV.

Concerning the angels and giants

. . . IF the poets and philosophers did not acknowledge that there is one God, and concerning these gods were not of opinion, some that they are demons, others that they are matter, and others that they once were men,—there might be some show of reason for our being harassed as we are, since we employ language which makes a distinction between God and matter, and the natures of the two. For, as we acknowledge a God, and a Son his Logos, and a Holy Spirit, united in essence,—the Father, the Son, the Spirit, because the Son is the Intelligence, Reason, Wisdom of the Father, and the Spirit an effluence, as light from fire; so also do we apprehend the existence of other powers, which exercise dominion about matter, and by means of it, and one in particular, which is hostile to God: not that anything is really opposed to God, like strife to friendship, according to Empedocles, and night to day, according to the appearing and disappearing of the stars (for even if anything *had* placed itself in opposition to God, it would have ceased to exist, its structure being destroyed by the power and might of God), but that to the good that is in God, which belongs of necessity to Him, and co-exists with Him, as colour with body, without which it has no existence (not as being part of it, but as an attendant property co-existing with it, united and blended, just as it is natural for fire to be yellow and the ether dark blue),—to the good that is in God, I say, the spirit which is about matter, who was created by God, just as the other angels were created by Him, and entrusted with the control of matter and the forms of matter, is opposed. For this is the office of the angels,—to exercise providence for God over the things created and ordered by Him; so that God may have the universal and general providence of the whole, while the particular parts are provided for by the angels appointed over them. Just as with men, who have freedom of choice as to both virtue and vice (for you would not either honour the good or punish the bad, unless vice and virtue were in their own power; and some are diligent in the matters entrusted to them by you, and others faithless), so is it among the angels. Some, free agents, you will observe, such as they were created by God, continued in those things for which God had made and over which He had ordained them; but some outraged both the constitution of their nature and the government entrusted to them: namely, this ruler of matter and its various forms, and others of those who were placed about this first firmament (you know that we say nothing without witnesses, but state the things which have been declared by the prophets); these fell into impure love of virgins, and were subjugated by the flesh, and he became negligent and wicked in the management of the things entrusted to him. Of these lovers of virgins, therefore, were begotten those who are called giants. And if something has been said by the poets, too, about the giants, be not surprised at this: worldly wisdom and divine differ as much from each other as truth and plausibility: the one is of heaven and the other of earth; and, indeed, according to the prince of matter,

"We know we oft speak lies that look like truths."[30]

---

[30]Hesoid, *Theog.* 27.

CHAPTER XXV.

The poets and philosophers have denied a divine Providence

THESE angels, then, who have fallen from heaven, and haunt the air and the earth, and are no longer able to rise to heavenly things, and the souls of the giants, which are the demons who wander about the world, perform actions similar, the one (that is, the demons) to the natures they have received, the other (that is, the angels) to the appetites they have indulged. But the prince of matter, as may be seen merely from what transpires, exercises a control and management contrary to the good that is in God. . . . Some who are of no mean reputation have therefore thought that this universe is constituted without any definite order, and is driven hither and thither by an irrational chance. But they do not understand, that of those things which belong to the constitution of the whole world there is nothing out of order or neglected, but that each one of them has been produced by reason, and that, therefore, they do not transgress the order prescribed to them; and that man himself, too, so far as He that made him is concerned, is well ordered, both by his original nature, which has one common character for all, and by the constitution of his body, which does not transgress the law imposed upon it, and by the termination of his life, which remains equal and common to all alike; but that, according to the character peculiar to himself and the operation of the ruling prince and of the demons his followers, he is impelled and moved in this direction or in that, notwithstanding that all possess in common the same original constitution of mind.[31]

CHAPTER XXVI.

The demons allure men to the worship of images

THEY who draw men to idols, then, are the aforesaid demons, who are eager for the blood of the sacrifices, and lick them; but the gods that please the multitude, and whose names are given to the images, were men, as may be learned from their history. And that it is the demons who act under their names, is proved by the nature of their operations. For some castrate, as Rhea; others wound and slaughter, as Artemis; the Tauric goddess puts all strangers to death. I pass over those who lacerate with knives and scourges of bones, and shall not attempt to describe all the kinds of demons; for it is not the part of a god to incite to things against nature.

---

[31]Or, "powers of reasoning" (λογισμός).

"But when the demon plots against a man,
He first inflicts some hurt upon his mind."[32]

But God, being perfectly good, is eternally doing good. . . .

CHAPTER XXVII.

Artifices of the demons

WHAT then? In the first place, the irrational and fantastic movements of the soul about opinions produce a diversity of images (εἴδωλα) from time to time: some they derive from matter, and some they fashion and bring forth for themselves. . . . These irrational and fantastic movements of the soul, then, give birth to empty visions in the mind, by which it becomes madly set on idols. When, too, a tender and susceptible soul, which has no knowledge or experience of sounder doctrines, and is unaccustomed to contemplate truth, and to consider thoughtfully the Father and Maker of all things, gets impressed with false opinions respecting itself, then the demons who hover about matter, greedy of sacrificial odours and the blood of victims, and ever ready to lead men into error, avail themselves of these delusive movements of the souls of the multitude; and, taking possession of their thoughts, cause to flow into the mind empty visions as if coming from the idols and the statues; and when, too, a soul of itself, as being immortal, moves conformably to reason, either predicting the future or healing the present, the demons claim the glory for themselves.

CHAPTER XXVIII.

The heathen gods were simply men

BUT it is perhaps necessary, in accordance with what has already been adduced, to say a little about their names. Herodotus, then, and Alexander the son of Philip, in his letter to his mother (and each of them is said to have conversed with the priests at Heliopolis, and Memphis, and Thebes), affirm that they learnt from them that the gods had been men. Herodotus speaks thus: "Of such a nature were, they said, the beings represented by these images, they were very far indeed from being gods. However, in the times anterior to them it was otherwise; then Egypt had gods for its rulers, who dwelt upon the earth with men, one being always supreme above the rest. The last of these was Horus the son of Osiris, called by the Greeks Apollo. He deposed Typhon, and ruled over Egypt as its last god-king. Osiris is named Dionysus (Bacchus) by the Greeks."[33] "Almost all the

---

[32]From an unknown tragedian.
[33]ii. 144. Mr. Rawlinson's translation is used in the extracts from Herodotus.

names of the gods came into Greece from Egypt."[34] Apollo was the son of Dionysus and Isis, as Herodotus likewise affirms: "According to the Egyptians, Apollo and Diana are the children of Bacchus and Isis; while Latona is their nurse and their preserver."[35] These beings of heavenly origin they had for their first kings: partly from ignorance of the true worship of the Deity, partly from gratitude for their government, they esteemed them as gods together with their wives. "The male kine, if clean, and the male calves, are used for sacrifice by the Egyptians universally; but the females, they are not allowed to sacrifice, since they are sacred to Isis. The statue of this goddess has the form of a woman, but with horns like a cow, resembling those of the Greek representations of Io."[36] And who can be more deserving of credit in making these statements, than those who in family succession, son from father, received not only the priesthood, but also the history? For it is not likely that the priests, who make it their business to commend the idols to men's reverence, would assert falsely that they were men. . . . That they were men, the most learned of the Egyptians also testify, who, while saying that ether, earth, sun, moon, are gods, regard the rest as mortal men, and the temples as their sepulchres. Apollodorus, too, asserts the same thing in his treatise concerning the gods. But Herodotus calls even their sufferings mysteries. "The ceremonies at the feast of Isis in the city of Busiris have been already spoken of. It is there that the whole multitude, both of men and women, many thousands in number, beat themselves at the close of the sacrifice in honour of a god whose name a religious scruple forbids me to mention."[37] If they are gods, they are also immortal; but if people are beaten for them, and their sufferings are mysteries, they are men. . . .

CHAPTER XXX.

Reasons why divinity has been ascribed to men

FOR if detestable and god-hated men had the reputation of being gods, and the daughter of Derceto, Semiramis, a lascivious and blood-stained woman, was esteemed a Syrian goddess; and if, on account of Derceto, the Syrians worship doves and Semiramis (for, a thing impossible, a woman was changed into a dove:

---

[34]ii. 50.
[35]ii. 156.
[36]ii. 41.
[37]ii. 61.

the story is in Ctesias), what wonder if some should be called gods by their people on the ground of their rule and sovereignty (the Sibyl, of whom Plato also makes mention, says:

> "It was the generation then the tenth,
> Of men endow'd with speech, since forth the flood
> Had burst upon the men of former times,
> And Kronos, Japetus, and Titan reigned,
> Whom men, of Ouranos and Gaia
> Proclaimed the noblest sons, and named them so, [38]
> Because of men endowed with gift of speech
> They were the first");[39]

and others for their strength, as Heracles and Perseus; and others for their art, as Asclepius? Those, therefore, to whom either the subjects gave honour or the rulers themselves [assumed it], obtained the name, some from fear, others from reverence. Thus Antinous, through the benevolence of your ancestors towards their subjects, came to be regarded as a god. But those who came after adopted the worship without examination.

> "The Cretans always lie; for they, O king,
> Have built a tomb to thee who art not dead."[40]

Though you believe, O Callimachus, in the nativity of Zeus, you do not believe in his sepulchre; and whilst you think to obscure the truth, you in fact proclaim him dead, even to those who are ignorant; and if you see the cave, you call to mind the childbirth of Rhea; but when you see the coffin, you throw a shadow over his death, not considering that the unbegotten God alone is eternal. For either the tales told by the multitude and the poets about the gods are unworthy of credit, and the reverence shown them is superfluous (for those do not exist, the tales concerning whom are untrue); or if the births, the amours, the murders, the thefts, the castrations, the thunderbolts, are true, they no longer exist, having ceased to be since they were born, having previously had no being. And on what principle must we believe some things and disbelieve others, when the poets have written their stories in order to gain greater veneration for them? For surely those through whom they have got to be considered gods, and who have striven to represent their deeds as worthy of reverence, cannot have invented their sufferings. That, therefore, we are not atheists, acknowledging as we do God the Maker of this universe and His Logos, has been proved according to my ability, if not according to the importance of the subject.

---

[38]*i.e.* after Gaia and Ouranos, *Earth* and *Heaven*.
[39]Oracc. *Sibyll.* iii. 108–113.
[40]Callim. *Hym. Jov.* 8 sq.

CHAPTER XXXI.

Confutation of the other charges brought against the Christians

BUT they have further also made up stories against us of impious feasts and forbidden intercourse between the sexes, both that they may appear to themselves to have rational grounds of hatred, and because they think either by fear to lead us away from our way of life, or to render the rulers harsh and inexorable by the magnitude of the charges they bring. But they lose their labour with those who know that from of old it has been the custom, and not in our time only, for vice to make war on virtue. Thus Pythagoras, with three hundred others, was burnt to death; Heraclitus and Democritus were banished, the one from the city of the Ephesians, the other from Abdera, because he was charged with being mad; and the Athenians condemned Socrates to death. But as they were none the worse in respect of virtue because of the opinion of the multitude, so neither does the undiscriminating calumny of some persons cast any shade upon us as regards rectitude of life, for with God we stand in good repute. Nevertheless, I will meet these charges also, although I am well assured that by what has been already said I have cleared myself to you. For as you excel all men in intelligence, you know that those whose life is directed towards God as its rule, so that each one among us may be blameless and irreproachable before Him, will not entertain even the thought of the slightest sin. For if we believed that we should live only the present life, then we might be suspected of sinning, through being enslaved to flesh and blood, or overmastered by gain or carnal desire; but since we know that God is witness to what we think and what we say both by night and by day, and that He, being Himself light, sees all things in our heart, we are persuaded that when we are removed from the present life we shall live another life, better than the present one, and heavenly, not earthly (since we shall abide near God, and with God, free from all change or suffering in the soul, not as flesh, even though we shall have flesh, but as heavenly spirit), or, falling with the rest, a worse one and in fire; for God has not made us as sheep or beasts of burden, a mere by-work, and that we should perish and be annihilated. On these grounds it is not likely that we should wish to do evil, or deliver ourselves over to the great Judge to be punished.

CHAPTER XXXII.

Elevated morality of the Christians

IT is, however, nothing wonderful that they should get up tales about us such as they tell of their own gods, of the incidents of whose lives they make mysteries. But it behoved them, if they meant to condemn shameless and promiscuous intercourse, to hate either Zeus, who begat children of his mother Rhea and his daughter Koré, and took his own sister to wife, or Orpheus, the inventor of these tales, which made Zeus more unholy and detestable than Thyestes himself; for the latter defiled his daughter in pursuance of an oracle, and when he wanted to obtain the kingdom and avenge himself. But we are so far from practising promiscuous intercourse, that it is not lawful among us to indulge even a lustful look. "For," saith He, "he that looketh on a woman to lust after her, hath committed adultery already in his heart" [Matt. 5:28]. Those, then, who are forbidden to look at anything more than that for which God formed the eyes, which were intended to be a light to us, and to whom a wanton look is adultery, the eyes being made for other purposes, and who are to be called to account for their very thoughts, how can any one doubt that such persons practise self-control? For our account lies not with human laws, which a bad man can evade (at the outset I proved to you, sovereign lords, that our doctrine is from the teaching of God), but we have a law which makes the measure of rectitude to consist in dealing with our neighbour as ourselves.[41] On this account, too, according to age, we recognise some as sons and daughters, others we regard as brothers and sisters, and to the more advanced in life we give the honour due to fathers and mothers. On behalf of those, then, to whom we apply the names of brothers and sisters, and other designations of relationship, we exercise the greatest care that their bodies should remain undefiled and uncorrupted; for the Logos again says to us, "If any one kiss a second time because it has given him pleasure, [he sins];" adding, "Therefore the kiss, or rather the salutation, should be given with the greatest care, since, if there be mixed with it the least defilement of thought, it excludes us from eternal life."[42]

CHAPTER XXXIII.

Chastity of the Christians with respect to marriage

THEREFORE, having the hope of eternal life, we despise the things of this life, even to the pleasures of the soul, each of us reckoning her his wife whom he has married according to the laws laid down by us, and that only for the purpose of having children. For as the husbandman throwing the seed into the ground awaits the harvest, not sowing more upon it, so to us the procreation of children is the measure of our indulgence in appetite. Nay, you would find many among us, both men and women, growing old unmarried, in the hope of living in closer communion with God. But if the remaining in virginity and in the state of an

---

[41]Otto translates: "which has made us and our neighbours attain the highest degree of rectitude." The text is obscure, but the above seems the probable meaning: comp. Matt. xxii. 39, etc.
[42]Probably from some apocryphal writing.

eunuch brings nearer to God, while the indulgence of carnal thought and desire leads away from Him, in those cases in which we shun the thoughts, much more do we reject the deeds. For we bestow our attention, not on the study of words, but on the exhibition and teaching of actions,—that a person should either remain as he was born, or be content with one marriage; for a second marriage is only a specious adultery. "For whosoever puts away his wife," says He, "and marries another, commits adultery" [Matt. 19:9]; not permitting a man to send her away whose virginity he has brought to an end, nor to marry again. For he who deprives himself of his first wife, even though she be dead, is a cloaked adulterer, resisting the hand of God, because in the beginning God made one man and one woman, and dissolving the strictest union of flesh with flesh, formed for the intercourse of the race.

CHAPTER XXXIV.

The vast difference in morals between the Christians and their accusers

BUT though such is our character (Oh! why should I speak of things unfit to be uttered?), the things said of us are an example of the proverb, "The harlot reproves the chaste." For those who have set up a market for fornication, and established infamous resorts for the young for every kind of vile pleasure,—who do not abstain even from males, males with males committing shocking abominations, outraging all the noblest and comeliest bodies in all sorts of ways, so dishonouring the fair workmanship of God (for beauty on earth is not self-made, but sent hither by the hand and will of God),—these men, I say, revile us for the very things which they are conscious of themselves, and ascribe to their own gods, boasting of them as noble deeds, and worthy of the gods. These adulterers and pederasts defame the eunuchs and the once-married (while they themselves live like fishes; for these gulp down whatever falls in their way, and the stronger chases the weaker: and, in fact, this is to feed upon human flesh, to do violence in contravention of the very laws which you and your ancestors, with due care for all that is fair and right, have enacted), so that not even the governors of the provinces sent by you suffice for the hearing of the complaints against those, to whom it even is not lawful, when they are struck, not to offer themselves for more blows, nor when defamed not to bless: for it is not enough to be just (and justice is to return like for like), but it is incumbent on us to be good and patient of evil.

CHAPTER XXXV.

The Christians condemn and detest all cruelty

WHAT man of sound mind, therefore, will affirm, while such is our character, that we are murderers? For we cannot eat human flesh till we have killed some one. The former charge, therefore, being false, if any one should ask them in regard to the second, whether they have seen what they assert, not one of them would be so barefaced as to say that he had. And yet we have slaves, some more and some fewer, by whom we could not help being seen; but even of these, not one has been found to invent even such things against us. For when they know that we cannot endure even to see a man put to death, though justly, who of them can accuse us of murder or cannibalism? Who does not reckon among the things of greatest interest the contests of gladiators and wild beasts, especially those which are given by you? But we, deeming that to see a man put to death is much the same as killing him, have abjured such spectacles. How, then, when we do not even look on, lest we should contract guilt and pollution, can we put people to death? And when we say that those women who use drugs to bring on abortion commit murder, and will have to give an account to God for the abortion, on what principle should we commit murder? For it does not belong to the same person to regard the very fetus in the womb as a created being, and therefore an object of God's care, and when it has passed into life, to kill it; and not to expose an infant, because those who expose them are chargeable with child-murder, and on the other hand, when it has been reared to destroy it. But we are in all things always like and the same, submitting ourselves to reason, and not ruling over it.

CHAPTER XXXVI.

Bearing of the doctrine of the resurrection on the practices of the Christians

WHO, then, that believes in a resurrection, would make himself into a tomb for bodies that will rise again? For it is not the part of the same persons to believe that our bodies will rise again, and to eat them as if they would not; and to think that the earth will give back the bodies held by it, but that those which a man has entombed in himself will not be demanded back. On the contrary, it is reasonable to suppose, that those who think they shall have no account to give of the present life, ill or well spent, and that there is no resurrection, but calculate on the soul perishing with the body, and being as it were quenched in it, will refrain from no deed of daring; but as for those who are persuaded that nothing will escape the scrutiny of God, but that even the body which has ministered to the irrational impulses of the soul, and to its desires, will be punished along with it, it is not likely that they will commit even the smallest sin. But if to any one it appears sheer nonsense that the body which has mouldered away, and been dissolved, and reduced to nothing, should be reconstructed, we certainly cannot with any reason be accused of wickedness with reference to those that believe not, but only of folly; for with the opinions by which we deceive ourselves we injure no one else. But that it is not our belief alone that bodies will rise again, but that many philosophers also hold the same view, it is out of place to show just now, lest we should be thought to introduce topics irrelevant to the matter in hand, either by speaking of the intelligible and the sensible, and the nature of these respectively, or by contending that the incorporeal is older than the corporeal, and that the intelligible precedes the sensible, although we become acquainted with the latter earliest, since the corporeal is formed from the incorporeal, by the combination with it of the intelligible, and that the sensible is formed from the intelligible; for nothing hinders, according to Pythagoras and Plato, that when the dissolution of bodies takes place, they should, from the very same elements of which they were constructed at first, be constructed again. But let us defer the discourse concerning the resurrection.

CHAPTER XXXVII.

Entreaty to be fairly judged

AND now do you, who are entirely in everything, by nature and by education, upright, and moderate, and benevolent, and worthy of your rule, now that I have disposed of the several accusations, and proved that we are pious, and gentle, and temperate in spirit, bend your royal head in approval. For who are more deserving to obtain the things they ask, than those who, like us, pray for your government, that you may, as is most equitable, receive the kingdom, son from father, and that your empire may receive increase and addition, all men becoming subject to your sway? And this is also for our advantage, that we may lead a peaceable and quiet life, and may ourselves readily perform all that is commanded us.

ᴄᴏᴏ 3 ᴄᴏᴏ

IRENAEUS
(A.D. 120–203)

A great deal of historical uncertainty surrounds the biographical information available to scholars concerning Irenaeus. It seems most reasonable to assume that he was born in or near Smyrna, the capital of Asia Minor. The first recorded mention of Irenaeus is in the year A.D. 177 when he was sent by the believers of Lyons to deliver a letter to Bishop Eleupherius of Rome. Upon his return, Irenaeus was made bishop of Lyons (A.D. 177–79). We know that the office of bishop was not given to younger men, and thus we can begin to estimate the date of his birth. Irenaeus gives us more evidence when he speaks about his personal recollections of Polycarp who lived from A.D. c69–155. These and other similar references in the writings of Irenaeus himself tend to establish his birth sometime between A.D. 115 and 130.

Clearly Irenaeus enjoyed the benefits of a good classical education. He was a student of Polycarp and obviously had read many of the Greek authors. He also refers to most of the major early Christian writings.

The city of Lyons was an important political and commercial center with an excellent system of roads and convenient waterways. It seems fairly obvious that Christianity had come to this region in southern Gaul very early. Some believe that the Christianity of the Rhone Valley (between Lyons and the Mediterranean) was derived from Ephesus. Thus for Irenaeus to go from the strong Christian area around Smyrna to Lyons was not as great a cultural shift as it might appear at first. It is known, however, that Lyons became one of the first cities to establish emperor worship. The city was burned by Emperor Lucius Septimius Severus in A.D. 197.

Irenaeus first came to Lyons as a missionary. His evangelistic spirit is clearly seen in his apologetic writings. Apparently he was also an unusually gifted preacher, though none of his sermons are extant.

Many scholars consider Irenaeus the most important theologian of the second century. This evaluation, however, is not due to his creative originality. Irenaeus would have considered it sinful if he had been justly accused of being theologically original; he goes to great lengths to prove that he was merely a faithful transmitter of the testimony that was handed down by the apostles. In fact, it is on the basis of this apostolic tradition that he fought against the heretics. Christianity, according to Irenaeus, must be guided by the "rule of faith." He held the church of Rome in highest esteem because of its obvious and definite adherence to theological orthodoxy. (One must be careful not to read into the claims of Irenaeus something that would be appropriate only at some later date. In the second century, the church at Rome was strongly evangelical and deeply committed to the apostolic faith.)

There is no question where Irenaeus stands with regard to the authority of the Scripture. He goes to great lengths to demonstrate that at no point were his own writings out of harmony with the teachings of Holy Scripture. He refers to every book in the New Testament (except Philemon and 3 John). This is an especially strong testimony because Irenaeus had been directly influenced by Polycarp who had himself been directly influenced by the apostle John.

The bishop whom Irenaeus replaced had been martyred. Thus he lived in a situation of constant physical danger. However, he considered the Gnostic heresies a more important danger, not to himself but to the church. In his mammoth five-volume work *Against Heresies* he attacks the system of Valentinus but then proceeds to systematically refute all of the current heresies in as much detail as possible. Some scholars have questioned his success in refuting the various heresies. Nevertheless, he is unsurpassed when he turns to his positive exposition of the faith. Irenaeus clearly recognizes that the fundamental issues are the doctrines of creation, redemption, and the unity of the Father, Son, and Holy Spirit.

One cannot fully understand the work of Irenaeus unless one places it in proper historical context. The Montanist controversy, the Quartodeciman Question, and Gnosticism are all prominent in Irenaeus's writings. Gnosticism is the primary theological issue that Irenaeus faced. It was perhaps the most difficult issue because of its great similarity with many points of orthodox theology. A subtle heresy, such as Gnosticism, is ultimately more dangerous for the church than is an outright denial of orthodoxy. Irenaeus realized that Gnosticism usually began with a false doctrine of creation and the relationship between creation and the existence of evil. If Irenaeus did not destroy all Gnostic thinking, he certainly delivered a fatal wound.

Almost nothing is known about the later life of Irenaeus. Jerome suggests that he may have lived until the reign of Commodus, thus giving him an estimated age of seventy or eighty years. The traditional date of his death is A.D. 203, but there is no solid historical foundation for this date. The most reasonable assumption is that Irenaeus died a natural death sometime before the end of the second century.

The section of *Against Heresies* reprinted in this chapter is from Books II and III. Irenaeus argues first for theism and the oneness of God. Since Irenaeus considered the gnostic heresy to be the most severe challenge to the true Christian faith, he next defends the fact of creation through the Word. The Gnostics taught that matter was inherently evil. They said that if God had created the world, He would have had to create evil and would thus be evil Himself. Therefore, some suggested that angels had created matter in opposition to God's will. Others thought that there must be a God beyond God. The biblical God was defiled by His relationship to matter (which was thought to be inherently evil), but their God beyond God was thought to be perfect. Irenaeus saw that this not only led to many logical contradictions (which in themselves show that the gnostic view is false) but that such views were not supported by positive evidence and were thus mere irrational speculations. True Christianity, however, is not subject to such logical absurdities, and, furthermore, there is a great body of evidence and a long tradition that supports it. The truth is there is only one God, and all things were created by His Word.

The existence of one sovereign God who created all things is what the apostles preached when they were endowed by the Holy Spirit from heaven. A heretic, on the other hand, will not preach what Scripture teaches nor what church tradition commends. One way heretics may be exposed, Irenaeus thought, is to show that they have no natural place in the perpetual succession of bishops who had kept the faith pure from apostolic times until the days in which he lived. According to Irenaeus, Christian truth is found only in this tradition.

Heretics do not correctly interpret the apostolic Scriptures, nor do they follow apostolic tradition. Irenaeus taught that heresy is to be refuted, therefore, by showing its divergence from the teachings of Christ and the apostles concerning the one true God—Creator of all things. Irenaeus believed that Scripture centers on Christ, who is the very Word of God, and that true preachers and spiritual teachers are those who fully preach Christ, clearly expound the meaning of the Scriptures to us, and increase our love for the Son of God who made atonement for our sins.

BIBLIOGRAPHY

Farrar, Frederic. *Lives of the Fathers*. New York: Macmillan, 1889. Vol. 1.

Grant, Robert M. "Irenaeus." In *Twentieth Century Encyclopedia of Religious Knowledge*. Edited by Lefferts A. Loetscher. Grand Rapids: Baker, 1955.

Hitchcock, Frances R. *Irenaeus, of Lugdunum: A Study of His Teaching*. Cambridge: At the University Press, 1914.

Leigh-Bennett, Ernest. *Handbook of the Early Christian Fathers*. London: Williams & Norgate, 1920.

Zahn, Franz Theodor Ritter von. "Irenaeus." In *The New Schaff-Herzog Encyclopedia of Religious Knowledge*. Edited by Samuel Macauley Jackson. Grand Rapids: Baker, 1950.

IRENAEUS AGAINST HERESIES

BOOK II.

PREFACE

1. IN the first book, which immediately precedes this, exposing "knowledge falsely so called," [1 Tim. 6:20] I showed thee, my very dear friend, that the whole system devised, in many and opposite ways, by those who are of the school of Valentinus, was false and baseless. I also set forth the tenets of their predecessors, proving that they not only differed among themselves, but had long previously swerved from the truth itself. . . .

2. In the present book, I shall establish those points which fit in with my design, so far as time permits, and overthrow, by means of lengthened treatment under distinct heads, their whole system; for which reason, since it is an exposure and subversion of their opinions, I have so entitled the composition of this work. . . .

CHAPTER I.

There is but one god: The impossibility of its being otherwise.

1. IT is proper, then, that I should begin with the first and most important head, that is, God the Creator, who made the heaven and the earth, and all things that are therein, . . . and to demonstrate that there is nothing either above Him or after Him; nor that, influenced by any one, but of His own free will, He created all things, since He is the only God, the only Lord, the only Creator, the

From Alexander Roberts and James Donaldson, eds., *The Ante-Nicene Fathers*, repr. ed. (New York: Scribner, 1903), 1:359–62, 414–19.

only Father, alone containing all things, and Himself commanding all things into existence.

2. For how can there be any other Fulness, or Principle, or Power, or God, above Him, since it is matter of necessity that God, the Pleroma (Fulness) of all these, should contain all things in His immensity, and should be contained by no one? But if there *is* anything beyond Him, He is not then the Pleroma of all, nor does He contain all. For that which they declare to be beyond Him will be wanting to the Pleroma, or, [in other words,] to that God who is above all things. But that which is wanting, and falls in any way short, is not the Pleroma of all things. . . .

3. Now, since there exists, according to them, also something else which they declare to be outside of the Pleroma, into which they further hold there descended that higher power who went astray, it is in every way necessary that the Pleroma either contains that which is beyond, yet is contained (for otherwise, it will not be beyond the Pleroma; for if there is anything beyond the Pleroma, there will be a Pleroma within this very Pleroma which they declare to be outside of the Pleroma, and the Pleroma will be contained by that which is beyond: and with the Pleroma is understood also the first God); or, again, they must be an infinite distance separated from each other—the Pleroma [I mean], and that which is beyond it. But if they maintain this, there will then be a third kind of existence, which separates by immensity the Pleroma and that which is beyond it. This third kind of existence will therefore bound and contain both the others, and will be greater both than the Pleroma, and than that which is beyond it, inasmuch as it contains both in its bosom. In this way, talk might go on for ever concerning those things which are contained, and those which contain. For if this third existence has its beginning above, and its end beneath, there is an absolute necessity that it be also bounded on the sides, either beginning or ceasing at certain other points, [where new existences begin.] These, again, and others which are above and below, will have their beginnings at certain other points, and so on *ad infinitum*; so that their thoughts would never rest in one God, but, in consequence of seeking after more than exists, would wander away to that which has no existence, and depart from the true God.

4. These remarks are, in like manner, applicable against the followers of Marcion. For his two gods will also be contained and circumscribed by an immense interval which separates them from one another. But then there is a necessity to suppose a multitude of gods separated by an immense distance from each other on every side, beginning with one another, and ending in one another. Thus, by that very process of reasoning on which they depend for teaching that there is a certain Pleroma or God above the Creator of heaven and earth, any one who chooses to employ it may maintain that there is another Pleroma above the

Pleroma, above that again another, and above Bythus another ocean of Deity, while in like manner the same successions hold with respect to the sides; and thus, their doctrine flowing out into immensity, there will always be a necessity to conceive of other Pleromata, and other Bythi, so as never at any time to stop, but always to continue seeking for others besides those already mentioned. Moreover, it will be uncertain whether these which we conceive of are below, or are, in fact, themselves the things which are above; and, in like manner, [it will be doubtful] respecting those things which are said by them to be above, whether they are really above or below; and thus our opinions will have no fixed conclusion or certainty, but will of necessity wander forth after worlds without limits, and gods that cannot be numbered.

5. . . . For it must be either that there is one Being who contains all things, and formed in His own territory all those things which have been created, according to His own will; or, again, that there are numerous unlimited creators and gods, who begin from each other, and end in each other on every side; and it will then be necessary to allow that all the rest are contained from without by some one who is greater, and that they are each of them shut up within their own territory, and remain in it. No one of them all, therefore, is God. For there will be [much] wanting to every one of them, possessing [as he will do] only a very small part when compared with all the rest. The name of the Omnipotent will thus be brought to an end, and such an opinion will of necessity fall into impiety.

CHAPTER II.

The world was not formed by angels, or by any other being, contrary to the will of the Most High God, but was made by the Father through the Word.[1]

1. THOSE, moreover, who say that the world was formed by angels, or by any other maker of it, contrary to the will of Him who is the Supreme Father, err first of all in this very point, that they maintain that angels formed such and so might a creation, contrary to the will of the Most High God. This would imply that angels were more powerful than God; or if not so, that He was either careless, or inferior, or paid no regard to those things which took place among His own possessions, whether they turned out ill or well, so that He might drive away and prevent the one, while He praised and rejoiced over the other. But if one would not ascribe such conduct even to a man of any ability, how much less to God!

. . .

---

[1][This noble chapter is a sort of homily on Hebrews 1.]

3. If, however, [the things referred to were done] not against His will, but with His concurrence and knowledge, as some [of these men] think, the angels, or the Former of the world [whoever that may have been], will no longer be the causes of that formation, but the will of God. For if He is the Former of the world, He too made the angels, or at least was the cause of their creation; and *He* will be regarded as having made the world who prepared the causes of its formation. Although they maintain that the angels were made by a long succession downwards, or that the Former of the world [sprang] from the Supreme Father, as Basilides asserts; nevertheless that which is the cause of those things which have been made will still be traced to Him who was the Author of such a succession. [The case stands] just as regards success in war, which is ascribed to the king who prepared those things which are the cause of victory; and, in like manner, the creation of any state, or of any work, is referred to him who prepared materials for the accomplishment of those results which were afterwards brought about. Wherefore, we do not say that it was the axe which cut the wood, or the saw which divided it; but one would very properly say that the *man* cut and divided it who formed the axe and the saw for this purpose, and [who also formed] at a much earlier date all the tools by which the axe and the saw themselves were formed. With justice, therefore, according to an analogous process of reasoning, the Father of all will be declared the Former of this world, and not the angels, nor any other [so-called] former of the world, other than He who was its Author, and had formerly[2] been the cause of the preparation for a creation of this kind.

4. This manner of speech may perhaps be plausible or persuasive to those who know not God, and who liken Him to needy human beings, and to those who cannot immediately and without assistance form anything, but require many instrumentalities to produce what they intend. But it will not be regarded as at all probable by those who know that God stands in need of nothing, and that He created and made all things by His Word, while He neither required angels to assist Him in the production of those things which are made, nor of any power greatly inferior to Himself, and ignorant of the Father, nor of any defect or ignorance, in order that he who should know Him might become man.[3] But He Himself in Himself, after a fashion which we can neither describe nor conceive,

---

[2]Vossius and others read "primus" instead of "prius," but on defective MS. authority.

[3]Harvey here observes: "Grabe misses the meaning by applying to the redeemed that which the author says of the Redeemer;" but it may be doubted if this is really the case. Perhaps Massuet's rendering of the clause, "that that man might be formed who should know Him," is, after all, preferable to that given above.

predestinating all things, formed them as He pleased, bestowing harmony on all things, and assigning them their own place, and the beginning of their creation. In this way He conferred on spiritual things a spiritual and invisible nature, on supercelestial things a celestial, on angels an angelical, on animals an animal, on beings that swim a nature suited to the water, and on those that live on the land one fitted for the land—on all, in short, a nature suitable to the character of the life assigned them—while He formed all things that were made by His Word that never wearies.

5. For this is a peculiarity of the pre-eminence of God, not to stand in need of other instruments for the creation of those things which are summoned into existence. His own Word is both suitable and sufficient for the formation of all things, even as John, the disciple of the Lord, declares regarding Him: "All things were made by Him, and without Him was nothing made" [John 1:3]. Now, among the "all things" our world must be embraced. It too, therefore, was made by His Word, as Scripture tells us in the book of Genesis that He made all things connected with our world by His Word. David also expresses the same truth [when he says], "For He spake, and they were made; He commanded, and they were created" [Pss. 33:9; 148:5]. Whom, therefore, shall we believe as to the creation of the world—these heretics who have been mentioned that prate so foolishly and inconsistently on the subject, or the disciples of the Lord, and Moses, who was both a faithful servant of God and a prophet? He at first narrated the formation of the world in these words: "In the beginning God created the heaven and the earth [Gen. 1:1]; and all other things in succession; but neither gods nor angels [had any share in the work].

Now, that this God is the Father of our Lord Jesus Christ, Paul the apostle also has declared, [saying,] "There is one God, the Father, who is above all, and through all things, and in us all."[4] I have indeed proved already that there is only one God; but I shall further demonstrate this from the apostles themselves, and from the discourses of the Lord. For what sort of conduct would it be, were we to forsake the utterances of the prophets, of the Lord, and of the apostles, that we might give heed to these persons, who speak not a word of sense?

.   .   .

---

[4]Eph. 4:6, differing somewhat from Text. Rec. of New Testament.

BOOK III.

PREFACE

THOU hast indeed enjoined upon me, my very dear friend, that I should bring to light the Valentinian doctrines, concealed, as their votaries imagine; that I should exhibit their diversity, and compose a treatise in refutation of them. I therefore have undertaken—showing that they spring from Simon, the father of all heretics—to exhibit both their doctrines and successions, and to set forth arguments against them all.

CHAPTER I.

The apostles did not commence to preach the gospel, or to place anything on record, until they were endowed with the gifts and power of the Holy Spirit. They preached one God alone, Maker of heaven and earth.

1. WE have learned from none others the plan of our salvation, than from those through whom the Gospel has come down to us, which they did at one time proclaim in public, and, at a later period, by the will of God, handed down to us in the Scriptures, to be the ground and pillar of our faith.[5] For it is unlawful to assert that they preached before they possessed "perfect knowledge," as some do even venture to say, boasting themselves as improvers of the apostles. For, after our Lord rose from the dead, [the apostles] were invested with power from on high when the Holy Spirit came down [upon them], were filled from all [His gifts], and had perfect knowledge: they departed to the ends of the earth, preaching the glad tidings of the good things [sent] from God to us, and proclaiming the peace of heaven to men, who indeed do all equally and individually possess the Gospel of God. Matthew also issued a written Gospel among the Hebrews[6] in their own dialect, while Peter and Paul were preaching at Rome, and laying the foundations of the Church. After their departure, Mark, the disciple and interpreter of Peter, did also hand down to us in writing what had been preached by Peter. Luke also, the companion of Paul, recorded in a book the Gospel preached by him. Afterwards, John, the disciple of the Lord, who also had leaned upon His breast, did himself publish a Gospel during his residence at Ephesus in Asia.

---

[5]See 1 Tim 3:15, where these terms are used in reference to the Church.

[6]On this and similar statements in the Fathers, the reader may consult Dr. Roberts's *Discussions on the Gospels*, in which they are fully criticised, and the Greek original of St. Matthew's Gospel maintained.

2. These have all declared to us that there is one God, Creator of heaven and earth, announced by the law and the prophets; and one Christ, the Son of God. If any one do [sic] not agree to these truths, he despises the companions of the Lord; nay more, he despises Christ Himself the Lord; yea, he despises the Father also, and stands self-condemned, resisting and opposing his own salvation, as is the case with all heretics.

CHAPTER II.
The heretics follow neither Scripture nor tradition.

1. WHEN, however, they are confuted from the Scriptures, they turn round and accuse these same Scriptures, as if they were not correct, nor of authority, and [assert] that they are ambiguous, and that the truth cannot be extracted from them by those who are ignorant of tradition. For [they allege] that the truth was not delivered by means of written documents, but *vivâ voce*: wherefore also Paul declared, "But we speak wisdom among those that are perfect, but not the wisdom of this world" [1 Cor. 2:6]. And this wisdom each one of them alleges to be the fiction of his own inventing, forsooth; so that, according to their idea, the truth properly resides at one time in Valentinus, at another in Marcion, at another in Cerinthus, then afterwards in Basilides, or has even been indifferently in any other opponent,[7] who could speak nothing pertaining to salvation. For every one of these men, being altogether of a perverse disposition, depraving the system of truth, is not ashamed to preach himself.

2. But, again, when we refer them to that tradition which originates from the apostles, [and] which is preserved by means of the successions of presbyters in the Churches, they object to tradition, saying that they themselves are wiser not merely than the presbyters, but even than the apostles, because they have discovered the unadulterated truth. For [they maintain] that the apostles intermingled the things of the law with the words of the Saviour; and that not the apostles alone, but even the Lord Himself, spoke as at one time from the Demiurge, at another from the intermediate place, and yet again from the Pleroma, but that they themselves, indubitably, unsulliedly, and purely, have knowledge of the hidden mystery: this is, indeed, to blaspheme their Creator after a most impudent manner! It comes to this, therefore, that these men do now consent neither to Scripture nor to tradition.

3. Such are the adversaries with whom we have to deal, my very dear

---

[7]This is Harvey's rendering of the old Latin, *in illo qui contra disputat.*

friend, endeavouring like slippery serpents to escape at all points. Wherefore they must be opposed at all points, if perchance, by cutting off their retreat, we may succeed in turning them back to the truth. For, though it is not an easy thing for a soul under the influence of error to repent, yet, on the other hand, it is not altogether impossible to escape from error when the truth is brought alongside it.

CHAPTER III.

A refutation of the heretics, from the fact that, in the various churches, a perpetual succession of bishops was kept up.

1. IT is within the power of all, therefore, in every Church, who may wish to see the truth, to contemplate clearly the tradition of the apostles manifested throughout the whole world; and we are in a position to reckon up those who were by the apostles instituted bishops in the Churches, and [to demonstrate] the succession of these men to our own times; those who neither taught nor knew of anything like what these [heretics] rave about. For if the apostles had known hidden mysteries, which they were in the habit of imparting to "the perfect" apart and privily from the rest, they would have delivered them especially to those to whom they were also committing the Churches themselves. For they were desirous that these men should be very perfect and blameless in all things, whom also they were leaving behind as their successors, delivering up their own place of government to these men; which men, if they discharged their functions honestly, would be a great boon [to the Church], but if they should fall away, the direst calamity.

2. Since, however, it would be very tedious, in such a volume as this, to reckon up the successions of all the Churches, we do put to confusion all those who, in whatever manner, whether by an evil self-pleasing, by vainglory, or by blindness and perverse opinion, assemble in unauthorized meetings; [we do this, I say,] by indicating that tradition derived from the apostles, of the very great, the very ancient, and universally known Church founded and organized at Rome by the two most glorious apostles, Peter and Paul; as also [by pointing out] the faith preached to men, which comes down to our time by means of the successions of the bishops. For it is a matter of necessity that every Church should agree with this Church, on account of its preeminent authority,[8] that is, the faithful every-

---

[8]The Latin text of this difficult but important clause is, "Ad hanc enim ecclesiam propter potiorem principalitatem necesse est omnem convenire ecclesiam." Both the text and meaning have here given rise to much discussion. It is impossible to say with certainty of what words in the Greek original "potiorem principalitatem" may be the translation. We are far from sure that the rendering given above is correct, but we have been unable to think of anything better. [A most extraordinary confession. It would be hard to find a worse; but

where, inasmuch as the apostolical tradition has been preserved continuously by those [faithful men] who exist everywhere.

3. The blessed apostles, then, having founded and built up the Church, committed into the hands of Linus the office of the episcopate. Of this Linus, Paul makes mention in the Epistles to Timothy. To him succeeded Anacletus; and after him, in the third place from the apostles, Clement was allotted the bishopric. This man, as he had seen the blessed apostles, and had been conversant with them, might be said to have the preaching of the apostles still echoing [in his ears], and their traditions before his eyes. Nor was he alone [in this], for there were many still remaining who had received instructions from the apostles. In the time of this Clement, no small dissension having occurred among the brethren at Corinth, the Church in Rome despatched a most powerful letter to the Corinthians, exhorting them to peace, renewing their faith, and declaring the tradition which it had lately received from the apostles, proclaiming the one God, omnipotent, and Maker of heaven and earth, the Creator of man, who brought on the deluge, and called Abraham, who led the people from the land of Egypt, spake with Moses, set forth the law, sent the prophets, and who has prepared fire for the devil and his angels. From this document, whosoever chooses to do so, may learn that He, the Father of our Lord Jesus Christ, was preached by the Churches, and may also understand the apostolical tradition of the Church, since this Epistle is of older date than these men who are now propagating falsehood, and who conjure into existence another god beyond the Creator and the Maker of all existing things. To this Clement there succeeded Evaristus. Alexander followed Evaristus; then, sixth from the apostles, Sixtus was appointed; after him, Telephorus, who was gloriously martyred; then Hyginus; after him, Pius; then after him, Anicetus. Soter having succeeded Anicetus, Eleutherius does now, in the twelfth place from the apostles, hold the inheritance of the episcopate. In this order, and by this succession, the ecclesiastical tradition from the apostles, and the preaching of the truth, have come down to us. And this is most abundant proof that there is one and the same vivifying faith, which has been preserved in the Church from the apostles until now, and handed down in truth.

---

take the following from a candid Roman Catholic, which is better and more literal: "For to this Church, on account of more potent principality, it is necessary that every Church (that is, those who are on every side faithful) *resort;* in which Church ever, *by those who are on every side,* has been preserved that tradition which is from the apostles." (Berington and Kirk, vol. i. p. 252.) Here it is obvious that the faith was kept at Rome, by *those who resort there* from all quarters. She was a mirror of the Catholic World, owing her orthodoxy to them; not the Sun, dispensing her own light to others, but the glass bringing their rays into a focus. [See note at end of book iii.] A discussion of the subject may be seen in chap. xii. of Dr. Wordsworth's St. *Hippolytus and the Church of Rome.*

4. But Polycarp also was not only instructed by apostles, and conversed with many who had seen Christ, but was also, by apostles in Asia, appointed bishop of the Church in Smyrna, whom I also saw in my early youth, for he tarried [on earth] a very long time, and, when a very old man, gloriously and most nobly suffering martyrdom,[9] departed this life, having always taught the things which he had learned from the apostles, and which the Church has handed down, and which alone are true. To these things all the Asiatic Churches testify, as do also those men who have succeeded Polycarp down to the present time,—a man who was of much greater weight, and a more stedfast witness of truth, than Valentinus, and Marcion, and the rest of the heretics. He it was who, coming to Rome in the time of Anicetus caused many to turn away from the aforesaid heretics to the Church of God, proclaiming that he had received this one and sole truth from the apostles,—that, namely, which is handed down by the Church.[10] There are also those who heard from him that John, the disciple of the Lord, going to bathe at Ephesus, and perceiving Cerinthus within, rushed out of the bath-house without bathing, exclaiming, "Let us fly, lest even the bath-house fall down, because Cerinthus, the enemy of the truth, is within." And Polycarp himself replied to Marcion, who met him on one occasion, and said, "Dost thou know me?" "I do know thee, the first-born of Satan." Such was the horror which the apostles and their disciples had against holding even verbal communication with any corrupters of the truth; as Paul also says, "A man that is an heretic, after the first and second admonition, reject; knowing that he that is such is subverted, and sinneth, being condemned of himself" [Titus 3:10–11]. There is also a very powerful[11] Epistle of Polycarp written to the Philippians, from which those who choose to do so, and are anxious about their salvation, can learn the character of his faith, and the preaching of the truth. Then, again, the Church in Ephesus, founded by Paul, and having John remaining among them permanently until the times of Trajan, is a true witness of the tradition of the apostles.

CHAPTER IV.

The truth is to be found nowhere else but in the Catholic Church, the sole depository of apostolical doctrine. Heresies are of recent formation, and cannot trace their origin up to the apostles.

1. SINCE therefore we have such proofs, it is not necessary to seek the truth among others which it is easy to obtain from the Church; since the apostles, like

---

[9]Polycarp suffered about the year 167, in the reign of Marcus Aurelius. His great age of eighty-six years implies that he was contemporary with St. John for nearly twenty years.
[10]So the Greek. The Latin reads: "which he also handed down to the Church."
[11]ἱκανωτάτη. Harvey translates this *all-sufficient*, and thus paraphrases: *But his Epistle is all-sufficient, to teach those that are desirous to learn.*

a rich man [depositing his money] in a bank, lodged in her hands most copiously all things pertaining to the truth: so that every man, whosoever will, can draw from her the water of life [Rev. 22:17]. For she is the entrance to life; all others are thieves and robbers. On this account are we bound to avoid *them*, but to make choice of the things pertaining to the Church with the utmost diligence, and to lay hold of the tradition of the truth. For how stands the case? Suppose there arise a dispute relative to some important question[12] among us, should we not have recourse to the most ancient Churches with which the apostles held constant intercourse, and learn from them what is certain and clear in regard to the present question? For how should it be if the apostles themselves had not left us writings? Would it not be necessary, [in that case,] to follow the course of the tradition which they handed down to those to whom they did commit the Churches?

2. To which course many nations of those barbarians who believe in Christ do assent, having salvation written in their hearts by the Spirit, without paper or ink, and carefully preserving the ancient tradition,[13] believing in one God, the Creator of heaven and earth, and all things therein, by means of Christ Jesus, the Son of God; who, because of His surpassing love towards His creation, condescended to be born of the virgin, He Himself uniting man through Himself to God, and having suffered under Pontius Pilate, and rising again, and having been received up in splendour, shall come in glory, the Saviour of those who are saved, and the Judge of those who are judged, and sending into eternal fire those who transform the truth, and despise His Father and His advent. Those who, in the absence of written documents,[14] have believed this faith, are barbarians, so far as regards our language; but as regards doctrine, manner, and tenor of life, they are, because of faith, very wise indeed; and they do please God, ordering their conversation in all righteousness, chastity, and wisdom. If any one were to preach to these men the inventions of the heretics, speaking to them in their own language, they would at once stop their ears, and flee as far off as possible, not enduring even to listen to the blasphemous address. Thus, by means of that ancient tradition of the apostles, they do not suffer their mind to conceive anything of the [doctrines suggested by the] portentous language of these teachers, among whom neither Church nor doctrine has ever been established.

3. For, prior to Valentinus, those who follow Valentinus had no existence;

---

[12]Latin, "modica quæstione."

[13][The uneducated barbarians must receive the Gospel on testimony. Irenæus puts *apostolic* traditions, genuine and uncorrupt, in this relation to the primary authority of the written word. 2 Thess. 2:15; 3:6.]

[14]Literally, "without letters;" equivalent to, "without paper and ink," a few lines previously.

nor did those from Marcion exist before Marcion; nor, in short, had any of those malignant-minded people, whom I have above enumerated, any being previous to the initiators and inventors of their perversity. For Valentinus came to Rome in the time of Hyginus, flourished under Pius, and remained until Anicetus. Cerdon, too, Marcion's predecessor, himself arrived in the time of Hyginus, who was the ninth bishop.[15] Coming frequently into the Church, and making public confession, he thus remained, one time teaching in secret, and then again making public confession; but at last, having been denounced for corrupt teaching, he was excommunicated[16] from the assembly of the brethren. Marcion, then, succeeding him, flourished under Anicetus, who held the tenth place of the episcopate. But the rest, who are called Gnostics, take rise from Menander, Simon's disciple, as I have shown; and each one of them appeared to be both the father and the high priest of that doctrine into which he has been initiated. But all these (the Marcosians) broke out into their apostasy much later, even during the intermediate period of the Church.

CHAPTER V.

Christ and His apostles, without any fraud, deception, or hypocrisy, preached that one God, the Father, was the Founder of all things. They did not accommodate their doctrine to the prepossessions of their hearers.

1. SINCE, therefore, the tradition from the apostles does thus exist in the Church, and is permanent among us, let us revert to the Scriptural proof furnished by those apostles who did also write the Gospel, in which they recorded the doctrine regarding God, pointing out that our Lord Jesus Christ is the truth [John 14:6], and that no lie is in Him. As also David says, prophesying His birth from a virgin, and the resurrection from the dead, "Truth has sprung out of the earth" [Ps. 85:11]. The apostles, likewise, being disciples of the truth, are above all falsehood; for a lie has no fellowship with the truth, just as darkness has none with light, but the presence of the one shuts out that of the other. Our Lord, therefore, being the truth, did not speak lies; and whom He knew to have taken origin from a defect, He never would have acknowledged as God, even the God of all, the Supreme King, too, and His own Father, an imperfect being as a

---

[15]The old Latin translation says the *eighth bishop*; but there is no discrepancy. Eusebius, who has preserved the Greek of this passage, probably counted the apostles as the *first step* in the episcopal succession. As Irenæus tells us in the preceding chapter, Linus is to be counted as the first bishop.

[16]It is thought that this does not mean excommunication properly so called, but a species of *self-excommunication*, i.e., anticipating the sentence of the Church, by quitting it altogether. See Valesius's note in his edition of Eusebius.

perfect one, an animal one as a spiritual, Him who was without the Pleroma as Him who was within it. Neither did His disciples make mention of any other God, or term any other Lord, except Him, who was truly the God and Lord of all, as these most vain sophists affirm that the apostles did with hypocrisy frame their doctrine according to the capacity of their hearers, and gave answers after the opinions of their questioners,—fabling blind things for the blind, according to their blindness; for the dull according to their dulness; for those in error according to their error. And to those who imagined that the Demiurge alone was God, they preached him; but to those who are capable of comprehending the unnameable Father, they did declare the unspeakable mystery through parables and enigmas: so that the Lord and the apostles exercised the office of teacher not to further the cause of truth, but even in hypocrisy, and as each individual was able to receive it!

2. Such [a line of conduct] belongs not to those who heal, or who give life: it is rather that of those bringing on diseases, and increasing ignorance; and much more true than these men shall the law be found, which pronounces every one accursed who sends the blind man astray in the way. For the apostles, who were commissioned to find out the wanderers, and to be for sight to those who saw not, and medicine to the weak, certainly did not address them in accordance with their opinion at the time, but according to revealed truth. For no persons of any kind would act properly, if they should advise blind men, just about to fall over a precipice, to continue their most dangerous path, as if it were the right one, and as if they might go on in safety. Or what medical man, anxious to heal a sick person, would prescribe in accordance with the patient's whims, and not according to the requisite medicine? But that the Lord came as the physician of the sick, He does Himself declare, saying, "They that are whole need not a physician, but they that are sick; I came not to call the righteous, but sinners to repentance" [Luke 5:31–32]. How then shall the sick be strengthened, or how shall sinners come to repentance? Is it by persevering in the very same courses? or, on the contrary, is it by undergoing a great change and reversal of their former mode of living, by which they have brought upon themselves no slight amount of sickness, and many sins? But ignorance, the mother of all these, is driven out by knowledge. Wherefore the Lord used to impart knowledge to His disciples, by which also it was His practice to heal those who were suffering, and to keep back sinners from sin. He therefore did not address them in accordance with their pristine notions, nor did He reply to them in harmony with the opinion of His questioners, but according to the doctrine leading to salvation, without hypocrisy or respect of person.

3. This is also made clear from the words of the Lord, who did truly reveal the Son of God to those of the circumcision—Him who had been foretold as

Christ by the prophets; that is, He set Himself forth, who had restored liberty to men, and bestowed on them the inheritance of incorruption. And again, the apostles taught the Gentiles that they should leave vain stocks and stones, which they imagined to be gods, and worship the true God, who had created and made all the human family, and, by means of His creation, did nourish, increase, strengthen, and preserve them in being; and that they might look for His Son Jesus Christ, who redeemed us from apostasy with His own blood, so that we should also be a sanctified people,—who shall also descend from heaven in His Father's power, and pass judgment upon all, and who shall freely give the good things of God to those who shall have kept His commandments. He, appearing in these last times, the chief cornerstone, has gathered into one, and united those that were far off and those that were near [Eph. 2:17]; that is, the circumcision and the uncircumcision, enlarging Japhet, and placing him in the dwelling of Shem [Gen. 9:27].

CHAPTER VI.

The Holy Ghost, throughout the Old Testament Scriptures, made mention of no other God or Lord, save Him who is the True God.

1. THEREFORE neither would the Lord, nor the Holy Spirit, nor the apostles, have ever named as God, definitely and absolutely, him who was not God, unless he were truly God; nor would they have named any one in his own person Lord, except God the Father ruling over all, and His Son who has received dominion from His Father over all creation, as this passage has it: "The LORD said unto my Lord, Sit Thou at my right hand, until I make Thine enemies Thy footstool" [Ps. 110:1]. Here the [Scripture] represents to us the Father addressing the Son; He who gave Him the inheritance of the heathen, and subjected to Him all His enemies. Since, therefore, the Father is truly Lord, and the Son truly Lord, the Holy Spirit has fitly designated them by the title of Lord. And again, referring to the destruction of the Sodomites, the Scripture says, "Then the LORD rained upon Sodom and upon Gomorrah fire and brimstone from the LORD out of heaven" [Gen. 19:24]. For it here points out that the Son, who had also been talking with Abraham, had received power to judge the Sodomites for their wickedness. And this [text following] does declare the same truth: "Thy throne, O God, is for ever and ever; the sceptre of Thy kingdom is a right sceptre. Thou hast loved righteousness, and hated iniquity: therefore God, Thy God, hath anointed Thee" [Ps. 45:6–7]. For the Spirit designates both [of them] by the name of God—both Him who is anointed as Son, and Him who does anoint, that is, the Father. And again: "God stood in the congregation of the gods, He judges among the gods" [Ps. 82:1]. He [here] refers to the Father and the Son, and those who have received the adoption; but these are the Church.

For she is the synagogue of God, which God—that is, the Son Himself—has gathered by Himself. Of whom He again speaks: "The God of gods, the Lord hath spoken, and hath called the earth" [Ps. 50:1]. Who is meant by God? He of whom He has said, "God shall come openly, our God, and shall not keep silence" [Ps. 50:3]; that is, the Son, who came manifested to men, who said, "I have openly appeared to those who seek Me not" [Isa. 65:1]. But of what gods [does he speak]? [Of those] to whom He says, "I have said, Ye are gods, and all sons of the Most High" [Ps. 82:6]. To those, no doubt, who have received the grace of the "adoption, by which we cry, Abba Father" [Rom. 8:15].

2. Wherefore, as I have already stated, no other is named as God, or is called Lord, except Him who is God and Lord of all, who also said to Moses, "I AM THAT I AM. And thus shalt thou say to the children of Israel: He who is, hath sent me unto you" [Ex. 3:14]; and His Son Jesus Christ our Lord, who makes those that believe in His name the sons of God. And again, when the Son speaks to Moses, He says, "I am come down to deliver this people" [Ex. 3:8]. For it is He who descended and ascended for the salvation of men. Therefore God has been declared through the Son, who is in the Father, and has the Father in Himself—HE WHO IS, the Father bearing witness to the Son, and the Son announcing the Father.—As also Esaias says, "I too am witness," he declares, "saith the LORD God, and the Son whom I have chosen, that ye may know, and believe, and understand that I AM" [Isa. 43:10].

3. When, however, the Scripture terms them [gods] which are no gods, it does not, as I have already remarked, declare them as gods in every sense, but with a certain addition and signification, by which they are shown to be no gods at all. As with David: "The gods of the heathen are idols of demons" [Ps. 96:5]; and, "Ye shall not follow other gods" [Ps. 81:9]. For in that he says "the gods of the heathen"—but the heathen are ignorant of the true God—and calls them "other gods," he bars their claim [to be looked upon] as gods at all. But as to what they are in their own person, he speaks concerning them; "for they are," he says, "the idols of demons." And Esaias: "Let them be confounded, all who blaspheme God, and carve useless things;[17] even I am witness, saith God" [Isa. 44:9]. He removes them from [the category of] gods, but he makes use of the word alone, for this [purpose], that we may know of whom he speaks. Jeremiah also says the same: "The gods that have not made the heavens and earth, let them perish from the earth which is under the heaven" [Jer. 10:11]. For, from the fact of his having subjoined their destruction, he shows them to be no gods at all. Elias, too, when all Israel was assembled at Mount Carmel, wishing to turn them from idolatry,

---

[17]These words are an interpolation: it is supposed they have been carelessly repeated from the preceding quotation of Isaiah.

says to them, "How long halt ye between two opinions?[18] If the LORD be God,[19] follow Him" [1 Kings 18:21]. And again, at the burnt-offering, he thus addresses the idolatrous priests: "Ye shall call upon the name of your gods, and I will call on the name of the LORD my God; and the Lord that will hearken by fire,[20] He is God." Now, from the fact of the prophet having said these words, he proves that these gods which were reputed so among those men, are no gods at all. He directed them to that God upon whom he believed, and who was truly God; whom invoking, he exclaimed, "LORD God of Abraham, God of Isaac, and God of Jacob, hear me to-day, and let all this people know that Thou art the God of Israel" [1 Kings 18:36–37].

4. Wherefore I do also call upon thee, LORD God of Abraham, and God of Isaac, and God of Jacob and Israel, who art the Father of our Lord Jesus Christ, the God who, through the abundance of Thy mercy, hast had a favour towards us, that we should know Thee, who has made heaven and earth, who rulest over all, who art the only and the true God, above whom there is none other God; grant, by our Lord Jesus Christ, the governing power of the Holy Spirit; give to every reader of this book to know Thee, that Thou art God alone, to be strengthened in Thee, and to avoid every heretical, and godless, and impious doctrine.

---

[18]Literally, "In both houghs," *in ambabus suffraginibus.*
[19]The old Latin translation has, "Si *unus* est Dominus Deus"—*If the Lord God is one;* which is supposed by the critics to have occurred through carelessness of the translator.
[20]The Latin version has, "that answereth to-day" (*hodie*),—an evident error for *igne.*

ᗱᗙ 4 ᗙᗱ
TERTULLIAN
(A.D. 155–235)

Tertullian was born into a pagan home in Carthage, Africa, sometime between A.D. 150 and 160. His father was a proconsular centurion. Tertullian describes his own youthful life as one in which he delighted in the brutalities of the arena and greatly enjoyed the vulgar theater. However, he was an ardent student of literature, law, and philosophy.

Very little is known about Tertullian's conversion. Most scholars date this experience around A.D. 185, about a year before his marriage. Apparently the Christian martyrs had made a strong impression on him.

While one must not overlook *Octavius* by Minucius Felix, it is not inappropriate to think of the writings of Tertullian as the beginning of the literature of Latin Christianity. Most of his books are polemical and apologetic. He directed his ideas in a vigorous literary style toward those who were enemies, persecutors, or heretics. He not only developed an unusual style but is often called the originator of ecclesiastical Latin. He formed a total of 982 new Latin words: 509 nouns, 284 adjectives, 28 adverbs, and 161 verbs.

Undoubtedly, Tertullian was one of the greatest of the early church apologists. In his famous work entitled *Against Marcion* Tertullian explains why he considered Marcion the arch heretic. Marcion, like many modern liberal theologians, claimed not to be able to harmonize the God of law and wrath in the Old Testament with the God of love and forgiveness in the New Testament. He made a radical distinction between the testaments, claiming that they spoke about two different Gods. Thus Marcion drew up his own Bible, containing only the passages he felt he could believe. Tertullian forthrightly condemns this system of theology. He considers Marcion utterly destitute of historical sense.

Other works by Tertullian include *Against Gnostic Systems* and *Against Monarchianism*. Perhaps his most famous work is *Prescription Against Heretics*; however, his most interesting work is *The Apology*.

Scholars disagree about the exact date when *The Apology* was written. Some authorities date it as early as A.D. 198; others as late as A.D. 217. The dating of this book is somewhat complicated by a most remarkable incident in Tertullian's life. Though he had been admitted to the priesthood about A.D. 192, sometime around A.D. 199 Tertullian seems to have become a Montanist. Apparently the church was in a rather lax state, and this probably made Montanism very attractive because of its energy and spiritual character.

Montanism was an enthusiastic, apocalyptic revival movement. Montanus was the prophetic leader. He was joined by two women, Maximilla and Priscilla, who believed themselves to be instruments of a new outpouring of the Holy Spirit. They taught that the kingdom of God was about to appear. They expected the heavenly Jerusalem to descend in Phrygia. It should be remembered, however, that the Montanists accepted both the Old and New Testament as the fully authoritative Word of God. They believed in the resurrection of the dead and maintained the orthodox doctrine of the Trinity. The Montanists' error is found in their claim to have a supposedly new revelation. They did not deny the basic truths that were believed by all true Christians in that day, but they did believe that the Holy Spirit had led them to new truths regarding the kingdom of God.

The writings of Tertullian do contain several indications of Montanist teaching. For example, on the authority of this "new prophecy" Tertullian calls for long fasts and for refraining from any second marriages. He sometimes exalts martydom by teaching Christians not to avoid persecution.

In *The Apology*, however, there is no indication of Montanist teaching. His doctrine in this work seems to be completely orthodox. From this some have concluded that *The Apology* was written prior to his shift toward Montanism. Be that as it may, Tertullian's *Apology* is one of the finest examples of an early Christian defense.

In the section reprinted in this chapter, Tertullian defends Christians against the standard charge of atheism by cleverly turning the argument around. Christians do not worship the gods, he says, for we have found them to be nonexistent; however, we do worship the one true God, Creator of the universe. God has given ample evidence of His existence, particularly through the miracle of the Bible itself and of fulfilled prophecy. Not only that, he contends, but the facts of the gospel, including the disappearance of the sun at the time of the Crucifixion, are fully documented in the publicly available historical records of that time period. Tertullian concludes that every fact and every truth point to the divinity of Christ.

Jerome tells us that Tertullian lived to be very old. There is some evidence that he broke with Montanism in his later life. Most scholars date his death some time prior to A.D. 240. Though he remained a dissenter, the old Latin church did not have a more educated or a more honest champion against its enemies.

BIBLIOGRAPHY

Campenhausen, Hans von. *The Fathers of the Latin Church.* Translated by Manfred Hoffman. London: Adam and Charles Black, 1964.

Donaldson, James, and Roberts, Alexander, eds. *Ante-Nicene Fathers: Latin Christianity: Its Founder Tertullian.* Grand Rapids: Eerdmans, 1951, vol. 3.

Kaye, John. *The Ecclesiastical History of the Second and Third Centuries, Illustrated from the Writings of Tertullian.* London: Griffith Farran, n.d.

Mackinnon, James. *From Christ to Constantine.* London: Longmans, Green, 1936.

Newman, Albert Henry. *A Manual of Church History.* Philadelphia: American Baptist Publication Society, 1901.

Plummer, Alfred. *The Church of the Early Fathers.* London: Longmans, Green, 1888.

THE APOLOGY

CHAPTER X.

"YOU do not worship the gods," you say; "and you do not offer sacrifices for the emperors." Well, we do not offer sacrifice for others, for the same reason that we do not for ourselves,—namely, that your gods are not at all the objects of our worship. So we are accused of sacrilege and treason. This is the chief ground of charge against us—nay, it is the sum-total of our offending; and it is worthy then of being inquired into, if neither prejudice nor injustice be the judge, the one of which has no idea of discovering the truth, and the other simply and at once rejects it. We do not worship your gods, because we know that there are no such beings. This, therefore, is what you should do: you should call on us to demonstrate their non-existence, and thereby prove that they have no claim to adoration; for only if your gods were truly so, would there be any obligation to render divine homage to them. And punishment even were [sic] due to Christians, if it were made plain that those to whom they refused all worship were indeed divine. But you say, They are gods. We protest and appeal from yourselves to your knowledge; let that judge us; let that condemn us, if it can deny that all these gods of yours were but men. If even it venture to deny that, it will be confuted by its own books of antiquities, from which it has got its information about them, bearing witness to this day, as they plainly do, both of the cities in which they were born, and the countries in which they have left traces of their exploits, as well as where also they are proved to have been buried. Shall I now, therefore, go over them one by one, so numerous and so various, new and old, barbarian, Grecian, Roman, foreign, captive and adopted, private and common, male and

From Alexander Roberts and James Donaldson, eds., *The Ante-Nicene Fathers*, vol. 3: *Latin Christianity: Its Founder, Tertullian*, trans. S. Thelwall, rev. A. Cleveland Coxe (1872; reprint ed., Grand Rapids: Eerdmans, 1951), pp. 26–27, 31–36.

female, rural and urban, naval and military? It were useless even to hunt out all their names: so I may content myself with a compend; and this not for your information, but that you may have what you know brought to your recollection, for undoubtedly you act as if you had forgotten all about them. No one of your gods is earlier than Saturn: from him you trace all your deities, even those of higher rank and better known. What, then, can be proved of the first, will apply to those that follow. So far, then, as books give us information, neither the Greek Diodorus or Thallus, neither Cassius Severus or Cornelius Nepos, nor any writer upon sacred antiquities, have ventured to say that Saturn was any but a man: so far as the question depends on facts, I find none more trustworthy than those — that in Italy itself we have the country in which, after many expeditions, and after having partaken of Attic hospitalities, Saturn settled, obtaining cordial welcome from Janus, or, as the Salii will have it, Janis. The mountain on which he dwelt was called Saturnius; the city he founded is called Saturnia to this day; last of all, the whole of Italy, after having borne the name of Oenotria, was called Saturnia from him. He first gave you the art of writing, and a stamped coinage, and thence it is he presides over the public treasury. But if Saturn were a man, he had undoubtedly a human origin; and having a human origin, he was not the off-spring of heaven and earth. As his parents were unknown, it was not unnatural that he should be spoken of as the son of those elements from which we might all seem to spring. For who does not speak of heaven and earth as father and moth-er, in a sort of way of veneration and honour? or from the custom which prevails among us of saying that persons of whom we have no knowledge, or who make a sudden appearance, have fallen from the skies? In this way it came about that Saturn, everywhere a sudden and unlooked-for guest, got everywhere the name of the Heaven-born. For even the common folk call persons whose stock is un-known, sons of earth. I say nothing of how men in these rude times were wont to act, when they were impressed by the look of any stranger happening to appear among them, as though it were divine, since even at this day men of culture make gods of those whom, a day or two before, they acknowledged to be dead men by their public mourning for them. Let these notices of Saturn, brief as they are, suffice. . . .

. . .

CHAPTER XVII.

THE object of our worship is the One God,[1] He who by His commanding word, His arranging wisdom, His mighty power, brought forth from nothing this

---

[1][Kaye, p. 168. Remarks on natural religion.]

entire mass of our world, with all its array of elements, bodies, spirits, for the glory of His majesty; whence also the Greeks have bestowed on it the name of Κόσμος. The eye cannot see Him, though He is (spiritually) visible. He is incomprehensible, though in grace He is manifested. He is beyond our utmost thought, though our human faculties conceive of Him. He is therefore equally real and great. But that which, in the ordinary sense, can be seen and handled and conceived, is inferior to the eyes by which it is taken in, and the hands by which it is tainted, and the faculties by which it is discovered; but that which is infinite is known only to itself. This it is which gives some notion of God, while yet beyond all our conceptions—our very incapacity of fully grasping Him affords us the idea of what He really is. He is presented to our minds in His transcendent greatness, as at once known and unknown. And this is the crowning guilt of men, that they will not recognize One, of whom they cannot possibly be ignorant. Would you have the proof from the works of His hands, so numerous and so great, which both contain you and sustain you, which minister at once to your enjoyment, and strike you with awe; or would you rather have it from the testimony of the soul itself? Though under the oppressive bondage of the body, though led astray by depraving customs, though enervated by lusts and passions, though in slavery to false gods; yet, whenever the soul comes to itself, as out of a surfeit, or a sleep, or a sickness, and attains something of its natural soundness, it speaks of God; using no other word, because this is the peculiar name of the true God. "God is great and good"—"Which may God give," are the words on every lip. It bears witness, too, that God is judge, exclaiming, "God sees," and, "I commend myself to God," and, "God will repay me," O noble testimony of the soul by nature[2] Christian! Then, too, in using such words as these, it looks not to the Capitol, but to the heavens. It knows that there is the throne of the living God, as from Him and from thence itself came down.

CHAPTER XVIII.

BUT, that we might attain an ampler and more authoritative knowledge at once of Himself, and of His counsels and will, God has added a written revelation for the behoof of every one whose heart is set on seeking Him, that seeking he may find, and finding believe, and believing obey. For from the first He sent messengers into the world,—men whose stainless righteousness made them worthy to know the Most High, and to reveal Him,—men abundantly endowed with the Holy Spirit, that they might proclaim that there is one God only who made all things, who formed man from the dust of the ground (for He is the true

---

[2][Though we are not by nature good, in our present estate; this is elsewhere demonstrated by Tertullian, as see cap. xviii.]

Prometheus who gave order to the world by arranging the seasons and their course),—these have further set before us the proofs He has given of His majesty in His judgments by floods and fires, the rules appointed by Him for securing His favour, as well as the retribution in store for the ignoring, forsaking and keeping them, as being about at the end of all to adjudge His worshippers to everlasting life, and the wicked to the doom of fire at once without ending and without break, raising up again all the dead from the beginning, reforming and renewing them with the object of awarding either recompense. Once these things were with us, too, the theme of ridicule. We are of your stock and nature: men are made, not born, Christians. The preachers of whom we have spoken are called prophets, from the office which belongs to them of predicting the future. Their words, as well as the miracles which they performed, that men might have faith in their divine authority, we have still in the literary treasures they have left, and which are open to all. Ptolemy, surnamed Philadelphus, the most learned of his race, a man of vast acquaintance with all literature, emulating, I imagine, the book enthusiasm of Pisistratus, among other remains of the past which either their antiquity or something of peculiar interest made famous, at the suggestion of Demetrius Phalereus, who was renowned above all grammarians of his time, and to whom he had committed the management of these things, applied to the Jews for their writings—I mean the writings peculiar to them and in their tongue, which they alone possessed, for from themselves, as a people dear to God for their fathers' sake, their prophets had ever sprung, and to them they had ever spoken. Now in ancient times the people we call Jews bare the name of Hebrews, and so both their writings and their speech were Hebrew. But that the understanding of their books might not be wanting, this also the Jews supplied to Ptolemy; for they gave him seventy-two interpreters—men whom the philosopher Menedemus, the well-known asserter of a Providence, regarded with respect as sharing in his views. The same account is given by Aristaeus. So the king left these works unlocked to all, in the Greek language.[3] To this day, at the temple of Serapis, the libraries of Ptolemy are to be seen, with the identical Hebrew originals in them. The Jews, too, read them publicly. Under a tribute-liberty, they are in the habit of going to hear them every Sabbath. Whoever gives ear will find God in them; whoever takes pains to understand, will be compelled to believe.

CHAPTER XIX.

THEIR high antiquity, first of all, claims authority for these writings. With you, too, it is a kind of religion to demand belief on this very ground. Well, all the substances, all the materials, the origins, classes, contents of your most an-

---

[3][Kaye, p. 291. See Elucidation I. Also Vol. II, p. 334.]

cient writings, even most nations and cities illustrious in the records of the past and noted for their antiquity in books of annals,—the very forms of your letters, those revealers and custodiers of events, nay (I think I speak still within the mark), your very gods themselves, your very temples and oracles, and sacred rites, are less ancient than the work of a single prophet, in whom you have the *thesaurus* of the entire Jewish religion, and therefore too of ours. If you happen to have heard of a certain Moses, I speak first of him: he is as far back as the Argive Inachus; by nearly four hundred years—only seven less—he precedes Danaus, your most ancient name; while he antedates by a millennium the death of Priam. I might affirm, too, that he is five hundred years earlier than Homer, and have supporters of that view. The other prophets also, though of later date, are, even the most recent of them, as far back as the first of your philosophers, and legislators, and historians. It is not so much the difficulty of the subject, as its vastness, that stands in the way of a statement of the grounds on which these statements rest; the matter is not so arduous as it would be tedious. It would require the anxious study of many books, and the fingers' busy reckoning. The histories of the most ancient nations, such as the Egyptians, the Chaldeans, the Phoenicians, would need to be ransacked; the men of these various nations who have information to give, would have to be called in as witnesses. Manetho the Egyptian, and Berosus the Chaldean, and Hieromus the Phoenician king of Tyre; their successors too, Ptolemy the Mendesian, and Demetrius Phalereus, and King Juba, and Apion, and Thallus, and their critic the Jew Josephus, the native vindicator of the ancient history of his people, who either authenticates or refutes the others. Also the Greek censors' lists must be compared, and the dates of events ascertained, that the chronological connections may be opened up, and thus the reckonings of the various annals be made to give forth light. We must go abroad into the histories and literature of all nations. And, in fact, we have already brought the proof in part before you, in giving those hints as to how it is to be effected. But it seems better to delay the full discussion of this, lest in our haste we do not sufficiently carry it out, or lest in its thorough handling we make too lengthened a digression.

CHAPTER XX.

TO make up for our delay in this, we bring under your notice something of even greater importance; we point to the majesty of our Scriptures, if not to their antiquity. If you doubt that they are as ancient as we say, we offer proof that they are divine. And you may convince yourselves of this at once, and without going very far. Your instructors, the world, and the age, and the event, are all before you. All that is taking place around you was fore-announced; all that you now see with your eye was previously heard by the ear. The swallowing up of cities by the earth; the theft of islands by the sea; wars, bringing external and internal convulsions; the collision of kingdoms with kingdoms; famines and pestilences, and local massacres, and widespread desolating mortalities; the exaltation of the lowly, and the humbling of the proud; the decay of righteousness, the growth of sin, the slackening interest in all good ways; the very seasons and elements going out of their ordinary course, monsters and portents taking the place of nature's forms—it was all foreseen and predicted before it came to pass. While we suffer the calamities, we read of them in the Scriptures; as we examine, they are proved. Well, the truth of a prophecy, I think, is the demonstration of its being from above. Hence there is among us an assured faith in regard to coming events as things already proved to us, for they were predicted along with what we have day by day fulfilled. They are uttered by the same voices, they are written in the same books—the same Spirit inspires them. All time is one to prophecy foretelling the future. Among men, it may be, a distinction of times is made while the fulfilment is going on: from being future we think of it as present, and then from being present we count it as belonging to the past. How are we to blame, I pray you, that we believe in things to come as though they already were, with the grounds we have for our faith in these two steps?

CHAPTER XXI.

BUT having asserted that our religion is supported by the writings of the Jews, the oldest which exist, though it is generally known, and we fully admit that it dates from a comparatively recent period—no further back indeed than the reign of Tiberius—a question may perhaps be raised on this ground about its standing, as if it were hiding something of its presumption under shadow of an illustrious religion, one which has at any rate undoubted allowance of the law, or because, apart from the question of age, we neither accord with the Jews in their peculiarities in regard to food, nor in their sacred days, nor even in their well-known bodily sign, nor in the possession of a common name, which surely behoved to be the case if we did homage to the same God as they. Then, too, the common people have now some knowledge of Christ, and think of Him as but a man, one indeed such as the Jews condemned, so that some may naturally enough have taken up the idea that we are worshippers of a mere human being. But we are neither ashamed of Christ—for we rejoice to be counted His disciples, and in His name to suffer—nor do we differ from the Jews concerning God. We must make, therefore, a remark or two as to Christ's divinity. In former times, the Jews enjoyed much of God's favour, when the fathers of their race were noted for their righteousness and faith. So it was that as a people they flourished greatly, and their kingdom attained to a lofty eminence; and so highly blessed were they, that for their instruction God spake to them in special revelations, pointing out to them beforehand how they should merit His favor and avoid His displeasure. But how deeply they have sinned, puffed up to their fall with a false trust in their noble ancestors, turning from God's way into a way of sheer impiety, though they themselves should refuse to admit it, their present national ruin would afford sufficient proof. Scattered abroad, a race of wanderers, exiles from their own land and clime, they roam over the whole world without either a human or a heavenly king, not possessing even the stranger's right to set so much as a simple footstep in their native country. The sacred writers withal, in giving previous warning of these things, all with equal clearness ever declared that, in the last days of the world, God would, out of every nation, and people, and country, choose for Himself more faithful worshippers, upon whom He would bestow His grace, and that indeed in ampler measure, in keeping with the enlarged capacities of a nobler dispensation. Accordingly, He appeared among us, whose coming to renovate and illuminate man's nature was pre-announced by God—I mean Christ, that Son of God. And so the supreme Head and Master of this grace and discipline, the Enlightener and Trainer of the human race, God's own Son, was announced among us, born—but not so born as to make Him ashamed of the name of Son or of His paternal origin. It was not His lot to have as His father, by incest with a sister, or by violation of a daughter or another's wife, a god in the shape of serpent, or ox, or bird, or lover, for his vile ends transmuting himself into the gold of Danaus. They are your divinities upon whom these base deeds of Jupiter were done. But the Son of God has no mother in any sense which involves impurity; she, whom men suppose to be His mother in the ordinary way, had never entered into the marriage bond.[4] But, first, I shall discuss His essential nature, and so the nature of His birth will be understood. We have already asserted that God made the world, and all which it contains, by His Word, and Reason, and Power. It is abundantly plain that your philosophers, too, regard the Logos—that is, the Word and Reason—as the Creator of the universe. For Zeno lays it down that he is the creator, having made all things according to a determinate plan; that his name is Fate, and God, and the soul of Jupiter, and the necessity of all things. Cleanthes ascribes all this to spirit, which he maintains pervades the universe. And we, in like manner, hold that the Word, and Reason, and Power, by which we have said God made all, have spirit as their proper and essential *substratum*, in which the Word has inbeing to give forth utterances, and reason abides to dispose and arrange, and power is over all to execute. We have been taught that He proceeds forth from God, and in that procession He is generated; so that He is the Son of God, and is called God from unity of substance with God. For God, too, is a Spirit. Even when the ray is shot from the sun, it is

---

[4][That is, by the consummation of her marriage with Joseph.]

still part of the parent mass; the sun will still be in the ray, because it is a ray of the sun—there is no division of substance, but merely an extension. Thus Christ is Spirit of Spirit, and God of God, as light of light is kindled.[5] The material matrix remains entire and unimpaired, though you derive from it any number of shoots possessed of its qualities; so, too, that which has come forth out of God is at once God and the Son of God, and the two are one. In this way also, as He is Spirit of Spirit and God of God, He is made a second in manner of existence—in position, not in nature; and He did not withdraw from the original source, but went forth. This ray of God, then, as it was always foretold in ancient times, descending into a certain virgin, and made flesh in their womb, is in His birth God and man united. The flesh formed by the Spirit is nourished, grows up to manhood, speaks, teaches, works, and is the Christ. Receive meanwhile this fable, if you choose to call it so—it is like some of your own—while we go on to show how Christ's claims are proved, and who the parties are with you by whom such fables have been set agoing to overthrow the truth, which they resemble. The Jews, too, were well aware that Christ was coming, as those to whom the prophets spake. Nay, even now His advent is expected by them; nor is there any other contention between them and us, than that they believe the advent has not yet occurred. For two comings of Christ having been revealed to us: a first, which has been fulfilled in the lowliness of a human lot; a second, which impends over the world, now near its close, in all the majesty of Deity unveiled; and, by mis-understanding the first, they have concluded that the second—which, as matter of more manifest prediction, they set their hopes on—is the only one. It was the merited punishment of their sin not to understand the Lord's first advent: for if they had, they would have believed; and if they had believed, they would have obtained salvation. They themselves read how it is written of them that they are deprived of wisdom and understanding—of the use of eyes and ears [Isa. 6:10]. As, then, under the force of their pre-judgment, they had convinced themselves from His lowly guise that Christ was no more than man, it followed from that, as a necessary consequence, that they should hold Him a magician from the powers which He displayed,—expelling devils from men by a word, restoring vision to the blind, cleansing the leprous, reinvigorating the paralytic, summoning the dead to life again, making the very elements of nature obey Him, stilling the storms and walking on the sea; proving that He was the Logos of God, that primordial first-begotten Word, accompanied by power and reason, and based on Spirit,—that He who was now doing all things by His word, and He who had done that of old, were one and the same. But the Jews were so exasperated by His

---

[5][Language common among Christians, and adopted afterward into the Creed.]

teaching, by which their rulers and chiefs were convicted of the truth, chiefly because so many turned aside to Him, that at last they brought Him before Pontius Pilate, at that time Roman governor of Syria; and, by the violence of their outcries against Him, extorted a sentence giving Him up to them to be crucified. He Himself had predicted this; which, however, would have signified little had not the prophets of old done it as well. And yet, nailed upon the cross, He exhibited many notable signs, by which His death was distinguished from all others. At His own free-will, He with a word dismissed from Him His spirit, anticipating the executioner's work. In the same hour, too, the light of day was withdrawn, when the sun at the very time was in his meridian blaze. Those who were not aware that this had been predicted about Christ, no doubt thought it an eclipse. You yourselves have the account of the world-portent still in your archives.[6] Then, when His body was taken down from the cross and placed in a sepulchre, the Jews in their eager watchfulness surrounded it with a large military guard, lest, as He had predicted His resurrection from the dead on the third day, His disciples might remove by stealth His body, and deceive even the incredulous. But, lo, on the third day there was a sudden shock of earthquake, and the stone which sealed the sepulchre was rolled away, and the guard fled off in terror: without a single disciple near, the grave was found empty of all but the clothes of the buried One. But nevertheless, the leaders of the Jews, whom it nearly concerned both to spread abroad a lie, and keep back a people tributary and submissive to them from the faith, gave it out that the body of Christ had been stolen by His followers. For the Lord, you see, did not go forth into the public gaze, lest the wicked should be delivered from their error; that faith also, destined to a great reward, might hold its ground in difficulty. But He spent forty days with some of His disciples down in Galilee, a region of Judea, instructing them in the doctrines they were to teach to others. Thereafter, having given them commission to preach the gospel through the world, He was encompassed with a cloud and taken up to heaven,—a fact more certain far than the assertions of your Proculi concerning Romulus.[7] All these things Pilate did to Christ; and now in fact a Christian in his own convictions, he sent word of Him to the reigning Caesar, who was at the time Tiberius. Yes, and the Caesars too would have believed on Christ, if either the Caesars had not been necessary for the world, or if Christians could have been Caesars. His disciples also, spreading over the world, did as their Divine Master bade them; and after suffering greatly themselves from the persecutions of the Jews, and with no unwilling heart, as having

---

[6]Elucidation V.

[7]Proculus was a Roman senator who affirmed that Romulus had appeared to him after his death.

faith undoubting in the truth, at last by Nero's cruel sword sowed the seed of Christian blood at Rome.[8] Yes, and we shall prove that even your own gods are effective witnesses for Christ. It is a great matter if, to give you faith in Christians, I can bring forward the authority of the very beings on account of whom you refuse them credit. Thus far we have carried out the plan we laid down. We have set forth this origin of our sect and name, with this account of the Founder of Christianity. Let no one henceforth charge us with infamous wickedness; let no one think that it is otherwise than we have represented, for none may give a false account of his religion. For in the very fact that he says he worships another god than he really does, he is guilty of denying the object of his worship, and transferring his worship and homage to another; and, in the transference, he ceases to worship the god he has repudiated. We say, and before all men we say, and torn and bleeding under your tortures, we cry out, "We worship God through Christ." Count Christ a man, if you please; by Him and in Him God would be known and be adored. If the Jews object, we answer that Moses, who was but a man, taught them their religion; against the Greeks we urge that Orpheus at Pieria, Musaeus at Athens, Melampus at Argos, Trophonius in Boeotia, imposed religious rites; turning to yourselves, who exercise sway over the nations, it was the man Numa Pompilius who laid on the Romans a heavy load of costly superstitions. Surely Christ, then, had a right to reveal Deity, which was in fact His own essential possession, not with the object of bringing boors and savages by the dread of multitudinous gods, whose favour must be won, into some civilization, as was the case with Numa; but as one who aimed to enlighten men already civilized, and under illusions from their very culture, that they might come to the knowledge of the truth. Search, then, and see if that divinity of Christ be true. If it be of such a nature that the acceptance of it transforms a man, and makes him truly good, there is implied in that the duty of renouncing what is opposed to it as false. . . .

---

[8][Chapter 1, at close. "The blood of Christians is the seed of the Church."]

⧞ 5 ⧞

ORIGEN
(A.D. c185–c253)

Emperor Septimius Severus is remembered for his fierce persecution of Christians in the early third century. When the persecution swept through Alexandria, among the martyrs was a certain Leonides, a faithful believer. The oldest of his seven children, filled with enthusiasm for the faith and burning with a desire to publicly demonstrate his commitment to the gospel of Christ, attempted to join his father in the martyrs' fate. In a desperate move to save her son, Origen's mother hid his clothes, preventing him from going outside due to his modesty, and thus she saved the life of the one who became the most outstanding theological writer of the persecuted church.

Origin was born in Alexandria some time around A.D. 185. In his early years he was carefully trained by his father Leonides in the truths of Christian doctrine. Following his father's death, Origen was taken in by a wealthy and benevolent woman of Alexandria. Soon, however, he entered a career as a teacher of grammar, as his father had done. His unfailing kindness expressed toward those who were victims of persecution and his own literary skill and theological insight soon brought him an appointment to the Catechetical School as headmaster (succeeding Clement of Alexandria). The post was not a salaried one; so he sold his library in order to eat.

Origen understood the Scripture to be literally relevant to every situation; therefore, he did not possess two coats, nor did he wear shoes, because of Jesus' words in Matthew 10:7–10. He also took Matthew 19:12 quite seriously and refrained from marrying. When he realized the temptations that he faced while privately tutoring young female students, he applied Matthew 5:27–30 to his situation and made himself a eunuch.

Origin traveled widely but eventually settled in Alexandria to devote himself to advanced study. Ambrose, a wealthy man who had been won to the true faith by Origen, showed his gratitude in a tangible way by providing secretaries (shorthand experts and copyists) for Origen's work.

Origen had been ordained as an elder in Palestine around A.D. 230. This soon made it impossible for him to continue his work in Alexandria since Demetrius, the bishop of Alexandria, made it quite plain that eunuchs were not allowed to be ordained. So Origen took Ambrose and the secretaries and moved to Palestine. He spent twenty years there in furious activity. The empire-wide persecution in the days of Emperor Decius, however, did not pass Origen by. He was relentlessly tortured, but he never denied Christ. He was released after the death of Decius, but the strain had been severe, and in about A.D. 253 Origen died.

Jerome says that Origen wrote more than any one person could read. That may be so, for Epiphanius tells us that Origen authored over six thousand volumes. His most famous contribution to the world of critical scholarship is the *Hexapla* (a six-columned Bible comparing the Hebrew Old Testament to the several Greek versions). His major work in systematic theology is *De Principiis* (*On First Principles*). Modern copies of this work seem to be based on copies that have been edited to make them more orthodox at crucial points. Jean Daniélou (1905–1974), a French theologian, historian, and cardinal of the Roman Catholic church, is quite correct to describe Origen as both a biblical theologian and a Neoplatonic philosopher who had much in common with Gnosticism. Orthodox Christianity has never been fully comfortable with Origen.

His great work of apologetics is *Against Celsus*. This is a point-by-point refutation of an anti-Christian treatise entitled *The True Doctrine* (*Logos*) that was written by Celsus in the generation that preceeded Origen's own. (Most scholars date this work of Origen about A.D. 178, near the end of the reign of Marcus Aurelius.) The book by Celsus had been found by Ambrose, and he had asked Origen to answer it. Origen did so in such detail and with such ability that many consider it to be the greatest single apologetic work of antiquity. It is extremely long and somewhat tedious, due to Origen's stated purpose—to answer every objection and to give the fullest possible answer (Preface 1–6). One can dip into this work at almost any point and find spiritual nourishment in the midst of intensive apologetic reasoning.

Celsus, one of the more thoughtful opponents of the Christian faith, had addressed his treatise to a broad readership of sensible, cultivated, educated people who were convinced that Christianity was a false and irrational belief system. Celsus was by far the strongest intellectual antagonist of biblical Christianity in antiquity even though Porphyry is more frequently given that title by Christian historians. It is doubtful that anyone other than Origen could have so successfully answered this masterly anti-Christian polemic.

Celsus argues in two ways: first, as a Jew; second, as himself, a pagan philosopher. In the first part the objections, though forcefully argued, were nevertheless easily answered. Celsus (writing as a Jew) complains that Christian doctrine and morality were not new and that Christians borrowed most of their beliefs and practices from others and believed many foolish things. Why, for example, would Christ as an infant have to be rushed into hiding in Egypt if He were in fact divine? Moreover, Celsus continued, Jesus could not have been a god. Why would a god have to go into hiding when humans turned against Him? And would a god allow Himself to be betrayed by His own disciples and then killed by ordinary soldiers? Even a prudent person, much more a god, would try to escape foreseen dangers. Celsus contends that Jesus never even won a convert during His lifetime, not even His own disciples. Even those who followed Him were only taxgatherers and sailors, men of the most worthless and untrustworthy character. Celsus further argues that Jesus was a sorcerer and that no satisfactory evidence of the Resurrection exists. Origen's reply to this point is included in the selections reprinted in this chapter (Book II: chaps. xlviii–lxvii).

In later sections, Celsus argues not as a Jew but as himself—a pagan philosopher. After all, he says, Jews and Christians attack each other over rather trivial matters. Both Jews and Christians believe that a savior was predicted; they simply differ over whether or not that saviour has actually come (Book III: chaps. i–iii). But as a thinking man who is not a Jew, Celsus says he can find no reason whatsoever to believe that a god or a son of a god has, will, or should come to earth at all. For if God were to become a man, He would have to change from best to worst, and this is not possible with God. Origen's answer to these charges is included in the reading selections in this chapter (Book IV: chaps. xiv–xviii).

Celsus further urges that Christ was historically insignificant and thus could never be accepted as the divine Son of God, the Savior of the world. Origen, however, faces every criticism with skill and insight (Book VI: chaps. lxxviii–lxxix; Book VII: chaps. liii–lvii). Origen looks forward to the establishment of the kingdom of God (Book VIII: chaps. lxxii), and he remains eager to answer any further objections on falsehoods that Celsus may produce (Book VIII: chap. lxxvi). In a real sense, Origen effectively silenced this kind of intellectual attack on Christian faith until it reappeared with a renewed strength in the modern, post-Reformation centuries.

BIBLIOGRAPHY

Bigg, Charles. *The Christian Platonists of Alexandria.* 2d ed. rev. Oxford: At the University Press, 1913.

Chadwick, Henry. *Early Christian Thought and the Classical Tradition.* Oxford: Clarendon, 1966.

Daniélou, Jean. *Origène.* Paris: La Table Ronde, 1948. English translation by Walter Mitchell. New York: Sheed and Ward, 1955.

Eusebius. *Historia Ecclesiastica* (VI).

Hanson, R. P. C. *Allegory and Event: A Study of the Sources and Significance of Origen's Interpretation of Scripture.* London: SCM, 1959.

Origen. *Contra Celsum.* Translated with an introduction and notes by Henry Chadwick. Cambridge: At the University Press, 1953. (Reprinted with corrections and minor revisions 1965 and 1980.)

DE PRINCIPIIS
(On First Principles)

PREFACE

1. ALL who believe and are assured that grace and truth were obtained through Jesus Christ, and who know Christ to be the truth, agreeably to His own declaration, "I am the truth" [John 14:6], derive the knowledge which incites men to a good and happy life from no other source than from the very words and teaching of Christ. And by the words of Christ we do not mean those only which He spake when He became man and tabernacled in the flesh; for before that time, Christ, the Word of God, was in Moses and the prophets. For without the Word of God, how could they have been able to prophesy of Christ? And were it not our purpose to confine the present treatise within the limits of all attainable brevity, it would not be difficult to show, in proof of this statement, out of the Holy Scriptures, how Moses or the prophets both spake and performed all they did through being filled with the Spirit of Christ. And therefore I think it sufficient to quote this one testimony of Paul from the Epistle to the Hebrews, in which he says: "By faith Moses, when he was come to years, refused to be called the son of Pharaoh's daughter; choosing rather to suffer affliction with the people of God, than to enjoy the pleasures of sin for a season; esteeming the reproach of Christ greater riches than the treasures of the Egyptians" [Heb. 11:24–26]. Moreover, that after His ascension into heaven He spake in His apostles, is shown by Paul in these words: "Or do you seek a proof of Christ, who speaketh in me?" [2 Cor. 13:3].

From Alexander Roberts and James Donaldson, eds., *Ante-Nicene Christian Library*, trans. Frederick Crombie (Edinburgh: T. & T. Clark, 1871), 10:1–5.

2. Since many, however, of those who profess to believe in Christ differ from each other, not only in small and trifling matters, but also on subjects of the highest importance, as *e.g.* regarding God, or the Lord Jesus Christ, or the Holy Spirit; and not only regarding these, but also regarding others which are created existences, viz. the powers[1] and the holy virtues;[2] it seems on that account necessary first of all to fix a definite limit and to lay down an unmistakeable rule regarding each one of these, and then to pass to the investigation of other points. For as we ceased to seek for truth (notwithstanding the professions of many among Greeks and Barbarians to make it known) among all who claimed it for erroneous opinions, after we had come to believe that Christ was the Son of God, and were persuaded that we must learn it from Himself; so, seeing there are many who think they hold the opinions of Christ, and yet some of these think differently from their predecessors, yet as the teaching of the church, transmitted in orderly succession from the apostles, and remaining in the churches to the present day, is still preserved, that alone is to be accepted as truth which differs in no respect from ecclesiastical and apostolical tradition.

3. Now it ought to be known that the holy apostles, in preaching the faith of Christ, delivered themselves with the utmost clearness on certain points which they believed to be necessary to every one, even to those who seem somewhat dull in the investigation of divine knowledge; leaving, however, the grounds of their statements to be examined into by those who should deserve the excellent gifts of the Spirit, and who, especially by means of the Holy Spirit Himself, should obtain the gift of language, of wisdom, and of knowledge: while on other subjects they merely stated the fact that things were so, keeping silence as to the manner or origin of their existence; clearly in order that the more zealous of their successors, who should be lovers of wisdom, might have a subject of exercise on which to display the fruit of their talents,—those persons, I mean, who should prepare themselves to be fit and worthy receivers of wisdom.

4. The particular points[3] clearly delivered in the teaching of the apostles are as follow:

First, That there is one God, who created and arranged all things, and who, when nothing existed, called all things into being—God from the first creation and foundation of the world—the God of all just men, of Adam, Abel, Seth, Enos, Enoch, Noe, Sem, Abraham, Isaac, Jacob, the twelve patriarchs, Moses, and the prophets; and that this God in the last days, as He had announced beforehand by His prophets, sent our Lord Jesus Christ to call in the first place

---

[1]Dominationes.
[2]Virtutes.
[3]Species.

Israel to Himself, and in the second place the Gentiles, after the unfaithfulness of the people of Israel. This just and good God, the Father of our Lord Jesus Christ, Himself gave the law, and the prophets, and the gospels, being also the God of the apostles and of the Old and New Testaments.

Secondly, That Jesus Christ Himself, who came [into the world], was born of the Father before all creatures; that, after He had been the servant of the Father in the creation of all things—"For by Him were all things made" [John 1:3]—He in the last times, divesting Himself [of His glory], became a man, and was incarnate although God, and while made a man remained the God which He was; that He assumed a body like to our own, differing in this respect only, that it was born of a virgin and of the Holy Spirit: that this Jesus Christ was truly born, and did truly suffer, and did not endure this death common [to man] in appearance only, but did truly die; that He did truly rise from the dead; and that after His resurrection He conversed with His disciples, and was taken up [into heaven].

Then, *thirdly,* the apostles related that the Holy Spirit was associated in honour and dignity with the Father and the Son. But in His case it is not clearly distinguished whether He is to be regarded as born or innate,[4] or also as a Son of God or not: for these are points which have to be inquired into out of sacred Scripture according to the best of our ability, and which demand careful investigation. And that this Spirit inspired each one of the saints, whether prophets or apostles; and that there was not one Spirit in the men of the old dispensation, and another in those who were inspired at the advent of Christ, is most clearly taught throughout the churches.

5. After these points, also, the apostolic teaching is that the soul, having a substance[5] and life of its own, shall, after its departure from the world, be rewarded according to its deserts, being destined to obtain either an inheritance of eternal life and blessedness, if its actions shall have procured this for it, or to be delivered up to eternal fire and punishments, if the guilt of its crimes shall have brought it down to this: and also, that there is to be a time of resurrection from the dead, when this body, which now "is sown in corruption, shall rise in incorruption," and that which "is sown in dishonour will rise in glory" [1 Cor. 15:42]. This also is clearly defined in the teaching of the church, that every rational soul

---

[4]Innatus. The words which Rufinus has rendered "natus an innatus" are rendered by Jerome in his Epistle to Avitus (94 *alias* 59), "factus an infectus." Criticising the errors in the first book of the *Principles*, he says: "Origen declares the Holy Spirit to be third in dignity and honour after the Father and the Son; and although professing ignorance whether he were created or not (factus an infectus), he indicated afterwards his opinion regarding him, maintaining that nothing was uncreated except God the Father." Jerome, no doubt, read γενητὸς ἢ ἀγένητος, and Rufinus γεννητὸς ἢ ἀγέννητος.—R.

[5]Substantia.

is possessed of free-will and volition; that it has a struggle to maintain with the devil and his angels, and opposing influences,[6] because they strive to burden it with sins; but if we live rightly and wisely, we should endeavour to shake ourselves free of a burden of that kind. From which it follows, also, that we understand ourselves not to be subject to necessity, so as to be compelled by all means, even against our will, to do either good or evil. For if we are our own masters, some influences perhaps may impel us to sin, and others help us to salvation; we are not forced, however, by any necessity either to act rightly or wrongly, which those persons think is the case who say that the courses and movements of the stars are the cause of human actions, not only of those which take place beyond the influence of the freedom of the will, but also of those which are placed within our own power. But with respect to the soul, whether it is derived from the seed by a process of traducianism, so that the reason or substance of it may be considered as placed in the seminal particles of the body themselves, or whether it has any other beginning; and this beginning itself, whether it be by birth or not, or whether bestowed upon the body from without or no, is not distinguished with sufficient clearness in the teaching of the church.

6. Regarding the devil and his angels, and the opposing influences, the teaching of the church has laid down that these beings exist indeed; but what they are, or how they exist, it has not explained with sufficient clearness. This opinion, however, is held by most, that the devil was an angel, and that, having become an apostate, he induced as many of the angels as possible to fall away with himself, and these up to the present time are called his angels.

7. This also is a part of the church's teaching, that the world was made and took its beginning at a certain time, and is to be destroyed on account of its wickedness. . . .

8. Then, finally, that the Scriptures were written by the Spirit of God, and have a meaning, not such only as is apparent at first sight, but also another, which escapes the notice of most.

.   .   .

---

[6]Virtutes.

AGAINST CELSUS
(Contra Celsum)

BOOK II.

CHAPTER XLVIII.

CELSUS, moreover, unable to resist the miracles which Jesus is recorded to have performed, has already on several occasions spoken of them slanderously as works of sorcery; and we also on several occasions have, to the best of our ability, replied to his statements. And now he represents us as saying that "we deemed Jesus to be the Son of God, because he healed the lame and the blind." And he adds: "Moreover, as you assert, he raised the dead." That He healed the lame and the blind, and that therefore we hold Him to be the Christ and the Son of God, is manifest to us from what is contained in the prophecies: "Then the eyes of the blind shall be opened, and the ears of the deaf shall hear; then shall the lame man leap as an hart [Isa. 35:5–6]. And that He also raised the dead, and that it is no fiction of those who composed the Gospels, is shown by this, that if it had been a fiction, *many* individuals would have been represented as having risen from the dead, and these, too, such as had been many years in their graves. But as it is no fiction, they are very easily counted of whom this is related to have happened; viz. the daughter of the ruler of the synagogue (of whom I know not why He said, "She is not dead, but sleepeth," stating regarding her something which does not apply to all who die); and the only son of the widow, on whom He took compassion and raised him up, making the bearers of the corpse to stand still; and the third instance, that of Lazarus, who had been four days in the grave.

From Alexander Roberts and James Donaldson, eds., *The Ante-Nicene Christian Library*, trans. Frederick Crombie (Edinburgh: T. & T. Clark, 1872), 23:49–71; 85–88; 174–78; 421–23; 475–79; 554–56; 558–59.

Now, regarding these cases we would say to all persons of candid mind, and especially to the Jew, that as there were many lepers in the days of Elisha the prophet, and none of them was healed save Naaman the Syrian, and many widows in the days of Elijah the prophet, to none of whom was Elijah sent save to Sarepta in Sidonia (for the widow there had been deemed worthy by a divine decree of the miracle which was wrought by the prophet in the matter of the bread); so also there were many dead in the days of Jesus, but those only rose from the grave whom the Logos knew to be fitted for a resurrection, in order that the works done by the Lord might not be merely symbols of certain things, but that by the very acts themselves He might gain over many to the marvelous doctrine of the gospel. I would say, moreover, that, agreeably to the promise of Jesus, His disciples performed even greater works than these miracles of Jesus, which were perceptible only to the senses.[1] For the eyes of those who are blind in soul are ever opened; and the ears of those who were deaf to virtuous words, listen readily to the doctrine of God, and of the blessed life with Him; and many, too, who were lame in the feet of the "inner man," as Scripture calls it, having now been healed by the word, do not simply leap, but leap as the hart, which is an animal hostile to serpents, and stronger than all the poison of vipers. And these lame who have been healed, receive from Jesus power to trample, with those feet in which they were formerly lame, upon the serpents and scorpions of wickedness, and generally upon all the power of the enemy; and though they tread upon it, they sustain no injury, for they also have become stronger than the poison of all evil and of demons.

CHAPTER XLIX.

JESUS, accordingly, in turning away the minds of His disciples, not merely from giving heed to sorcerers in general, and those who profess in any other manner to work miracles—for His disciples did not need to be so warned—but from such as gave themselves out as the Christ of God, and who tried by certain apparent[2] miracles to gain over to them the disciples of Jesus, said in a certain passage: "Then, if any man shall say unto you, Lo, here is Christ, or there; believe it not. For there shall arise false Christs and false prophets, and shall show great signs and wonders; insomuch that, if it were possible, they shall deceive the very elect. Behold, I have told you before. Wherefore, if they shall say unto you, Behold, he is in the desert, go not forth; behold, he is in the secret chambers, believe it not. For as the lightning cometh out of the east, and shineth even to the west, so also shall the coming of the Son of man be" [Matt. 24:23-27]. And

---

[1]ὧν Ἰησοῦς αἰσθητῶν.
[2]φαντασιῶν.

in another passage: "Many will say unto me in that day, Lord, Lord, have we not eaten and drunk in Thy name, and by Thy name have cast out demons, and done many wonderful works? And then will I say unto them, Depart from me, because ye are workers of iniquity."[3] But Celsus, wishing to assimilate the miracles of Jesus to the works of human sorcery, says in express terms as follows: "O light and truth! he distinctly declares, with his own voice, as ye yourselves have recorded, that there will come to you even others, employing miracles of a similar kind, who are wicked men, and sorcerers; and he calls him who makes use of such devices, one Satan. So that Jesus himself does not deny that these works at least are not at all divine, but are the acts of wicked men; and being compelled by the force of truth, he at the same time not only laid open the doings of others, but convicted himself of the same acts. Is it not, then, a miserable inference, to conclude from the same works that the one is God and the others sorcerers? Why ought the others, because of these acts, to be accounted wicked rather than this man, seeing they have him as their witness against himself? For he has himself acknowledged that these are not the works of a divine nature, but the inventions of certain deceivers, and of thoroughly wicked men." Observe, now, whether Celsus is not clearly convicted of slandering the gospel by such statements, since what Jesus says regarding those who are to work signs and wonders is different from what this Jew of Celsus alleges it to be. For if Jesus had simply told His disciples to be on their guard against those who professed to work miracles, without declaring what they would give themselves out to be, then perhaps there would have been some ground for his suspicion. But since those against whom Jesus would have us to be on our guard give themselves out as the Christ—which is not a claim put forth by sorcerers—and since he says that even some who lead wicked lives will perform miracles in the name of Jesus, and expel demons out of men, sorcery in the case of these individuals, or any suspicion of such, is rather, if we may so speak, altogether banished, and the divinity of Christ established, as well as the divine mission[4] of His disciples; seeing that it is possible that one who makes use of His name, and who is wrought upon by some power, in some way unknown, to make the pretence that he is the Christ, should seem to perform miracles like those of Jesus, while others through His name should do works resembling those of His genuine disciples.

CHAPTER L.

PAUL, moreover, in the Second Epistle to the Thessalonians, shows in what manner there will one day be revealed "the man of sin, the son of perdi-

---

[3]Cf. Matt. 7:22–23, with Luke 13:26–27.
[4]θειότης, lit. divinity.

tion, who opposeth and exalteth himself above all that is called God, or that is worshipped; so that he sitteth in the temple of God, showing himself that he is God" [2 Thess. 2:3–4]. And again he says to the Thessalonians: "And now ye know what withholdeth that he might be revealed in his time. For the mystery of iniquity doth already work: only He who now letteth will let, until he be taken out of the way: and then shall that Wicked be revealed, whom the Lord will consume with the spirit of His mouth, and shall destroy with the brightness of His coming: even him, whose coming is after the working of Satan, with all power, and signs, and lying wonders, and with all deceivableness of unrighteousness in them that perish" [2 Thess 2:6–10]. And in assigning the reason why the man of sin is permitted to continue in existence, he says: "Because they received not the love of the truth, that they might be saved. And for this cause God shall send them strong delusion, that they should believe a lie; that they all might be damned who believed not the truth, but had pleasure in unrighteousness" [2 Thess. 2:10–12]. Let any one now say whether any of the statements in the Gospel, or in the writings of the apostle, could give occasion for the suspicion that there is therein contained any prediction of sorcery. Any one, moreover, who likes may find the prophecy in Daniel respecting antichrist.[5] But Celsus falsifies the words of Jesus, since He did not say that others would come working similar miracles to Himself, but who are wicked men and sorcerers, although Celsus asserts that He uttered such words. For as the power of the Egyptian magicians was not similar to the divinely bestowed grace of Moses, but the issue clearly proved that the acts of the former were the effect of magic, while those of Moses were wrought by divine power; so the proceedings of the antichrists, and of those who feign that they can work miracles as being the disciples of Christ, are said to be lying signs and wonders, prevailing with all deceivableness of unrighteousness among them that perish; whereas the works of Christ and His disciples had for their fruit, not deceit, but the salvation of human souls. And who would rationally maintain that an improved moral life, which daily lessened the number of a man's offenses, could proceed from a system of deceit?

CHAPTER LI.

CELSUS, indeed, evinced a slight knowledge of Scripture when he made Jesus say, that it is "a certain Satan who contrives such devices;" although he begs the question[6] when he asserts that "Jesus did not deny that these works have in them nothing of divinity, but proceed from wicked men," for he makes things which differ in kind to be the same. Now, as a wolf is not of the same species as a

---

[5]Cf. Dan. 7:26.

[6]συναρφάζει τὸν λόγον.

dog, although it may appear to have some resemblance in the figure of its body and in its voice, nor a common wood-pigeon[7] the same as a dove,[8] so there is no resemblance between what is done by the power of God and what is the effect of sorcery. And we might further say, in answer to the calumnies of Celsus, Are those to be regarded as miracles which are wrought through sorcery by wicked demons, but those not which are performed by a nature that is holy and divine? and does human life endure the worse, but never receive the better? Now it appears to me that we must lay it down as a general principle, that as, wherever anything that is evil would make itself to be of the same nature with the good, there must by all means be something that is good opposed to the evil; so also, in opposition to those things which are brought about by sorcery, there must also of necessity be some things in human life which are the result of divine power. And it follows from the same, that we must either annihilate both, and assert that neither exists, or, assuming the one, and particularly the evil, admit also the reality of the good. Now, if one were to lay it down that works are wrought by means of sorcery, but would not grant that there are also works which are the product of divine power, he would seem to me to resemble him who should admit the existence of sophisms and plausible arguments, which have the appearance of establishing the truth, although really undermining it, while denying that truth had anywhere a home among men, or a dialectic which differed from sophistry. But if we once admit that it is consistent with the existence of magic and sorcery (which derive their power from evil demons, who are spell-bound by elaborate incantations, and become subject to sorcerers) that some works must be found among men which proceed from a power that is divine, why shall we not test those who profess to perform them by their lives and morals, and the consequences of their miracles, viz. whether they tend to the injury of men or to the reformation of conduct? What minister of evil demons, *e.g.*, can do such things? and by means of what incantations and magic arts? And who, on the other hand, is it that, having his soul and his spirit, and I imagine also his body, in a pure and holy state, receives a divine spirit, and performs such works in order to benefit men, and to lead them to believe on the true God? But if we must once investigate (without being carried away by the miracles themselves) who it is that performs them by help of a good, and who by help of an evil power, so that we may neither slander all without discrimination, nor yet admire and accept all as divine, will it not be manifest, from what occurred in the times of Moses and Jesus, when entire nations were established in consequence of their miracles, that these men wrought by means of divine power what they are recorded to have

---

[7]φύσσα.
[8]πεοιστεϱά.

performed? For wickedness and sorcery would not have led a whole nation to rise not only above idols and images erected by men, but also above all created things, and to ascend to the uncreated origin of the God of the universe.

CHAPTER LII.

BUT since it is a Jew who makes these assertions in the treatise of Celsus, we would say to him: Pray, friend, why do you believe the works which are recorded in your writings as having been performed by God through the instrumentality of Moses to be really divine, and endeavour to refute those who slanderously assert that they were wrought by sorcery, like those of the Egyptian magicians; while, in imitation of your Egyptian opponents, you charge those which were done by Jesus, and which, you admit, were actually performed, with not being divine? For if the final result, and the founding of an entire nation by the miracles of Moses, manifestly demonstrate that it was God who brought these things to pass in the time of Moses the Hebrew lawgiver, why should not such rather be shown to be the case with Jesus, who accomplished far greater works than those of Moses? For the former took those of his own nation, the descendants of Abraham, who had observed the rite of circumcision transmitted by tradition, and who were careful observers of the Abrahamic usages, and led them out of Egypt, enacting for them those laws which you believe to be divine; whereas the latter ventured upon a greater undertaking, and superinduced upon the pre-existing constitution, and upon ancestral customs and modes of life agreeable to the existing laws, a constitution in conformity with the gospel. And as it was necessary, in order that Moses should find credit not only among the elders, but the common people, that there should be performed those miracles which he is recorded to have performed, why should not Jesus also, in order that He may be believed on by those of the people who had learned to ask for signs and wonders, require to work such miracles as, on account of their greater grandeur and divinity (in comparison with those of Moses), were able to convert men from Jewish fables, and from the human traditions which prevailed among them, and make them admit that He who taught and did such things was greater than the prophets? For how was not He greater than the prophets, who was proclaimed by them to be the Christ, and the Saviour of the human race?

CHAPTER LIII.

ALL the arguments, indeed, which this Jew of Celsus advances against those who believe on Jesus, may, by parity of reasoning, be urged as ground of accusation against Moses: so that there is no difference in asserting that the sorcery practised by Jesus and that by Moses were similar to each other,⁹—both of them, so far as the language of this Jew of Celsus is concerned, being liable to the same charge; as, *e.g.*, when this Jew says of Christ, "But, O light and truth! Jesus with his own voice expressly declares, as you yourselves have recorded, that there will appear among you others also, who will perform miracles like mine, but who are wicked men and sorcerers," some one, either Greek or Egyptian, or any other party who disbelieved the Jew, might say respecting Moses, "But, O light and truth! Moses with his own voice expressly declares, as ye also have recorded, that there will appear among you others also, who will perform miracles like mine, but who are wicked men and sorcerers. For it is written in your law, 'If there arise among you a prophet, or a dreamer of dreams, and giveth thee a sign or a wonder, and the sign or wonder come to pass whereof he spake unto thee, saying, Let us go after other gods which thou hast not known, and let us serve them; thou shalt not hearken to the words of that prophet or dreamer of dreams' [Deut. 13:1–3]," etc. Again, perverting the words of Jesus, he says, "And he terms him who devises such things, one Satan;" while one, applying this to Moses, might say, "And he terms him who devises such things, a prophet who dreams dreams." And as this Jew asserts regarding Jesus, that "even he himself does not deny that these works have in them nothing of divinity, but are the acts of wicked men;" so any one who disbelieves the writings of Moses might say, quoting what has been already said, the same thing, viz., that "even Moses does not deny that these works have in them nothing of divinity, but are the acts of wicked men." And he will do the same thing also with respect to this: "Being compelled by the force of truth, Moses at the same time both exposed the doings of others, and convicted himself of the same." And when the Jew says, "Is it not a wretched inference from the same acts, to conclude that the one is a God, and the others sorcerers?" one might object to him, on the ground of those words of Moses already quoted, "Is it not then a wretched inference from the same acts, to conclude that the one is a prophet and servant of God, and the others sorcerers?" But when, in addition to those comparisons which I have already mentioned, Celsus, dwelling upon the subject, adduces this also: "Why from these works should the others be accounted wicked, rather than this man, seeing they have him as a witness against himself?"—we, too, shall adduce the following, in addition to what has been already said: "Why, from those passages in which Moses forbids us to believe those who exhibit signs and wonders, ought we to consider such persons as wicked, rather than Moses, because he calumniates some of them in respect of their signs and

⁹ὥστε μηδὲν διαφέρειν παραπλήσιον εἶναι λέγειν γοητείαν τὴν Ἰησοῦ τῇ Μωύσεως.

wonders?" And urging more to the same effect, that he may appear to strengthen his attempt, he says: "He himself acknowledged that these were not the works of a divine nature, but were the inventions of certain deceivers, and of very wicked men." Who, then, is "himself?" You, O Jew, say that it is Jesus; but he who accuses you as liable to the same charges, will transfer this "himself" to the person of Moses.

CHAPTER LIV.

AFTER this, forsooth, the Jew of Celsus, to keep up the character assigned to the Jew from the beginning, in his address to those of his countrymen who had become believers, says: "By what, then, were you induced [to become his followers]? Was it because he foretold that after his death he would rise again?" Now this question, like the others, can be retorted upon Moses. For we might say to the Jew: "By what, then, were *you* induced [to become the follower of Moses]? Was it because he put on record the following statement about his own death: 'And Moses, the servant of the Lord, died there, in the land of Moab, according to the word of the Lord; and they buried him in Moab, near the house of Phogor: and no one knoweth his sepulchre until this day?' [Deut. 34:5–6]." For as the Jew casts discredit upon the statement, that "Jesus foretold that after His death He would rise again," another person might make a similar assertion about Moses, and would say in reply, that Moses also put on record (for the book of Deuteronomy is his composition) the statement, that "no one knoweth his sepulchre until this day," in order to magnify and enhance the importance of his place of burial, as being unknown to mankind.

CHAPTER LV.

THE Jew continues his address to those of his countrymen who are converts, as follows: "Come now, let us grant to you that the prediction was actually uttered. Yet how many others are there who practise such juggling tricks, in order to deceive their simple hearers, and who make gain by their deception?—as was the case, they say, with Zamolxis[10] in Scythia, the slave of Pythagoras; and with Pythagoras himself in Italy; and with Rhampsinitus[11] in Egypt (the latter of whom, they say, played at dice with Demeter in Hades, and returned to the upper world with a golden napkin which he had received from her as a gift); and also with Orpheus[12] among the Odrysians, and Protesilaus in Thessaly, and Hercules[13] at Cape Tenarus, and Theseus. But the question is, whether any one

---

[10]Cf. Herodot. iv. 95.
[11]Cf. Herodot. ii. 122.
[12]Cf. Diodor. iv. *Bibl. Hist.*
[13]Cf. Diodor. iv. *Bibl. Hist.*

who was really dead ever rose with a veritable body.[14] Or do you imagine the statements of others not only to be myths, but to have the appearance of such, while you have discovered a becoming and credible termination to your drama in the voice from the cross, when he breathed his last, and in the earthquake and the darkness? That while alive he was of no assistance to himself, but that when dead he rose again, and showed the marks of his punishment, and how his hands were pierced with nails: who beheld this? A half-frantic[15] woman, as you state, and some other one, perhaps, of those who were engaged in the same system of delusion, who had either dreamed so, owing to a peculiar state of mind,[16] or under the influence of a wandering imagination had formed to himself an appearance according to his own wishes,[17] which has been the case with numberless individuals; or, which is most probable, one who desired to impress others with this portent, and by such a falsehood to furnish an occasion to impostors like himself."

Now, since it is a Jew who makes these statements, we shall conduct the defence of our Jesus as if we were replying to a Jew, still continuing the comparison derived from the accounts regarding Moses, and saying to him: "How many others are there who practise similar juggling tricks to those of Moses, in order to deceive their silly hearers, and who make gain by their deception?" Now this objection would be more appropriate in the mouth of one who did not believe in Moses (as we might quote the instances of Zamolxis and Pythagoras, who were engaged in such juggling tricks) than in that of a Jew, who is not very learned in the histories of the Greeks. An Egyptian, moreover, who did not believe the miracles of Moses, might credibly adduce the instance of Rhampsinitus, saying that it was far more credible that he had descended to Hades, and had played at dice with Demeter, and that after stealing from her a golden napkin he exhibited it as a sign of his having been in Hades, and of his having returned thence, than that Moses should have recorded that he entered into the darkness, where God was, and that he alone, above all others, drew near to God. For the following is his statement: "Moses alone shall come near the Lord; but the rest shall not come nigh" [Ex. 24:2]. We, then, who are the disciples of Jesus, say to the Jew who urges these objections: "While assailing our belief in Jesus, defend yourself, and answer the Egyptian and the Greek objectors: what will you say to those charges which you brought against our Jesus, but which also might be brought against Moses first? And if you should make a vigorous effort to defend Moses, as indeed

---

[14]αὐτῷ σώματι.
[15]γυνὴ πάροιστρος.
[16]κατά τινα διαθεσιν ὀνειρώξας.
[17]ἢ κατὰ τὴν αὐτοῦ βούλησιν δοξῇ πεπλανημένη φαντασιωθείς.

his history does admit of a clear and powerful defence, you will unconsciously, in your support of Moses, be an unwilling assistant in establishing the greater divinity of Jesus."

CHAPTER LVI.

BUT since the Jew says that these histories of the alleged descent of heroes to Hades, and of their return thence, are juggling impositions,[18] maintaining that these heroes disappeared for a certain time, and secretly withdrew themselves from the sight of all men, and gave themselves out afterwards as having returned from Hades,—for such is the meaning which his words seem to convey respecting the Odrysian Orpheus, and the Thessalian Protesilaus, and the Taenarian Hercules, and Theseus also,—let us endeavour to show that the account of Jesus being raised from the dead cannot possibly be compared to these. For each one of the heroes respectively mentioned might, had he wished, have secretly withdrawn himself from the sight of men, and returned again, if so determined, to those whom he had left; but seeing that Jesus was crucified before all the Jews, and His body slain in the presence of His nation, how can they bring themselves to say that He practised a similar deception[19] with those heroes who are related to have gone down to Hades, and to have returned thence? But we say that the following consideration might be adduced, perhaps, as a defence of the public crucifixion of Jesus, especially in connection with the existence of those stories of heroes who are supposed to have been compelled[20] to descend to Hades: that if we were to suppose Jesus to have died an obscure death, so that the fact of His decease was not patent to the whole nation of the Jews, and afterwards to have actually risen from the dead, there would, in such a case, have been ground for the same suspicion entertained regarding the heroes being also entertained regarding Himself. Probably, then, in addition to other causes for the crucifixion of Jesus, this also may have contributed to His dying a conspicuous death upon the cross, that no one might have it in his power to say that He voluntarily withdrew from the sight of men, and seemed only to die, without really doing so; but, appearing again, made a juggler's trick[21] of the resurrection from the dead. But a clear and unmistakeable proof of the fact I hold to be the undertaking of His disciples, who devoted themselves to the teaching of a doctrine which was attended with danger to human life,—a doctrine which they would not have taught with such courage had they invented the resurrection of Jesus from the dead; and who also, at the

---

[18]τερατείας.

[19]πῶς οἴονται τὸ παραπλήσιον πλάσασθαι λέγειν αὐτὸν τοῖς ἱστορουμένοις, etc.

[20]καταβεβηκέναι βιᾷ. Bohereau proposes the omission of βιᾷ.

[21]ἐτερατεύσατο.

same time, not only prepared others to despise death, but were themselves the first to manifest their disregard for its terrors.

CHAPTER LVII.

BUT observe whether this Jew of Celsus does not talk very blindly, in saying that it is impossible for any one to rise from the dead with a veritable body, his language being: "But this is the question, whether any one who was really dead ever rose again with a veritable body?" Now a Jew would not have uttered these words, who believed what is recorded in the third and fourth books of Kings regarding little children, of whom the one was raised up by Elijah [1 Kings 17:21-22], and the other by Elisha [2 Kings 4:34-35]. And on this account, too, I think it was that Jesus appeared to no other nation than the Jews, who had become accustomed to miraculous occurrences; so that, by comparing what they themselves believed with the works which were done by Him, and with what was related of Him, they might confess that He, in regard to whom greater things were done, and by whom mightier marvels were performed, was greater than all those who preceded Him.

CHAPTER LVIII.

FURTHER, after these Greek stories which the Jew adduced respecting those who were guilty of juggling practices,[22] and who pretended to have risen from the dead, he says to those Jews who are converts to Christianity: "Do you imagine the statements of others not only to be myths, but to have the appearance of such, while you have discovered a becoming and credible termination to your drama in the voice from the cross, when he breathed his last?" We reply to the Jew: "What you adduce as myths, we regard also as such; but the statements of the Scriptures which are common to us both, in which not you only, but we also, take pride, we do not at all regard as myths. And therefore we accord our belief to those who have therein related that some rose from the dead, as not being guilty of imposition; and to Him especially there mentioned as having risen, who both predicted the event Himself, and was the subject of prediction by others. And His resurrection is more miraculous than that of the others in this respect, that they were raised by the prophets Elijah and Elisha, while He was raised by none of the prophets, but by His Father in heaven. And therefore His resurrection also produced greater results than theirs. For what great good has accrued to the world from the resurrection of the children through the instrumentality of Elijah and Elisha, such as has resulted from the preaching of the

---

[22]τερατευομένοις.

resurrection of Jesus, accepted as an article of belief, and as effected through the agency of divine power?"

CHAPTER LIX.

HE imagines also that both the earthquake and the darkness were an invention;[23] but regarding these, we have in the preceding pages made our defence, according to our ability, adducing the testimony of Phlegon, who relates that these events took place at the time when our Saviour suffered. And he goes on to say, that "Jesus, while alive, was of no assistance to himself, but that he arose after death, and exhibited the marks of his punishment, and showed how his hands had been pierced by nails." We ask him what he means by the expression, "was of no assistance to himself?" For if he means it to refer to want of virtue, we reply that He *was* of very great assistance. For He neither uttered nor committed anything that was improper, but was truly "led as a sheep to the slaughter, and was dumb as a lamb before the shearer" [Isa. 53:7]; and the Gospel testifies that He opened not His mouth. But if Celsus applies the expression to things indifferent and corporeal,[24] [meaning that in such Jesus could render no help to Himself,] we say that we have proved from the Gospels that He went voluntarily to encounter His sufferings. Speaking next of the statements in the Gospels, that after His resurrection He showed the marks of His punishment, and how His hands had been pierced, he asks, "Who beheld this?" And discrediting the narrative of Mary Magdalene, who is related to have seen Him, he replies, "A half-frantic woman, as ye state." And because she is not the only one who is recorded to have seen the Saviour after His resurrection, but others also are mentioned, this Jew of Celsus calumniates these statements also in adding, "And some one else of those engaged in the same system of deception!"

CHAPTER LX.

IN the next place, as if this were possible, viz. that the image of a man who was dead could appear to another as if he were still living, he adopts this opinion as an Epicurean, and says, "That some one having so dreamed owing to a peculiar state of mind, or having, under the influence of a perverted imagination, formed such an appearance as he himself desired, reported that such had been seen; and this," he continues, "has been the case with numberless individuals." But even if this statement of his seems to have a considerable degree of force, it is nevertheless only fitted to confirm a necessary doctrine, that the soul of the dead exists in a separate state [from the body]; and he who adopts such an opinion does

---

[23]τερατείαν.
[24]εἰ δὲ τὸ "ἐπήρκεσεν" ἀπὸ τῶν μέσων καὶ σωματικῶν λαμβάνει.

not believe without good reason in the immortality, or at least continued existence, of the soul, as even Plato says in his treatise on the Soul that shadowy phantoms of persons already dead have appeared to some around their sepulchres. Now the phantoms which exist about the soul of the dead are produced by some substance, and this substance is in the soul, which exists apart in a body said to be of splendid appearance.[25] But Celsus, unwilling to admit any such view, will have it that some dreamed a waking dream,[26] and, under the influence of a perverted imagination, formed to themselves such an image as they desired. Now it is not irrational to believe that a dream may take place while one is asleep; but to suppose a waking vision in the case of those who are not altogether out of their senses, and under the influence of delirium or hypochondria, is incredible. And Celsus, seeing this, called the woman "half-mad,"—a statement which is not made by the history recording the fact, but from which he took occasion to charge the occurrences with being untrue.

CHAPTER LXI.

JESUS accordingly, as Celsus imagines, exhibited after His death only the appearance of wounds received on the cross, and was not in reality so wounded as He is described to have been; whereas, according to the teaching of the Gospel— some portions of which Celsus arbitrarily accepts, in order to find ground of accusation, and other parts of which he rejects—Jesus called to Him one of His disciples who was sceptical, and who deemed the miracle an impossibility. That individual had, indeed, expressed his belief in the statement of the woman who said that she had seen Him, because he did not think it impossible that the soul of a dead man could be seen; but he did not yet consider the report to be true that He had been raised in a body, which was the antitype of the former.[27] And therefore he did not merely say, "Unless I see, I will not believe;" but he added, "Unless I put my hand into the print of the nails, and lay my hands upon His side, I will not believe." These words were spoken by Thomas, who deemed it possible that the body of the soul[28] might be seen by the eye of sense, resembling in all respects its former appearance,

"Both in size, and in beauty of eyes,
And in voice;"

and frequently, too,

---

[25]τὰ μὲν οὖν γινόμεθα περὶ ψυχῆς τεθνηκότων φαντάσματα ἀπό τινος ὑποκειμίνου γίνεται, τοῦ κατὰ τὴν ὑφεστηκυῖαν ἐν τῷ καλουμένῳ αὐγοειδεῖ σώματι ψυχήν. Cf. note in Benedictine ed.

[26]ὕπαρ.

[27]ἐν σώματι ἀντιτύπῳ ἐγηγέρθαι.

[28]ψυχῆς σῶμα.

"Having, also, such garments around the person[29] [as when alive]."

Jesus accordingly, having called Thomas, said, "Reach hither thy finger, and behold my hands; and reach hither thy hand, and thrust it into my side: and be not faithless, but believing" [John 20:27].

CHAPTER LXII.

NOW it followed from all the predictions which were uttered regarding Him—amongst which was this prediction of the resurrection—and from all that was done by Him, and from all the events which befell Him, that this event should be marvellous above all others. For it had been said beforehand by the prophet in the person of Jesus: "My flesh shall rest in hope, and Thou wilt not leave my soul in Hades, and wilt not suffer Thine Holy One to see corruption" [Ps. 16;9–10]. And truly, after His resurrection, He existed in a body intermediate, as it were, between the grossness of that which He had before His sufferings, and the appearance of a soul uncovered by such a body. And hence it was, that when His disciples were together, and Thomas with them, there "came Jesus, the doors being shut, and stood in the midst, and said, Peace be unto you. Then saith He to Thomas, Reach hither thy finger" [John 20:26–27], etc. And in the Gospel of Luke also, while Simon and Cleopas were conversing with each other respecting all that had happened to them, Jesus "drew near, and went with them. And their eyes were holden, that they should not know Him. And He said unto them, What manner of communications are these that ye have one to another, as ye walk?" And when their eyes were opened, and they knew Him, then the Scripture says, in express words, "And He vanished out of their sight" [Luke 24:15–17, 31]. And although Celsus may wish to place what is told of Jesus, and of those who saw Him after His resurrection, on the same level with imaginary appearances of a different kind, and those who have invented such, yet to those who institute a candid and intelligent examination, the events will appear only the more miraculous.

CHAPTER LXIII.

AFTER these points, Celsus proceeds to bring against the Gospel narrative a charge which is not to be lightly passed over, saying that "if Jesus desired to show that his power was really divine, he ought to have appeared to those who had ill-treated him, and to him who had condemned him, and to all men universally." For it appears to us also to be true, according to the Gospel account, that He was not seen after His resurrection in the same manner as He used formerly to show Himself—publicly, and to all men. But it is recorded in the Acts, that "being

---

[29]Cf. Homer, *Iliad*, xxiii. 66, 67.

seen during forty days," He expounded to His disciples "the things pertaining to the kingdom of God" [Acts 1:3]. And in the Gospels it is not stated that He was always with them; but that on one occasion He appeared in their midst, after eight days, when the doors were shut [John 20:26], and on another in some similar fashion. And Paul also, in the concluding portions of the first Epistle to the Corinthians, in reference to His not having publicly appeared as He did in the period before He suffered, writes as follows: "For I delivered unto you first of all that which I also received, how that Christ died for our sins according to the Scriptures; and that He was seen of Cephas, then of the twelve: after that He was seen of above five hundred brethren at once, of whom the greater part remain unto the present time, but some are fallen asleep. After that He was seen of James, then of all the apostles. And last of all He was seen of me also, as of one born out of due time" [1 Cor. 15:3–8]. I am of opinion now that the statements in this passage contain some great and wonderful mysteries, which are beyond the grasp not merely of the great multitude of ordinary believers, but even of those who are far advanced [in Christian knowledge], and that in them the reason would be explained why He did not show Himself, after His resurrection from the dead, in the same manner as before that event. And in a treatise of this nature, composed in answer to a work directed against the Christians and their faith, observe whether we are able to adduce a few rational arguments out of a greater number, and thus make an impression upon the hearers of this apology.

CHAPTER LXIV.

ALTHOUGH Jesus was only a single individual, He was nevertheless more things than one, according to the different standpoint from which He might be regarded;[30] nor was He seen in the same way by all who beheld Him. Now, that He was more things than one, according to the varying point of view, is clear from this statement, "I am the way, and the truth, and the life;" and from this, "I am the bread;" and this, "I am the door," and innumerable others. And that when seen He did not appear in like fashion to all those who saw Him, but according to their several ability to receive Him, will be clear to those who notice why, at the time when He was about to be transfigured on the high mountain, He did not admit all His apostles [to this sight], but only Peter, and James, and John, because they alone were capable of beholding His glory on that occasion, and of observing the glorified appearance of Moses and Elijah, and of listening to their conversation, and to the voice from the heavenly cloud. I am of opinion, too, that before He ascended the mountain where His disciples came to Him alone, and where He taught them the beatitudes, when He was somewhere in the

---

[30]πλείονα τῇ ἐπινοίᾳ ἦν.

lower part of the mountain, and when, as it became late, He healed those who were brought to Him, freeing them from all sickness and disease, He did not appear the same person to the sick, and to those who needed His healing aid, as to those who were able by reason of their strength to go up the mountain along with Him. Nay, even when He interpreted privately to His own disciples the parables which were delivered to the multitudes without, from whom the explanation was withheld, as they who heard them explained were endowed with higher organs of hearing than they who heard them without explanation, so was it altogether the same with the eyes of their soul, and, I think, also with those of their body.[31] And the following statement shows that He had not always the same appearance, viz. that Judas, when about to betray Him, said to the multitudes who were setting out with him, as not being acquainted with Him, "Whomsoever I shall kiss, the same is he" [Matt. 26:48]. And I think that the Saviour Himself indicates the same thing by the words: "I was daily with you, teaching in the temple, and ye laid no hold on me" [Matt. 26:55]. Entertaining, then, such exalted views regarding Jesus, not only with respect to the Deity within, and which was hidden from the view of the multitude, but with respect to the transfiguration of His body, which took place when and to whom He would, we say, that before Jesus had "put off the governments and powers,"[32] and while as yet He was not dead unto sin, all men were capable of seeing Him; but that, when He had "put off the governments and powers," and had no longer anything which was capable of being seen by the multitude, all who had formerly seen Him were not now able to behold Him. And therefore, sparing them, He did not show Himself to all after His resurrection from the dead.

CHAPTER LXV.

AND why do I say "to all?" For even with His own apostles and disciples He was not perpetually present, nor did He constantly show Himself to them, because they were not able without intermission[33] to receive His divinity. For His deity was more resplendent after He had finished the economy[34] [of salvation]: and this Peter, surnamed Cephas, the first-fruits as it were of the apostles, was enabled to behold, and along with him the twelve (Matthias having been substituted in room [sic] of Judas); and after them He appeared to the five hundred brethren at once, and then to James, and subsequently to all the others besides the twelve apostles, perhaps to the seventy also, and lastly to Paul, as to one born out of due time, and who knew well how to say, "Unto me, who am less than the

---

[31]οὕτω καὶ ταῖς ὄψεσι πάντως μὲν τῆς ψυχῆς, ἐγὼ δ' ἡγοῦμαι, ὅτι καὶ τοῦ σώματος.
[32]τὸν μὴ ἀπεκδυσάμενον, etc. Cf. Alford, *in loco* (Col. ii. 15).
[33]διηνεκῶς.
[34]τὴν οἰκονομίαν τελέσαντος.

least of all saints, is this grace given;" and probably the expression "least of all" has the same meaning with "one born out of due time." For as no one could reasonably blame Jesus for not having admitted all His apostles to the high mountain, but only the three already mentioned, on the occasion of His transfiguration, when He was about to manifest the splendour which appeared in His garments, and the glory of Moses and Elias talking with Him, so none could reasonably object to the statements of the apostles, who introduce the appearance of Jesus after His resurrection as having been made not to all, but to those only whom He knew to have received eyes capable of seeing His resurrection. I think, moreover, that the following statement regarding Him has an apologetic value[35] in reference to our subject, viz.: "For to this end Christ died, and rose again, that He might be Lord both of the dead and living" [Rom. 14:9]. For observe, it is conveyed in these words, that Jesus died that He might be Lord of the dead; and that He rose again to be Lord not only of the dead, but also of the living. And the apostle understands, undoubtedly, by the dead over whom Christ is to be Lord, those who are so called in the first Epistle to the Corinthians, "For the trumpet shall sound, and the dead shall be raised incorruptible" [1 Cor. 15:52]; and by the living, those who are to be changed, and who are different from the dead who are to be raised. And respecting the living the words are these, "And we shall be changed;" an expression which follows immediately after the statement, "The dead shall be raised first."[36] Moreover, in the first Epistle to the Thessalonians, describing the same change in different words, he says that they who sleep are not the same as those who are alive; his language being, "I would not have you to be ignorant, brethren, concerning them who are asleep, that ye sorrow not, even as others which have no hope. For if we believe that Jesus died, and rose again, even so them also that sleep in Jesus will God bring with Him. For this we say unto you by the word of the Lord, that we who are alive and remain unto the coming of the Lord, shall not prevent them that are asleep." [1 Thess. 4:13–15]. The explanation which appeared to us to be appropriate to this passage, we gave in the exegetical remarks which we have made on the first Epistle to the Thessalonians.

CHAPTER LXVI.

AND be not surprised if all the multitudes who have believed on Jesus do not behold His resurrection, when Paul, writing to the Corinthians, can say to them, as being incapable of receiving greater matters, "For I determined not to know anything among you, save Jesus Christ, and Him crucified [1 Cor. 2:2]; which is the same as saying, "Hitherto ye were not able, neither yet now are ye

---

[35]χρήσιμον δ' οἶμαι πρὸς ἀπολογίαν τῶν προκειμένων.
[36]Cf. 1 Cor. 15:52 with 1 Thess. 4:16.

able, for ye are still carnal" [1 Cor. 3:2–3]. The Scripture, therefore, doing everything by appointment of God, has recorded of Jesus, that before His sufferings He
appeared to all indifferently, but not always; while after His sufferings He no
longer appeared to all in the same way, but with a certain discrimination which
measured out to each his due. And as it is related that "God appeared to Abraham," or to one of the saints, and this "appearance" was not a thing of constant
occurrence, but took place at intervals, and not to all, so understand that the Son
of God appeared in the one case on the same principle that God appeared to the
latter.[37]

CHAPTER LXVII.

TO the best of our ability, therefore, as in a treatise of this nature, we have
answered the objection, that "if Jesus had really wished to manifest his divine
power, he ought to have shown himself to those who ill-treated him, and to the
judge who condemned him, and to all without reservation." There was, however,
no obligation on Him to appear either to the judge who condemned Him, or to
those who ill-treated Him. For Jesus spared both the one and the other, that they
might not be smitten with blindness, as the men of Sodom were when they
conspired against the beauty of the angels entertained by Lot. And here is the
account of the matter: "But the men put forth their hand, and pulled Lot into the
house to them, and shut to the door. And they smote the men who were at the
door of the house with blindness, both small and great; so that they wearied
themselves to find the door" [Gen. 19:10–11]. Jesus, accordingly, wished to show
that His power was divine to each one who was capable of seeing it, and according to the measure of His capability. And I do not suppose that He guarded
against being seen on any other ground than from a regard to the fitness of those
who were incapable of seeing Him. And it is in vain for Celsus to add, "For he
had no longer occasion to fear any man after his death, being, as you say, a God;
nor was he sent into the world at all for the purpose of being hid." Yet He was
sent into the world not only to become known, but also to be hid. For all that He
was, was not known even to those to whom He was known, but a certain part of
Him remained concealed even from them; and to some He was not known at all.
And He opened the gates of light to those who were the sons of darkness and of
night, and had devoted themselves to becoming the sons of light and of the day.
For our Saviour Lord, like a good physician, came rather to us who were full of
sins, than to those who were righteous.

· · ·

[37]οὕτω μοι νόει καὶ τὸν υἱὸν τοῦ Θεοῦ ὦθαι τῇ παραπλησίᾳ εἰς τὸ περὶ ἐκείν-
ων, εἰς τὸ ὦφθαι αὐτοῖς τὸν Θεόν, κρίσει.

BOOK III.

CHAPTER I.

IN the first book of our answer to the work of Celsus, who had boastfully entitled the treatise which he had composed against us A *True Discourse*, we have gone through, as you enjoined, my faithful Ambrosius, to the best of our ability, his preface, and the parts immediately following it, testing each one of his assertions as he went along, until we finished with the tirade[38] of this Jew of his, feigned to have been delivered against Jesus. And in the second book we met, as we best could, all the charges contained in the invective[39] of the said Jew, which were levelled at us who are believers in God through Christ; and now we enter upon this third division of our discourse, in which our object is to refute the allegations which he makes in his own person.

He gives it as his opinion, that "the controversy between Jews and Christians is a most foolish one," and asserts that "the discussions which we have with each other regarding Christ differ in no respect from what is called in the proverb 'a fight about the shadow of an ass;' "[40] and thinks that "there is nothing of importance[41] in the investigations of the Jews and Christians: for both believe that it was predicted by the Divine Spirit that one was to come as a Saviour to the human race, but do not yet agree on the point whether the person predicted has actually come or not." For we Christians, indeed, have believed in Jesus, as He who came according to the predictions of the prophets. But the majority of the Jews are so far from believing in Him, that those of them who lived at the time of His coming conspired against Him; and those of the present day, approving of what the Jews of former times dared to do against Him, speak evil of Him, asserting that it was by means of sorcery[42] that he passed himself off for Him who was predicted by the prophets as the One who was to come, and who was called, agreeably to the traditions of the Jews,[43] the Christ.

CHAPTER II.

BUT let Celsus, and those who assent to his charges, tell us whether it is at all like "an ass's shadow," that the Jewish prophets should have predicted the

---

[38]δημηγορία; cf. book i. c. 71.
[39]Ibid.
[40]κατὰ τὴν παροιμίαν καλουμένης ὄνου σκιᾶς μάχης. On this proverb, see Zenobius, *Centuria Sexta*, adag. 28, and the note of Schottius. Cf. also Suidas, *s.v.* ὄνου σκία.—DE LA RUE.
[41]σεμνόν.
[42]διά τινος γοητείας.
[43]κατὰ τὰ 'Ιουδαίων πάτρια.

birth-place of Him who was to be the ruler of those who had lived righteous lives, and who are called the "heritage" of God;[44] and that Emmanuel should be conceived by a virgin; and that such signs and wonders should be performed by Him who was the subject of prophecy; and that His word should have such speedy course, that the voice of His apostles should go forth into all the earth; and that He should undergo certain sufferings after His condemnation by the Jews; and that He should rise again from the dead. For was it by chance[45] that the prophets made these announcements, with no persuasion of their truth in their minds,[46] moving them not only to speak, but to deem their announcements worthy of being committed to writing? And did so great a nation as that of the Jews, who had long ago received a country of their own wherein to dwell, recognise certain men as prophets, and reject others as utterers of false predictions, without any conviction of the soundness of the distinction?[47] And was there no motive which induced them to class with the books of Moses, which were held as sacred, the words of those persons who were afterwards deemed to be prophets? And can those who charge the Jews and Christians with folly, show us how the Jewish nation could have continued to subsist, had there existed among them no promise of the knowledge of future events? and how, while each of the surrounding nations believed, agreeably to their ancient institutions, that they received oracles and predictions from those whom they accounted gods, this people alone, who were taught to view with contempt all those who were considered gods by the heathen, as not being gods, but demons, according to the declaration of the prophets, "For all the gods of the nations are demons,[48] had among them no one who professed to be a prophet, and who could restrain such as, from a desire to know the future, were ready to desert[49] to the demons[50] of other nations? Judge, then, whether it were not a necessity, that as the whole nation had been taught to despise the deities of other lands, they should have had an abundance of prophets, who made known events which were of far greater importance in themselves,[51] and which surpassed the oracles of all other countries.

---

[44]τῶν χρηματιζόντων μερίδος Θεοῦ.

[45]ἆρα γὰρ ὡς ἔτυχε.

[46]σὺν οὐδεμιᾷ πιθανότητι.

[47]Ibid.

[48]Ps. 96:5, δαιμόνια; "idols," Auth. Vers. We have in this passage, and in many others, the identification of the δαίμονες or gods of the heathen with the δαίμονες or δαιμόνια, "evil spirits," or angels, supposed to be mentioned in Gen. 6:2.

[49]The reading in the text is αὐτομολεῖν, on which Bohereau, with whom the Benedictine editor agrees, remarks that we must either read αὐτομολήσοντας, or understand some such word as ἑτοίμους before αυτομολεῖν.

[50]Ps. 96:5, see footnote 48.

[51]το μεῖζον αυτόθεν.

CHAPTER III.

IN the next place, miracles were performed in all countries, or at least in many of them, as Celsus himself admits, instancing the case of Esculapius, who conferred benefits on many, and who foretold future events to entire cities, which were dedicated to him, such as Tricca, and Epidaurus, and Cos, and Pergamus; and along with Esculapius he mentions Aristeas of Proconnesus, and a certain Clazomenian, and Cleomedes of Astypalaea. But among the Jews alone, who say they are dedicated to the God of all things, there was wrought no miracle or sign which might help to confirm their faith in the Creator of all things, and strengthen their hope of another and better life! But how can they imagine such a state of things? For they would immediately have gone over to the worship of those demons which gave oracles and performed cures, and deserted the God who was believed, as far as words went,[52] to assist them, but who never manifested to them His visible presence. But if this result has not taken place, and if, on the contrary, they have suffered countless calamities rather than renounce Judaism and their law, and have been cruelly treated, at one time in Assyria, at another in Persia, and at another under Antiochus, is it not in keeping with the probabilities of the case[53] for those to suppose who do not yield their belief to their miraculous histories and prophecies, that the events in question could not be inventions, but that a certain divine Spirit being in the holy souls of the prophets, as of men who underwent any labour for the cause of virtue, *did* move them to prophesy some things relating to their contemporaries, and others to their posterity, but chiefly regarding a certain personage who was to come as a Saviour to the human race?

.   .   .

BOOK IV.

CHAPTER XIV.

BUT let us look at what Celsus next with great ostentation announces in the following fashion: "And again," he says, "let us resume the subject from the beginning, with a larger array of proofs. And I make no new statement, but say what has been long settled. God is good, and beautiful, and blessed, and that in

---

[52]μέχοι λόγου.
[53]πῶς οὐχὶ ἐξ εἰκότων κατασκευάζεται.

the best and most beautiful degree. [54] But if he come down among men, he must undergo a change, and a change from good to evil, from virtue to vice, from happiness to misery, and from best to worst. Who, then, would make choice of such a change? It is the nature of a mortal, indeed, to undergo change and remoulding, but of an immortal to remain the same and unaltered. God, then, could not admit of such a change." Now it appears to me that the fitting answer has been returned to these objections, when I have related what is called in Scripture the "condescension"[55] of God to human affairs; for which purpose He did not need to undergo a transformation, as Celsus thinks we assert, nor a change from good to evil, nor from virtue to vice, nor from happiness to misery, nor from best to worst. For, continuing unchangeable in His essence, He condescends to human affairs by the economy of His providence. [56] We show, accordingly, that the Holy Scriptures represent God as unchangeable, both by such words as "Thou art the same," [Ps. 102:27] and "I change not;" [Mal. 3:6] whereas the gods of Epicurus, being composed of atoms, and, so far as their structure is concerned, capable of dissolution, endeavour to throw off the atoms which contain the elements of destruction. Nay, even the god of the Stoics, as being corporeal, at one time has his whole essence composed of the guiding principle[57] when the conflagration [of the world] takes place; and at another, when a rearrangement of things occurs, he again becomes partly material. [58] For even the Stoics were unable distinctly to comprehend the natural idea of God, as of a being altogether incorruptible and simple, and uncompounded and indivisible.

CHAPTER XV.

AND with respect to His having descended among men, He was "previously in the form of God;"[59] and through benevolence, divested Himself [of His glory], that He might be capable of being received by men. But He did not, I imagine, undergo any change from "good to evil," for "He did no *sin*" [1 Pet. 2:22] nor from "virtue to vice," for "He knew no *sin*" [2 Cor. 5:21]. Nor did He pass from "happiness to misery," but He humbled Himself, and nevertheless was blessed, even when His humiliation was undergone in order to benefit our race. Nor was there any change in Him from "best to worst," for how can goodness and benev-

---

[54]Ὁ Θεὸς ἀγαθός ἐστι, καὶ καλὸς, καὶ εὐδαίμων, καὶ ἐν τῷ καλλίστῳ καὶ ἀρίστῳ..
[55]κατάβασιν.
[56]τῇ προνοίᾳ καὶ τῇ οἰκονομίᾳ.
[57]ἡγεμονικὸν.
[58]The reading in the text is, ἐπὶ μέρους γίνεται αὐτῆς, which is thus corrected by Guietus: ἐπιμερὴς γίνεται αὐτός.
[59]Cf. Phil. 2:6–7.

olence be of "the worst?" Is it befitting to say of the physician, who looks on dreadful sights and handles unsightly objects in order to cure the sufferers, that he passes from "good to evil," or from "virtue to vice," or from "happiness to misery?" And yet the physician, in looking on dreadful sights and handling unsightly objects, does not wholly escape the possibility of being involved in the same fate. But He who heals the wounds of our souls, through the word of God that is in Him, is Himself incapable of admitting any wickedness. But if the immortal God—the Word—by assuming a mortal body and a human soul, appears to Celsus to undergo a change and transformation, let him learn that the Word, still remaining essentially the Word, suffers none of those things which are suffered by the body or the soul; but, condescending occasionally to [the weakness of] him who is unable to look upon the splendours and brilliancy of Deity, He becomes as it were flesh, speaking with a literal voice, until he who has received Him in such a form is able, through being elevated in some slight degree by the teaching of the Word, to gaze upon what is, so to speak, His real and pre-eminent appearance.[60]

CHAPTER XVI.

FOR there are different appearances, as it were, of the Word, according as He shows himself to each one of those who come to His doctrine; and this in a manner corresponding to the condition of him who is just becoming a disciple, or of him who has made a little progress, or of him who has advanced further, or of him who has already *nearly* attained to virtue, or who has even *already* attained it. And hence it is not the case, as Celsus and those like him would have it, that our God was transformed, and ascending the lofty mountain, showed that His real appearance was something different, and far more excellent than what those who remained below, and were unable to follow Him on high, beheld. For those below did not possess eyes capable of seeing the transformation of the Word into His glorious and more divine condition. But with difficulty were they able to receive Him as He was; so that it might be said of Him by those who were unable to behold His more excellent nature: "We saw Him, and He had no form nor comeliness; but His form was mean,[61] and inferior to that of the sons of men.[62] And let these remarks be an answer to the suppositions of Celsus, who does not understand the changes or transformations of Jesus, as related in the histories, nor His mortal and immortal nature.

---

[60]προηγουμένην.
[61]ἄτιμον.
[62]ἐκλεῖπον.

CHAPTER XVII.

BUT will not those narratives, especially when they are understood in their proper sense, appear far more worthy of respect than the story that Dionysus was deceived by the Titans, and expelled from the throne of Jupiter, and torn in pieces by them, and his remains being afterwards put together again, he returned as it were once more to life, and ascended to heaven? Or are the Greeks at liberty to refer such stories to the doctrine of the soul, and to interpret them figuratively, while the door of a consistent explanation, and one everywhere in accord and harmony with the writings of the Divine Spirit, who had His abode in pure souls, is closed against *us?* Celsus, then, is altogether ignorant of the purpose of our writings, and it is therefore upon his own acceptation of them that he casts discredit, and not upon their real meaning; whereas, if he had reflected on what is appropriate[63] to a soul which is to enjoy an everlasting life, and on the opinion which we are to form of its essence and principles, he would not so have ridiculed the entrance of the immortal into a mortal body, which took place not according to the metempsychosis of Plato, but agreeably to another and higher view of things. And he would have observed one "descent," distinguished by its great benevolence, undertaken to convert (as the Scripture mystically terms them) the "lost sheep of the house of Israel," which had strayed down from the mountains, and to which the Shepherd is said in certain parables to have gone down, leaving on the mountains those "which had not strayed."

CHAPTER XVIII.

BUT Celsus, lingering over matters which he does not understand, leads us to be guilty of tautology, as we do not wish even in appearance to leave any one of his objections unexamined. He proceeds, accordingly, as follows: "God either really changes himself, as these assert, into a mortal body, and the impossibility of that has been already declared; or else he does *not* undergo a change, but only causes the beholders to imagine so, and thus deceives them, and is guilty of falsehood. Now deceit and falsehood are nothing but evils, and would only be employed as a medicine, either in the case of sick and lunatic friends, with a view to their cure, or in that of enemies when one is taking measures to escape danger. But no sick man or lunatic is a friend of God, nor does God fear any one to such a degree as to shun danger by leading him into error." Now the answer to these statements might have respect partly to the nature of the Divine Word, who is God, and partly to the soul of Jesus. As respects the nature of the Word, in the

---

[63]τί ἀκολουθεῖ.

same way as the quality of the food changes in the nurse into milk with reference to the nature of the child, or is arranged by the physician with a view to the good of his health in the case of a sick man, or [is specially] prepared for a stronger man, because he possesses greater vigour, so does God appropriately change, in the case of each individual, the power of the Word to which belongs the natural property of nourishing the human soul. And to one is given, as the Scripture terms it, "the sincere milk of the word;" and to another, who is weaker, as it were, "herbs;" and to another who is full-grown, "strong meat." And the Word does not, I imagine, prove false to His own nature, in contributing nourishment to each one, according as he is capable of receiving Him. Nor does He mislead or prove false. But if one were to take the change as referring to the soul of Jesus after it had entered a body, we would inquire in what sense the term "change" is used. For if it be meant to apply to its essence, such a supposition is inadmissible, not only in relation to the soul of Jesus, but also to the rational soul of any other being. And if it be alleged that it suffers anything from the body when united with it, or from the place to which it has come, then what inconvenience[64] can happen to the Word who, in great benevolence, brought down a Saviour to the human race?—seeing none of those who formerly professed to effect a cure could accomplish so much as that soul showed *it* could do, by what it performed, even by voluntarily descending to the level of human destinies for the benefit of our race. And the Divine Word, well knowing this, speaks to that effect in many passages of Scripture, although it is sufficient at present to quote one testimony of Paul to the following effect: "Let this mind be in you which was also in Christ Jesus; who, being in the form of God, thought it not robbery to be equal with God, but made Himself of no reputation, and took upon Him the form of a servant, and was made in the likeness of men; and being found in fashion as a man, He humbled Himself, and became obedient unto death, even the death of the cross. Wherefore God also hath highly exalted Him, and given Him a name which is above every name" [Phil. 2:5–9].

.   .   .

---

[64]τί ἄτοπον.

BOOK VI.

CHAPTER LXXVIII.

CELSUS next makes certain observations of the following nature: "Again, if God, like Jupiter in the comedy, should, on awaking from a lengthened slumber, desire to rescue the human race from evil, why did He send this Spirit of which you speak into one corner [of the earth]? He ought to have breathed it alike into many bodies, and have sent them out into all the world. Now the comic poet, to cause laughter in the theatre, wrote that Jupiter, after awakening, despatched Mercury to the Athenians and Lacedaemonians; but do not you think that you have made the Son of God more ridiculous in sending Him to the Jews?" Observe in such language as this the irreverent character of Celsus, who, unlike a philosopher, takes the writer of a comedy, whose business is to cause laughter, and compares our God, the Creator of all things, to the being who, as represented in the play, on awakening, despatches Mercury [on an errand]! We stated, indeed, in what precedes, that it was not as if awakening from a lengthened slumber that God sent Jesus to the human race, who has now, for good reasons, fulfilled the economy of His incarnation, but who has always conferred benefits upon the human race. For no noble deed has ever been performed amongst men, where the divine Word did not visit the souls of those who were capable, although for a little time, of admitting such operations of the divine Word. Moreover, the advent of Jesus apparently to one corner [of the earth] was founded on good reasons, since it was necessary that He who was the subject of prophecy should make His appearance among those who had become acquainted with the doctrine of one God, and who perused the writings of His prophets, and who had come to know the announcement of Christ, and that He should come to them at a time when the Word was about to be diffused from one corner over the whole world.

CHAPTER LXXIX.

AND therefore there was no need that there should everywhere exist many bodies, and many spirits like Jesus, in order that the whole world of men might be enlightened by the Word of God. For the one Word was enough, having arisen as the "Sun of righteousness," to send forth from Judea His coming rays into the soul of all who were willing to receive Him. But if any one desires to see many bodies filled with a divine Spirit, similar to the one Christ, ministering to the salvation of men everywhere, let him take note of those who teach the gospel of Jesus in all lands in soundness of doctrine and uprightness of life, and who are themselves termed "christs" by the Holy Scriptures, in the passage, "Touch not mine anointed,[65] and do not my prophets any harm" [1 Chron. 16:22; Ps. 105:15]. For as we have heard that Antichrist cometh, and yet have learned that there are many antichrists in the world, in the same way, knowing that Christ has come, we see that, owing to Him, there are many christs in the world, who, like Him, have loved righteousness and hated iniquity, and therefore God, the God of Christ, anointed them also with the "oil of gladness." But inasmuch as He loved righteousness and hated iniquity above those who were His partners,[66] He also obtained the first-fruits of His anointing, and, if we must so term it, the entire unction of the oil of gladness; while they who were His partners shared also in His unction, in proportion to their individual capacity. Therefore, since Christ is the head of the church, so that Christ and the church form one body, the ointment descended from the head to the beard of Aaron,—the symbols of the perfect man,—and this ointment in its descent reached to the very skirt of his garment. This is my answer to the irreverent language of Celsus when he says, "He ought to have breathed [His Spirit] alike into many bodies, and have sent it forth into all the world." The comic poet, indeed, to cause laughter, has represented Jupiter asleep and awaking from slumber, and despatching Mercury to the Greeks; but the Word, knowing that the nature of God is unaffected by sleep, may teach us that God administers in due season, and as right reason demands, the affairs of the world. It is not, however, a matter of surprise that, owing to the greatness and incomprehensibility[67] of the divine judgments, ignorant persons should make mistakes, and Celsus among them. There is therefore nothing ridiculous in the Son of God having been sent to the Jews, amongst whom the prophets had appeared, in order that, making a commencement among them in a bodily shape, He might arise with might and power upon a world of souls, which no longer desired to remain deserted by God.

.   .   .

---

[65] τῶν χριστῶν μου.
[66] τοὺς μετόχους αὐτοῦ.
[67] δυσδιηγήτους τὰς κρίσεις.

BOOK VII.

CHAPTER LIII.

AFTER these remarks of Celsus, which we have done our best to refute, he goes on to address us thus: "Seeing you are so eager for some novelty, how much better it would have been if you had chosen as the object of your zealous homage some one of those who died a glorious death, and whose divinity might have received the support of some myth to perpetuate his memory! Why, if you were not satisfied with Hercules or Aesculapius, and other heroes of antiquity, you had Orpheus, who was confessedly a divinely inspired man, who died a violent death. But perhaps some others have taken him up before you. You may then take Anaxarchus, who, when cast into a mortar, and beaten most barbarously, showed a noble contempt for his suffering, and said, 'Beat, beat the shell of Anaxarchus, for himself you do not beat,—a speech surely of a spirit truly divine. But others were before you in following his interpretation of the laws of nature. Might you not, then, take Epictetus, who, when his master was twisting his leg, said, smiling and unmoved, 'You will break my leg;' and when it was broken, he added, 'Did I not tell you that you would break it?' What saying equal to these did your god utter under suffering? If you had said even of the Sibyl, whose authority some of you acknowledge, that she was a child of God, you would have said something more reasonable. But you have had the presumption to include in her writings many impious things, and set up as a god one who ended a most infamous life by a most miserable death. How much more suitable than he would have been Jonah in the whale's belly, or Daniel delivered from the wild beasts, or any of a still more portentous kind!"

CHAPTER LIV.

BUT since he sends us to Hercules, let him repeat to us any of his sayings, and let him justify his shameful subjection to Omphale. Let him show that divine honours should be paid to one who, like a highway robber, carries off a farmer's ox by force, and afterwards devours it, amusing himself meanwhile with the curses of the owner; in memory of which even to this day sacrifices offered to the demon of Hercules are accompanied with curses. Again he proposes Aesculapius to us, as if to oblige us to repeat what we have said already; but we forbear. In regard to Orpheus, what does he admire in him to make him assert that, by common consent, he was regarded as a divinely inspired man, and lived a noble life? I am greatly deceived if it is not the desire which Celsus has to oppose us and put down Jesus that leads him to sound forth the praises of Orpheus; and whether, when he made himself acquainted with his impious fables about the gods, he did not cast them aside as deserving, even more than the poems of Homer, to be excluded from a well-ordered state. For, indeed, Orpheus says much worse things than Homer of those whom they call gods. Noble, indeed, it was in Anaxarchus to say to Aristocreon, tyrant of Cyprus, "Beat on, beat the shell of Anaxarchus," but it is the one admirable incident in the life of Anaxarchus known to the Greeks; and although, on the strength of that, some like Celsus might deservedly honour the man for his courage, yet to look up to Anaxarchus as a god is not consistent with reason. He also directs us to Epictetus, whose firmness is justly admired, although his saying when his leg was broken by his master is not to be compared with the marvellous acts and words of Jesus which Celsus refuses to believe; and these words were accompanied by such a divine power, that even to this day they convert not only some of the more ignorant and simple, but many also of the most enlightened of men.

CHAPTER LV.

WHEN, to his enumeration of those to whom he would send us, he adds, "What saying equal to these did your god utter under sufferings?" we would reply, that the silence of Jesus under scourgings, and amidst all His sufferings, spoke more for His firmness and submission than all that was said by the Greeks when beset by calamity. Perhaps Celsus may believe what was recorded with all sincerity by trustworthy men, who, while giving a truthful account of all the wonders performed by Jesus, specify among these the silence which He preserved when subjected to scourgings; showing the same singular meekness under the insults which were heaped upon Him, when they put upon Him the purple robe, and set the crown of thorns upon His head, and when they put in His hand a reed in place of a sceptre: no unworthy or angry word escaped Him against those who subjected Him to such outrages. Since, then, He received the scourgings with silent firmness, and bore with meekness all the insults of those who outraged Him, it cannot be said, as is said by some, that it was in cowardly weakness that He uttered the words: "Father, if it be possible, let this cup pass from me: nevertheless, not as I will, but as Thou wilt" [Matt. 26:39]. The prayer which seems to be contained in these words for the removal of what He calls "the cup" bears a sense which we have elsewhere examined and set forth at large. But taking it in its more obvious sense, consider if it be not a prayer offered to God with all piety. For no man naturally regards anything which may befall him as necessary and inevitable; though he may submit to what is not inevitable, if occasion requires. Besides, these words, "nevertheless, not as I will, but as Thou wilt," are not the language of one who yielded to necessity, but of one who was contented with what was befalling Him, and who submitted with reverence to the arrangements of Providence.

CHAPTER LVI.

CELSUS then adds, for what reason I know not, that instead of calling Jesus the Son of God, we had better have given that honour to the Sibyl, in whose books he maintains we have interpolated many impious statements, though he does not mention what those interpolations are. He might have proved his assertion by producing some older copies which are free from the interpolations which he attributes to us; but he does not do so even to justify his statement that these passages are of an impious character. Moreover, he again speaks of the life of Jesus as "a most infamous life," as he has done before, not once or twice, but many times, although he does not stay to specify any of the actions of His life which he thinks most infamous. He seems to think that he may in this way make assertions without proving them, and rail against one of whom he knows nothing. Had he set himself to show what sort of infamy he found in the actions of Jesus, we should have repelled the several charges brought against Him. Jesus did indeed meet with a most sad death; but the same might be said of Socrates, and of Anaxarchus, whom he had just mentioned, and a multitude of others. If the death of Jesus was a miserable one, was not that of the others so too? And if their death was not miserable, can it be said that the death of Jesus was? You see from this, then, that the object of Celsus is to vilify the character of Jesus; and I can only suppose that he is driven to it by some spirit akin to those whose power has been broken and vanquished by Jesus, and which now finds itself deprived of the smoke and blood on which it lived, whilst deceiving those who sought for God here upon earth in images, instead of looking up to the true God, the Governor of all things.

CHAPTER LVII.

AFTER this, as though his object was to swell the size of his book, he advises us "to choose Jonah rather than Jesus as our God;" thus setting Jonah, who preached repentance to the single city of Nineveh, before Jesus, who has preached repentance to the whole world, and with much greater results. He would have us to regard as God a man who, by a strange miracle, passed three days and three nights in the whale's belly; and he is unwilling that He who submitted to death for the sake of men, He to whom God bore testimony through the prophets, and who has done great things in heaven and earth, should receive on that ground honour second only to that which is given to the Most High God. Moreover, Jonah was swallowed by the whale for refusing to preach as God had commanded him; while Jesus suffered death for men after He had given the instructions which God wished Him to give. Still further, he adds that Daniel rescued from the lions is more worthy of our adoration than Jesus, who subdued the fierceness of every opposing power, and gave to us "authority to tread on serpents and scorpions, and over all the power of the enemy" [Luke 10:19]. Finally, having no other names to offer us, he adds, "and others of a still more monstrous kind,"—thus casting a slight upon both Jonah and Daniel; for the spirit which is in Celsus cannot speak well of the righteous.

.　.　.

BOOK VIII.

CHAPTER LXXII.

AFTERWARDS he says: "If it were possible," implying at the same time that he thought it most desirable, "that all the inhabitants of Asia, Europe, and Libya, Greeks and barbarians, all to the uttermost ends of the earth, were to come under one law;" but judging this quite impossible, he adds, "Any one who thinks this possible, knows nothing." It would require careful consideration and lengthened argument to prove that it is not only possible, but that it will surely come to pass, that all who are endowed with reason shall come under one law. However, if we must refer to this subject, it will be with great brevity. The Stoics, indeed, hold that, when the strongest of the elements prevails, all things shall be turned into fire. But our belief is, that the Word shall prevail over the entire rational creation, and change every soul into His own perfection; in which state every one, by the mere exercise of his power, will choose what he desires, and obtain what he chooses. For although, in the diseases and wounds of the body, there are some which no medical skill can cure, yet we hold that in the mind there is no evil so strong that it may not be overcome by the Supreme Word and God. For stronger than all the evils in the soul is the Word, and the healing power that dwells in Him; and this healing He applies, according to the will of God, to every man. The consummation of all things is the destruction of evil, although as to the question whether it shall be so destroyed that it can never anywhere arise again, it is beyond our present purpose to say. Many things are said obscurely in the prophecies on the total destruction of evil, and the restoration to righteousness of every soul; but it will be enough for our present purpose to quote the following passage from Zephaniah: "Prepare and rise early; all the gleanings of their vineyards are destroyed. Therefore wait ye upon me, saith the Lord, on the day that I rise up for a testimony; for my determination is to gather the nations, that I may assemble the kings, to pour upon them mine indignation, even all my fierce anger: for all the earth shall be devoured with the fire of my jealousy. For then will I turn to the people a pure language, that they may all call upon the name of the Lord, to serve Him with one consent. From beyond the rivers of Ethiopia my suppliants, even the daughter of my dispersed, shall bring my offering. In that day shalt thou not be ashamed for all thy doings, wherein thou hast transgressed against me: for then I will take away out of the midst of thee them that rejoice in thy pride; and thou shalt no more be haughty because of my holy mountain. I will also leave in the midst of thee an afflicted and poor people, and they shall trust in the name of the Lord. The remnant of Israel shall not do iniquity, nor speak lies; neither shall a deceitful tongue be found in their mouth: for they shall feed and lie down, and none shall make them afraid" [Zeph. 3:7–13]. I leave it to those who are able, after a careful study of the whole subject, to unfold the meaning of this prophecy, and especially to inquire into the signification of the words, "When the whole earth is destroyed, there will be turned upon the peoples a language according to their race,"[68] as things were before the confusion of tongues. Let them also carefully consider the promise, that all shall call upon the name of the Lord, and serve Him with one consent; also that all contemptuous reproach shall be taken away, and there shall be no longer any injustice, or vain speech, or a deceitful tongue. And thus much it seemed needful for me to say briefly, and without entering into elaborate details, in answer to the remark of Celsus, that he considered any agreement between the inhabitants of Asia, Europe, and Libya, as well Greeks as barbarians, was impossible. And perhaps such a result would indeed be impossible to those who are still in the body, but not to those who are released from it.

· · ·

CHAPTER LXXVI.

YOU have here, reverend Ambrosius, the conclusion of what we have been enabled to accomplish by the power given to us in obedience to your command. In eight books we have embraced all that we considered it proper to say in reply to that book of Celsus which he entitles *A True Discourse*. And now it remains for the readers of his discourse and of my reply to judge which of the two breathes most of the Spirit of the true God, of piety towards Him, and of that truth which leads men by sound doctrines to the noblest life. You must know, however, that Celsus had promised another treatise as a sequel to this one, in which he engaged to supply practical rules of living to those who felt disposed to embrace his opin-

---

[68]"A language to last as long as the world."—BOUHEREAU.

ions. If, then, he has not fulfilled his promise of writing a second book, we may well be contented with those eight books which we have written in answer to his discourse. But if he has begun and finished that second book, pray obtain it and send it to us, that we may answer it as the Father of truth may give us ability, and either overthrow the false teaching that may be in it, or laying aside all jealousy, we may testify our approval of whatever truth it may contain.

GLORY BE TO THEE, OUR GOD; GLORY BE TO THEE.

❦ 6 ❧
ATHANASIUS
(A.D. c298–373)

Most scholars believe that Athanasius was born in Alexandria, Egypt, in A.D. 298. Apparently his was a family of some wealth and rank. It is obvious from his writings that Athanasius received a liberal education in the Greek tradition. He is well versed in the philosophical schools and is acquainted with the classical writers. However, it is his saturation in the Holy Scripture that sets him apart for the unique mission to which God called him.

Every student of church history studies the so-called Arian Controversy and the resulting Council of Nicea (A.D. 325). Over 250 bishops representing many nationalities met at Nicea to settle the controversy. Arius so emphasized monotheism (the belief in the existence of only one God) that he essentially denied that there was an eternal Trinity. This doctrinal stance appealed to many who had become Christians out of a polytheistic background. Arius contended that there must have been a time when the Son of God did not exist. In the Bible Jesus was clearly proclaimed as the first born over all creation, he said. Moreover, Jesus was the only begotten Son of the Father, according to the Gospel of John. Thus Arius concluded that the Bible itself taught that Jesus had not always existed as part of the Trinity but had come into existence by an act of creation at some time in the past.

Athanasius was the champion for the orthodox view. He opposed the Arians by contending that Christ was eternally divine. He used the Greek word *homoousios* (meaning, "of exactly the same essence") to describe the relationship between the Father and the Son. It was the stance of Athanasius that was finally accepted by the council. Arius and his followers were declared to be unorthodox in their theological perspective.

Not long after this, Athanasius was elected bishop of Alexandria. Arius had been exiled because of his heretical theology. However, Constantine later brought Arius out of exile and directed Athanasius to receive Arius at the communion table. Athanasius steadfastly refused and thus was called before the Council at Tyre in A.D. 335. Realizing that he was not receiving a fair hearing at Tyre, Athanasius went to Constantinople where he met the emperor and pleaded his case. In response to this, Constantine called the council to meet at Constantinople. The Arian element was still strong, however, and this time Athanasius was banished into exile.

Nevertheless, Athanasius was not replaced as the bishop of Alexandria. After Constantine's death (A.D. 337), Athanasius returned to Alexandria and remained there nine years, fulfilling his work of ministry among the people. During this time he wrote his *Apology Against the Arians* and *On the Nicene Formula*.

The political and theological battles in the church, however, had not yet disappeared. The Arian influence continued to grow, and many of the bishops who were loyal to the Nicene Creed were exiled. Just before Athanasius himself was to be arrested, he was taken by some of his fellow bishops out into the desert, where he remained in hiding for six years. During this period he wrote several apologetic works.

In A.D. 362, the year after Julian had become the new emperor of the Roman Empire, Athanasius returned to his place of ministry in Egypt. Julian was a pagan emperor who believed that Christianity would crumble because of its internal conflicts. Athanasius, on the other hand, headed up a movement toward internal peace. Therefore Julian ordered Athanasius into exile, but again he hid in the desert. After Emperor Julian died, Athanasius once again carried on a public ministry in Alexandria.

The new emperor, Valentinian, appointed his brother Valens as the emperor of the East. Valens was clearly sympathetic with Arianism; he forced Athanasius to leave Alexandria. Once again Athanasius went into hiding. Apparently Valens later changed his mind, as Athanasius was allowed to return to Alexandria and carry on a peaceful ministry. This time he remained in Alexandria until his death on May 2, 373.

Perhaps his greatest apologetic works are those from which excerpts are reprinted in this chapter. The two essays that follow (*Against the Heathen* and *The Incarnation of the Word*) were written prior to the Council of Nicea and probably come from the pen of Athanasius when he was in his mid-twenties. However, they show a characteristic maturity of theological thought.

In *Against the Heathen* Athanasius is greatly concerned to prove that humans have an innate ability and a responsibility to worship the almighty God. As artists are known by their works, so God is known by His creation. This natural theology is built on the order and harmony of the universe.

The same straightforward logical approach is found in his defense of the Incarnation. That Word through which the creation was brought into being is the same Word by which redemption is made available to the human race. Repentance alone, he said, is not enough to restore what was lost because of sin. A re-creation was necessary to accomplish the restoration of our incorruptible nature. Thus the Redeemer must also be the Creator. This was his argument for the deity of Christ and for his strong denial of Arian teachings. To say anything less than that Jesus is God is to strike at the very heart of Christianity. Therefore, Jesus Christ is always central in the theological writings of Athanasius.

In the reading reprinted in this chapter from *Incarnation of the Word* there are four parts, each of which could be read separately. Chapters i–iv argue for the necessity of the incarnation of Christ. Chapters xxi–xxvi and xxx–xxxii defend the necessity of the Cross and the reality of the Resurrection. This is a classic defense of the truthfulness of the heart of the gospel. Then chapters xxxiii–xl use the fulfillment of biblical prophecy as a persuasive argument directed toward orthodox Jews who read and believe the Hebrew Scriptures. Finally, chapters xli–liv are directed toward unbelieving Gentiles, pressing upon their minds the evidence for the truthfulness of the Christian claims. The reading also includes the summary (chaps. lv–lvii) in which Athanasius, like an evangelist, pleads for a decision by speaking of the second coming of Jesus and calling individuals to repentance and faith in Christ.

Without question Athanasius was an outstanding personality.

Like so many other great historical figures of the past, he seems to have had his greatest impact on Christianity before he was thirty years of age. At the Council of Nicea, Athanasius was probably no more than twenty-seven years old, and yet God had blessed him with a deep insight into the true nature of Christian faith. His writings remain as standard examples of classical Christianity.

BIBLIOGRAPHY

Athanasius. *Contre Gentes* and *De Incarnation*. Edited and translated by Robert W. Thompson. Oxford: At the University Press, 1971.
Bush, R. Wheler. *St. Athanasius: His Life and Times*. New York: E. & J. B. Young, 1888.
Hough, Lynn Harold. *Athanasius: The Hero*. Cincinnati, Ohio: Jennings and Graham, 1906.
Robertson, Archibald, ed. *St. Athanasius*. Nicene and Post-Nicene Fathers, edited by Henry Wace and Philip Schaff. Vol. 4. Oxford: Parker, 1892.

AGAINST THE HEATHEN
(Contra Gentes)

CHAPTER I.

Introduction: The purpose of the book a vindication of Christian doctrine, and especially of the Cross, against the scoffing objection of Gentiles. The effects of this doctrine its main vindication.

1. THE knowledge of our religion and of the truth of things is independently manifest rather than in need of human teachers, for almost day by day it asserts itself by facts, and manifests itself brighter than the sun by the doctrine of Christ.

2. Still, as you nevertheless desire to hear about it, Macarius,[1] come let us as we may be able set forth a few points of the faith of Christ: able though you are to find it out from the divine oracles, but yet generously desiring to hear from others as well.

3. For although the sacred and inspired Scriptures are sufficient[2] to declare the truth . . . we must communicate in writing to you . . . the faith, namely, of Christ the Saviour; lest any should hold cheap the doctrine taught among us, or think faith in Christ unreasonable. For this is what the Gentiles traduce and scoff at, and laugh loudly at us, insisting on the one fact of the Cross of Christ; and it is just here that one must pity their want of sense, because when they traduce the

---

From Archibald Robertson, ed., *St. Athanasius*, trans. Cardinal Newman, A Select Library of Nicene and Post-Nicene Fathers of the Christian Church, ed. Henry Wace and Philip Schaff (Oxford: Parker, 1892), 4:4, 22–23, 24–26, 28–30.

[1]See *de Incarn.* I and note there.
[2]Constantly insisted on by Athan.

Cross of Christ they do not see that its power has filled all the world, and that by it the effects of the knowledge of God are made manifest to all.

4. For they would not have scoffed at such a fact, had they, too, been men who genuinely gave heed to His divine Nature. On the contrary, they in their turn would have recognised this man as Saviour of the world, and that the Cross has been not a disaster, but a healing of Creation.

5. For if after the Cross all idolatry was overthrown, while every manifestation of demons is driven away by this Sign,[3] and Christ alone is worshipped and the Father known through Him, and, while gainsayers are put to shame, He daily invisibly wins over the souls of these gainsayers,[4]—how, one might fairly ask them, is it still open to us to regard the matter as human, instead of confessing that He Who ascended the Cross is Word of God and Saviour of the World? But these men seem to me quite as bad as one who should traduce the sun when covered by clouds, while yet wondering at his light, seeing how the whole of creation is illumined by him.

6. For as the light is noble, and the sun, the chief cause of light, is nobler still, so, as it is a divine thing for the whole world to be filled with his knowledge, it follows that the orderer and chief cause of such an achievement is God and the Word of God.

7. We speak then as lies within our power, first refuting the ignorance of the unbelieving; so that what is false being refuted, the truth may then shine forth of itself, and that you yourself, friend, may be reassured that you have believed what is true, and in coming to know Christ have not been deceived. . . .

.   .   .

PART III.

Chapter XXXV.

Creation a revelation of God; especially in the order and harmony pervading the whole.

1. FOR God, being good and loving to mankind, and caring for the souls made by Him,—since He is by nature invisible and incomprehensible, having

---

[3]Cf. *de Incarn.* 47.2, 48.3, Vit. Ant. passim.
[4]Cf. *de Incarn.* 50.3, 51.3, etc.

His being beyond all created existence,[5] for which reason the race of mankind was likely to miss the way to the knowledge of Him, since they are made out of nothing while He is unmade,—for this cause God by His own Word gave the Universe the Order it has, in order that since He is by nature invisible, men might be enabled to know Him at any rate by His works.[6] For often the artist even when not seen is known by his works.

2. And as they tell of Phidias the Sculptor that his works of art by their symmetry and by the proportion of their parts betray Phidias to those who see them although he is not there, so by the order of the Universe one ought to perceive God its maker and artificer, even though He be not seen with the bodily eyes. . . .

3. And I say this not on my own authority, but on the strength of what I learned from men who have spoken of God, among them Paul, who thus writes to the Romans: "for the invisible things of Him since the creation of the world are clearly seen, being understood by the things that are made" [Rom. 1:20]. . . .

4. For who that sees the circle of heaven and the course of the sun and the moon, and the positions and movements of the other stars, as they take place in opposite and different directions, while yet in their difference all with one accord observe a consistent order, can resist the conclusion that these are not ordered by themselves, but have a maker distinct from themselves who orders them? or who that sees the sun rising by day and the moon shining by night, and waning and waxing without variation exactly according to the same number of days, and some of the stars running their courses and with orbits various and manifold, while others move[7] without wandering, can fail to perceive that they certainly have a creator to guide them?

. . .

CHAPTER XXXVIII.

The Unity of God shewn by the Harmony of the order of Nature.

1. SINCE then, there is everywhere not disorder but order . . . we needs must infer and be led to perceive the Master that put together and compacted all things, and produced harmony in them.

---

[5] Cf. below, 40.2.
[6] Cf. *Orat.* ii. 32.
[7] The 'fixed' stars as distinct from the planets. For the argument, cf. Plato, *Legg.* 966 E.

2. For in like manner as if we saw a city, consisting of many and diverse people, great and small, rich and poor, old and young, male and female, in an orderly condition, and its inhabitants, while different from one another, yet at unity among themselves, and not the rich set against the poor, the great against the small, nor the young against the old, but all at peace in the enjoyment of equal rights,—if we saw this, the inference surely follows that the presence of a ruler enforces concord, even if we do not see him; (for disorder is a sign of absence of rule, while order shews the governing authority: for when we see the mutual harmony of the members in the body, that the eye does not strive with the hearing, nor is the hand at variance with the foot, but that each accomplishes its service without variance, we perceive from this that certainly there is a soul in the body that governs these members, though we see it not); so in the order and harmony of the Universe, we needs must perceive God the governor of it all, and that He is one and not many.

3. . . . For if there were more than one Ruler of Creation, such an universal order would not be maintained, but all things would fall into confusion because of their plurality, each one biasing the whole to his own will, and striving with the other. . . . The rule of more than one is the rule of none. For each one would cancel the rule of the other, and none would appear ruler, but there would be anarchy everywhere. But where no ruler is, there disorder follows of course.

4. And conversely, the single order and concord of the many and diverse shews that the ruler too is one. For just as though one were to hear from a distance a lyre, composed of many diverse strings, and marvel at the concord of its symphony, in that its sound is composed neither of low notes exclusively, nor high nor intermediate only, but all combine their sounds in equal balance,—and would not fail to perceive from this that the lyre was not playing itself, nor even being struck by more persons than one, but that there was one musician, even if he did not see him, who by his skill combined the sound of each string into the tuneful symphony; so, the order of the whole universe being perfectly harmonious, and there being no strife of the higher against the lower or the lower against the higher, and all things making up one order, it is consistent to think that the Ruler and King of all Creation is one and not many, Who by His own light illumines and gives movement to all.

CHAPTER XXXIX.

Impossibility of a plurality of Gods.

1. FOR we must not think there is more than one ruler and maker of Creation: but it belongs to correct and true religion to believe that its Artificer is one, while Creation herself clearly points to this. For the fact that there is one Universe only

and not more is a conclusive proof that its Maker is one. For if there were a plurality of gods, there would necessarily be also more universes than one. For neither were it reasonable for more than one God to make a single universe, nor for the one universe to be made by more than one, because of the absurdities which would result from this.

2. Firstly, if the one universe were made by a plurality of gods, that would mean weakness on the part of those who made it, because many contributed to a single result; which would be a strong proof of the imperfect creative skill of each. For if one were sufficient, the many would not supplement each other's deficiency. But to say that there is any deficiency in God is not only impious, but even beyond all sacrilege. For even among men one would not call a workman perfect if he were unable to finish his work, a single piece, by himself and without the aid of several others.

3. But if, although each one was able to accomplish the whole, yet all worked at it in order to claim a share in the result, we have the laughable conclusion that each worked for reputation, lest he should be suspected of inability. But, once more, it is most grotesque to ascribe vainglory to gods.

4. Again, if each one were sufficient for the creation of the whole, what need of more than one, one being self-sufficient for the universe? . . .

5. And this you must know, that if the universe had been made by a plurality of gods, its movements would be diverse and inconsistent. For having regard to each one of its makers, its movements would be correspondingly different. . . .

6. Creation, then, being one, and the Universe one, and its order one, we must perceive that its King and Artificer also is one. For this is why the Artificer Himself made the whole universe one, lest by the coexistence of more than one a plurality of makers should be supposed; but that as the work is one, its Maker also may be believed to be One. Nor does it follow from the unity of the Maker that the Universe must be one, for God might have made others as well. But because the Universe that has been made is one, it is necessary to believe that its Maker also is one.

CHAPTER XL.

The rationality and order of the Universe proves that it is the work of the Reason or Word of God.

1. WHO then might this Maker be? for this is a point most necessary to make plain, lest, from ignorance with regard to him, a man should suppose the wrong maker, and fall once more into the same old godless error, but I think no one is really in doubt about it. For if our argument has proved that the gods of

the poets are no gods, and has convicted of error those that deify creation, and in general has shewn that the idolatry of the heathen is godlessness and impiety, it strictly follows from the elimination of these that the true religion is with us, and that the God we worship and preach is the only true One, Who is Lord of Creation and Maker of all existence.

2. Who then is this, save the Father of Christ, most holy and above all created existence,[8] Who like an excellent pilot, by His own Wisdom and His own Word, our Lord and Saviour Christ, steers and preserves and orders all things, and does as seems to Him best? But that is best which has been done, and which we see taking place, since that is what He wills; and this a man can hardly refuse to believe.

3. For if the movement of creation were irrational, and the universe were borne along without plan, a man might fairly disbelieve what we say. But if it subsist in reason and wisdom and skill, and is perfectly ordered throughout, it follows that He that is over it and has ordered it is none other than the [reason or] Word of God.

4. But by Word I mean, not that which is involved and inherent in all things created, which some are wont to call the seminal[9] principle, which is without soul and has no power of reason or thought, but only works by external art, according to the skill of him that applies it,—nor such a word as belongs to rational beings and which consists of syllables, and has the air as its vehicle of expression,—but I mean the living and powerful Word of the good God, the God of the Universe, the very Word which is God [John 1:1], Who while different from things that are made, and from all Creation, is the One own Word of the good Father, Who by His own providence ordered and illumines this Universe.

5. For being the good Word of the Good Father He produced the order of all things, combining one with another things contrary, and reducing them to one harmonious order. He being the Power of God and Wisdom of God causes the heaven to revolve, and has suspended the earth, and made it fast, though resting upon nothing, by His own nod.[10] Illumined by Him, the sun gives light to the world, and the moon has her measured period of shining. By reason of Him the water is suspended in the clouds, the rains shower upon the earth, and the sea is kept within bounds, while the earth bears grasses and is clothed with all manner of plants.

6. And if a man were incredulously to ask, as regards what we are saying, if

---

[8]Cf. above 35.1.
[9]σπερματικός.
[10]νεῦμα, i.e. act of will, or fiat.

there be a Word of God at all,[11] such an one would indeed be mad to doubt concerning the Word of God, but yet demonstration is possible from what is seen, because all things subsist by the Word and Wisdom of God, nor would any created thing have had a fixed existence had it not been made by reason, and that reason the Word of God, as we have said.

. . .

CHAPTER XLV.

Conclusion. Doctrine of Scripture on the subject of Part 1.

1. FOR just as by looking up to the heaven and seeing its order and the light of the stars, it is possible to infer the Word Who ordered these things, so by beholding the Word of God, one needs must behold also God His Father, proceeding from Whom He is rightly called His Father's Interpreter and Messenger.

2. And this one may see from our own experience; for if when a word proceeds from men[12] we infer that the mind is its source, and, by thinking about the word, see with our reason the mind which it reveals, by far greater evidence and incomparably more, seeing the power of the Word, we receive a knowledge also of His good Father, as the Saviour Himself says, "He that hath seen Me hath seen the Father" [John 14:9]. But this all inspired Scripture also teaches more plainly and with more authority, so that we in our turn write boldy to you as we do, and you, if you refer to them, will be able to verify what we say.

3. For an argument when confirmed by higher authority is irresistibly proved. From the first then the divine Word firmly taught the Jewish people about the abolition of idols when it said: "Thou shalt not make to thyself a graven image, nor the likeness of anything that is in the heaven above or in the earth beneath" [Ex. 20:4]. But the cause of their abolition another writer declares, saying: "The idols of the heathen are silver and gold, the works of men's hands: a mouth have they and will not speak, eyes have they and will not see, ears have they and will not hear, noses have they and will not smell, hands have they and will not handle, feet have they and will not walk" [Ps. 115:4–7]. Nor has it passed over in silence the doctrine of creation; but, knowing well its beauty, lest any attending solely to this beauty should worship things as if they were gods, instead

---

[11]*De Incarn.* 41.3.
[12]Cf. *de Sent. Dionys.* 23.

of God's works, it teaches men firmly beforehand when it says: "And do not when thou lookest up with thine eyes and seest the sun and moon and all the host of heaven, go astray and worship them, which the Lord thy God hath given to all nations under heaven" [Deut. 4:19]. But He gave them, not to be their gods, but that by their agency the Gentiles should know, as we have said, God the Maker of them all.

4. For the people of the Jews of old had abundant teaching, in that they had the knowledge of God not only from the works of Creation, but also from the divine Scriptures. And in general to draw men away from the error and irrational imagination of idols, He saith: "Thou shalt have none other gods but Me" [Ex. 20:3]. Not as if there were other gods does He forbid them to have them, but lest any, turning from the true God, should begin to make himself gods of what were not, such as those who in the poets and writers are called gods, though they are none. . . .

CHAPTER XLVI.

Doctrine of Scripture on the subject of Part 3.

1. HAS then the divine teaching, which abolished the godlessness of the heathen or the idols, passed over in silence, and left the race of mankind to go entirely unprovided with the knowledge of God? Not so: rather it anticipates their understanding when it says: "Hear, O Israel, the Lord thy God is one God;" and again, "Thou shalt love the Lord thy God with all thy heart and with all thy strength;" and again, "Thou shalt worship the Lord thy God, and Him only shalt thou serve, and shalt cleave to Him" [Deut. 6:4–5, 13].

2. But that the providence and ordering power of the Word also, over all and toward all, is attested by all inspired Scripture, this passage suffices to confirm our argument, where men who speak of God say: "Thou hast laid the foundation of the earth and it abideth. The day continueth according to Thine ordinance" [Ps. 119:90]. And again: "Sing to our God upon the harp, that covereth the heaven with clouds, that prepareth rain for the earth, that bringeth forth grass upon the mountains, and green herb for the service of man, and giveth food to the cattle" [Ps. 147:7–9].

3. But by whom does He give it, save by Him through Whom all things were made? For the providence over all things belongs naturally to Him by Whom they were made; and who is this save the Word of God, concerning Whom in another psalm he says: "By the Word of the Lord were the heavens made, and all the host of them by the Breath of His mouth" [Ps. 33:6]. For He tells us that all things were made in Him and through Him.

4. Wherefore He also persuades us and says, "He spake and they were made, He commanded and they were created" [Ps. 148:5]; as the illustrious Moses also at the beginning of his account of Creation confirms what we say by his narrative, saying: and God said, "let us make man in our image and after our likeness" [Gen. 1:26] for also when He was carrying out the creation of the heaven and earth and all things, the Father said to Him, "Let the heaven be made," and "let the waters be gathered together and let the dry land appear," and "let the earth bring forth herb" and "every green thing:" [Gen. 1:6–11], so that one must convict Jews also of not genuinely attending to the Scriptures.

5. For one might ask them to whom was God speaking, to use the imperative mood? If He were commanding and addressing the things He was creating, the utterance would be redundant, for they were not yet in being, but were about to be made; but no one speaks to what does not exist, nor addresses to what is not yet made a command to be made. For if God were giving a command to the things that were to be, He must have said, "Be made, heaven, and be made, earth, and come forth, green herb, and be created, O man." But in fact He did not do so; but He gives the command thus: "Let us make man," and "let the green herb come forth." By which God is proved to be speaking about them to some one at hand: it follows then that some one was with Him to Whom He spoke when He made all things.

6. Who then could it be, save His Word? For to whom could God be said to speak, except His Word? Or who was with Him when He made all created Existence, except His Wisdom, which says: "When He was making the heaven and the earth I was present with Him" [Prov. 8:27]? But in the mention of heaven and earth, all created things in heaven and earth are included as well.

7. But being present with Him as His Wisdom and His Word, looking at the Father He fashioned the Universe, and organised it and gave it order; and, as He is the power of the Father, He gave all things strength to be, as the Saviour says: "What things soever I see the Father doing, I also do in like manner" [John 5:19]. And His holy disciples teach that all things were made "through Him and unto Him" [Col. 1:16].

8. And, being the good Offspring of Him that is good, and true Son, He is the Father's Power and Wisdom and Word, not being so by participation,[13] nor as if these qualities were imparted to Him from without, as they are to those who

---

[13]μετοχή, cf. *de Syn.* 48, 51, 53. This was held by Arians, but in common with Paul Samos, and many of the Monarchian heretics. The same principle in Orig. on Ps. 135 (Lomm. xiii. 134) οὐ κατὰ μετουσίαν ἀλλὰ κατ' οὐσίαν θεός.

partake of Him and are made wise by Him, and receive power and reason in Him; but He is the very Wisdom, very Word, and very own Power of the Father, very Light, very Truth, very Righteousness, very Virtue, and in truth His express Image, and Brightness, and Resemblance. And to sum all up, He is the wholly perfect Fruit of the Father, and is alone the Son, and unchanging Image of the Father.

CHAPTER LVII.

Necessity of a return to the Word if our corrupt nature is to be restored.

1. WHO then, who can declare the Father by number, so as to discover the powers of His Word? For like as He is the Father's Word and Wisdom, so too condescending to created things, He becomes, to impart the knowledge and apprehension of Him that begat Him, His very Brightness and very Life, and the Door, and the Shepherd, and the Way, and King and Governor, and Saviour over all, and Light, and Giver of Life, and Providence over all. Having them such a Son begotten of Himself, good, and Creator, the Father did not hide Him out of the sight of His creatures, but even day by day reveals Him to all by means of the organisation and life of all things, which is His work.

2. But in and through Him He reveals Himself also, as the Saviour says: "I in the Father and the Father in Me" [John 14:10]: so that it follows that the Word is in Him that begat Him, and that He that is begotten lives eternally with the Father. But this being so, and nothing being outside Him, but both heaven and earth and all that in them is being dependent on Him, yet men in their folly have set aside the knowledge and service of Him, and honoured things that are not instead of things that are: and instead of the real and true God deified things that were not, "serving the creature rather than the Creator" [Rom. 1:25], thus involving themselves in foolishness and impiety.

3. For it is just as if one were to admire the works more than the workman, and being awestruck at the public works in the city, were to make light of their builder, or as if one were to praise a musical instrument but to despise the man who made and tuned it. Foolish and sadly disabled in eyesight! For how else had they known the building, or ship, or lyre, had not the ship-builder made it, the architect built it, or the musician fashioned it?

4. As then he that reasons in such a way is mad, and beyond all madness, even so affected in mind, I think, are those who do not recognise God or worship His Word, our Lord Jesus Christ the Saviour of all, through Whom the Father orders, and holds together all things, and exercises providence over the Universe; having faith and piety towards Whom, my Christ-loving friend, be of good cheer and of good hope, because immortality and the kingdom of heaven is the fruit of

faith and devotion towards Him, if only the soul be adorned according to His laws. For just as for them who walk after His example, the prize is life everlasting, so for those who walk the opposite way, and not that of virtue, there is great shame, and peril without pardon in the day of judgment, because although they knew the way of truth their acts were contrary to their knowledge.

ON THE INCARNATION OF THE WORD
(De Incarnatione Verbi Dei)

CHAPTER I.

Introductory. The subject of this treatise: the humiliation and incarnation of the Word. Presupposes the doctrine of Creation, and that by the Word. The Father has saved the world by Him through Whom He first made it.

1. WHEREAS in what precedes we have drawn out—choosing a few points from among many—a sufficient account of the error of the heathen concerning idols, and of the worship of idols, and how they originally came to be invented; how, namely, out of wickedness men devised for themselves the worshipping of idols: and whereas we have by God's grace noted somewhat also of the divinity of the Word of the Father, and of His universal Providence and power, and that the Good Father through Him orders all things, and all things are moved by Him, and in Him are quickened: come now, Macarius,[1] (worthy of that name), and true lover of Christ, let us follow up the faith of our religion,[2] and set forth also what relates to the Word's becoming Man, and to His divine Appearing amongst us, which Jews traduce and Greeks laugh to scorn, but we worship; in order that, all the more for the seeming low estate of the Word, your piety toward Him may be increased and multiplied.

From Archibald Robertson, ed., *St. Athanasius*, trans. Cardinal Newman, A Select Library of Nicene and Post-Nicene Fathers of the Christian Church, ed. Henry Wace and Philip Schaff (Oxford: Parker, 1892), 4:36–38, 48–50, 52–67.

[1]See *Contra Gentes*, i. The word (Μακάριε) may be an adjective only, but its occurrence in *both* places seems decisive. The name was very common (*Apol. c. Ar.* passim). 'Macarius' was a Christian as the present passage shews: he is presumed (*c. Gent.* i. 7) to have access to Scripture.

[2]τῆς εὐσεβείας. See 1 Tim. 3:16.

2. For the more He is mocked among the unbelieving, the more witness does He give of His own Godhead; inasmuch as He not only Himself demonstrates as possible what men mistake, thinking impossible, but what men deride as unseemly, this by His own goodness He clothes with seemliness, and what men, in their conceit of wisdom, laugh at as merely human, He by His own power demonstrates to be divine, subduing the pretensions of idols by His supposed humiliation—by the Cross—and those who mock and disbelieve invisibly winning over to recognise His divinity and power.

3. But to treat this subject it is necessary to recall what has been previously said; in order that you may neither fail to know the cause of the bodily appearing of the Word of the Father, so high and so great, nor think it a consequence of His own nature that the Saviour has worn a body; but that being incorporeal by nature, and Word from the beginning, He has yet of the loving-kindness and goodness of His own Father been manifested to us in a human body for our salvation.

4. It is, then, proper for us to begin the treatment of this subject by speaking of the creation of the universe, and of God its Artificer, that so it may be duly perceived that the renewal of creation has been the work of the self-same Word that made it at the beginning. For it will appear not inconsonant for the Father to have wrought its salvation in Him by Whose means He made it.

CHAPTER II.

Erroneous views of Creation rejected. (1) Epicurean (fortuitous generation). But diversity of bodies and parts argues a creating intellect. (2) Platonists (pre-existent matter.) But this subjects God to human limitations, making Him not a creator but a mechanic. (3) Gnostics (an alien Demiurge). Rejected from Scripture.

1. OF the making of the universe and the creation of all things many have taken different views, and each man has laid down the law just as he pleased. For some say that all things have come into being of themselves, and in a chance fashion; as, for example, the Epicureans, who tell us in their self-contempt, that universal providence does not exist speaking right in the face of obvious fact and experience.

2. For if, as they say, everything has had its beginning of itself, and independently of purpose, it would follow that everything had come into[3] mere being, so as to be alike and not distinct. For it would follow in virtue of the unity of

---

[3]Or, "been made in one way only." In the next clause I formerly translated the difficult words ὡς ἐπὶ σώματος ἕνος 'as in the case of the universe;' but although the rendering has commended itself to others I now reluctantly admit that it puts too much into the Greek (in spite of § 41. 5).

body that everything must be sun or moon, and in the case of men it would follow that the whole must be hand, or eye, or foot. But as it is this is not so. On the contrary, we see a distinction of sun, moon, and earth; and again, in the case of human bodies, of foot, hand, and head. Now, such separate arrangement as this tells us not of their having come into being of themselves, but shews that a cause preceded them; from which cause it is possible to apprehend God also as the Maker and Orderer of all.

3. But others, including Plato, who is in such repute among the Greeks, argue that God has made the world out of matter previously existing and without beginning. For God could have made nothing had not the material existed already; just as the wood must exist ready at hand for the carpenter, to enable him to work at all.

4. But in so saying they know not that they are investing God with weakness. For if He is not Himself the cause of the material, but makes things only of previously existing material, He proves to be weak, because unable to produce anything He makes without the material; just as it is without doubt a weakness of the carpenter not to be able to make anything required without his timber. For, *ex hypothesi*, had not the material existed, God would not have made anything. And how could He in that case be called Maker and Artificer, if He owes His ability to make to some other source—namely, to the material? So that if this be so, God will be on their theory a Mechanic only, and not a Creator out of nothing;[4] if, that is, He works at existing material, but is not Himself the cause of the material. For he could not in any sense be called Creator unless He is Creator of the material of which the things created have in their turn been made.

5. But the sectaries imagine to themselves a different artificer of all things, other than the Father of our Lord Jesus Christ, in deep blindness even as to the words they use.

6. For whereas the Lord says to the Jews: "Have ye not read that from the beginning He which created them made them male and female, and said, For this cause shall a man leave his father and mother, and shall cleave to his wife, and they twain shall become one flesh?" [Matt. 19:4] and then, referring to the Creator says, "What, therefore, GOD hath joined together let not man put asunder" [Matt. 19:6]: how come these men to assert that the creation is independent of the Father? Or if, in the words of John, who says, making no exception, "All things were made by Him, and "without Him was not anything made" [John 1:3], how could the artificer be another, distinct from the Father of Christ?

---

[4]εἰς τὸ εἶναι.

CHAPTER III.

The true doctrine. Creation out of nothing, of God's lavish bounty of being. Man created above the rest, but incapable of independent perseverance. Hence the exceptional and supra-natural gift of being in God's Image, with the promise of bliss conditionally upon his perseverance in grace.

1. THUS do they vainly speculate. But the godly teaching and the faith according to Christ brands their foolish language as godlessness. For it knows that it was not spontaneously, because forethought is not absent; nor of existing matter, because God is not weak; but that out of nothing, and without its having any previous existence, God made the universe to exist through His word, as He says firstly through Moses: "In the beginning God created the heaven and the earth" [Gen. 1:1]; secondly, in the most edifying book of the Shepherd, "First of all believe that God is one, which created and framed all things, and made them to exist out of nothing."[5]

2. To which also Paul refers when he says, "By faith we understand that the worlds have been framed by the Word of God, so that what is seen hath not been made out of things which do appear" [Heb. 11:3].

3. For God is good, or rather is essentially the source of goodness: nor[6] could one that is good be niggardly of anything: whence, grudging existence to none, He has made all things out of nothing by His own Word, Jesus Christ our Lord. And among these, having taken especial pity, above all things on earth, upon the race of men, and having perceived its inability, by virtue of the condition of its origin, to continue in one stay, He gave them a further gift, and He did not barely create man, as He did all the irrational creatures on the earth, but made them after His own image, giving them a portion even of the power of His own Word; so that having as it were a kind of reflexion of the Word, and being made rational, they might be able to abide ever in blessedness, living the true life which belongs to the saints in paradise.

4. But knowing once more how the will of man could sway to either side, in anticipation He secured the grace given them by a law and by the spot where He placed them. For He brought them into His own garden, and gave them a law: so that, if they kept the grace and remained good, they might still keep the life in paradise without sorrow or pain or care, besides having the promise of incorruption in heaven; but that if they transgressed and turned back, and became evil, they might know that they were incurring that corruption in death which was

---

[5]Herm. *Mand.* 1.
[6]c. *Gent.* xli. and Plato, *Timaeus* 29 E.

theirs by nature: no longer to live in paradise, but cast out of it from that time forth to die and to abide in death and in corruption.

5. Now this is that of which Holy Writ also gives warning, saying in the Person of God: "Of every tree that is in the garden, eating thou shalt eat: but of the tree of the knowledge of good and evil, ye shall not eat of it, but on the day that ye eat, dying ye shall die" [Gen. 2:16–17]. But by "dying ye shall die," what else could be meant than not dying merely, but also abiding ever in the corruption of death?

CHAPTERS IV, V.

Our creation and God's Incarnation most intimately connected. As by the Word man was called from non-existence into being, and further received the grace of a divine life, so by the one fault which forfeited that life they again incurred corruption and untold sin and misery filled the world.

1. YOU are wondering, perhaps, for what possible reason, having proposed to speak of the Incarnation of the Word, we are at present treating of the origin of mankind. But this, too, properly belongs to the aim of our treatise.

2. For in speaking of the appearance of the Saviour amongst us, we must needs speak also of the origin of men, that you may know that the reason of His coming down was because of us, and that our transgression[7] called forth the loving-kindness of the Word, that the Lord should both make haste to help us and appear among men.

3. For of His becoming Incarnate we were the object, and for our salvation He dealt so lovingly as to appear and be born even in a human body. . . .

.   .   .

CHAPTER XXI.

Death brought to nought by the death of Christ. Why then did not Christ die privately, or in a more honourable way? He was not subject to natural death, but had to die at the hands of others. Why then did He die? Nay but for that purpose He came, and but for that, He could not have risen.

6. . . . SINCE it was not fit, either, that the Lord should fall sick, who healed the diseases of others; nor again was it right for that body to lose its strength, in which He gives strength to the weaknesses of others also.

---

[7]Cf. *Orat.* ii. 54, note 4.

7. Why, then, did He not prevent death, as He did sickness? Because it was for this that He had the body, and it was unfitting to prevent it, lest the Resurrection also should be hindered, while yet it was equally unfitting for sickness to precede His death, lest it should be thought weakness on the part of Him that was in the body. Did He not then hunger? Yes; He hungered, agreeably to the properties of His body. But He did not perish of hunger, because of the Lord that wore it. Hence, even if He died to ransom all, yet He saw not corruption. For [His body] rose again in perfect soundness, since the body belonged to none other, but to the very Life.

CHAPTER XXII.

But why did He not withdraw His body from the Jews, and so guard its immortality? (1) It became Him not to inflict death on Himself, and yet not to shun it. (2) He came to receive death as the due of others, therefore it should come to Him from without. (3) His death must be certain, to guarantee the truth of His Resurrection. Also, He could not die from infirmity, lest He should be mocked in His healing of others.

1. BUT it were better, one might say, to have hidden from the designs of the Jews, that He might guard His body altogether from death. Now let such an one be told that this too was unbefitting the Lord. For as it was not fitting for the Word of God, being the Life, to inflict death Himself on His own body, so neither was it suitable to fly from death offered by others, but rather to follow it up unto destruction, for which reason He naturally neither laid aside His body of His own accord, nor, again, fled from the Jews when they took counsel against Him.

2. But this did not shew weakness on the Word's part, but, on the contrary, shewed Him to be Saviour and Life; in that He both awaited death to destroy it, and hasted to accomplish the death offered Him for the salvation of all.

3. And besides, the Saviour came to accomplish not His own death, but the death of men; whence He did not lay aside His body by a death of His own—for He was Life and had none—but received that death which came from men, in order perfectly to do away with this when it met Him in His own body [John 10:17–18].

4. Again, from the following also one might see the reasonableness of the Lord's body meeting this end. The Lord was especially concerned for the resurrection of the body which He was set to accomplish. For what He was to do was to manifest it as a monument of victory over death, and to assure all of His having effected the blotting out of corruption, and of the incorruption of their bodies from thenceforward; as a gage of which and a proof of the resurrection in store for all, He has preserved His own body incorrupt.

5. If, then, once more, His body had fallen sick, and the word had been sundered from it in the sight of all, it would have been unbecoming that He who healed the diseases of others should suffer His own instrument to waste in sickness. For how could His driving out the diseases of others have been believed[8] in if His own temple fell sick in Him?[9] For either He had been mocked as unable to drive away diseases, or if He could, but did not, He would be thought insensible toward others also.

CHAPTER XXIII.

Necessity of a public death for the doctrine of the Resurrection.

1. BUT even if, without any disease and without any pain, He had hidden His body away privily and by Himself "in a corner" [Acts 26:26], or in a desert place, or in a house, or anywhere, and afterwards suddenly appeared and said that He had been raised from the dead, He would have seemed on all hands to be telling idle tales [Luke 24:11], and what He said about the Resurrection would have been all the more discredited, as there was no one at all to witness to His death. Now, death must precede resurrection, as it would be no resurrection did not death precede; so that if the death of His body had taken place anywhere in secret, the death not being apparent nor taking place before witnesses, His Resurrection too had been hidden and without evidence.

2. Or why, while when He had risen He proclaimed the Resurrection, should He cause His death to take place in secret? or why, while He drove out evil spirits in the presence of all, and made the man blind from his birth recover his sight, and changed the water into wine, that by these means He might be believed to be the Word of God, should He not manifest His mortal nature as incorruptible in the presence of all, that He might be believed Himself to be the Life?

3. Or how were His disciples to have boldness in speaking of the Resurrection, were they not able to say that He first died? Or how could they be believed, saying that death had first taken place and then the Resurrection, had they not had as witnesses of His death the men before whom they spoke with boldness? For if, even as it was, when His death and Resurrection had taken place in the sight of all, the Pharisees of that day would not believe, but compelled even those who had seen the Resurrection to deny it, why, surely, if these things had happened in secret, how many pretexts for disbelief would they have devised?

4. Or how could the end of death, and the victory over it be proved, unless

---

[8]Cf. Matt. 27:42.
[9]*i.e.* when sustained by its union with Him.

challenging it before the eyes of all He had shewn it to be dead, annulled for the future by the incorruption of His body?

CHAPTER XXIV.

Further objections anticipated. He did not choose His manner of death; for He was to prove Conqueror of death in all or any of its forms: (simile of a good wrestler). The death chosen to disgrace Him proved the Trophy against death: moreover it preserved His body undivided.

1. BUT what others also might have said, we must anticipate in reply. For perhaps a man might say even as follows: If it was necessary for His death to take place before all, and with witnesses, that the story of His Resurrection also might be believed, it would have been better at any rate for Him to have devised for Himself a glorious death, if only to escape the ignominy of the Cross.

2. But had He done even this, He would give ground for suspicion against Himself, that He was not powerful against every death, but only against the death devised for[10] Him; and so again there would have been a pretext for disbelief about the Resurrection all the same. So death came to His body, not from Himself, but from hostile counsels, in order that whatever death they offered to the Saviour, this He might utterly do away.

3. And just as a noble wrestler, great in skill and courage, does not pick out his antagonists for himself, lest he should raise a suspicion of his being afraid of some of them, but puts it in the choice of the onlookers, and especially so if they happen to be his enemies, so that against whomsoever they match him, him he may throw, and be believed superior to them all; so also the Life of all, our Lord and Saviour, even Christ, did not devise a death for His own body, so as not to appear to be fearing some other death; but He accepted on the Cross, and endured, a death inflicted by others, and above all by His enemies, which they thought dreadful and ignominious and not to be faced; so that this also being destroyed, both He Himself might be believed to be the Life, and the power of death be brought utterly to nought.

4. So something surprising and startling has happened; for the death, which they thought to inflict as a disgrace, was actually a monument of victory against death itself. Whence neither did He suffer the death of John, his head being severed, nor, as Esaias, was He sawn in sunder; in order that even in death He might still keep His body undivided and in perfect soundness, and no pretext be afforded to those that would divide the Church.

---

[10]*i.e.* suggested as ἔνδοξον (*supra*, 1); a reading παρ' ἑαυτοῦ has been suggested: (devised) "by Himself."

CHAPTER XXV.

Why the Cross, of all deaths? (1) *He had to bear the curse for us.* (2) *On it He held out His hands to unite all, Jews and Gentiles, in Himself.* (3) *He defeated the "Prince of the powers of the air" in his own region, clearing the way to heaven and opening for us the everlasting doors.*

1. AND thus much in reply to those without who pile up arguments for themselves. But if any of our own people also inquire, not from love of debate, but from love of learning, why He suffered death in none other way save on the Cross, let him also be told that no other way than this was good for us, and that it was well that the Lord suffered this for our sakes.

2. For if He came Himself to bear the curse laid upon us, how else could He have "become a curse" [Gal. 3:13], unless He received the death set for a curse? and that is the Cross. For this is exactly what is written: "Cursed is he that hangeth on a tree" [Deut. 21:23].

3. Again, if the Lord's death is the ransom of all, and by His death "the middle wall of partition" [Eph. 2:14] is broken down, and the calling of the nations is brought about, how would He have called us to Him, had He not been crucified? For it is only on the cross that a man dies with his hands spread out. Whence it was fitting for the Lord to bear this also and to spread out His hands, that with the one He might draw the ancient people, and with the other those from the Gentiles, and unite both in Himself.

4. For this is what He Himself has said, signifying by what manner of death He was to ransom all: "I, when I am lifted up," He saith, "shall draw all men unto Me" [John 12:32].

5. And once more, if the devil, the enemy of our race, having fallen from heaven, wanders about our lower atmosphere, and there bearing rule over his fellow-spirits, as his peers in disobedience, not only works illusions by their means in them that are deceived, but tries to hinder them that are going up (and about this[11] the Apostle says: "According to the prince of the power of the air, of the spirit that now worketh in the sons of disobedience"); while the Lord came to cast down the devil, and clear the air and prepare the way for us up into heaven, as said the Apostle: "Through the veil, that is to say, His flesh" [Heb. 10:20]— and this must needs be by death—well, by what other kind of death could this have come to pass, than by one which took place in the air, I mean the cross? for only he that is perfected on the cross dies in the air. Whence it was quite fitting that the Lord suffered this death.

---

[11]Eph. 2:2, and see the curious visions of Antony, *Vit. Ant.*, 65, 66.

6. For thus being lifted up He cleared the air[12] of the malignity both of the devil and of demons of all kinds, as He says: "I beheld Satan as lightning fall from heaven" [Luke 10:18]; and made a new opening of the way up into heaven, as He says once more: "Lift up your gates, O ye princes, and be ye lift up, ye everlasting doors."[13] For it was not the Word Himself that needed an opening of the gates, being Lord of all; nor were any of His works closed to their Maker; but we it was that needed it, whom He carried up by His own body. For as He offered it to death on behalf of all, so by it He once more made ready the way up into the heavens.

CHAPTER XXVI.

Reasons for His rising on the Third Day. (1) *Not sooner, for else His real death would be denied, nor* (2) *later; to (a) guard the identity of His body, (b) not to keep His disciples too long in suspense, nor (c) to wait till the witnesses of His death were dispersed, or its memory faded.*

1. THE death on the Cross, then, for us has proved seemly and fitting, and its cause has been shewn to be reasonable in every respect; and it may justly be argued that in no other way than by the Cross was it right for the salvation of all to take place. For not even thus—not even on the Cross—did He leave Himself concealed; but far otherwise, while He made creation witness to the presence of its Maker, He suffered not the temple of His body to remain long, but having merely shewn it to be dead, by the contact of death with it, He straightway raised it up on the third day, bearing away, as the mark of victory and the triumph over death, the incorruptibility and impassibility which resulted to His body.

2. For He could, even immediately on death, have raised His body and shewn it alive; but this also the Saviour, in wise foresight, did not do. For one might have said that He had not died at all, or that death had not come into perfect contact with Him, if He had manifested the Resurrection at once.

3. Perhaps, again, had the interval of His dying and rising again been one of two days[14] only, the glory of His incorruption would have been obscure. So in order that the body might be proved to be dead, the Word tarried yet one intermediate day, and on the third shewed it incorruptible to all.

---

[12]Cf. Lightfoot on Coloss. 2:15, also the fragment of *Letter* 22, and *Letter* 60.7.
[13]Ps. 24:7, Septuagint.
[14]Literally 'at an even' [distance], as contrasted with (a) the same day (2, above), (b) the third day (ἐν τριταίῳ διαστήματι (6, below). ἐν ἴσῳ must therefore be equivalent *in sense* to δευτεραίου. Possibly the literal sense is '[had the Resurrection taken place] at an equal interval between the Death and the [actual day of] the Resurrection.'

4. So then, that the death on the Cross might be proved, He raised His body on the third day.

5. But lest, by raising it up when it had remained a long time and been completely corrupted, He should be disbelieved, as though He had exchanged it for some other body—for a man might also from lapse of time distrust what he saw, and forget what had taken place—for this cause He waited not more than three days; nor did He keep long in suspense those whom He had told about the Resurrection;

6. but while the word was still echoing in their ears and their eyes were still expectant and their mind in suspense, and while those who had slain Him were still living on earth, and were on the spot and could witness to the death of the Lord's body, the Son of God Himself, after an interval of three days, shewed His body, once dead, immortal and incorruptible; and it was made manifest to all that it was not from any natural weakness of the Word that dwelt in it that the body had died, but in order that in it death might be done away by the power of the Saviour.

.   .   .

CHAPTER XXX.

The reality of the Resurrection proved by facts: (1) the victory over death described above: (2) the Wonders of Grace are the work of one Living, of One who is God: (3) if the gods be (as alleged) real and living, a fortiori He Who shatters their power is alive.

1. WHAT we have so far said, then, is no small proof that death has been brought to nought, and that the Cross of the Lord is a sign of victory over him. But of the Resurrection of the body to immortality thereupon accomplished by Christ, the common Saviour and true Life of all the demonstration by facts is clearer than arguments to those whose mental vision is sound.

2. For if, as our argument shewed, death has been brought to nought, and because of Christ all tread him under foot, much more did He Himself first tread him down with His own body, and bring him to nought. But supposing death slain by Him, what could have happened save the rising again of His body, and its being displayed as a monument of victory against death? or how could death have been shewn to be brought to nought unless the Lord's body had risen? But if this demonstration of the Resurrection seem to any one insufficient, let him be assured of what is said even from what takes place before his eyes.

3. For whereas on a man's decease he can put forth no power, but his

influence lasts to the grave and thenceforth ceases; and actions, and power over men, belong to the living only; let him who will, see and be judge, confessing the truth from what appears to sight.

4. For now that the Saviour works so great things among men, and day by day is invisibly persuading so great a multitude from every side, both from them that dwell in Greece and in foreign lands, to come over to His faith, and all to obey His teaching, will any one still hold his mind in doubt whether a Resurrection has been accomplished by the Saviour, and whether Christ is alive, or rather is Himself the Life?

5. Or is it like a dead man to be pricking the consciences of men, so that they deny their hereditary laws and bow before the teaching of Christ? Or how, if he is no longer active (for this is proper to one dead), does he stay from their activity those who are active and alive, so that the adulterer no longer commits adultery, and the murderer murders no more, nor is the inflicter of wrong any longer grasping, and the profane is henceforth religious? Or how, if He be not risen but is dead, does He drive away, and pursue, and cast down those false gods said by the unbelievers to be alive, and the demons they worship?

6. For where Christ is named, and His faith, there all idolatry is deposed and all imposture of evil spirits is exposed, and any spirit is unable to endure even the name, nay even on barely hearing it flies and disappears. But this work is not that of one dead, but of one that lives—and especially of God.

7. In particular, it would be ridiculous to say that while the spirits cast out by Him and the idols brought to nought are alive, He who chases them away, and by His power prevents their even appearing, yea, and is being confessed by them all to be Son of God, is dead.

CHAPTER XXXI.

If Power is the sign of life, what do we learn from the impotence of idols, for good or evil, and the constraining power of Christ and of the Sign of the Cross? Death and the demons are by this proved to have lost their sovereignty. Coincidence of the above argument from facts with that from the Personality of Christ.

1. BUT they who disbelieve in the Resurrection afford a strong proof against themselves, if instead of all the spirits and the gods worshipped by them casting out Christ, Who, they say, is dead, Christ on the contrary proves them all to be dead.

2. For if it be true that one dead can exert no power, while the Saviour does daily so many works, drawing men to religion, persuading to virtue, teaching of immortality, leading on to a desire for heavenly things, revealing the knowledge of the Father, inspiring strength to meet death, shewing Himself to each one, and displacing the godlessness of idolatry, and the gods and spirits of the unbelievers

can do none of these things, but rather shew themselves dead at the presence of Christ, their pomp being reduced to impotence and vanity; whereas by the sign of the Cross all magic is stopped, and all witchcraft brought to nought, and all the idols are being deserted and left, and every unruly pleasure is checked, and every one is looking up from earth to heaven: Whom is one to pronounce dead? Christ, that is doing so many works? But to work is not proper to one dead. Or him that exerts no power at all, but lies as it were without life? which is essentially proper to the idols and spirits, dead as they are.

3. For the Son of God is "living and active" [Heb. 4:12], and works day by day, and brings about the salvation of all. But death is daily proved to have lost all his power, and idols and spirits are proved to be dead rather than Christ, so that henceforth no man can any longer doubt of the Resurrection of His body.

4. But he who is incredulous of the Resurrection of the Lord's body would seem to be ignorant of the power of the Word and Wisdom of God. For if He took a body to Himself at all, and—in reasonable consistency, as our argument shewed—appropriated it as His own, what was the Lord to do with it? or what should be the end of the body when the Word had once descended upon it? For it could not but die, inasmuch as it was mortal, and to be offered unto death on behalf of all: for which purpose it was that the Saviour fashioned it for Himself. But it was impossible for it to remain dead, because it had been made the temple of life. Whence, while it died as mortal, it came to life again by reason of the Life in it; and of its Resurrection the works are a sign.

CHAPTER XXXII.

But who is to see Him risen, so as to believe? Nay, God is ever invisible and known by His works only: and here the works cry out in proof. If you do not believe, look at those who do, and perceive the Godhead of Christ. The demons see this, though men be blind. Summary of the argument so far.

1. BUT if, because He is not seen, His having risen at all is disbelieved, it is high time for those who refuse belief to deny the very course of Nature. For it is God's peculiar property at once to be invisible and yet to be known from His works, as has been already stated above.

2. If, then, the works are not there, they do well to disbelieve what does not appear. But if the works cry aloud and shew it clearly, why do they choose to deny the life so manifestly due to the Resurrection? For even if they be maimed in their intelligence, yet even with the external senses men may see the unimpeachable power and Godhead of Christ.

3. For even a blind man, if he see not the sun, yet if he but take hold of the warmth the sun gives out, knows that there is a sun above the earth. Thus let our opponents also, even if they believe not as yet, being still blind to the truth, yet at

least knowing His power by others who believe, not deny the Godhead of Christ and the Resurrection accomplished by Him.

4. For it is plain that if Christ be dead, He could not be expelling demons and spoiling idols; for a dead man the spirits would not have obeyed. But if they be manifestly expelled by the naming of His name, it must be evident that He is not dead; especially as spirits, seeing even what is unseen by men, could tell if Christ were dead and refuse Him any obedience at all.

5. But as it is, what irreligious men believe not, the spirits see—that He is God,—and hence they fly and fall at His feet, saying just what they uttered when He was in the body: "We know Thee Who Thou art, the Holy One of God" [Luke 4:34]; and, "Ah, what have we to do with Thee, Thou Son of God? I pray Thee, torment me not" [Mark 5:7].

6. As then demons confess Him, and His works bear Him witness day by day, it must be evident, and let none brazen it out against the truth, both that the Saviour raised His own body, and that He is the true Son of God, being from Him, as from His Father, His own Word, and Wisdom, and Power, Who in ages later took a body for the salvation of all, and taught the world concerning the Father, and brought death to nought, and bestowed incorruption upon all by the promise of the Resurrection, having raised His own body as a first-fruits of this, and having displayed it by the sign of the Cross as a monument of victory over death and its corruption.

CHAPTER XXXIII.

UNBELIEF OF JEWS AND SCOFFING OF GREEKS. THE FORMER confounded by their own Scriptures. Prophecies of His coming as God and as Man.

1. THESE things being so, and the Resurrection of His body and the victory gained over death by the Saviour being clearly proved, come now, let us put to rebuke both the disbelief of the Jews and the scoffing of the Gentiles.

2. For these, perhaps, are the points where Jews express incredulity, while Gentiles laugh, finding fault with the unseemliness of the Cross, and of the Word of God becoming man. But our argument shall not delay to grapple with both, especially as the proofs at our command against them are clear as day.

3. For Jews in their incredulity may be refuted from the Scriptures, which even themselves read; for this text and that, and, in a word, the whole inspired Scripture, cries aloud concerning these things, as even its express words abundantly shew. For prophets proclaimed beforehand concerning the wonder of the Virgin and the birth from her, saying: "Lo, the Virgin shall be with child, and shall bring forth a Son, and they shall call his name Emmanuel, which is, being interpreted, God with us" [Matt. 1:23; Isa. 7:14].

4. But Moses, the truly great, and whom they believe to speak truth, with

reference to the Saviour's becoming man, having estimated what was said as important, and assured of its truth, set it down in these words: "There shall rise a star out of Jacob, and a man out of Israel, and he shall break in pieces the captains of Moab" [Num. 24:17]. And again: "How lovely are thy habitations O Jacob, thy tabernacles O Israel, as shadowing gardens, and as parks by the rivers, and as tabernacles which the Lord hath fixed, as cedars by the waters. A man shall come forth out of his seed, and shall be Lord over many peoples" [Num. 24:5–9]. And again, Esaias: "Before the Child know how to call father or mother, he shall take the power of Damascus and the spoils of Samaria before the king of Assyria" [Isa. 8:4].

5. That a man, then, shall appear is foretold in those words. But that He that is to come is Lord of all, they predict once more as follows: "Behold the Lord sitteth upon a light cloud, and shall come into Egypt, and the graven images of Egypt shall be shaken" [Isa. 19:1]. For from thence also it is that the Father calls Him back, saying: "I called My Son out of Egypt" [Hos. 11:1].

CHAPTER XXXIV.

Prophecies of His passion and death in all its circumstances.

1. NOR is even His death passed over in silence: on the contrary, it is referred to in the divine Scriptures, even exceeding clearly. For to the end that none should err for want of instruction in the actual events, they feared not to mention even the cause of His death,—that He suffers it not for His own sake, but for the immortality and salvation of all, and the counsels of the Jews against Him and the indignities offered Him at their hands.

2. They say then: "A man in stripes, and knowing how to bear weakness, for his face is turned away: he was dishonoured and held in no account. He beareth our sins, and is in pain on our account; and we reckoned him to be in labour, and in stripes, and in ill-usage; but he was wounded for our sins, and made weak for our wickedness. The chastisement of our peace was upon him, and by his stripes we were healed" [Isa. 53:3–5]. O marvel at the loving-kindness of the Word, that for our sakes He is dishonoured, that we may be brought to honour. "For all we," it says, "like sheep were gone astray; man had erred in his way; and the Lord delivered him for our sins; and he openeth not his mouth, because he hath been evilly intreated. As a sheep was he brought to the slaughter, and as a lamb dumb before his shearer, so openeth he not his mouth: in his abasement his judgment was taken away"[15] [Isa. 53:6–8].

3. Then lest any should from His suffering conceive Him to be a common

---

[15]Or, "exalted."

man, Holy Writ anticipates the surmises of man, and declares the power (which worked) for Him,[16] and the difference of His nature compared with ourselves saying: "But who shall declare his generation? For his life is taken away from the earth. From the wickedness of the people was he brought to death. And I will give the wicked instead of his burial, and the rich instead of his death; for he did no wickedness, neither was guile found in his mouth. And the Lord will cleanse him from his stripes."

CHAPTER XXXV.

Prophecies of the Cross. How these prophecies are satisfied in Christ alone.

1. BUT, perhaps, having heard the prophecy of His death, you ask to learn also what is set forth concerning the Cross. For not even this is passed over: it is displayed by the holy men with great plainness.

2. For first Moses predicts it, and that with a loud voice, when he says: "Ye shall see[17] your Life hanging before your eyes, and shall not believe."

3. And next, the prophets after him witness of this, saying: "But I as an innocent lamb brought to be slain" [Jer. 11:19], "knew it not; they counselled an evil counsel against me, saying, Hither and let us cast a tree upon his[18] bread, and efface him from the land of the living."

4. And again: "They pierced my hands and my feet, they numbered all my bones . . . they parted my garments among them, and for my vesture they cast lots" [Ps. 22:16–18].

5. Now a death raised aloft, and that takes place on a tree, could be none other than the Cross: and again, in no other death are the hands and feet pierced, save on the Cross only.

6. But since by the sojourn of the Saviour among men all nations also on every side began to know God; they did not leave this point, either, without a reference: but mention is made of this matter as well in the Holy Scriptures. For "there shall be," he saith "the root of Jesse, and he that riseth to rule the nations,

---

[16]τὴν ὑπὲρ αὐτοῦ δύναμιν. The Ben. version simplifies this difficult expression by ignoring the ὑπέρ. Mr. E. N. Bennett has suggested to me that the true reading may be ὑπεράϋλον for ὑπὲρ αὐτοῦ (ὑπεραϋλως in Philo). I would add the suggestion that αὐτοῦ stood after ὑπεράϋλον, and that the similarity of the five letters in MS. caused the second word to be dropped out. 'His exceeding immaterial power' would be the resulting sense. (See Class. Review, 1890, No. iv. p. 182.)

[17]Deut. 28:66, see *Orat.* ii. 16, note 1.

[18]Properly "let us destroy the tree with its bread" (*i.e.* fruit). The Septuagint translates belaḥmô '*upon* his bread,' which is possible in itself; but they either mistook the verb, or followed some wrong reading. Their rendering is followed by all the Latin versions. For a comment on the latter see Tertull. *adv. Marc.* iii. 19, iv. 40.

on him shall the nations hope" [Isa. 11:10]. This then is a little in proof of what has happened.

7. But all Scripture teems with refutations of the disbelief of the Jews. For which of the righteous men and holy prophets, and patriarchs, recorded in the divine Scriptures, ever had his corporal birth of a virgin only? Or what woman has sufficed without man for the conception of human kind? Was not Abel born of Adam, Enoch of Jared, Noe of Lamech, and Abraham of Tharra, Isaac of Abraham, Jacob of Isaac? Was not Judas born of Jacob, and Moses and Aaron of Ameram? Was not Samuel born of Elkana, was not David of Jesse, was not Solomon of David, was not Ezechias of Achaz, was not Josias of Amos, was not Esaias of Amos, was not Jeremy of Chelchias, was not Ezechiel of Buzi? Had not each a father as author of his existence? Who then is he that is born of a virgin only? For the prophet made exceeding much of this sign.

8. Or whose birth did a star in the skies forerun, to announce to the world him that was born? For when Moses was born, he was hid by his parents: David was not heard of, even by those of his neighbourhood, inasmuch as even the great Samuel knew him not, but asked, had Jesse yet another son? Abraham again became known to his neighbours as[19] a great man only subsequently to his birth. But of Christ's birth the witness was not man, but a star in that heaven whence He was descending.

CHAPTER XXXVI.

Prophecies of Christ's sovereignty, flight into Egypt, etc.

1. BUT what king that ever was, before he had strength to call father or mother, reigned and gained triumphs over his enemies?[20] Did not David come to the throne at thirty years of age, and Solomon, when he had grown to be a young man? Did not Joas enter on the kingdom when seven years old, and Josias, a still later king, receive the government about the seventh year of his age? And yet they at that age had strength to call father or mother.

2. Who, then, is there that was reigning and spoiling his enemies almost before his birth? Or what king of this sort has ever been in Israel and in Juda—let the Jews, who have searched out the matter, tell us—in whom all the nations have placed their hopes and had peace, instead of being at enmity with them on every side?

3. For as long as Jerusalem stood there was war without respite betwixt them, and they all fought with Israel; the Assyrians oppressed them, the Egyp-

---

[19]Or 'only after he had grown great,' i.e. to man's estate.
[20]Isa. 8:4, where note Septuagint.

tians persecuted them, the Babylonians fell upon them; and, strange to say, they had even the Syrians their neighbours at war against them. Or did not David war against them of Moab, and smite the Syrians, Josias guard against his neighbours, and Ezechias quail at the boasting of Senacherim, and Amalek make war against Moses, and the Amorites oppose him, and the inhabitants of Jericho array themselves against Jesus son of Naue? And, in a word, treaties of friendship had no place between the nations and Israel. Who, then, it is on whom the nations are to set their hope, it is worth while to see. For there must be such an one, as it is impossible for the prophet to have spoken falsely.

4. But which of the holy prophets or of the early patriarchs has died on the Cross for the salvation of all? Or who was wounded and destroyed for the healing of all? Or which of the righteous men, or kings, went down to Egypt, so that at his coming the idols of Egypt fell?[21] For Abraham went thither, but idolatry prevailed universally all the same. Moses was born there, and the deluded worship of the people was there none the less.

CHAPTER XXXVII.
Psalm 22:16, etc. Majesty of His birth and death. Confusion of oracles and demons in Egypt.

1. OR who among those recorded in Scripture was pierced in the hands and feet, or hung at all upon a tree, and was sacrificed on a cross for the salvation of all? For Abraham died, ending his life on a bed; Isaac and Jacob also died with their feet raised on a bed; Moses and Aaron died on the mountain; David in his house, without being the object of any conspiracy at the hands of the people; true, he was pursued by Saul, but he was preserved unhurt. Esaias was sawn asunder, but not hung on a tree. Jeremy was shamefully treated, but did not die under condemnation; Ezechiel suffered, not however for the people, but to indicate what was to come upon the people.

2. Again, these, even where they suffered, were men resembling all in their common nature; but he that is declared in Scripture to suffer on behalf of all is called not merely man, but the Life of all, albeit He was in fact like men in nature. For "ye shall see," it says, "your Life hanging before your eyes;" [Deut. 28:66] and "who shall declare his generation?" [Isa. 53:8]. For one can ascertain the genealogy of all the saints, and declare it from the beginning, and of whom each was born; but the generation of Him that is the Life the Scriptures refer to as not to be declared.

3. Who then is he of whom the Divine Scriptures say this? Or who is so

---

[21]Cf. *Letter* 61.4.

great that even the prophets predict of him such great things? None else, now, is found in the Scriptures but the common Saviour of all, the Word of God, our Lord Jesus Christ. For He it is that proceeded from a virgin and appeared as man on the earth, and whose generation after the flesh cannot be declared. For there is none that can tell His father after the flesh, His body not being of a man, but of a virgin alone;

4. so that no one can declare the corporal generation of the Saviour from a man, in the same way as one can draw up a genealogy of David and of Moses and of all the patriarchs. For He it is that caused the star also to mark the birth of His body; since it was fit that the Word, coming down from heaven, should have His constellation also from heaven, and it was fitting that the King of Creation when He came forth should be openly recognized by all creation.

5. Why, He was born in Judea, and men from Persia came to worship Him. He it is that even before His appearing in the body won the victory over His demon adversaries and a triumph over idolatry. All heathen at any rate from every region, abjuring their hereditary tradition and the impiety of idols, are now placing their hope in Christ, and enrolling themselves under Him, the like of which you may see with your own eyes.

6. For at no other time has the impiety of the Egyptians ceased, save when the Lord of all, riding as it were upon a cloud, came down there in the body and brought to nought the delusion of idols, and brought over all to Himself, and through Himself to the Father.

7. He it is that was crucified before the sun and all creation as witnesses, and before those who put Him to death: and by His death has salvation come to all, and all creation been ransomed. He is the Life of all, and He it is that as a sheep yielded His body to death as a substitute, for the salvation of all, even though the Jews believe it not.

CHAPTER XXXVIII.

Other clear prophecies of the coming of God in the flesh. Christ's miracles unprecedented.

1. FOR if they do not think these proofs sufficient, let them be persuaded at any rate by other reasons, drawn from the oracles they themselves possess. For of whom do the prophets say: "I was made manifest to them that sought me not, I was found of them that asked not for me: I said Behold, here am I, to the nation that had not called upon my name; I stretched out my hands to a disobedient and gainsaying people" [Isa. 65:1–2; Rom. 10:20–21].

2. Who, then, one might say to the Jews, is he that was made manifest? For if it is the prophet, let them say when he was hid, afterward to appear again. And what manner of prophet is this, that was not only made manifest from obscurity,

but also stretched out his hands on the Cross? None surely of the righteous, save the Word of God only, Who, incorporeal by nature, appeared for our sakes in the body and suffered for all.

3. Or if not even this is sufficient for them, let them at least be silenced by another proof, seeing how clear its demonstrative force is. For the Scripture says: "Be strong ye hands that hang down, and feeble knees; comfort ye, ye of faint mind; be strong, fear not. Behold, our God recompenseth judgment; He shall come and save us. Then shall the eyes of the blind be opened, and the ears of the deaf shall hear; then shall the lame man leap as an hart, and the tongue of the stammerers shall be plain" [Isa. 35:3–6].

4. Now what can they say to this, or how can they dare to face this at all? For the prophecy not only indicates that God is to sojourn here, but it announces the signs and the time of His coming. For they connect the blind recovering their sight, and the lame walking, and the deaf hearing, and the tongue of the stammerers being made plain, with the Divine Coming which is to take place. Let them say, then, when such signs have come to pass in Israel, or where in Jewry anything of the sort has occurred.

5. Naaman, a leper, was cleansed, but no deaf man heard nor lame walked. Elias raised a dead man; so did Eliseus; but none blind from birth regained his sight. For in good truth, to raise a dead man is a great thing, but it is not like the wonder wrought by the Saviour. Only, if Scripture has not passed over the case of the leper, and of the dead son of the widow, certainly, had it come to pass that a lame man also had walked and a blind man recovered his sight, the narrative would not have omitted to mention this also. Since then nothing is said in the Scriptures, it is evident that these things had never taken place before.

6. When, then, have they taken place, save when the Word of God Himself came in the body? Or when did He come, if not when lame men walked, and stammerers were made to speak plain, and deaf men heard, and men blind from birth regained their sight? For this was the very thing the Jews said who then witnessed it, because they had not heard of these things having taken place at any other time: "Since the world began it was never heard that any one opened the eyes of a man born blind. If this man were not from God, He could do nothing" [John 9:32–33].

CHAPTER XXXIX.

Do you look for another? But Daniel foretells the exact time. Objections to this removed.

1. BUT perhaps, being unable, even they, to fight continually against plain facts, they will, without denying what is written, maintain that they are looking for these things, and that the Word of God is not yet come. For this it is on

which they are for ever harping, not blushing to brazen it out in the face of plain facts.

2. But on this one point, above all, they shall be all the more refuted, not at our hands, but at those of the most wise Daniel, who marks both the actual date, and the divine sojourn of the Saviour, saying: "Seventy weeks are cut short upon thy people, and upon the holy city, for a full end to be made of sin, and for sins to be sealed up, and to blot out iniquities, and to make atonement for iniquities, and to bring everlasting righteousness, and to seal vision and prophet, and to anoint a Holy of Holies; and thou shalt know and understand from the going forth of the word to restore[22] and to build Jerusalem unto Christ the Prince" [Dan. 9:24–25].

3. Perhaps with regard to the other (prophecies) they may be able even to find excuses and to put off what is written to a future time. But what can they say to this, or can they face it at all? Where not only is the Christ referred to, but He that is to be anointed is declared to be not man simply, but Holy of Holies; and Jerusalem is to stand till His coming, and thenceforth, prophet and vision cease in Israel.

4. David was anointed of old, and Solomon and Ezechias; but then, nevertheless, Jerusalem and the place stood, and prophets were prophesying: Gad and Asaph and Nathan; and, later, Esaias and Osee and Amos and others. And again, the actual men that were anointed were called holy, and not Holy of Holies.

5. But if they shield themselves with the captivity, and say that because of it Jerusalem was not, what can they say about the prophets too? For in fact when first the people went down to Babylon, Daniel and Jeremy were there, and Ezechiel and Aggaeus and Zachary were prophesying.

CHAPTER XL.

Argument (1) from the withdrawal of prophecy and destruction of Jerusalem, (2) from the conversion of the Gentiles, and that to the God of Moses. What more remains for the Messiah to do, that Christ has not done?

1. SO the Jews are trifling, and the time in question, which they refer to the future, is actually come. For when did prophet and vision cease from Israel, save when Christ came, the Holy of Holies? For it is a sign, and an important proof, of the coming of the Word of God, that Jerusalem no longer stands, nor is any prophet raised up nor vision revealed to them,—and that very naturally.

---

[22]Lit. "answer," a misrendering of the Hebrew.

2. For when He that was signified was come, what need was there any longer of any to signify Him? When the truth was there, what need any more of the shadow? For this was the reason of their prophesying at all,—namely, till the true Righteousness should come, and He that was to ransom the sins of all. And this was why Jerusalem stood till then—namely, that there they might be exercised in the types as a preparation for the reality.

3. So when the Holy of Holies was come, naturally vision and prophecy were sealed and the kingdom of Jerusalem ceased. For kings were to be anointed among them only until the Holy of Holies should have been anointed; and Jacob prophesies that the kingdom of the Jews should be established until Him, as follows:—"The ruler shall not fail from Juda, nor the Prince from his loins, until that which is laid up for him shall come; and he is the expectation of the nations" [Gen. 49:10].

4. Whence the Saviour also Himself cried aloud and said: "The law and the prophets prophesied until John" [Matt. 11:13; Luke 16:16]. If then there is now among the Jews king or prophet or vision, they do well to deny the Christ that is come. But if there is neither king nor vision, but from that time forth all prophecy is sealed and the city and temple taken, why are they so irreligious and so perverse as to see what has happened, and yet to deny Christ, Who has brought it all to pass? Or why, when they see even heathens deserting their idols, and placing their hope, through Christ, on the God of Israel, do they deny Christ, Who was born of the root of Jesse after the flesh and henceforth is King? For if the nations were worshipping some other God, and not confessing the God of Abraham and Isaac and Jacob and Moses, then, once more, they would be doing well in alleging that God had not come.

5. But if the Gentiles are honouring the same God that gave the law to Moses and made the promise to Abraham, and Whose word the Jews dishonoured,—why are they ignorant, or rather why do they choose to ignore, that the Lord foretold by the Scriptures has shone forth upon the world, and appeared to it in bodily form, as the Scripture said: "The Lord God hath shined upon us;"[23] and again: "He sent His Word and healed them" [Ps. 107:20]; and again: "Not a messenger, not an angel, but the Lord Himself saved them?"[24]

6. Their state may be compared to that of one out of his right mind, who sees the earth illumined by the sun, but denies the sun that illumines it. For what more is there for him whom they expect to do, when he is come? To call the heathen? But they are called already. To make prophecy, and king, and vision to cease? This too has already come to pass. To expose the godlessness of

---

[23]Cf. Ps. 118:27, and for the literal sense, Num. 6:25.
[24]Isa. 63:9 (Septuagint), and the note in the (Queen's Printers') 'Varlorum' Bible.

idolatry? It is already exposed and condemned. Or to destroy death? He is already destroyed.

7. What then has not come to pass, that the Christ must do? What is left unfulfilled, that the Jews should now disbelieve with impunity? For if, I say,—which is just what we actually see,—there is no longer king nor prophet nor Jerusalem nor sacrifice nor vision among them, but even the whole earth is filled with the knowledge of God, and gentiles, leaving their godlessness, are now taking refuge with the God of Abraham, through the Word, even our Lord Jesus Christ, then it must be plain, even to those who are exceedingly obstinate, that the Christ is come, and that He has illumined absolutely all with His light, and given them the true and divine teaching concerning His Father.

8. So one can fairly refute the Jews by these and by other arguments from the Divine Scriptures.

CHAPTER XLI.

ANSWER TO THE GREEKS. *Do they recognise the Logos? If He manifests Himself in the organism of the Universe, why not in one Body? For a human body is a part of the same whole.*

1. BUT one cannot but be utterly astonished at the Gentiles, who, while they laugh at what is no matter for jesting, are themselves insensible to their own disgrace, which they do not see that they have set up in the shape of stocks and stones.

2. Only, as our argument is not lacking in demonstrative proof, come let us put them also to shame on reasonable grounds,—mainly from what we ourselves also see. For what is there on our side that is absurd, or worthy of derision? Is it merely our saying that the Word has been made manifest in the body? But this even they will join in owning to have happened without any absurdity, if they shew themselves friends of truth.

3. If then they deny that there is a Word of God at all, they do so gratuitously,[25] jesting at what they know not.

4. But if they confess that there is a Word of God, and He ruler of the universe, and that in Him the Father has produced the creation, and that by His Providence the whole receives light and life and being, and that He reigns over all, so that from the works of His providence He is known, and through Him the

---

[25]Athan. here assumes, for the purpose of his argument, the principles of the Neo-platonist schools. They were influenced, in regard to the Logos, by Philo, but even on this subject the germ of their teaching may be traced in Plato, especially in the *Timaeus*, (See Drummond's *Philo.* i. 65–88, Bigg's *Bamp. Lect.* 14, 18, 248–253, and St. Aug. *Confess.* in 'Nicene Fathers,' Series 1, vol. 1, p. 107 and notes.)

Father,—consider, I pray you, whether they be not unwittingly raising the jest against themselves.

5. The philosophers of the Greeks say that the universe is a great body;[26] and rightly so. For we see it and its parts as objects of our senses. If, then, the Word of God is in the Universe, which is a body, and has united Himself with the whole and with all its parts, what is there surprising or absurd if we say that He has united Himself[27] with man also.

6. For if it were absurd for Him to have been in a body at all, it would be absurd for Him to be united with the whole either, and to be giving light and movement to all things by His providence. For the whole also is a body.

7. But if it beseems Him to unite Himself with the universe, and to be made known in the whole, it must beseem Him also to appear in a human body, and that by Him it should be illumined and work. For mankind is part of the whole as well as the rest. And if it be unseemly for a part to have been adopted as His instrument to teach men of His Godhead, it must be most absurd that He should be made known even by the whole universe.

CHAPTER XLII.

His union with the body is based upon His relation to Creation as a whole. He used a human body, since to man it was that He wished to reveal Himself.

1. FOR just as, while the whole body is quickened and illumined by man, supposing one said it were absurd that man's power should also be in the toe, he would be thought foolish; because, while granting that he pervades and works in the whole, he demurs to his being in the part also; thus he who grants and believes that the Word of God is in the whole Universe, and that the whole is illumined and moved by Him, should not think it absurd that a single human body also should receive movement and light from Him.

2. But if it is because the human race is a thing created and has been made out of nothing, that they regard that manifestation of the Saviour in man, which we speak of, as not seemly, it is high time for them to eject Him from creation also; for it too has been brought into existence by the Word out of nothing.

3. But if, even though creation be a thing made, it is not absurd that the Word should be in it, then neither is it absurd that He should be in man. For

---

[26]Especially Plato, *Tim.* 30, etc.

[27]ἐπιβεβηκέναι. The Union of God and Man in Christ is of course 'hypostatic' or personal, and thus different in kind from the union of the Word with Creation. His argument is *ad homines*. It was not for thinkers who identified the Universe with God to take exception to the idea of Incarnation.

whatever idea they form of the whole, they must necessarily apply the like idea to the part. For man also, as I said before, is a part of the whole.

4. Thus it is not at all unseemly that the Word should be in man, while all things are deriving from Him their light and movement and light, as also their authors say, "In him we live and move and have our being" [Acts 17:28].

5. So, then, what is there to scoff at in what we say, if the Word has used that, wherein He is, as an instrument to manifest Himself? For were He not in it, neither could He have used it; but if we have previously allowed that He is in the whole and in its parts, what is there incredible in His manifesting Himself in that wherein He is?

6. For by His own power He is united[28] wholly with each and all, and orders all things without stint, so that no one could have called it out of place for Him to speak, and make known Himself and His Father, by means of sun, if He so willed, or moon, or heaven, or earth, or waters, or fire;[29] inasmuch as He holds in one all things at once, and is in fact not only in all, but also in the part in question, and there invisibly manifests Himself. In like manner, it cannot be absurd if, ordering as He does the whole, and giving life to all things, and having willed to make Himself known through men, He has used as His instrument a human body to manifest the truth and knowledge of the Father. For humanity, too, is an actual part of the whole.

7. And as Mind, pervading man all through, is interpreted by a part of the body, I mean the tongue, without any one saying, I suppose, that the essence of the mind is on that account lowered, so if the Word, pervading all things, has used a human instrument, this cannot appear unseemly. For, as I have said previously, if it be unseemly to have used a body as an instrument, it is unseemly also for Him to be in the Whole.

CHAPTER XLIII.

He came in human rather than in any nobler form, because (1) He came to save, not to impress; (2) Man alone of creatures had sinned. As men would not recognise His works in the Universe, He came and worked among them as Man; in the sphere to which they had limited themselves.

1. NOW, if they ask, Why then did He not appear by means of other and nobler parts of creation, and use some nobler instrument, as the sun, or moon, or stars, or fire, or air, instead of man merely? let them know that the Lord came not to make a display, but to heal and teach those who were suffering.

---

[28]ἐπιβαίνων, see supra, note 24.
[29]The superfluous πεποιηκέναι is ignored, being untranslateable as the text stands. For a less simple conjecture, see the Bened. note.

2. For the way for one aiming at display would be, just to appear, and to dazzle the beholders; but for one seeking to heal and teach the way is, not simply to sojourn here, but to give himself to the aid of those in want, and to appear as they who need him can bear it; that he may not, by exceeding the requirements of the sufferers, trouble the very persons that need him, rendering God's appearance useless to them.

3. Now, nothing in creation had gone astray with regard to their notions of God, save man only. Why, neither sun, nor moon, nor heaven, nor the stars, nor water, nor air had swerved from their order; but knowing their Artificer and Sovereign, the Word, they remain as they were made.[30] But men alone, having rejected what was good, then devised things of nought instead of the truth, and have ascribed the honour due to God, and their knowledge of Him, to demons and men in the shape of stones.

4. With reason, then, since it were unworthy of the Divine Goodness to overlook so grave a matter, while yet men were not able to recognise Him as ordering and guiding the whole, He takes to Himself as an instrument a part of the whole, His human body, and unites[31] Himself with that, in order that since men could not recognise Him in the whole, they should not fail to know Him in the part; and since they could not look up to His invisible power, might be able, at any rate, from what resembled themselves to reason to Him and to contemplate Him.

5. For, men as they are, they will be able to know His Father more quickly and directly by a body of like nature and by the divine works wrought through it, judging by comparison that they are not human, but the works of God, which are done by Him.

6. And if it were absurd, as they say, for the Word to be known through the works of the body, it would likewise be absurd for Him to be known through the works of the universe. For just as He is in creation, and yet does not partake of its nature in the least degree, but rather all things partake[32] of His power; so while He used the body as His instrument He partook of no corporeal property, but, on the contrary, Himself sanctified even the body.

---

[30]This thought is beautifully expressed by Keble:—
'All true, all faultless, all in tune, Creation's wondrous choir
Opened in mystic unison, to last till time expire.
And still it lasts: by day and night with one consenting voice
All hymn Thy glory, Lord, aright, all worship and rejoice:
Man only mars the sweet accord'. . . .
('Christian Year,' Fourth Sunday after Trinity.)
[31]Cf. 41.5, note 27.
[32]Cf. Orig. *c. Cels.* vi.64, where there is the same contrast between μετέχειν and μετέχεσθαι.

7. For if even Plato, who is in such repute among the Greeks, says[33] that its author, beholding the universe tempest-tossed, and in peril of going down to the place of chaos, takes his seat at the helm of the soul and comes to the rescue and corrects all its calamities; what is there incredible in what we say, that mankind being in error, the Word lighted down[34] upon it and appeared as man, that He might save it in its tempest by His guidance and goodness?

CHAPTER XLIV.

As God made man by a word, why not restore him by a word? But (1) creation out of nothing is different from reparation of what already exists. (2) Man was there with a definite need, calling for a definite remedy. Death was ingrained in man's nature: He then must wind life closely to human nature. Therefore the Word became Incarnate that He might meet and conquer death in His usurped territory. (Simile of straw and asbestos.)

1. BUT perhaps, shamed into agreeing with this, they will choose to say that God, if He wished to reform and to save mankind, ought to have done so by a mere fiat,[35] without His word taking a body, in just the same way as He did formerly, when He produced them out of nothing.

2. To this objection of theirs a reasonable answer would be: that formerly, nothing being in existence at all, what was needed to make everything was a fiat and the bare will to do so. But when man had once been made, and necessity demanded a cure, not for things that were not, but for things that had come to be, it was naturally consequent that the Physician and Saviour should appear in what had come to be, in order also to cure the things that were. For this cause, then, He has become man, and used His body as a human instrument.

3. For if this were not the right way, how was the Word, choosing to use an instrument, to appear? or whence was He to take it, save from those already in being, and in need of His Godhead by means of one like themselves? For it was not things without being that needed salvation, so that a bare command should suffice, but man, already in existence, was going to corruption and ruin.[36] It was then natural and right that the Word should use a human instrument and reveal Himself everywhither.

4. Secondly, you must know this also, that the corruption which had set in

---

[33]Ath. paraphrases loosely Plat. *Politic.* 273 D. See Jowett's Plato (ed. 2), vol. iv. pp. · 515, 553.

[34]Lit. "sate down," as three lines above.

[35]With this discussion compare that upon 'repentance' above 7. (esp. 7. note 33).

[36]Restoration by a mere fiat would have shewn God's *power*, the Incarnation shews His *Love*. See *Orat.* i.52, note 1, ii.68, note 1.

was not external to the body, but had become attached to it; and it was required that, instead of corruption, life should cleave to it; so that, just as death has been engendered in the body, so life may be engendered in it also.

5. Now if death were external to the body, it would be proper for life also to have been engendered externally to it. But if death was wound closely to the body and was ruling over it as though united to it, it was required that life also should be wound closely to the body, that so the body, by putting on life in its stead, should cast off corruption. Besides, even supposing that the Word had come outside the body, and not in it, death would indeed have been defeated by Him, in perfect accordance with nature, inasmuch as death has no power against the Life; but the corruption attached to the body would have remained in it none the less.[37]

6. For this cause the Saviour reasonably put on Him a body, in order that the body, becoming wound closely to the Life, should no longer, as mortal, abide in death, but, as having put on immortality, should thenceforth rise again and remain immortal. For, once it had put on corruption, it could not have risen again unless it had put on life. And death likewise could not, from its very nature, appear, save in the body. Therefore He put on a body, that He might find death in the body, and blot it out. For how could the Lord have been proved at all to be the Life, had He not quickened what was mortal?

7. And just as, whereas stubble is naturally destructible by fire, supposing (firstly) a man keeps fire away from the stubble, though it is not burned, yet the stubble remains, for all that, merely stubble, fearing the threat of the fire—for fire has the natural property of consuming it; while if a man (secondly) encloses it with a quantity of asbestos, the substance said[38] to be an antidote to fire, the stubble no longer dreads the fire, being secured by its enclosure in incombustible matter;

8. in this very way one may say, with regard to the body and death, that if death had been kept from the body by a mere command on His part, it would none the less have been mortal and corruptible, according to the nature of bodies; but, that this should not be, it put on the incorporeal Word of God, and thus no longer fears either death or corruption, for it has life as a garment, and corruption is done away in it.

CHAPTER XLV.

Thus once again every part of creation manifests the glory of God. Nature, the witness to her Creator, yields (by miracles) a second testimony to God Incarnate.

---

[37]Cf. *Orat.* i.56, note 5, 65, note 3.
[38]He appears not to have seen the substance.

The witness of Nature, perverted by man's sin, was thus forced back to truth. If these reasons suffice not, let the Greeks look at facts.

1. CONSISTENTLY, therefore, the Word of God took a body and has made use of a human instrument, in order to quicken the body also, and as He is known in creation by His works so to work in man as well, and to shew Himself everywhere, leaving nothing void of His own divinity, and of the knowledge of Him.

2. For I resume, and repeat what I said before, that the Saviour did this in order that, as He fills all things on all sides by His presence, so also He might fill all things with the knowledge of Him, as the divine Scripture also says: "The whole earth was filled with the knowledge of the Lord."[39]

3. For if a man will but look up to heaven, he sees its Order, or if he cannot raise his face to heaven, but only to man, he sees His power, beyond comparison with that of men, shewn by His works, and learns that He alone among men is God the Word. Or if a man is gone astray among demons, and is in fear of them, he may see this man drive them out, and make up his mind that He is their Master. Or if a man has sunk to the waters,[40] and thinks that they are God,—as the Egyptians, for instance, reverence the water,—he may see its nature changed by Him, and learn that the Lord is Creator of the waters.

4. But if a man is gone down even to Hades, and stands in awe of the heroes who have descended thither, regarding them as gods, yet he may see the fact of Christ's Resurrection and victory over death, and infer that among them also Christ alone is true God and Lord.

5. For the Lord touched all parts of creation, and freed and undeceived all of them from every illusion; as Paul says: "Having put off from Himself the principalities and the powers, He triumphed on the Cross" [Col. 2:15]: that no one might by any possibility be any longer deceived, but everywhere might find the true Word of God.

6. For thus man, shut in on every side,[41] and beholding the divinity of the Word unfolded everywhere, that is, in heaven, in Hades, in man, upon earth, is no longer exposed to deceit concerning God, but is to worship Christ alone, and through Him come rightly to know the Father.

7. By these arguments, then, on grounds of reason, the Gentiles in their turn will fairly be put to shame by us. But if they deem the arguments insufficient

---

[39]Isa. 11:9.
[40]See Döllinger, *Gentile and Jew*, i.449.
[41]The Incarnation completes the circle of God's self-witness and of man's responsibility.

to shame them, let them be assured of what we are saying at any rate by facts obvious to the sight of all.

CHAPTER XLVI.

Discredit, from the date of the Incarnation, of idol-cultus, oracles, mythologies, demoniacal energy, magic, and Gentile philosophy. And whereas the old cults were strictly local and independent, the worship of Christ is catholic and uniform.

1. WHEN did men begin to desert the worshipping of idols, save since God, the true Word of God, has come among men? Or when have the oracles among the Greeks, and everywhere, ceased and become empty, save when the Saviour has manifested Himself upon earth?

2. Or when did those who are called gods and heroes in the poets begin to be convicted of being merely mortal men,[42] save since the Lord effected His conquest of death, and preserved incorruptible the body he had taken, raising it from the dead?

3. Or when did the deceitfulness and madness of demons fall into contempt, save when the power of God, the Word, the Master of all these as well, condescending because of man's weakness, appeared on earth? Or when[43] did the art and the schools of magic begin to be trodden down, save when the divine manifestation of the Word took place among men?

4. And, in a word, at what time has the wisdom of the Greeks become foolish, save when the true Wisdom of God manifested itself on earth? For formerly the whole world and every place was led astray by the worshipping of idols, and men regarded nothing else but the idols as gods. But now, all the world over, men are deserting the superstition of the idols, and taking refuge with Christ; and, worshipping Him as God, are by His means coming to know that Father also Whom they knew not.

5. And, marvellous fact, whereas the objects of worship were various and of vast number, and each place had its own idol, and he who was accounted a god among them had no power to pass over to the neighbouring place, so as to persuade those of neighbouring peoples to worship him, but was barely served even among his own people; for no one else worshipped his neighbour's god—on the contrary, each man kept to his own idol,[44] thinking it to be lord of all;—Christ alone is worshipped as one and the same among all peoples; and what the

---

[42]Cf. notes on *c. Gent.* 10, and 12.2.

[43]On the following argument see Döllinger ii.—240 *sqq.*, and Bigg. *Bampt. Lect.* 248, note 1.

[44]On the local character of ancient religions, see Döllinger i.109, etc., and Coulanges, *La Cité Antique*, Book III. ch. vi., and V. iii (the substance in Barker's *Aryan Civilisation*).

weakness of the idols could not do—to persuade, namely, even those dwelling close at hand,—this Christ has done, persuading not only those close at hand, but simply the entire world, to worship one and the same Lord, and through Him God, even His Father.

CHAPTER XLVII.

The numerous oracles,—fancied apparitions in sacred places, etc., dispelled by the sign of the Cross. The old gods prove to have been mere men. Magic is exposed. And whereas Philosophy could only persuade select and local cliques of Immortality and goodness,—men of little intellect have infused into the multitudes of the churches the principle of supernatural life.

1. AND whereas formerly every place was full of the deceit of the oracles,[45] and the oracles at Delphi and Dodona, and in Boeotia[46] and Lycia[47] and Libya[48] and Egypt and those of the Cabiri,[49] and the Pythoness, were held in repute by men's imagination, now, since Christ has begun to be preached everywhere, their madness also has ceased and there is none among them to divine any more.

2. And whereas formerly demons used to deceive[50] men's fancy, occupying springs or rivers, trees or stones, and thus imposed upon the simple by their juggleries; now, after the divine visitation of the Word, their deception has ceased. For by the Sign of the Cross, though a man but use it, he drives out their deceits.

3. And while formerly men held to be gods the Zeus and Cronos and Apollo and the heroes mentioned in the poets, and went astray in honouring them; now that the Saviour has appeared among men, those others have been exposed as mortal men,[51] and Christ alone has been recognised among men as the true God, the Word of God.

4. And what is one to say of the magic[52] esteemed among them? that before the Word sojourned among us this was strong and active among Egyptians, and Chaldees, and Indians, and inspired awe in those who saw it; but that by the presence of the Truth, and the Appearing of the Word, it also has been thoroughly confuted, and brought wholly to nought.

---

[45]On these, see Döllinger, i.216, etc., and Milton's *Ode on the Nativity*, stanza xix.
[46]i.e. that of Trophonius.
[47]Patara.
[48]Ammon.
[49]See Döllinger, i.73, 164–70: the Cabiri were pre-Hellenic deities, worshipped in many ancient sanctuaries, but principally in Samothrace and Lemnos.
[50]Cf. *Vit. Ant.* xvi.–xliii., also Döllinger ii.212, and a curious catena of extracts from early Fathers, collected by Hurter in 'Opuscula S.S. Patrum Selecta,' vol. 1, appendix.
[51]For this opinion, see note 1 on *c. Gent.* 12.
[52]See Döllinger, ii.210, and (on Julian) 215.

5. But as to Gentile wisdom, and the sounding pretensions of the philosophers, I think none can need our argument, since the wonder is before the eyes of all, that while the wise among the Greeks had written so much, and were unable to persuade even a few[53] from their own neighbourhood, concerning immortality and a virtuous life, Christ alone, by ordinary language, and by men not clever with the tongue, has throughout all the world persuaded whole churches full of men to despise death, and to mind the things of immortality; to overlook what is temporal and to turn their eyes to what is eternal; to think nothing of earthly glory and to strive only for the heavenly.

CHAPTER XLVIII.

Further facts. Christian continence of virgins and ascetics. Martyrs. The power of the Cross against demons and magic. Christ by His Power shews Himself more than a man, more than a magician, more than a spirit. For all these are totally subject to Him. Therefore He is the Word of God.

1. NOW these arguments of ours do not amount merely to words, but have in actual experience a witness to their truth.

2. For let him that will, go up and behold the proof of virtue in the virgins of Christ and in the young men that practise holy chastity,[54] and the assurance of immortality in so great a band of His martyrs.

3. And let him come who would test by experience what we have now said, and in the very presence of the deceit of demons and the imposture of oracles and the marvels of magic, let him use the Sign of that Cross which is laughed at among them, and he shall see how by its means demons fly, oracles cease, all magic and witchcraft is brought to nought.

4. Who, then, and how great is this Christ, Who by His own Name and Presence casts into the shade and brings to nought all things on every side, and is alone strong against all, and has filled the whole world with His teaching? Let the Greeks tell us, who are pleased to laugh, and blush not.

5. For if He is a man, how then has one man exceeded the power of all whom even themselves hold to be gods, and convicted them by His own power of being nothing? But if they call Him a magician, how can it be that by a magician all magic is destroyed, instead of being confirmed? For if He conquered particular magicians, or prevailed over one only, it would be proper for them to hold that He excelled the rest by superior skill;

---

[53]In Plato's ideal Republic, the notion of any direct influence of the highest ideals upon the masses is quite absent. Their happiness is to be in passive obedience to the few whom those ideals inspire. (Contrast Isa. 54:13, Jer. 31:34.)

[54]Cf. *Hist. Arian.* 25, *Apol. Const.* 33.

6. but if His Cross has won the victory over absolutely all magic, and over the very name of it, it must be plain that the Saviour is not a magician, seeing that even those demons who are invoked by the other magicians fly from Him as their Master.

7. Who He is, then, let the Greeks tell us, whose only serious pursuit is jesting. Perhaps they might say that He, too, was a demon, and hence His strength. But say this as they will, they will have the laugh against them, for they can once more be put to shame by our former proofs. For how is it possible that He should be a demon who drives the demons out?

8. For if He simply drove out particular demons, it might properly be held that by the chief of demons He prevailed against the lesser, just as the Jews said to Him when they wished to insult Him. But if, by His Name being named, all madness of the demons is uprooted and chased away, it must be evident that here, too, they are wrong, and that our Lord and Saviour Christ is not, as they think, some demoniacal power.

9. Then, if the Saviour is neither a man simply, nor a magician, nor some demon, but has by His own Godhead brought to nought and cast into the shade both the doctrine found in the poets and the delusion of the demons and the wisdom of the Gentiles, it must be plain and will be owned by all, that this is the true Son of God, even the Word and Wisdom and Power of the Father from the beginning. For this is why His works also are no works of man, but are recognised to be above man, and truly God's works, both from the facts in themselves, and from comparison with [the rest of] mankind.

CHAPTER XLIX.

His Birth and Miracles. You call Asclepius, Heracles, and Dionysus gods for their works. Contrast their works with His, and the wonders at His death, etc.

1. FOR what man, that ever was born, formed a body for himself from a virgin alone? Or what man ever healed such diseases as the common Lord of all? Or who has restored what was wanting to man's nature, and made one blind from his birth to see?

2. Asclepius was deified among them, because he practised medicine and found out herbs for bodies that were sick; not forming them himself out of the earth, but discovering them by science drawn from nature. But what is this to what was done by the Saviour, in that, instead of healing a wound, He modified a man's original nature, and restored the body whole.

3. Heracles is worshipped as a god among the Greeks because he fought against men, his peers, and destroyed wild beasts by guile. What is this to what was done by the Word, in driving away from man diseases and demons and death itself? Dionysus is worshipped among them because he has taught man drunken-

ness; but the true Saviour and Lord of all, for teaching temperance, is mocked by these people.

4. But let these matters pass. What will they say to the other miracles of His Godhead? At what man's death was the sun darkened and the earth shaken? Lo even to this day men are dying, and they died also of old. When did any such-like wonder happen in their case?

5. Or, to pass over the deeds done through His body, and mention those after its rising again: what man's doctrine that ever was has prevailed everywhere, one and the same, from one end of the earth to the other, so that his worship has winged its way through every land?

6. Or why, if Christ is, as they say, a man, and not God the Word, is not His worship prevented by the gods they have from passing into the same land where they are? Or why on the contrary does the Word Himself, sojourning here, by His teaching stop their worship and put their deception to shame? .

CHAPTER L.

Impotence and rivalries of the Sophists put to shame by the Death of Christ. His Resurrection unparalleled even in Greek legend.

1. MANY before this Man have been kings and tyrants of the world, many are on record who have been wise men and magicians, among the Chaldeans and Egyptians and Indians; which of these, I say, not after death, but while still alive, was ever able so far to prevail as to fill the whole earth with his teaching and reform so great a multitude from the superstition of idols, as our Saviour has brought over from idols to Himself?

2. The philosophers of the Greeks have composed many works with plausibility and verbal skill; what result, then, have they exhibited so great as has the Cross of Christ? For the refinements they taught were plausible enough till they died; but even the influence they seemed to have while alive was subject to their mutual rivalries; and they were emulous, and declaimed against one another.

3. But the Word of God, most strange fact, teaching in meaner language, has cast into the shade the choice sophists; and while He has, by drawing all to Himself, brought their schools to nought, He has filled His own churches; and the marvellous thing is, that by going down as man to death, He has brought to nought the sounding utterances of the wise[55] concerning idols.

4. For whose death ever drove out demons? or whose death did demons ever fear, as they did that of Christ? For where the Saviour's name is named, there every demon is driven out. Or who has so rid men of the passions of the natural

---

[55]*e.g.* Iamblichus, etc., cf. Introd. to *c. Gent.*

man, that whoremongers are chaste, and murderers no longer hold the sword, and those who were formerly mastered by cowardice play the man?

5. And, in short, who persuaded men of barbarous countries and heathen men in divers places to lay aside their madness, and to mind peace, if it be not the Faith of Christ and the Sign of the Cross? Or who else has given men such assurance of immortality, as has the Cross of Christ, and the Resurrection of His Body?

6. For although the Greeks have told all manner of false tales, yet they were not able to feign a Resurrection of their idols,—for it never crossed their mind, whether it be at all possible for the body again to exist after death. And here one would most especially accept their testimony, inasmuch as by this opinion they have exposed the weakness of their own idolatry, while leaving the possibility open to Christ, so that hence also He might be made known among all as Son of God.

CHAPTER LI.

The new virtue of continence. Revolution of Society, purified and pacified by Christianity.

1. WHICH of mankind, again, after his death, or else while living, taught concerning virginity, and that this virtue was not impossible among men? But Christ, our Saviour and King of all, had such power in His teaching concerning it, that even children not yet arrived at the lawful age vow that virginity which lies beyond the law.

2. What man has ever yet been able to pass so far as to come among Scythians and Ethiopians, or Persians or Armenians or Goths, or those we hear of beyond the ocean or those beyond Hyrcania, or even the Egyptians and Chaldees, men that mind magic and are superstitious beyond nature and savage in their ways, and to preach at all about virtue and self-control, and against the worshipping of idols, as has the Lord of all, the Power of God, our Lord Jesus Christ?

3. Who not only preached by means of His own disciples, but also carried persuasion to men's mind, to lay aside the fierceness of their manners, and no longer to serve their ancestral gods, but to learn to know Him, and through Him to worship the Father.

4. For formerly, while in idolatry, Greeks and Barbarians used to war against each other, and were actually cruel to their own kin. For it was impossible for any one to cross sea or land at all, without arming the hand with swords,[56] because of their implacable fighting among themselves.

---

[56]Cf. Thucy. i.5, 6: 'πᾶσα γὰρ ἡ ῞Ελλας ἐσιδηροφόρει,' etc.

5. For the whole course of their life was carried on by arms, and the sword with them took the place of a staff, and was their support in every emergency; and still, as I said before, they were serving idols, and offering sacrifices to demons, while for all their idolatrous superstition they could not be reclaimed from this spirit.

6. But when they have come over to the school of Christ, then, strangely enough, as men truly pricked in conscience, they have laid aside the savagery of their murders and no longer mind the things of war: but all is at peace with them, and from henceforth what makes for friendship is to their liking.

CHAPTER LII.

Wars, etc., roused by demons, lulled by Christianity.

1. WHO then is He that has done this, or who is He that has united in peace men that hated one another, save the beloved Son of the Father, the common Saviour of all, even Jesus Christ, Who by His own love underwent all things for our salvation? For even from of old it was prophesied of the peace He was to usher in, where the Scripture says: "They shall beat their swords into ploughshares, and their pikes into sickles, and nation shall not take the sword against nation, neither shall they learn war any more" [Isa. 2:4].

2. And this is at least not incredible, inasmuch as even now those barbarians who have an innate savagery of manners, while they still sacrifice to the idols of their country, are mad against one another, and cannot endure to be a single hour without weapons:

3. but when they hear the teaching of Christ, straightway instead of fighting they turn to husbandry, and instead of arming their hands with weapons they raise them in prayer, and in a word, in place of fighting among themselves, henceforth they arm against the devil and against evil spirits, subduing these by self-restraint and virtue of soul.

4. Now this is at once a proof of the divinity of the Saviour, since what men could not learn among idols[57] they have learned from Him; and no small exposure of the weakness and nothingness of demons and idols. For demons, knowing their own weakness, for this reason formerly set men to make war against one another, lest, if they ceased from mutual strife, they should turn to battle against demons.

5. Why, they who become disciples of Christ, instead of warring with each other, stand arrayed against demons by their habits and their virtuous actions: and

---

[57]St. Augustine, Civ. D. IV. xvi. commenting on the fact that the temple of 'Repose' (Quies) at Rome was not within the city walls, suggests 'qui illam turbam colere perseveraret . . . doemoniorum, eum Quietem habere non posse.'

they rout them, and mock at their captain the devil; so that in youth they are self-restrained, in temptations endure, in labours persevere, when insulted are patient, when robbed make light of it: and, wonderful as it is, they despise even death and become martyrs of Christ.

CHAPTER LIII.

The whole fabric of Gentilism levelled at a blow by Christ secretly addressing the conscience of man.

1. AND to mention one proof of the divinity of the Saviour, which is indeed utterly surprising,—what mere man or magician or tyrant or king was ever able by himself to engage with so many, and to fight the battle against all idolatry and the whole demoniacal host and all magic, and all the wisdom of the Greeks, while they were so strong and still flourishing and imposing upon all, and at one onset to check them all, as was our Lord, the true Word of God, Who, invisibly exposing each man's error, is by Himself bearing off all men from them all, so that while they who were worshipping idols now trample upon them, those in repute for magic burn their books, and the wise prefer to all studies the interpretation of the Gospels?

2. For whom they used to worship, them they are deserting, and Whom they used to mock as one crucified, Him they worship as Christ, confessing Him to be God. And they that are called gods among them are routed by the Sign of the Cross, while the Crucified Saviour is proclaimed in all the world as God and the Son of God. And the gods worshipped among the Greeks are falling into ill repute at their hands, as scandalous beings; while those who receive the teaching of Christ live a chaster life than they.

3. If, then, these and the like are human works, let him who will point out similar works on the part of men of former time, and so convince us. But if they prove to be, and are, not men's works, but God's, why are the unbelievers so irreligious as not to recognise the Master that wrought them?

4. For their case is as though a man, from the works of creation, failed to know God their Artificer. For if they knew His Godhead from His power over the universe, they would have known that the bodily works of Christ also are not human, but are the works of the Saviour of all, the Word of God. And did they thus know, "they would not," as Paul said, "have crucified the Lord of glory" [1 Cor. 2:8].

CHAPTER LIV.

The Word Incarnate, as is the case with the Invisible God, is known to us by His works. By them we recognise His deifying mission. Let us be content to enumerate a few of them, leaving their dazzling plentitude to him who will behold.

1. AS, then, if a man should wish to see God, Who is invisible by nature and not seen at all, he may know and apprehend Him from His works: so let him who fails to see Christ with his understanding, at least apprehend Him by the works of His body, and test whether they be human works or God's works.

2. And if they be human, let him scoff; but if they are not human, but of God, let him recognise it, and not laugh at what is no matter for scoffing; but rather let him marvel that by so ordinary a means things divine had been manifested to us, and that by death immortality has reached to all, and that by the Word becoming man, the universal Providence has been known, and its Giver and Artificer the very Word of God.

3. For He was made man that we might be made God;[58] and He manifested Himself by a body that we might receive the idea of the unseen Father; and He endured the insolence of men that we might inherit immortality. For while He Himself was in no way injured, being impassible and incorruptible and very Word and God, men who were suffering, and for whose sakes He endured all this, He maintained and preserved in His own impassibility.

4. And, in a word, the achievements of the Saviour, resulting from His becoming man, are of such kind and number, that if one should wish to enumerate them, he may be compared to men who gaze at the expanse of the sea and wish to count its waves. For as one cannot take in the whole of the waves with his eyes, for those which are coming on baffle the sense of him that attempts it; so for him that would take in all the achievements of Christ in the body, it is impossible to take in the whole, even by reckoning them up, as those which go beyond his thought are more than those he thinks he has taken in.

5. Better is it, then, not to aim at speaking of the whole, where one cannot do justice even to a part, but, after mentioning one more, to leave the whole for you to marvel at. For all alike are marvellous, and wherever a man turns his glance, he may behold on that side the divinity of the Word, and he struck with exceeding great awe.

---

[58]Θεοποιηθῶμεν. See *Orat.* ii.70, note 1, and many other passages in those Discourses, as well as *Letters* 60.4, 61.2 (Eucharistic reference), *de Synodis* 51, note 7. (Compare also Iren. IV. xxxviii.4, 'non ab initio dii facti sumus, sed primo quidem homines, tunc demum dii,' cf. *ib.* praef. 4 *fin.* also V. ix.2, 'sublevat in vitam Dei.' Origen *Cels.* iii.28 *fin.* touches the same thought, but Ath. is here in closer affinity to the idea of Irenaeus than to that of Oirgen.) The New Test. reference is 2 Pet. 1:4, rather than Heb. 2:9 sqq.; the Old Test., Ps. 82:6, which seems to underlie *Orat.* iii.25 (note 5). In spite of the last mentioned passage, 'God' is far preferable as a rendering, in most places, to 'gods,' which has heathenish associations. To us (1 Cor. 8:6) there are no such things as 'gods.' (The best summary of patristic teaching on this subject is given by Harnack *Dg.* ii. p. 46 note.)

CHAPTER LV.

Summary of foregoing. Cessation of pagan oracles, etc.: propagation of the faith. The true King has come forth and silenced all usurpers.

1. THIS, then, after what we have so far said, it is right for you to realize, and to take as the sum of what we have already stated, and to marvel at exceedingly; namely, that since the Saviour has come among us, idolatry not only has no longer increased, but what there was is diminishing and gradually coming to an end: and not only does the wisdom of the Greeks no longer advance, but what there is is now fading away: and demons, so far from cheating any more by illusions and prophecies and magic arts, if they so much as dare to make the attempt, are put to shame by the sign of the Cross.

2. And to sum the matter up: behold how the Saviour's doctrine is everywhere increasing, while all idolatry and everything opposed to the faith of Christ is daily dwindling, and losing power, and falling. And thus beholding, worship the Saviour, "Who is above all" and mighty, even God the Word; and condemn those who are being worsted and done away by Him.

3. For as, when the sun is come, darkness no longer prevails, but if any be still left anywhere it is driven away; so, now that the divine Appearing of the Word of God is come, the darkness of the idols prevails no more, and all parts of the world in every direction are illumined by His teaching.

4. And as, when a king is reigning in some country without appearing but keeps at home in his own house, often some disorderly persons, abusing his retirement, proclaim themselves; and each of them, by assuming the character, imposes on the simple as king, and so men are led astray by the name, hearing that there is a king, but not seeing him, if for no other reason, because they cannot enter the house; but when the real king comes forth and appears, then the disorderly impostors are exposed by his presence, while men, seeing the real king, desert those who previously led them astray:

5. in like manner, the evil spirits formerly used to deceive men, investing themselves with God's honour; but when the Word of God appeared in a body, and made known to us His own Father, then at length the deceit of the evil spirits is done away and stopped, while men, turning their eyes to the true God, Word of the Father, are deserting the idols, and now coming to know the true God.

6. Now this is a proof that Christ is God the Word, and the Power of God. For whereas human things cease, and the Word of Christ abides, it is clear to all eyes that what ceases is temporary, but that He Who abides is God, and the true Son of God, His only-begotten Word.

CHAPTER LVI.

Search then, the Scriptures, if you can, and so fill up this sketch. Learn to look for the Second Advent and Judgment.

1. LET this, then, Christ-loving man, be our offering to you, just for a rudimentary sketch and outline, in a short compass, of the faith of Christ and of His Divine appearing to usward. But you, taking occasion by this, if you light upon the text of the Scriptures, by genuinely applying your mind to them, will learn from them more completely and clearly the exact detail of what we have said.

2. For they were spoken and written by God, through men who spoke of God. But we impart of what we have learned from inspired teachers who have been conversant with them, who have also become martyrs for the deity of Christ, to your zeal for learning, in turn.

3. And you will also learn about His second glorious and truly divine appearing to us, when no longer in lowliness, but in His own glory,—no longer in humble guise, but in His own magnificence,—He is to come, no more to suffer, but thenceforth to render to all the fruit of His own Cross, that is, the resurrection and incorruption; and no longer to be judged, but to judge all, by what each has done in the body, whether good or evil; where there is laid up for the good the kingdom of heaven, but for them that have done evil everlasting fire and outer darkness.

4. For thus the Lord Himself also says: "Henceforth ye shall see the Son of Man sitting at the right hand of power, and coming on the clouds of heaven in the glory of the Father" [Matt. 26:64].

5. And for this very reason there is also a word of the Saviour to prepare us for that day, in these words: "Be ye ready and watch, for He cometh at an hour ye know not" [Matt. 24:42].[59] For, according to the blessed Paul: "We must all stand before the judgment-seat of Christ, that each one may receive according as he hath done in the body, whether it be good or bad" [2 Cor. 5:10].[60]

CHAPTER LVII.

Above all, so live that you may have the right to eat of this tree of knowledge and life, and so come to eternal joys. Doxology.

1. BUT for the searching of the Scriptures and true knowledge of them, an honourable life is needed, and a pure soul, and that virtue which is according to

---

[59]Cf. Mark 13:35.
[60]Cf. Rom. 14:10.

Christ; so that the intellect guiding its path by it, may be able to attain what it desires, and to comprehend it, in so far as it is accessible to human nature to learn concerning the Word of God.

2. For without a pure mind and a modelling of the life after the saints, a man could not possibly comprehend the words of the saints.

3. For just as, if a man wished to see the light of the sun, he would at any rate wipe and brighten his eye, purifying himself in some sort like what he desires, so that the eye, thus becoming light, may see the light of the sun; or as, if a man would see a city or country, he at any rate comes to the place to see it;— thus he that would comprehend the mind of those who speak of God must needs begin by washing and cleansing his soul, by his manner of living, and approach the saints themselves by imitating their works; so that, associated with them in the conduct of a common life, he may understand also what has been revealed to them by God, and thenceforth, as closely knit to them, may escape the peril of the sinners and their fire at the day of judgment, and receive what is laid up for the saints in the kingdom of heaven, which "Eye hath not seen, nor ear heard, neither have entered into the heart of man" [1 Cor. 2:9], whatsoever things are prepared for them that live a virtuous life, and love the God and Father, in Christ Jesus our Lord: through Whom and with Whom be to the Father Himself, with the Son Himself, in the Holy Spirit, honour and might and glory for ever and ever. Amen.

↜ 7 ↝

AUGUSTINE OF HIPPO
(A.D. 354–430)

Undoubtedly Augustine was the greatest of the Fathers of the Western church. His Neoplatonist teachings dominated Christian philosophy and theology until the rise of Aristotelianism in the days of Thomas Aquinas. It is not an overstatement to say that his philosophy had a formative influence on Descartes and, thus, on the whole development of modern philosophy. In addition, the Protestant Reformers, especially Calvin, were guided in their theological views to a great extent by the published works of Augustine.

Patricius, the pagan, and Monica, the Christian, were living in the small city of Tagaste, located not far to the west of Carthage and some fifty miles south of the Mediterranean in North Africa, when on November 13, 354, they welcomed the birth of their son, Augustine. Eventually Augustine's father became a Christian, but family life in the days of Augustine's childhood was not always as pleasant as it could have been.

At the age of twelve Augustine was sent by his parents to the advanced schools in Madaura, a center of pagan culture. During the four years he spent there his education was greatly expanded, but at the same time he was thoroughly exposed to the pagan lifestyle. After his father died in 370, he was sent to study rhetoric at Carthage. There he mastered the Latin classics and studied translations of many of the dialogues of Plato. Augustine was deeply impressed with Plato and with his "spiritual" philosophy. He was also attracted to the teachings of Mani who taught that the world was governed by the two principles of light and darkness (or good and evil). For Augustine this offered a solution to the problem of evil that plagued his mind. According to Manicheism the human soul was like a fragment of light encased in a material, thus an evil, body. Christ was viewed as a powerful prophet, but Mani did not affirm Christ's divine nature or His redemptive mission. Augustine freely admits that in his youthful thinking he was unable to conceive of a spiritual being, much less a spiritual God.

While in Carthage he continued to live according to his pre-Christian sensuality, constantly searching for sexual gratification. He began to teach rhetoric in Carthage and increasingly gave himself to Manicheism. However, his "higher self" resisted his tendencies toward sensual immorality, and doubts began to grow in his mind. In 383, after a discussion with a Manichean bishop named Faustus, Augustine began to abandon Manichean thought.

Moving to Milan in 384, Augustine became a teacher of rhetoric there. For a time he remained skeptical toward religion, but the philosophical writings of Cicero and the Neoplatonists gradually convinced him that ultimate reality was spiritual rather than material as Mani had taught. Augustine's great admiration for Neoplatonism, however, was not a blind faith, and he gradually came to realize that ultimate answers were not to be found there.

After a period of careful reading of the Bible, particularly the Gospel of John, Augustine became convinced that only the grace of God could save people from their sins. His *Confessions*, his personal theological testimony, is unique among the great spiritual autobiographies. In this work he intimately describes the inward conflict of the volitional and the intellectual aspects of his life.

His mother never ceased to love him and pray for him, though his life had so deeply disappointed her. While in Milan, Augustine heard the sermons of Bishop Ambrose. These powerful messages and the prayers of his mother were combined by the Holy Spirit to speak a convicting word to Augustine's heart and mind. In 386 Augustine finally acknowledged the saving grace of God directed toward him and, upon a profession of his faith in the Lord Jesus Christ, he was baptized by Ambrose the next year at the age of thirty-three.

The following year Augustine returned to Africa, and three years later, in 391, he was ordained as an elder in the church. The bishop of Hippo (modern Bône, Algeria) asked Augustine to preach and expound the Scripture, and everyone was greatly impressed with his skill and dedication. In 395 he was consecrated as the new bishop of Hippo.

Though his work load was extremely heavy, he did not cease his writing until the very year of his death. He was deliberate, incessant, and effective in his struggle against all heretics. Augustine's apologetic approach to theology can be seen quite clearly in his writings against the Manicheans, the Pelagians, and the Donatists.

Though he began to write during his teaching years at Carthage, Augustine's literary career is usually dated as beginning in 385 when he wrote *Contra Academicos*, an attack on the academic skeptics. Nevertheless, most of his major works were written after his ordination as bishop of Hippo. Perhaps the two most famous works of Augustine are his *Confessions* and the *City of God*. Christian apologists have found his proof for the existence of God in *The Free Choice of the Will* to be of special interest. Selections from all three are included in this chapter.

The Free Choice of the Will contains a theistic argument from truth. There are absolute truths, claims Augustine. We, for example, cannot doubt the proposition that affirms our existence or our thoughts. Nor can we doubt the facts of mathematics ($2 + 2 = 4$). These truths are held in common by all people and yet are not caused by finite minds. Our minds acknowledge these truths, but we do not cause them. These truths are not caused by changing, contingent circumstances, since dependent things cannot cause independent realities to be. There must then be a totally independent and unchanging source for these absolute truths. Truths are ideas, and ideas come from minds; therefore, there must be an absolute Mind—God. Whenever anyone affirms truth, that person is implicitly affirming the existence of Truth (God).

The selection chosen from the *Confessions* is not from the autobiographical section but from the later part in which Augustine discusses God, memory, and time. The particular section reprinted in this chapter is his attempt to expound Genesis 1:1; it precedes his famous discussion about time itself. His method of exposition and manner of treating objections is most instructive for students of apologetics today.

Finally a selection from Augustine's *City of God* is included

that contains his defense of Christianity in light of the stiff opposition to the faith that arose following the sack of Rome by Alaric
and his Goths in 410. The destructive force of the Vandals in 455
was more severe, and perhaps the sack by the Normans in 1084
was worse still. The events in 410, however, were the first hard
evidences that the Empire was at its end. Moreover, Rome fell just
as Christianity seemed to triumph, and the pagans argued cause
and effect at that point. Here then was the great question to which
the Christian apologist Augustine must address himself. Was the
decline of the Empire the result of the abandonment of the old
gods and the civil religion of Rome? How could Christians explain
the flow of history?

On August 28, 430, Augustine died. The city of Hippo,
where he had lived more than half of his life, was under siege by
the Vandals and had been for eight months. Augustine died before
the city fell. He had just completed a list of passages in ninety-
three of his works that he thought needed revision. His library
escaped destruction, a special providence of God; and we have
almost a complete set of his writings.

Few men have ever had the lasting influence that Augustine
has had. By God's grace it has been an influence for good.

BIBLIOGRAPHY

Andresen, C. *Bibliographia Augustiniana.* 2d ed. Darmstadt: Wissenschaftliche
    Buchgesellschaft, 1973.
Battenhouse, R. W., ed. A *Companion to the Study of Augustine.* New York:
    Oxford University Press, 1955.
Bonner, G. *St. Augustine of Hippo: Life and Controversies.* Philadelphia: West-
    minster, 1963.
Brown, Peter. *Augustine of Hippo: A Biography.* London: Faber & Faber, 1967.
Gilson, E. *The Christian Philosophy of Saint Augustine.* New York: Random,
    1960.
Marrou, H. I. *St. Augustine and His Influence Through the Ages.* New York:
    Harper & Row, 1957.
Portalie, E. A *Guide to the Thought of St. Augustine.* Chicago: Regnery, 1960.

Concerning the Freedom of the Will (De Libero Arbitrio)

BOOK II.

A New English Version Edited by L. Russ Bush

Preface

THIS new English version of excerpts from Book II, chapters 3–4, 6, 8–10, 12–15, was prepared by L. Russ Bush specially for this publication. The text has been edited so as to focus attention on Augustine's argument for God's real existence, a fundamental apologetic theme. Students interested in the context of these excerpts or in Augustine's fuller development of the argument should study one of the standard translations.

II 3.7

Augustine. What clear evidence do we have that God exists? In order to answer this question, let me begin at a point which *is* clearly evident. Do you yourself exist? (Perhaps you are afraid to answer such a question because it sounds like a trick question. But you could not possibly be tricked by such a question if you did not exist.)

Euodius. Go on to the next point.

A. Since it is quite clearly evident that you do exist, and since this would not be so clearly evident to you if you were dead, it seems to be equally clear that you must be alive. Do you recognize that these two points must be absolutely true?

E. I understand that quite well.

The Latin text used in preparing this new English edition is found in *Corpus Scriptorum Ecclesiasticorum Latinorum*, Vol. LXXIV, Sancti Aureli Augustini Opera, Sect. VI, Pars III, De Libero Arbitrio. Recensuit Guilelmus M. Green, Vindebonae; Hoelder-Pichler-Tempsky, 1956.

A. Then my third point is also clearly evident. You do rationally understand things.

E. Evidently so!

A. In your opinion, which of these three (existence, life, or understanding) is the most important?

E. Understanding!

A. Why do you think that?

E. Because, of those three (existence, life, and understanding) it can be said that a stone exists and an animal lives. But I do not think that a stone lives or that an animal has rational understanding. However, a person who does have rational understanding also exists and is alive. Therefore, without hesitation, I conclude that to have all three is better than to lack one or two. Whatever is alive certainly exists, but it is not true that a living being always has rational understanding. (Life without rationality is, in my opinion, what animal life is.) But it is certainly not correct to argue that whatever exists also has life and understanding. Surely a corpse exists, but no one says that a corpse is alive. Much less could anyone believe that something not alive could have rational understanding.

A. We agree then that two of these three are lacking in a corpse, one in an animal, and none in a human being.

E. That is right.

A. We also agree that understanding is the most important of the three, because someone who has understanding must also exist and be alive.

E. Indeed so!

II 3.8

A. Now tell me whether or not you know that you have the common bodily senses of sight, hearing, smell, taste, and touch?

E. I do.

A. What do you think is the nature of sight? That is, what do you think we perceive when we see?

E. Physical things.

A. Do we see hardness and softness?

E. No.

A. Then what is the proper function of the eyes? What do we see through them?

E. Color.

A. What is the proper function of ears?

E. Sound.

A. Of smell?

E. Odor.

A. Of taste?

E. Flavor.

A. Of touch?

E. Soft or hard, smooth or rough, and many other similar qualities.

A. What about shape? Do we not perceive by both touch and sight that things are large or small, square or round, and so forth? Therefore, we cannot assign the perception of shape to sight or touch alone. It must be said to be a function of both sight and touch.

E. I understand that.

A. You understand then that while each of the senses uniquely relates to the perception of some particular properties of things, that some senses may perceive certain other properties in common.

E. Yes, I understand that also.

A. Which of these senses do we use to perceive what the proper function of each sense is and what properties are perceived by some or all of them in common?

E. None of them. We distinguish that by an inner sense.

A. Might not that inner sense be reason itself, the very thing that the animals lack? It seems to me that it is by reason that we understand and come to know these things.

.   .   .

II 3.9

A. Reason itself distinguishes between its servants [the senses] and the perceptions they convey to it. In the same way, reason can also recognize the differences between itself and the bodily senses, and reason proves itself to be superior. But how does reason know itself unless it is by reason. In other words, it is only by reason that you know that you have reason.

E. That is very true.

A. When we see a color, we do not through our sense of sight perceive our perception of color. Nor do we hear ourselves hearing a sound, or smell ourselves smelling a rose, or taste our tasting, or touch our touching. The five bodily senses perceive all bodily things, but the senses are not themselves perceived by any one of the senses.

E. That is manifestly correct.

II 4.10

A. . . . These points are clear: (1) physical things are perceived by a bodily sense; (2) this bodily sense cannot perceive itself; (3) there is an inner sense that can and does perceive the bodily sense and the fact that physical things are perceived by a bodily sense; (4) reason, thus, makes sense perceptions known, and it makes reason itself known, and together this is knowledge. Do you agree?

E. I do indeed.

.   .   .

II 6.13

A. Next let us consider whether reason judges this inner sense. I am not asking whether you think reason is better than the inner sense. It must be the case that reason judges the inner sense, because what else but reason can tell us that one thing is better than another thing when we are referring to physical things, bodily senses, or the inner sense. In fact, it is reason itself that tells us that reason is superior to all of these other things.

E. That is clearly right.

A. . . . I am really asking you to consider whether there is any thing in man's nature that is superior to reason.

E. I know of absolutely nothing that is superior to reason.

II 6.14

A. But what if we could find something that you could know without doubt both exists and is superior to reason? Would you hesitate to call it, whatever it may be, God?

E. If I were to find something to be superior to what is best in my nature, I would not necessarily call it God. I do not want to call something God simply because my reason happens to be inferior to it. God is that reality to which nothing else is superior.

A. Exactly! For God Himself gave your reason this reverent and true way of thinking about Him. But, if I may press the point, what if you find that there is nothing superior to our reason except the eternal and changeless reality? Would you hesitate to call that God? You know that physical reality is subject to change, and the life that animates physical bodies is subject to change. Reason itself changes, for sometimes reason strives for truth and sometimes it doesn't, sometimes it reaches truth and sometimes it doesn't. Surely if reason were to recognize (not through bodily senses such as touch, smell, taste, sight, or hearing but through itself alone) itself to be inferior to something that is eternal and unchangeable, then it must confess that this reality is God.

E. I will openly acknowledge that God is that reality to which there is nothing known to be superior.

A. That is good enough. Now all I have to do is show that such a being does exist. Either you will admit that this being is God or else, if there is something higher, you will admit that the higher reality is God. So whichever the case may be, if I can show, with God's help, that there is something higher than reason, then I will have demonstrated that God exists.

E. Then get on with the demonstration that you are promising.

.   .   .

II 8.20

A. Let me, then, have your close attention. Do you think that there is anything that can be found that all rational people, each with their own reason and mind, may perceive, some object that can be seen to be present to everyone (but not something like food or drink that undergoes change for the use of those to whom it is present), something that remains uncorrupted and whole whether it is actually seen by everyone or not? Or would you say that there is nothing like this?

E. Oh, no, I can think of many things like that. For example, mathematical truth is held in common by all rational people. Everyone who tries to solve a mathematical equation tries to grasp the solution by reason and understanding. One person may find the problem to be simple, another may find it difficult, still another may not be able to solve it at all. Nevertheless, the mathematical relationships are equally available to anyone who can grasp them. When someone perceives the truth involved, he does not thereby change it (in other words, he does not eat it up like food). Nor does that truth cease to be true just because someone makes an error in calculation; instead the error is no more and no less than the degree to which the truth is not properly perceived.

II 8.21

A. Quite right! I can see that you are familiar with these kinds of things for you found an answer quickly. But suppose I were to argue that the concept of number was not impressed on our minds by any inherent feature of numbers themselves but came rather from things that we perceive with the bodily senses so that number becomes, so to speak, a sensory-image of visible things. What would you reply to such a view, or is that perhaps the view you hold?

E. No, I certainly do not hold that view. Even if I did perceive the meaning of numerals through one of the bodily senses, I would not grasp the meaning of addition or division through a bodily sense. It is by the light of my mind that I recognize whether someone has made an error in their addition or subtraction. When I perceive something with my bodily senses, whether it is the heavens or the earth or any physical thing they contain, I do not know how long they will last. But seven plus three are ten not only now but for evermore. There never was a time when seven plus three were not ten, and there never will be such a time. Therefore, as I see it, mathematical truths are incorruptible, and they are common to me and to all other rational persons.

II 8.22

A. I fully agree with your answer. It is absolutely correct. But you can easily see that even the meanings of the numerals themselves are not perceived directly by the bodily senses. If you think about it you will realize that every number represents a given amount of units. For example, the number two represents twice as many units as the number one; three is one unit tripled; a number representing ten units is called ten. However many units any numeral contains is the name of that number. But a true notion of what "one" means cannot arise from the bodily senses. Anything perceived by the bodily senses is a physical thing and thus it is proved not to be "one." All physical bodies are made up of many parts. It is not necessary to discuss every small and almost undetectable particle, because no matter how small the tiny particle may be, it must have one part on the right, one on the left, one above and another below, one of the far side and another on the near side, parts at the ends and parts at the middle. No matter how small a thing is, it will be made up of such parts, and consequently we can regard no physical thing as truly and simply one. Yet it would be impossible to count those parts unless they could be differentiated into units.

Whenever I seek a simple unit (oneness) in a physical thing, even though I know that I will not find it, nevertheless I do know what I am looking for, and I know what it is that I do not find. Furthermore, I know that it cannot be found because it is not there at all. When I know that a physical object is not simply one, I know what oneness means. If I did not know what "one" meant, I would not be able to count "many" in a physical thing. Wherever my concept of oneness comes from, it does not come from the bodily senses, for by my senses I can only come to know physical things, which, as I have argued, are not truly and simply one. Moreover, if we have not perceived oneness through the bodily senses, then neither have we perceived any numbers by the bodily senses (none at least of those numbers that we understand by our reason), because all of those numbers are made up of combinations of one, and the bodily senses do not directly perceive the simple unit one.

Any small body can be divided in half, and each half can be divided into half. In other words, any physical thing has two halves, yet even they are not simply two. But the number two is exactly twice the number one and therefore has one for its half (that is, that which is truly and simply one), and simple oneness cannot be further divided into halves or thirds or any other fraction because oneness lacks parts and thus is truly one.

II 8.23

Furthermore, when we follow the accepted numerical order, we find that one is followed by two (which is the double of one). But the double of two is not the next number in the series. The double of two is four (which follows two after the interposition of three). This relational pattern runs through all the other numbers by a certain and unchangeable law. . . .

What, then, is the source of our recognition of these mathematical relationships that we can clearly see run through all numbers in an absolutely regular way? No one of us has perceived all numbers with any bodily sense (numbers go on forever, they are innumerable). How then could we know that these mathematical relationships hold throughout all of them? By what idea or by what image do we see with such assurance that these mathematical relationships are an absolute law that holds throughout innumerable instances, unless we know these things through an inner light unknown to the bodily senses?

II 8.24

By these and many similar arguments, it must be clear to those to whom God has given rationality, and who are not blinded by obstinacy, (1) that the orderliness and the truth of mathematics are not perceived by the bodily senses, (2) that they are absolutely unchangeable and indestructible, and (3) that they are perceived by all rational people in common. . . .

It is not without significance that in the Holy Scriptures number and wisdom are associated where it says: "I and my heart have longed [lit. "gone around"] to know and consider and seek after wisdom and number." [Eccl. 7:26 Septuagint]

II 9.25

But let me ask this: In your opinion, what do you think about wisdom itself? Does each person have an individual wisdom or is there one wisdom that we all share in common with each person becoming wiser the more fully he shares in it?

E. I cannot answer that unless I know what you mean by wisdom. Not everyone agrees on what actions or what words are wise. For example, those who go to war think they are acting wisely, while those who despise war and spend their time farming praise this way of life as the way of wisdom. Those who are shrewd businessmen think they are wise. Those who give up all temporal interests and devote themselves entirely to a search for truth through introspective meditation and theological study also believe this to be the path of wisdom. . . . There are literally countless other groups that believe that their ideas and theirs alone are truly wise.

Therefore, since the issue before us [concerning God's existence] is not a question of what we may happen to believe but rather what we may hold by clear understanding, I am not able to answer your question based on what I personally may believe wisdom to be unless I also come to know what wisdom is through contemplation and rational discernment.

II 9.26

A. Do you think that wisdom is ever found apart from truth that enables us to discern and know the supreme good? In the examples you have given of people seeking different goals, they all sought the good and shunned evil, but they sought different goals because they had different concepts of what the good is. Anyone who seeks what should not be sought is in error even though he would not seek it if he did not think that his aim was good. Someone who seeks nothing or who seeks that which ought to be sought is not in error. For instance, no one errs by seeking happiness. But one may err by choosing a pattern of life that does not lead to true happiness even though his motive for choosing that lifestyle may have been an honest search for happiness. We are in error whenever we choose to follow a path that does not lead us where we want to go. The more one errs in his way of life, the less wise he is, because his error leads him further away from the truth in which the supreme good is discerned and known. Only the supreme good will bring the real happiness that we all deserve.

Certainly we all wish to be happy. So in the same way we all wish to be wise, because no one is happy without wisdom. No one is happy without the supreme good that is discerned and known by wisdom. Therefore, just as the notion of happiness is in our minds before we ever actually experience happiness (for it is this prior notion of happiness that gives us the confidence to state without reservation that we desire to be happy), so in the same way we have the notion of wisdom in our minds even before we are wise. If anyone were to be asked whether he wants to be happy, it is this notion that enables him to confidently reply that he does.

II 9.27

Though you were unable to express it in words, it seems that we actually agree about the nature of wisdom. If you did not have a concept of wisdom in your mind, you could not know that you want to be wise or that you ought to be (which I am sure you will not deny). Therefore, tell me whether you think of wisdom as being a single reality equally available to all people in the same way mathematical truths are, or do you think (since each of us has his own mind and no one uses someone else's mind to perceive things) that there are as many wisdoms as there are people capable of becoming wise?

E. If the highest good is the same for all, then I suppose that the truth by which we discern and know that good, namely wisdom, must also be one and common to all.

A. Do you have any doubt about the supreme good, whatever it is, being the same for all people?

E. Yes, I really do, because it is quite obvious that different people enjoy different things.

A. I wish that no one had any doubts about the supreme good, just as no one doubts that if he achieved it (whatever it is) that he would be happy. But this is an important question and we may need to discuss it at length. Let us take the extreme case and suppose that there are as many different supreme goods as there are different things sought by different people as their supreme good. It would not necessarily follow that wisdom itself is not a single reality known in common by all rational persons simply because the goods which they choose to seek in the light of this common wisdom are varied. To argue that way would be like saying there must be many suns since we see so many varied things in its light. . . . People do see many different things which they may freely choose to enjoy, but there is only one sun by whose light these different things are seen and chosen. . . .

E. Well, of course it is possible that a single wisdom common to all could nevertheless allow individual choice of different goods, but what I want to know is whether or not this is the actual case. To grant that something is possible is not necessarily to agree that it is actually the case.

A. Nevertheless, we do agree that wisdom exists. But whether there is one common wisdom or whether there is a separate wisdom for each mind is a point that is still open for discussion.

E. That is correct.

II 10.28

A. Well, then, how do we know for sure that wisdom or wise men exist or that all men want to be happy? I have no doubt that you agree that this is true. Do you know that this is true in the same way that you know your own thoughts (which, of course, are totally secret from me unless you tell me what you are thinking)? Or do you see this truth in such a way that you think it could be seen by me as well (even if you do not tell me)?

E. Undoubtedly you could also see it even against my will.

A. In other words, this is at least one truth that we have in common yet we both see it with our individual minds.

E. Yes, that is clearly the case.

A. You surely agree that we should earnestly seek after wisdom. This is also clearly true, is it not?

E. Certainly I agree with that.

A. Can we possibly deny that this truth is one and is commonly accepted by all who know it even though each individual must contemplate it in his own mind, not in my mind or yours or any other person's. This truth is surely present in common to all who think about it.

E. No, we could never deny that.

A. Is it not also absolutely true for all people that each person should seek to live justly, that the perfect is better than the imperfect, that equals should be treated as equals, that every man should be given what is due him?

E. Yes, it is.

A. Can you deny that an uncorrupted thing is better than a corrupted thing, or that the eternal is better than the temporal, or that something which cannot be injured is better than something that can be injured.

E. No one can deny that.

A. Then, can anyone say that this truth is private truth and that it is not available to any rational person who desires to think along these lines.

E. No one could claim that such truth belonged only to him since it is as available to all rational minds as it is true.

A. Or again, who could deny that we should turn ourselves away from corruption and turn in love toward that which is incorrupt? Or how can anyone recognize that something is true and then fail to understand that it is by nature absolute (unchangeable) and equally available to all who are able to see it?

E. What you say is certainly correct.

A. Well then, will anyone doubt that it is better to live by an unshakable moral conviction than to live by a code of ethics that changes with every difficulty of life?

E. Everyone would agree on that.

II 10.29

A. We need no more examples. It is enough that you and I agree on this point, that it is absolutely certain that such principles and insights into virtue are true and changeless and that individually or collectively they are able to be seen by any rational person with his own unaided mind. But what I want to know is whether you think that these things are related to wisdom. I believe that you consider a man to be wise if he has attained wisdom.

E. Yes, I do think that.

A. Could a man live righteously if he could not distinguish what were lower things so that he could subordinate them to the higher things, or if he could not recognize what things were equal, or what was due to each?

E. No, he could not.

A. Then you would agree that one who understands these things does so wisely?

E. Yes, of course. . . .

A. And the one who is not deterred by difficulties from the course he wisely chose also acts wisely, does he not?

E. He does.

A. It seems clear to me, then, that all those truths that we call principles and insights into virtue pertain to wisdom. The more someone uses these insights in his daily life, the more wisely does he live and act, and we surely cannot separate wise actions from wisdom itself.

E. Certainly not.

A. Therefore, just as there are mathematical truths that cannot be changed and that are available to the minds of any who can understand them, so, too, there are, as you have agreed in response to my questions, true and changeless principles of wisdom equally available for all to see who are capable of understanding them.

.   .   .

II 12.30

In light of all this, then, you surely would not deny that absolute (unchangeable) truth does exist that contains all those things that are unchangeable true and that does not belong to any individual but rather is equally available to all who see it. . . . If two people perceive something at the same time, that something is not identified with the eyes of either person but is known to be a third something toward which both of them direct their sight.

E. That is quite clear and surely correct.

A. Do you think that this one truth by which we see so many things (which we have been discussing for such a long time) is higher than, equal to, or lower than our minds? If it were inferior to our minds we would be making judgments about it, not according to it. We do, for example, make judgments about physical objects because they are lower. We often make not only descriptive comments about them, but we say what we think ought to be the case. . . . We make these judgments according to the principles of truth within us, but no one ever makes these principles an object of judgment. Whenever anyone assumes that the eternal ought to be valued above the temporal, or that seven plus three are ten, no one argues that such things ought not to be so. We all simply recognize that these principles are so. . . . On the other hand, if this truth stood on a plane equal to our minds, it would be subject to change and thus would not be absolute. Sometimes our minds do change as we come to see things more or less clearly. But the truth that abides in itself does not increase or decrease because we understand more or less of it. The truth remains whole and uncorrupted. It brings joy to those who understand it and stands in judgment over those who are blinded to it. Why is it that we even judge our own minds according to truth? We surely can in no way stand in judgment over truth. We say, "My mind understands such-and-such a thing correctly," or we say, "My mind does not yet fully grasp the truth of such-and-such." But the amount that a mind ought to understand depends on how near that mind has been able to move toward the absolute truth. Therefore, if truth is not inferior to our minds nor equal to them, it must be higher than and superior to our minds.

II 13.35

As you may remember, I had promised to show you that there is something higher than our mind or our reason. Well, this is it—truth itself! If you are able, embrace it and enjoy it! "Delight in the Lord, and He will grant the desires of your heart" (Ps. 36:4). What more do you want than to be happy? And who is happier than the person who enjoys the firm, changeless, and most excellent truth?

Men with passionate desires claim that they are happy when they embrace the sensual bodies of their wives (or even of harlots). Can we doubt that we are happy when we embrace truth itself? Men with parched throats claim to be happy when they find an abundant supply of pure water, or when hungry discover a big dinner or a sumptuous supper. Shall we deny that we are happy when we quench our thirst and feed on truth? We often hear someone claim that they are happy if they can lie in a garden and smell the sweetness of the roses and other flowers. But what is more fragrant or more sweet smelling than the breath of truth? And shall we hesitate to say we are happy when we are inspired by (filled with the breath of) truth? Many claim to find their life's happiness in song or in instrumental music. When there is no music, these people count themselves to be unhappy. When there is music playing, they are thrilled with joy. When the truth, however, in melodious silence steals into our minds without the noise of singing, shall we seek happiness elsewhere rather than enjoy that which is so certain and so near at hand? People delight in gleaming gold and shining silver and in sparkling gems and in various colors. And they find pleasure in the visible splendor and the clarity of light itself, whether it is the light from a fire, or the light from the stars, or from the sun or the moon. Neither trouble nor poverty can prevent them from enjoying the pleasure of light itself, and for the sake of delights of this kind they want to go on living forever. Shall we then be afraid to find the happiness of life in the light of truth?

II 13.36

Since the highest good is known and possessed through truth, and since wisdom is that truth, let us see wisdom as the highest good, and let us grasp it and enjoy it. Happy indeed is the person who delights in the highest good.

This truth reveals all truly good things to each person. Each one understands these things according to his own capacity, and based upon that understanding chooses one or more of them for his own enjoyment.

The light of the sun enables us to see things in which we take great pleasure. Weak eyes find pleasure in the sun-lit objects above. But if someone possessed eyes that were strong enough, healthy enough, and vigorous enough, he would want to gaze directly at the sun itself. In the same way, when the keen and vigorous eyes of the mind see with certainty many absolute truths, they desire to turn their gaze upon the one truth by which all truths are illuminated. The mind, then, should cling to truth itself, forgetting everything else and enjoy all truly good things in it, for the goodness of all things is directly due to the supreme goodness of truth itself.

II 13.37

Freedom is found in the submission to truth. God Himself frees us from death, that is, from the state of sin. It is Truth Himself, speaking to men as a man, who says to those who believe in Him: "If you continue in my word, then are you my disciples indeed, and you shall know the truth and the truth shall make you free" (John 8:31–32).

But nothing can be enjoyed with freedom unless there is also the assurance of security.

II 14

Nothing, however, is secure if someone can lose it against his will. But no one can lose truth and wisdom against his will, because no one can be physically separated from them. When we speak of a loss of truth we are speaking of a deliberate choice by the perverted will of someone who wants to love inferior things. No one ever wills something against his will.

Truth, then, is a possession that all of us can enjoy equally in common. There is nothing lacking nor defective in it. It receives all its lovers without producing envy in any of them. It is totally available to everyone and yet is chaste with each. No one has to say to the other, "Move back so that I can get closer," or "Take away your hands so that I may embrace it." All may cling to it and touch it at the same time. It is a food that is never divided into portions, a drink that is equally available to all. When you share in it, no part of it becomes your private possession. What you take from it does not diminish it for me. I do not have to wait for you to exhale the breath of truth that you have before I may be inspired by that same breath. Truth in the whole or in part never becomes the private possession of any one person or any group. It is always completely available to everyone at any time.

II 14.38

Therefore, what we can touch, taste, or smell is less like truth than that which we see and hear. Every word is heard completely by all who hear it, and they all hear it at the same time. Every sight seen by men is seen at the same time as much by one as by the other.

But the analogy is actually quite weak. No spoken word, for instance, is sounded instantaneously. Words are sounded over a period of time (some sounds come before other sounds). The visibility of an object spreads out through space, so to speak, so that no single object is visible everywhere at all times. And certainly all these things may be taken away from us against our will, and these are difficulties that arise that may prevent us from enjoying them. Even if, for example, the beautiful music of a singer could last forever, his fans would earnestly try to be present to hear him, and they would be crowded together, and as their number grew there would be fighting over the seats nearest the entertainer. They would try to concentrate on the music but the sounds would always only touch their ear and then die away. Or to take another example, if I wanted and was able to gaze continuously at the sun, it would disappear when it sets or when a cloud passes by, and many other obstacles might arise that would prevent me (against my will) from gazing at it. And even if I could forever see the beauty of light or hear the beauty of sound, what great advantage would I have in that since any animal could do the same?

But provided there is the steadfast willingness to seek them, no one is ever prevented from approaching the beauty of truth and wisdom because too many people are already crowded around. This beauty does not pass away with time nor move from place to place. It is not interrupted by nightfall nor hidden by shadows; nor is it subject to the limitations of the physical senses. It is near to anyone anywhere who earnestly desires to enjoy it, and it is theirs to enjoy fully forever. It is in no place and yet is nowhere absent. Outwardly it admonishes us, inwardly it teaches us. It changes all who see it for the better, but it is itself never changed for the worse. No one judges it, yet no one judges rightly without it.

Undoubtedly, then, it is clear that truth is superior to our minds. Truth is one, and each mind is made wise by truth alone. You cannot judge truth, but by truth you can judge everything else.

II 15.39

You said that if I could show that there was something superior to our minds that you would confess that it was God (provided that there was nothing still more excellent). I accepted those conditions and agreed that it would be enough for me to show that much. For if there is anything superior to truth then that would be God, but if there is nothing else superior to it, then Truth itself is God. Whichever is the case, you cannot deny that God exists, and this was the question we set out to discuss.

If you are still uneasy about our faith-assumption (received from the holy teaching of Christ) that there is a Father of Wisdom, remember that it is also a faith-assumption that the Wisdom begotten of the eternal Father is equal to Him. (It is not necessary to go into these matters further now for they must be firmly accepted by faith alone.)

God does exist. Indeed He exists truly and supremely. In my view we not only hold this as certain by our faith, but we also come to grasp it intellectually by a sure (though admittedly a tenuous) form of knowledge. . . . Do you have any further objections to raise?

E. Oh, no! I accept all that you have said with an incredible joy that I cannot express in words. To me your arguments are convincingly certain. My inner being recognizes and cries out to this Truth wishing to cling to it, for I now see that it is not only good, but it is the Supreme Good and the Source of happiness.

BIBLIOGRAPHY OF STANDARD TRANSLATIONS

St. Augustine. *The Problem of Free Choice.* Translated and annotated by Dom Marx Pontifex. No. 22 of Ancient Christian Writers: The Works of the Fathers in Translation. Edited by Johannes Quasten and Joseph C. Plumpe. Westminster, Maryland: Newman; London: Longmans, Green, 1955.

_____. *The Free Choice of the Will*. Translated by Robert P. Russell. Vol. 59 of The Fathers of the Church: A New Translation. Washington, D.C.: The Catholic University of America Press, 1968.

_____. *On the Free Will*. In Selections from Medieval Philosophers: Augustine to Albert the Great. Translated and edited by Richard McKeon. New York: Scribner, 1929.

CONFESSIONS OF SAINT AUGUSTINE

BOOK XI.

CHAPTER III.

He begins from the creation of the world—not understanding the Hebrew text.

5. LET me hear and understand how in the beginning Thou didst make the heaven and the earth [Gen. 1:1]. Moses wrote this; he wrote and departed,— passed hence from Thee to Thee. Nor now is he before me; for if he were I would hold him, and ask him, and would adjure him by Thee that he would open unto me these things, and I would lend the ears of my body to the sounds bursting forth from his mouth. And should he speak in the Hebrew tongue, in vain would it beat on my senses, nor would aught touch my mind; but if in Latin, I should know what he said. But whence should I know whether he said what was true? But if I knew this even, should I know it from him? Verily within me, within in the chamber of my thought, Truth, neither Hebrew,[1] nor Greek,

---

From Marcus Dods, ed., *The Works of Aurelius Augustine, Bishop of Hippo. A New Translation*, trans. and annotated by J. G. Pilkington (Edinburgh: T. & T. Clark, 1876), 14:293–300.

[1]Augustine was not singular amongst the early Fathers in not knowing Hebrew, for of the Greeks only Origen, and of the Latins Jerome, knew anything of it. We find him confessing his ignorance both here and elsewhere (*Enarr. in Ps.* cxxxvi. 7, and *De Doctr. Christ.* ii. 22); and though he recommends a knowledge of Hebrew as well as Greek, to correct "the endless diversity of the Latin translators" (*De Doctr. Christ.* ii. 16), he speaks as strongly as does Grinfield, in his *Apology for the Septuagint*, in favour of the claims of that version to "biblical and canonical authority" (*Eps.* xxviii., lxxi., and lxxv.; *De Civ. Dei*, xviii. 42, 43; *De Doctr. Christ.* ii. 22). He discountenanced Jerome's new translation, probably from fear of giving offence, and, as we gather from *Ep.* lxxi. 5, not without cause. From the tumult he there describes as ensuing upon Jerome's version being read, the outcry would appear to have been as great as when, on the change of the old style of reckoning to the new, the ignorant mob clamoured to have back their eleven days!

nor Latin, nor barbarian, without the organs of voice and tongue, without the sound of syllables, would say, "He speaks the truth," and I, forthwith assured of it, confidently would say unto that man of Thine, "Thou speakest the truth." As, then, I cannot inquire of him, I beseech Thee,—Thee, O Truth, full of whom he spake truth,—Thee, my God, I beseech, forgive my sins; and do Thou, who didst give to that Thy servant to speak these things, grant to me also to understand them.

CHAPTER IV.

Heaven and earth cry out that they have been created by God.

6. BEHOLD, the heaven and earth are; they proclaim that they were made, for they are changed and varied. Whereas whatsoever hath not been made, and yet hath being, hath nothing in it which there was not before; this is what it is to be changed and varied. They also proclaim that they made not themselves; "therefore we are, because we have been made; we were not therefore before we were, so that we could have made ourselves." And the voice of those that speak is in itself an evidence. Thou, therefore, Lord, didst make these things; Thou who art beautiful, for they are beautiful; Thou who art good, for they are good; Thou who art, for they are. Nor even so are they beautiful, nor good, nor are they, as Thou their Creator art; compared with whom they are neither beautiful, nor good, nor are at all.[2] These things we know, thanks be to Thee. And our knowledge, compared with Thy knowledge, is ignorance.

CHAPTER V.

God created the world not from any certain matter, but in His own word.

7. BUT how didst Thou make the heaven and the earth, and what was the instrument of Thy so mighty work? For it was not as a human worker fashioning body from body, according to the fancy of his mind, in somewise able to assign a form which it perceives in itself by its inner eye.[3] And whence should he be able to do this, hadst not Thou made that mind? And he assigns to it already existing, and as it were having a being, a form, as clay, or stone, or wood, or gold, or such like. And whence should these things be, hadst not Thou appointed them? Thou

---

[2]It was the doctrine of Aristotle that excellence of character is the proper object of love, and in proportion as we recognise such excellence in others are we attracted to become like them (see Sidgwick's *Methods of Ethics*, book iv. c. 5, sec. 4). If this be true of the creature, how much more should it be so of the Creator, who is the perfection of all that we can conceive of goodness and truth. Compare *De Trin.* viii. 3–6, *De Vera Relig.* 57, and an extract from Athanese Coquerel in Archbishop Thomson's *Bampton Lectures*, note 73.

[3]See x. sec. 40, note 4, and sec. 53, above.

didst make for the workman his body,—Thou the mind commanding the limbs,—Thou the matter whereof he makes anything,[4]—Thou the capacity whereby he may apprehend his art, and see within what he may do without,— Thou the sense of his body, by which, as by an interpreter, he may from mind unto matter convey that which he doeth, and report to his mind what may have been done, that it within may consult the truth, presiding over itself, whether it be well done. All these things praise Thee, the Creator of all. But how dost Thou make them? How, O God, didst Thou make heaven and earth? Truly, neither in the heaven nor in the earth didst Thou make heaven and earth; nor in the air, nor in the waters, since these also belong to the heaven and the earth; nor in the whole world didst Thou make the whole world; because there was no place wherein it could be made before it was made, that it might be; nor didst Thou hold anything in Thy hand wherewith to make heaven and earth. For whence couldest Thou have what Thou hadst not made, whereof to make anything? For what is, save because Thou art? Therefore Thou didst speak and they were made [Ps. 33:9], and in Thy Word Thou madest these things [Ps. 33:6].

CHAPTER VI.

He did not, however, create it by a sounding and passing word.

8. BUT how didst Thou speak? Was it in that manner in which the voice came from the cloud, saying, "This is my beloved Son" [Matt. 17:5]? For that voice was uttered and passed away, began and ended. The syllables sounded and passed by, the second after the first, the third after the second, and thence in order, until the last after the rest, and silence after the last. Hence it is clear and plain that the motion of a creature expressed it, itself temporal, obeying Thy eternal will. And these thy words formed at the time, the outer ear conveyed to the intelligent mind, whose inner ear lay attentive to Thy eternal word. But it compared these words sounding in time with Thy eternal word in silence, and said, "It is different, very different. These words are far beneath me, nor are they, since they flee and pass away; but the Word of my Lord remaineth above me for ever." If, then, in sounding and fleeting words Thou didst say that heaven and earth should be made, and didst thus make heaven and earth, there was already a

---

[4]That is, the artificer makes, God creates. The creation of matter is distinctively a doctrine of revelation. The ancient philosophers believed in the eternity of matter. As Lucretius puts it (i. 51): "Nullam rem e nihilo gigni divinitus unquam." See Burton, *Bampton Lectures*, lect. iii. and notes 18–21, and Mansel, *Bampton Lectures*, lec. iii. note 12. See also p. 77, note, above, for the Manichaean doctrine as to the ὕλη; and *The Unseen Universe*, arts. 85, 86, 151, and 160, for the modern doctrine of "continuity." See also Kalisch, *Commentary* on Gen. i. 1.

corporeal creature before heaven and earth by whose temporal motions that voice might take its course in time. But there was nothing corporeal before heaven and earth; or if there were, certainly Thou without a transitory voice hadst created that whence Thou wouldest make the passing voice, by which to say that the heaven and the earth should be made. For whatsoever that were of which such a voice was made, unless it were made by Thee, it could not be at all. By what word of Thine was it decreed that a body might be made, whereby these words might be made?

CHAPTER VII.

By His co-eternal Word He speaks, and all things are done.

9. THOU callest us, therefore, to understand the Word, God with Thee, God [John 1:1], which is spoken eternally, and by it are all things spoken eternally. For what was spoken was not finished, and another spoken until all were spoken; but all things at once and for ever. For otherwise have we time and change, and not a true eternity, nor a true immortality. This I know, O my God, and give thanks. I know, I confess to Thee, O Lord, and whosoever is not unthankful to certain truth, knows and blesses Thee with me. We know, O Lord, we know; since in proportion as anything is not what it was, and is what it was not, in that proportion does it die and arise. Not anything therefore, of Thy Word giveth place and cometh into place again, because it is truly immortal and eternal. And, therefore, unto the Word co-eternal with Thee, Thou dost at once and for ever say all that Thou dost say; and whatever Thou sayest shall be made, is made; nor dost Thou make otherwise than by speaking; yet all things are not made both together and everlasting which Thou makest by speaking.

CHAPTER VIII.

That Word itself is the beginning of all things, in the which we are instructed as to evangelical truth.

10. WHY is this, I beseech Thee, O Lord my God? I see it, however; but how I shall express it, I know not, unless that everything which begins to be and ceases to be, then begins and ceases when in Thy eternal Reason it is known that it ought to begin or cease where nothing beginneth or ceaseth. The same is Thy Word, which is also "the Beginning," because also It speaketh unto us.[5] Thus, in

---

[5]John 8:25, *Old Ver.* Though some would read, *Qui et loquitur*, making it correspond to the Vulgate, instead of *Quia et loquitur*, as above, the latter is doubtless the correct reading, since we find the text similarly quoted *In Ev. Joh. Tract.* xxxviii. 11, where he enlarges on "The Beginning," comparing *principium* with ἀρχή. It will assist to the understanding of this section to refer to the early part of the note on p. 153, above, where the

the gospel He speaketh through the flesh; and this sounded outwardly in the ears of men, that it might be believed and sought inwardly, and that it might be found in the eternal Truth, where the good and only Master teacheth all His disciples. There, O Lord, I hear Thy voice, the voice of one speaking unto me, since He speaketh unto us who teacheth us. But He that teacheth us not, although He speaketh, speaketh not to us. Moreover, who teacheth us, unless it be the immutable Truth? For even when we are admonished through a changeable creature, we were led to the Truth immutable? There we learn truly while we stand and hear Him, and rejoice greatly "because of the Bridegroom's voice" [John 3:29], restoring us to that whence we are. And, therefore, the Beginning, because unless It remained, there would not, where we strayed, be whither to return. But when we return from error, it is by knowing that we return. But that we may know, He teacheth us, because He is the Beginning and speaketh unto us.

CHAPTER IX.

Wisdom and the Beginning.

11. IN this Beginning, O God, hast Thou made heaven and earth,—in Thy Word, in Thy Son, in Thy Power, in Thy Wisdom, in Thy Truth, wondrously speaking and wondrously making. Who shall comprehend? who shall relate it? What is that which shines through me, and strikes my heart without injury, and I both shudder and burn? I shudder inasmuch as I am unlike it; and I burn inasmuch as I am like it. It is Wisdom itself that shines through me, clearing my cloudiness, which again overwhelms me, fainting from it, in the darkness and amount of my punishment. For my strength is brought down in need [Ps. 31:10], so that I cannot endure my blessings, until Thou, O Lord, who hast been gracious to all mine iniquities, heal also all mine infirmities; because Thou shalt also redeem my life from corruption, and crown me with Thy loving-kindness and mercy, and shalt satisfy my desire with good things, because my youth shall be renewed like the eagle's [Ps. 103:3–5]. For by hope we are saved; and through

---

Platonic view of the *Logos*, as ἐνδιάθετος and προφορικός, or in the "bosom of the Father" and "made flesh," is given; which terminology, as Dr. Newman tells us (*Arians*, pt. i. c. 2, sec. 4), was accepted by the Church. Augustine, consistently with this idea, says (on John viii. 25, as above); "For if the Beginning, as it is in itself, had remained so with the Father as not to receive the form of a servant and speak as man with men, how could they have believed in Him, since their weak hearts could not have heard the word intelligently without some voice that would appeal to their senses? Therefore, said He, believe me to be the Beginning; for that you may believe, I not only am, but also speak to you." Newman, as quoted above, may be referred to for the significance of ἀρχή as applied to the Son, and *ibid.* sec. 3, also, on the "Word." For the difference between a mere "voice" and the "Word," compare Aug. *Serm.* ccxciii. sec. 3, and Origen, *In Joann.* ii. 36.

patience we await Thy promises [Rom. 8:24–25]. Let him that is able hear Thee discoursing within. I will with confidence cry out from Thy oracle, How wonderful are Thy works, O Lord, in Wisdom hast Thou made them all [Ps. 104:24]. And this Wisdom is the Beginning, and in that Beginning hast Thou made heaven and earth.

CHAPTER X.

The rashness of those who inquire what God did before He created heaven and earth.

12. LO, are they not full of their ancient way, who say to us, "What was God doing before He made heaven and earth? For if," say they, "He were unoccupied, and did nothing, why does He not for ever also, and from henceforth, cease from working, as in times past He did? For if any new motion has arisen in God, and a new will, to form a creature which He had never before formed, however can that be a true eternity where there ariseth a will which was not before? For the will of God is not a creature, but before the creature; because nothing could be created unless the will of the Creator were before it. The will of God, therefore, pertaineth to His very Substance. But if anything hath arisen in the Substance of God which was not before, that Substance is not truly called eternal. But if it was the eternal will of God that the creature should be, why was not the creature also from eternity?"

CHAPTER XI.

They who ask this have not as yet known the eternity of God, which is exempt from the relation of time.

13. THOSE who say these things do not as yet understand Thee, O Thou Wisdom of God, Thou light of souls; not as yet do they understand how these things be made which are made by and in Thee. They even endeavour to comprehend things eternal; but as yet their heart flieth about in the past and future motions of things, and is still wavering. Who shall hold it and fix it, that it may rest a little, and by degrees catch the glory of that ever-standing eternity, and compare it with the times which never stand, and see that it is incomparable; and that a long time cannot become long, save from the many motions that pass by, which cannot at the same instant be prolonged; but that in the Eternal nothing passeth away, but that the whole is present; but no time is wholly present; and let him see that all time past is forced on by the future, and that all the future followeth from the past, and that all, both past and future, is created and issues from that which is always present? Who will hold the heart of man, that it may stand still, and see how the still-standing eternity, itself neither future nor past,

uttereth the times future and past? Can my hand accomplish this, or the hand of my mouth by persuasion bring about a thing so great?

CHAPTER XII.

What God did before the creation of the world.

14. BEHOLD, I answer to him who asks, "What was God doing before He made heaven and earth?" I answer not, as a certain person is reported to have done facetiously (avoiding the pressure of the question), "He was preparing hell," saith he, "for those who pry into mysteries." It is one thing to perceive, another to laugh,—these things I answer not. For more willingly would I have answered, "I know not what I know not," than that I should make him a laughing-stock who asketh deep things, and gain praise as one who answereth false things. But I say that Thou, our God, art the Creator of every creature; and if by the term "heaven and earth" every creature is understood, I boldly say, "That before God made heaven and earth, He made not anything. For if He did, what did He make unless the creature?" And would that I knew whatever I desire to know to my advantage, as I know that no creature was made before any creature was made.

.　　.　　.

THE CITY OF GOD

BOOK I.

Argument

Augustin censures the pagans, who attributed the calamities of the world, and especially the recent sack of Rome by the Goths, to the Christian Religion, and its prohibition of the worship of the gods. He speaks of the blessings and ills of life, which then, as always, happened to good and bad men alike. Finally, he rebukes the shamelessness of those who cast up to the Christians that their women had been violated by the soldiers.

PREFACE, EXPLAINING HIS DESIGN IN UNDERTAKING THIS WORK

THE glorious city of God[1] is my theme in this work, which you, my dearest son Marcellinus,[2] suggested, and which is due to you by my promise. I have undertaken its defence against those who prefer their own gods to the Founder of

---

From Philip Schaff, ed., *The Nicene and Post-Nicene Fathers of the Christian Church*, trans. Marcus Dods (Buffalo: The Christian Literature Company, 1887), vol. 2.

[1][Augustin uses the term *civitas Dei* (πόλις θεοῦ) of the church universal as a commonwealth and community founded and governed by God. It is applied in the Bible to Jerusalem or the church of the Old Covenant (Ps. xl.6, 4; xlviii. 1, 8; lxxxvii. 3), and to the heavenly Jerusalem or the church perfect (Heb. xi. 10, 16; xii. 22; Rev. iii. 12; xxi. 2; xxii. 14, 19). Augustin comprehends under the term the whole Kingdom of God under the Jewish and Christian dispensation both in its militant and triumphant state, and contrasts it with the perishing kingdoms of this *world*. His work treats of both, but he calls it, *a meliore*, *The City of God.*—P.S.]

[2][Marcellinus was a friend of Augustin, and urged him to write this work. He was commissioned by the Emperor Honorius to convene a conference of Catholic and schismatic Donatist bishops in the summer of 411, and conceded the victory to the Catholics; but on account of his rigor in executing the laws against the Donatists, he fell a victim to their revenge, and was honored by a place among the martyrs. See the Letters of Augustin, 133, 136, 138, 139, 143, 151, the notes in this ed., vol. 1., 470 and 505, and the Translator's Preface.—P.S.]

this city,—a city surpassingly glorious, whether we view it as it still lives by faith in this fleeting course of time, and sojourns as a stranger in the midst of the ungodly, or as it shall dwell in the fixed stability of its eternal seat, which it now with patience waits for, expecting until "righteousness shall return unto judgment,"[3] and it obtain, by virtue of its excellence, final victory and perfect peace. A great work this, and an arduous; but God is my helper. For I am aware what ability is requisite to persuade the proud how great is the virtue of humility, which raises us, not by a quite human arrogance, but by a divine grace, above all earthly dignities that totter on this shifting scene. For the King and Founder of this city of which we speak, has in Scripture uttered to His people a dictum of the divine law in these words: "God resisteth the proud, but giveth grace unto the humble" [James 4:6; 1 Peter 5:5]. But this, which is God's prerogative, the inflated ambition of a proud spirit also affects, and dearly loves that this be numbered among its attributes, to

"Show pity to the humbled soul,
And crush the sons of pride."[4]

And therefore, as the plan of this work we have undertaken requires, and as occasion offers, we must speak also of the earthly city, which, though it be mistress of the nations, is itself ruled by its lust of rule.

CHAPTER I.

Of the adversaries of the Name of Christ, whom the Barbarians for Christ's sake spared when they stormed the city.

FOR to this earthly city belong the enemies against whom I have to defend the city of God. Many of them, indeed, being reclaimed from their ungodly error, have become sufficiently creditable citizens of this city; but many are so inflamed with hatred against it, and are so ungrateful to its Redeemer for His signal benefits, as to forget that they would now be unable to utter a single word to its prejudice, had they not found in its sacred places, as they fled from the enemy's steel, that life in which they now boast themselves.[5] Are not those very

---

[3]Ps. xciv. 15, rendered otherwise in Eng. ver. [In the Revised Vers: "Judgment shall return unto righteousness." In the Old Testament quotations, Augustin, being ignorant of Hebrew, had to rely on the imperfect Latin version of his day, and was at first even opposed to the revision of Jerome.—P.S.]

[4]Virgil, *Aeneid*, vi. 854. [*Parcere subjectis et debellare superbos.*—P.S.]

[5][Aug. refers to the sacking of the city of Rome by the West Gothic King Alaric, 410. He was the most humane of the barbaric invaders and conquerors of Rome, and had embraced Arian Christianity (probably from the teaching of Ulphilas, the Arian bishop and translator of the Bible). He spared the Catholic Christians.—For particulars see Gibbon's *Decline and Fall*, and Millman's *Latin Christianity.*—P.S.]

Romans, who were spared by the barbarians through their respect for Christ, become enemies to the name of Christ? The reliquaries of the martyrs and the churches of the apostles bear witness to this; for in the sack of the city they were open sanctuary for all who fled to them, whether Christian or Pagan. To their very threshold the blood-thirsty enemy raged; there his murderous fury owned a limit. Thither did such of the enemy as had any pity convey those to whom they had given quarter, lest any less mercifully disposed might fall upon them. And, indeed, when even those murderers who everywhere else showed themselves pitiless came to those spots where that was forbidden which the license of war permitted in every other place, their furious rage for slaughter was bridled, and their eagerness to take prisoners was quenched. Thus escaped multitudes who now reproach the Christian religion, and impute to Christ the ills that have befallen their city; but the preservation of their own life—a boon which they owe to the respect entertained for Christ by the barbarians—they attribute not to our Christ, but to their own good luck. They ought rather, had they any right perceptions, to attribute the severities and hardships inflicted by their enemies, to that divine providence which is wont to reform the depraved manners of men by chastisement, and which exercises with similar afflictions the righteous and praiseworthy,—either translating them, when they have passed through the trial, to a better world, or detaining them still on earth for ulterior purposes. And they ought to attribute it to the spirit of these Christian times, that, contrary to the custom of war, these bloodthirsty barbarians spared them, and spared them for Christ's sake, whether this mercy was actually shown in promiscuous places, or in those places specially dedicated to Christ's name, and of which the very largest were selected as sanctuaries, that full scope might thus be given to the expansive compassion which desired that a large multitude might find shelter there. Therefore ought they to give God thanks, and with sincere confession flee for refuge to His name, that so they may escape the punishment of eternal fire—they who with lying lips took upon them this name, that they might escape the punishment of present destruction. For of those whom you see insolently and shamelessly insulting the servants of Christ, there are numbers who would not have escaped that destruction and slaughter had they not pretended that they themselves were Christ's servants. Yet now, in ungrateful pride and most impious madness, and at the risk of being punished in everlasting darkness, they perversely oppose that name under which they fraudulently protected themselves for the sake of enjoying the light of this brief life.

CHAPTER II.

That it is quite contrary to the usage of war, that the victors should spare the vanquished for the sake of their gods.

THERE are histories of numberless wars, both before the building of Rome and since its rise and the extension of its domination; let these be read, and let one instance be cited in which, when a city had been taken by foreigners, the victors spared those who were found to have fled for sanctuary to the temples of their gods;[6] or one instance in which a barbarian general gave orders that none should be put to the sword who had been found in this or that temple. . . .

.   .   .

CHAPTER VI.

That not even the Romans, when they took cities, spared the conquered in their temples.

WHY, then, need our argument take note of the many nations who have waged wars with one another, and have nowhere spared the conquered in the temples of their gods? Let us look at the practice of the Romans themselves: let us, I say, recall and review the Romans, whose chief praise it has been "to spare the vanquished and subdue the proud," and that they preferred "rather to forgive than to revenge an injury;"[7] and among so many and great cities which they have stormed, taken, and overthrown for the extension of their dominion, let us be told what temples they were accustomed to exempt, so that whoever took refuge in them was free. Or have they really done this, and has the fact been suppressed by the historians of these events? Is it to be believed, that men who sought out with the greatest eagerness points they could praise, would omit those which, in their own estimation, are the most signal proofs of piety? Marcus Marcellus, a distinguished Roman, who took Syracuse, a most splendidly adorned city, is reported to have bewailed its coming ruin, and to have shed his own tears over it before he spilt its blood. He took steps also to preserve the chastity even of his enemy. For before he gave orders for the storming of the city, he issued an edict forbidding the violation of any free person. Yet the city was sacked according to the custom of war; nor do we anywhere read, that even by so chaste and gentle a commander orders were given that no one should be injured who had fled to this or that temple. And this certainly would by no means have been omitted, when neither his weeping nor his edict preservative of chastity could be passed in silence. Fabius, the conqueror of the city of Tarentum, is praised for abstaining

---

[6]The Benedictines remind us that Alexander and Xenophon, at least on some occasions, did so.
[7]Sallust, *Cat. Conj.* ix.

from making booty of the images. For when his secretary proposed the question to him, what he wished done with the statues of the gods, which had been taken in large numbers, he veiled his moderation under a joke. For he asked of what sort they were; and when they reported to him that there were not only many large images, but some of them armed, "Oh," says he, "let us leave with the Tarentines their angry gods." Seeing, then, that the writers of Roman history could not pass in silence, neither the weeping of the one general nor the laughing of the other, neither the chaste pity of the one nor the facetious moderation of the other, on what occasion would it be omitted, if, for the honor of any of their enemy's gods, they had shown this particular form of leniency, that in any temple slaughter or captivity was prohibited?

CHAPTER VII.

That the cruelties which occurred in the sack of Rome were in accordance with the custom of war, whereas the acts of clemency resulted from the influence of Christ's name.

ALL the spoiling, then, which Rome was exposed to in the recent calamity—all the slaughter, plundering, burning, and misery—was the result of the custom of war. But what was novel, was that savage barbarians showed themselves in so gentle a guise, that the largest churches were chosen and set apart for the purpose of being filled with the people to whom quarter was given, and that in them none were slain, from them none forcibly dragged; that into them many were led by their relenting enemies to be set at liberty, and that from them none were led into slavery by merciless foes. Whoever does not see that this is to be attributed to the name of Christ, and to the Christian temper, is blind; whoever sees this, and gives no praise, is ungrateful; whoever hinders any one from praising it, is mad. Far be it from any prudent man to impute this clemency to the barbarians. Their fierce and bloody minds were awed, and bridled, and marvellously tempered by Him who so long before said by His prophet, "I will visit their transgression with the rod, and their iniquities with stripes; nevertheless my loving-kindness will I not utterly take from them" [Ps. 89:32–33].

CHAPTER VIII.

Of the advantages and disadvantages which often indiscriminately accrue to good and wicked men.

WILL some one say, Why, then, was this divine compassion extended even to the ungodly and ungrateful? Why, but because it was the mercy of Him who daily "maketh His sun to rise on the evil and on the good, and sendeth rain on the just and on the unjust" [Matt. 5:45]. For though some of these men, taking thought of this, repent of their wickedness and reform, some, as the apostle says, "despising the riches of His goodness and long-suffering, after their hardness and impenitent heart, treasure up unto themselves wrath against the day of wrath and revelation of the righteous judgment of God, who will render to every man according to his deeds:" [Rom. 2:4–6] nevertheless does the patience of God still invite the wicked to repentance, even as the scourge of God educates the good to patience. And so, too, does the mercy of God embrace the good that it may cherish them, as the severity of God arrests the wicked to punish them. To the divine providence it has seemed good to prepare in the world to come for the righteous good things, which the unrighteous shall not enjoy; and for the wicked evil things, by which the good shall not be tormented. But as for the good things of this life, and its ills, God has willed that these should be common to both; that we might not too eagerly covet the things which wicked men are seen equally to enjoy, nor shrink with an unseemly fear from the ills which even good men often suffer.

There is, too, a very great difference in the purpose served both by those events which we call adverse and those called prosperous. For the good man is neither uplifted with the good things of time, nor broken by its ills; but the wicked man, because he is corrupted by this world's happiness, feels himself punished by its unhappiness.[8] Yet often, even in the present distribution of temporal things, does God plainly evince His own interference. For if every sin were now visited with manifest punishment, nothing would seem to be reserved for the final judgment; on the other hand, if no sin received now a plainly divine punishment, it would be concluded that there is no divine providence at all. And so of the good things of this life: if God did not by a very visible liberality confer these on some of those persons who ask for them, we should say that these good things were not at His disposal; and if He gave them to all who sought them, we should suppose that such were the only rewards of His service; and such a service would make us not godly, but greedy rather, and covetous. Wherefore, though good and bad men suffer alike, we must not suppose that there is no difference between the men themselves, because there is no difference in what they both suffer. For even in the likeness of the sufferings, there remains an unlikeness in the sufferers; and though exposed to the same anguish, virtue and vice are not the same thing. For as the same fire causes gold to glow brightly, and chaff to smoke; and under the same flail the straw is beaten small, while the grain is cleansed; and as the lees are not mixed with the oil, though squeezed out of the vat by the

---

[8]So Cyprian (*Contra Demetrianum*) says: *Paenam de adversis mundi ille sentit, cui et loetitia et gloria omnis in mundo est.*

same pressure, so the same violence of affliction proves, purges, clarifies the good, but damns, ruins, exterminates the wicked. And thus it is that in the same affliction the wicked detest God and blaspheme, while the good pray and praise. So material a difference does it make, not what ills are suffered, but what kind of man suffers them. For, stirred up with the same movement, mud exhales a horrible stench, and ointment emits a fragrant odor.

CHAPTER IX.

Of the reasons for administering correction to bad and good together.

WHAT, then, have the Christians suffered in that calamitous period, which would not profit everyone who duly and faithfully considered the following circumstances? First of all, they must humbly consider those very sins which have provoked God to fill the world with such terrible disasters; for although they be far from the excesses of wicked, immoral, and ungodly men, yet they do not judge themselves so clean removed from all faults as to be too good to suffer for these even temporal ills. For every man, however, laudably he lives, yet yields in some points to the lust of the flesh. Though he do [*sic*] not fall into gross enormity of wickedness, and abandoned viciousness, and abominable profanity, yet he slips into some sins, either rarely or so much the more frequently as the sins seem of less account. But not to mention this, where can we readily find a man who holds in fit and just estimation those persons on account of whose revolting pride, luxury, and avarice, and cursed iniquities and impiety, God now smites the earth as His predictions threatened? Where is the man who lives with them in the style in which it becomes us to live with them? For often we wickedly blind ourselves to the occasions of teaching and admonishing them, sometimes even of reprimanding and chiding them, either because we shrink from the labor or are ashamed to offend them, or because we fear to lose good friendships, lest this should stand in the way of our advancement, or injure us in some worldly matter, which either our covetous disposition desires to obtain, or our weakness shrinks from losing. So that, although the conduct of wicked men is distasteful to the good, and therefore they do not fall with them into that damnation which in the next life awaits such persons, yet, because they spare their damnable sins through fear, therefore, even though their own sins be slight and venial, they are justly scourged with the wicked in this world, though in eternity they quite escape punishment. Justly, when God afflicts them in common with the wicked, do they find this life bitter, through love of whose sweetness they declined to be bitter to these sinners.

If any one forbears to reprove and find fault with those who are doing wrong, because he seeks a more seasonable opportunity, or because he fears they may be made worse by his rebuke, or that other weak persons may be disheartened from endeavoring to lead a good and pious life, and may be driven from the faith; this man's omission seems to be occasioned not by covetousness, but by a charitable consideration. But what is blameworthy is, that they who themselves revolt from the conduct of the wicked, and live in quite another fashion, yet spare those faults in other men which they ought to reprehend and wean them from; and spare them because they fear to give offence, lest they should injure their interests in those things which good men may innocently and legitimately use,—though they use them more greedily than becomes persons who are strangers in this world, and profess the hope of a heavenly country. For not only the weaker brethren who enjoy married life, and have children (or desire to have them), and own houses and establishments, whom the apostle addresses in the churches, warning and instructing them how they should live, both the wives with their husbands, and the husbands with their wives, the children with their parents, and parents with their children, and servants with their masters, and masters with their servants,—not only do these weaker brethren gladly obtain and grudgingly lose many earthly and temporal things on account of which they dare not offend men whose polluted and wicked life greatly displeases them; but those also who live at a higher level, who are not entangled in the meshes of married life, but use meagre food and raiment, do often take thought of their own safety and good name, and abstain from finding fault with the wicked, because they fear their wiles and violence. And although they do not fear them to such an extent as to be drawn to the commission of like iniquities, nay, not by any threats or violence soever; yet those very deeds which they refuse to share in the commission of, they often decline to find fault with, when possibly they might by finding fault prevent their commission. They abstain from interference, because they fear that, if it fail of good effect, their own safety or reputation may be damaged or destroyed; not because they see that their preservation and good name are needful, that they may be able to influence those who need their instruction, but rather because they weakly relish the flattery and respect of men, and fear the judgments of the people, and the pain or death of the body; that is to say, their non-intervention is the result of selfishness, and not of love.

Accordingly this seems to me to be one principal reason why the good are chastised along with the wicked, when God is pleased to visit with temporal punishments the profligate manners of a community. They are punished together, not because they have spent an equally corrupt life, but because the good as well as the wicked, though not equally with them, love this present life; while they ought to hold it cheap, that the wicked, being admonished and reformed by their example, might lay hold of life eternal. And if they will not be the companions of the good in seeking life everlasting, they should be loved as enemies, and be dealt with patiently. For so long as they live, it remains uncertain whether they may not come to a better mind. These selfish persons have more cause to fear than those to whom it was said through the prophet, "He is taken away in his iniquity, but his blood will I require at the watchman's hand" [Ezek. 33:6]. For watchmen or overseers of the people are appointed in churches, that they may unsparingly rebuke sin. Nor is that man guiltless of the sin we speak of, who, though he be not a watchman, yet sees in the conduct of those with whom the relationships of this life bring him into contact, many things that should be blamed, and yet overlooks them, fearing to give offence, and lose such worldly blessings as may legitimately be desired, but which he too eagerly grasps. Then, lastly, there is another reason why the good are afflicted with temporal calamities—the reason which Job's case exemplifies: that the human spirit may be proved, and that it may be manifested with what fortitude of pious trust, and with how unmercenary a love, it cleaves to God.[9]

.   .   .

CHAPTER XI.

Of the end of this life, whether it is material that it be long delayed.

BUT, it is added, many Christians were slaughtered, and were put to death in a hideous variety of cruel ways. Well, if this be hard to bear, it is assuredly the common lot of all who are born into this life. Of this at least I am certain, that no one has ever died who was not destined to die some time. Now the end of life puts the longest life on a par with the shortest. For of two things which have alike ceased to be, the one is not better, the other worse—the one greater, the other less.[10] And of what consequence is it what kind of death puts an end to life, since he who has died once is not forced to go through the same ordeal a second time? And as in the daily casualties of life every man is, as it were, threatened with numberless deaths, so long as it remains uncertain which of them is his fate, I would ask whether it is not better to suffer one and die, than to live in fear of all? I am not unaware of the poor-spirited fear which prompts us to choose rather to live long in fear of so many deaths, than to die once and so escape them all; but the weak and cowardly shrinking of the flesh is one thing, and the well-considered and reasonable persuasion of the soul quite another. That death is not to be

---

[9]Compare with this chapter the first homily of Chrysostom to the people of Antioch.

[10]Much of a kindred nature might be gathered from the Stoics. Antoninus says (ii. 14): "Though thou shouldest be going to live 3000 years, and as many times 10,000 years, still remember that no man loses any other life than this which he now lives, nor lives any other than this which he now loses. The longest and the shortest are thus brought to the same."

judged an evil which is the end of a good life; for death becomes evil only by the retribution which follows it. They, then, who are destined to die, need not be careful to inquire what death they are to die, but into what place death will usher them. And since Christians are well aware that the death of the godly pauper whose sores the dogs licked was far better than of the wicked rich man who lay in purple and fine linen, what harm could these terrific deaths do to the dead who had lived well?

.   .   .

CHAPTER XIV.

Of the captivity of the saints, and that Divine Consolation never failed them therein.

BUT, say they, many Christians were even led away captive. This indeed were a most pitiable fate, if they could be led away to any place where they could not find their God. But for this calamity also sacred Scripture affords great consolation. The three youths were captives; Daniel was a captive; so were other prophets: and God, the comforter, did not fail them [Dan. 3]. And in like manner He has not failed His own people in the power of a nation which, though barbarous, is yet human,—He who did not abandon the prophet [Jonah] in the belly of a monster. These things, indeed, are turned to ridicule rather than credited by those with whom we are debating; though they believe what they read in their own books, that Arion of Methymna, the famous lyrist,[11] when he was thrown overboard, was received on a dolphin's back and carried to land. But that story of ours about the prophet Jonah is far more incredible,—more incredible because more marvellous, and more marvellous because a greater exhibition of power.

.   .   .

CHAPTER XXVIII.

By what judgment of God the enemy was permitted to indulge his lust on the bodies of continent Christians.

LET not your life, then, be a burden to you, ye faithful servants of Christ, though your chastity was made the sport of your enemies. You have a grand and

---

[11]"Second to none," as he is called by Herodotus, who first of all tells his well-known story (*Clio.* 23, 24).

true consolation, if you maintain a good conscience, and know that you did not consent to the sins of those who were permitted to commit sinful outrage upon you. And if you should ask why this permission was granted, indeed it is a deep providence of the Creator and Governor of the world; and "unsearchable are His judgments, and His ways past finding out" [Rom. 11:33]. Nevertheless, faithfully interrogate your own souls, whether ye have not been unduly puffed up by your integrity, and continence, and chastity; and whether ye have not been so desirous of the human praise that is accorded to these virtues, that ye have envied some who possessed them. I, for my part, do not know your hearts, and therefore I make no accusation; I do not even hear what your hearts answer when you question them. And yet, if they answer that it is as I have supposed it might be, do not marvel that you have lost that by which you can win men's praise, and retain that which cannot be exhibited to men. If you did not consent to sin, it was because God added His aid to His grace that it might not be lost, and because shame before men succeeded to human glory that it might not be loved. But in both respects even the faint-hearted among you have a consolation, approved by the one experience, chastened by the other; justified by the one, corrected by the other. As to those whose hearts, when interrogated, reply that they have never been proud of the virtue of virginity, widowhood, or matrimonial chastity, but, condescending to those of low estate, rejoiced with trembling in these gifts of God, and that they have never envied any one the like excellences of sanctity and purity, but rose superior to human applause, which is wont to be abundant in proportion to the rarity of the virtue applauded, and rather desired that their own number be increased, than that by the smallness of their numbers each of them should be conspicuous;—even such faithful women, I say, must not complain that permission was given to the barbarians so grossly to outrage them; nor must they allow themselves to believe that God overlooked their character when He permitted acts which no one with impunity commits. For some most flagrant and wicked desires are allowed free play at present by the secret judgment of God, and are reserved to the public and final judgment. Moreover, it is possible that those Christian women, who are unconscious of any undue pride on account of their virtuous chastity, whereby they sinlessly suffered the violence of their captors, had yet some lurking infirmity which might have betrayed them into a proud and contemptuous bearing, had they not been subjected to the humiliation that befell them in the taking of the city. As, therefore, some men were removed by death, that no wickedness might change their disposition, so these women were outraged lest prosperity should corrupt their modesty. Neither those women, then, who were already puffed up by the circumstance that they were still virgins, nor those who might have been so puffed up had they not been exposed to the violence of the enemy, lost their chastity, but rather gained humility; the former were saved from pride already cherished, the latter from pride that would shortly have grown upon them.

We must further notice that some of those suffers may have conceived that continence is a bodily good, and abides so long as the body is inviolate, and did not understand that the purity both of the body and the soul rests on the steadfastness of the will strengthened by God's grace, and cannot be forcibly taken from an unwilling person. From this error they are probably now delivered. For when they reflect how conscientiously they served God, and when they settle again to the firm persuasion that He can in nowise desert those who so serve Him, and so invoke His aid; and when they consider, what they cannot doubt, how pleasing to Him is chastity, they are shut up to the conclusion that He could never have permitted these disasters to befall His saints, if by them that saintliness could be destroyed which He Himself had bestowed upon them, and delights to see in them.

CHAPTER XXIX.

What the servants of Christ should say in reply to the unbelievers who cast in their teeth that Christ did not rescue them from the fury of their enemies.

THE whole family of God, most high and most true, has therefore a consolation of its own,—a consolation which cannot deceive, and which has in it a surer hope than the tottering and falling affairs of earth can afford. They will not refuse the discipline of this temporal life, in which they are schooled for life eternal; nor will they lament their experience of it, for the good things of earth they use as pilgrims who are not detained by them, and its ills either prove or improve them. As for those who insult over them in their trials, and when ills befall them say, "Where is thy God?" [Ps. 42:10] we may ask them where their gods are when they suffer the very calamities for the sake of avoiding which they worship their gods, or maintain they ought to be worshipped; for the family of Christ is furnished with its reply: our God is everywhere present, wholly everywhere; not confined to any place. He can be present unperceived, and be absent without moving; when He exposes us to adversities, it is either to prove our perfections or correct our imperfections; and in return for our patient endurance of the sufferings of time, He reserves for us an everlasting reward. But who are you, that we should deign to speak with you even about your own gods, much less about our God, who is "to be feared above all gods? For all the gods of the nations are idols; but the Lord made the heavens" [Ps. 96:4–5].

CHAPTER XXX.

That those who complain of christianity really desire to live without restraint in shameful luxury.

IF the famous Scipio Nasica were now alive, who was once your pontiff, and was unanimously chosen by the senate, when, in the panic created by the Punic war, they sought for the best citizen to entertain the Phrygian goddess, he would curb this shamelessness of yours, though you would perhaps scarcely dare to look upon the countenance of such a man. For why in your calamities do you complain of Christianity, unless because you desire to enjoy your luxurious license unrestrained, and to lead an abandoned and profligate life without the interruption of any uneasiness or disaster? For certainly your desire for peace, and prosperity, and plenty is not prompted by any purpose of using these blessings honestly, that is to say, with moderation, sobriety, temperance, and piety; for your purpose rather is to run riot in an endless variety of sottish pleasures, and thus to generate from your prosperity a moral pestilence which will prove a thousandfold more disastrous than the fiercest enemies. It was such a calamity as this that Scipio, your chief pontiff, your best man in the judgment of the whole senate, feared when he refused to agree to the destruction of Carthage, Rome's rival; and opposed Cato, who advised its destruction. He feared security, that enemy of weak minds, and he perceived that a wholesome fear would be a fit guardian for the citizens. And he was not mistaken; the event proved how wisely he had spoken. For when Carthage was destroyed, and the Roman republic delivered from its great cause of anxiety, a crowd of disastrous evils forthwith resulted from the prosperous condition of things. First concord was weakened, and destroyed by fierce and bloody seditions; then followed, by a concatenation of baleful causes, civil wars, which brought in their train such massacres, such bloodshed, such lawless and cruel proscription and plunder, that those Romans who, in the days of their virtue, had expected injury only at the hands of their enemies, now that their virtue was lost, suffered greater cruelties at the hands of their fellow-citizens. The lust of rule, which with other vices existed among the Romans in more unmitigated intensity than among any other people, after it had taken possession of the more powerful few, subdued under its yoke the rest, worn and wearied.

.   .   .

CHAPTER XXXIII.

That the overthrow of Rome has not corrected the vices of the Romans.

OH infatuated men, what is this blindness, or rather madness, which possesses you? How is it that while, as we hear, even the eastern nations are bewailing your ruin, and while powerful states in the most remote parts of the earth are mourning your fall as a public calamity, ye yourselves should be crowding to the theatres, should be pouring into them and filling them; and, in short, be playing a madder part now than ever before? This was the foul plague-spot, this the wreck of virtue and honor that Scipio sought to preserve you from when he prohibited the construction of theatres; this was his reason for desiring that you might still have an enemy to fear, seeing as he did how easily prosperity would corrupt and destroy you. He did not consider that republic flourishing whose walls stand, but whose morals are in ruins. But the seductions of evil-minded devils had more influence with you than the precautions of prudent men. Hence the injuries you do, you will not permit to be imputed to you: but the injuries you suffer, you impute to Christianity. Depraved by good fortune, and not chastened by adversity, what you desire in the restoration of a peaceful and secure state, is not the tranquillity of the commonwealth, but the impunity of your own vicious luxury. Scipio wished you to be hard pressed by an enemy, that you might not abandon yourselves to luxurious manners; but so abandoned are you, that not even when crushed by the enemy is your luxury repressed. You have missed the profit of your calamity; you have been made most wretched, and have remained most profligate.

CHAPTER XXXIV.

Of God's clemency in moderating the ruin of the city.

AND that you are yet alive is due to God, who spares you that you may be admonished to repent and reform your lives. It is He who has permitted you, ungrateful as you are, to escape the sword of the enemy, by calling yourselves His servants, or by finding asylum in the sacred places of the martyrs.

It is said that Romulus and Remus, in order to increase the population of the city they founded, opened a sanctuary in which every man might find asylum and absolution of all crime,—a remarkable foreshadowing of what has recently occurred in honor of Christ. The destroyers of Rome followed the example of its founders. But it was not greatly to their credit that the latter, for the sake of increasing the number of their citizens, did that which the former have done, lest the number of their enemies should be diminished.

CHAPTER XXXV.

Of the sons of the church who are hidden among the wicked, and of false Christians within the church.

LET these and similar answers (if any fuller and fitter answers can be found) be given to their enemies by the redeemed family of the Lord Christ, and by the pilgrim city of King Christ. But let this city bear in mind, that among her enemies lie hid those who are destined to be fellow-citizens, that she may not think it a fruitless labor to bear what they inflict as enemies until they become confessors of the faith. So, too, as long as she is a stranger in the world, the city of God has in her communion, and bound to her by the sacraments, some who shall not eternally dwell in the lot of the saints. Of these, some are not now recognized; others declare themselves, and do not hesitate to make common cause with our enemies in murmuring against God, whose sacramental badge they wear. These men you may to-day see thronging the churches with us, to-morrow crowding the theatres with the godless. But we have the less reason to despair of the reclamation even of such persons, if among our most declared enemies there are now some, unknown to themselves, who are destined to become our friends. In truth, these two cities are entangled together in this world, and intermixed until the last judgment effects their separation. I now proceed to speak, as God shall help me, of the rise, progress, and end of these two cities; and what I write, I write for the glory of the city of God, that, being placed in comparison with the other, it may shine with a brighter lustre.

.   .   .

∽ 8 ∽

ANSELM OF CANTERBURY (1033–1109)

Anselm was born in 1033 in the village of Aosta located in what is now Italy, but what was then the border between Burgundy and Lombardy. Almost nothing is known about his parents or about his life as a youth. Apparently he dearly loved his mother. She died, however, when he was in his early twenties. Unable to get along with his father, Anselm left home at the age of twenty-three. It seems that his father's family lived in Lombardy; so he went north into Burgundy, perhaps seeking support from his mother's family who were among the nobility of that region.

Anselm spent several years in Burgundy and France, but the reputation of Lanfranc drew Anselm to Normandy in 1059. Lanfranc was the master of the famous school at the Benedictine Abbey of Bec, and he became Anselm's mentor.

After his father's death, Anselm decided to enter the monastery at Bec to become a monk. In a very short time Anselm rose to positions of authority in the monastery. When Lanfranc went to a new monastery, Anselm succeeded him as prior of Bec and held the post for fifteen years (1063–78). When Herluin, the abbot of the monastery, died, Anselm succeeded him. Under Anselm's guidance Bec became one of the outstanding religious center in all of Europe.

During his thirty years at Bec, 1063–93, Anselm wrote many of his most famous works. The *Proslogion* was written during the year just prior to his becoming abbot. Unquestionably Augustine was the predominant influence on Anselm and the major source of ideas in Anselm's writings. Many of the examples, problems, and arguments used by Anselm are found in precisely the same form in Augustine's work. Actually the influence of Augustine is the most characteristic feature of the age in which Anselm lived.

In 1078 Anselm visited his old teacher Lanfranc who had become the archbishop of Canterbury. Anselm was very well received by the Christians in England, and when Lanfranc died in 1089, Anselm was their overwhelming choice to succeed him as the new archbishop. However, the English king, William Rufus, attempted to keep the position vacant so that he could profit financially from the Canterbury revenues. Thus it was not until 1093 that Anselm was actually offered the position of archbishop.

Anselm adamantly refused to accept the position of archbishop because he was dedicated to scholarly work and claimed to be unfit for the necessary secular responsibilities that would be his in such a position. As the story goes, the English bishops physically had to pry open Anselm's fingers in order to force the official staff into his hand. Then they literally dragged him to the church to be inducted into the office.

The ensuing relationship between Anselm and William Rufus could only be described as a violent one. William II may well have been morally the worst king ever to sit on the throne of England. His personal morals, however, were not as severe a problem for Anselm as were his attempts to dominate the church. Lanfranc had for the most part accepted William's control of the church, but Anselm was determined to assert the liberty of the church.

When Anselm disobeyed the king and visited Rome without permission, he became an exile. In the third year of his exile, 1100, William Rufus was killed, and the new king, Henry I, invited Anselm to return. Henry's demands, however, were not much different from those of William, and Anselm's attitude toward them remained the same. So in 1103 Anselm was exiled again. In 1107 a difficult and controversial compromise was reached, in which neither side was an obvious victor; however, Anselm did return to Canterbury.

The remarkable fact in all of this is that Anselm never ceased his scholarly work. In fact more than half of Anselm's writing was done after he became the archbishop of Canterbury. Like many great scholars, however, his work had little noticeable influence until one hundred years after his death.

Anselm died on the Wednesday before Easter—April 21, 1109. The story is told that some of his friends and disciples were sitting around his bed on Palm Sunday. One of them said, "Father and Lord, as far as it is given to us to know, you are leaving this world and are going to keep the Easter Court with your Lord."

Anselm, in his gracious way, replied, "If it is His will I shall gladly obey, but if He should prefer me to stay with you just long enough to solve the question of the origin of the soul which I have been turning over in my mind, I would gratefully accept the chance, for I doubt that anybody else will solve it while I am gone."

In his *Monologion*, written in about 1076 when Anselm was forty-three years old, he systematically set out to prove the existence of God by rational reflection alone. Principally the essay was an attempt to answer a number of questions that had arisen out of meditations on the being of God. Anselm did not intend, at this stage, to formulate a comprehension system of apologetic theology. He simply wanted to answer certain questions either that were put to him or that arose in his own mind—questions that caused the brothers of the monastery difficulty while they were trying to meditate.

Lanfranc apparently found the *Monologion* to be weak because Anselm had not based his arguments on Scripture or on the authority of the church fathers, such as Augustine. This caused Anselm some distress, but it did not prevent publication. In a real sense, however, the work is preliminary and does not express the confident settling of issues for Anselm that the later *Proslogion* does.

The original title of the *Monologion* was *An Example of Meditating about the Rational Basis of Faith*, whereas the *Proslogion* was originally called *Faith Seeking Understanding*. Thus, perhaps not surprisingly, the arguments in the *Monologion* are cosmological rather than ontological. In the section printed in this chapter, Anselm argues for God's existence from goodness, from perfection, and from existence itself. The identification of the Creator with the Supreme Good is found also in Plotinus, but Anselm is quick to emphasize that God is not merely the cause of the forms of being—but of being itself. Thus he formulates a distinctly biblical form of the cosmological argument in contrast to the Platonic or Aristotelian forms of the argument.

The *Proslogion*, written in 1078, contains Anselm's famous "ontological argument" for the existence of God. Within a short time, Gaunilo, a monk of Marmoutier known only for his reply entitled *In Behalf of the Fool*, wrote a critique of chapters II and III of the *Proslogion*. Anselm offered a defense of his reasoning and, because of the importance of this extended clarification, directed that all subsequent printings of the *Proslogion* include the exchange with Gaunilo as well.

Of the classic proofs for theism, Anselm's argument is perhaps the most difficult for a novice to grasp. Kant rejected the argument, yet he considered it the common basis of all metaphysical arguments for God's existence. Anselm's central idea was that perfection implies existence, a view quite compatible with Augustinian Platonism. The so-called argument is addressed to God and thus is not simply an argument whose conclusion proves God's existence. Anselm already believes, as does Gaunilo. The argument actually is an attempt to understand that which Anselm already believed. Yet Anselm did intend to produce a philosophically persuasive proof that should convince the atheist if only the existence of the *concept* of God be granted. This necessary concept is that of "a being than which nothing greater can be conceived." A being so described could not fail to exist, Anselm claimed.

Traditional interpreters have concentrated almost exclusively on what they take to be a logically complete argument in *Proslogion* II, and the controversy over the validity or the fallacy involved in that section continues. Recently several modern interpreters have found an independent, self-contained argument in *Proslogion* III and have suggested that the two arguments stand or fall independently. Richard R. La Croix contends that neither section contains a logically complete argument but that the two chapters must be taken together to form an adequate basis for the deductions concerning God's existence that Anselm wants to make.

Ontological arguments are popular with idealist philosophers even today. Anselm's arguments were soundly denounced by Aquinas but were repeated with new fervor by Descartes and Leibniz. Kant considered the ontological argument to be the necessary yet inconclusive step in all theistic reasoning. In recent times Charles

Hartshorne, a philosopher from the University of Texas, has most vigorously defended Anselm's argument, while Karl Barth and many, more conservative, Reformed theologians have taken the priority of faith as an essential premise for their theological formulations. You must believe in order to understand, they say. Faith preceeds knowledge. And so it did from Augustine until Aquinas.

BIBLIOGRAPHY

Anselm of Canterbury. Vol. 1. *Monologion, Proslogion, Debate with Gaunilo, and a Meditation on Human Redemption.* Edited and translated by Jasper Hopkins and Herbert Richardson. Toronto: Mellen, 1974.

Barth, Karl. *Anselm: Fides Quaerens Intellectum.* Translated by Ian W. Robertson, Richmond: John Knox, 1960.

Cambell, Richard. *From Belief to Understanding.* Canberra: The Australian National University, 1976.

Hartshorne, Charles. *Anselm's Discovery: A Re-examination of the Ontological Proof for God's Existence.* LaSalle: Open Court, 1965.

Hick, John, and McGill, Arthur C., eds. *The Many-Faced Argument: Recent Studies on the Ontological Argument for the Existence of God.* New York: Macmillan, 1967.

Hopkins, Jasper. *A Companion to the Study of St. Anselm.* Minneapolis: University of Minnesota Press, 1972.

La Croix, Richard R. *Proslogion II and III: A Third Interpretation of Anselm's Argument.* Leiden: Brill, 1972.

Plantinga, Alvin, ed. *The Ontological Argument From St. Anselm to Contemporary Philosophers.* With an Introduction by Richard Taylor. Garden City: Doubleday, Anchor, 1965.

St. Anselm's Proslogion. Translated with an Introduction and Philosophical Commentary by M. J. Charlesworth. Notre Dame: University of Notre Dame Press, 1965.

Southern, R. W. *Saint Anselm and His Biographer.* Cambridge: At the University Press, 1963.

MONOLOGIUM
ON THE BEING OF GOD

Preface

CERTAIN brethren have often and earnestly entreated me to put in writing some thoughts that I had offered them in familiar conversation, regarding meditation on the Being of God, and on some other topics connected with this subject, under the form of a meditation on these themes. It is in accordance with their wish, rather than with my ability, that they have prescribed such a form for the writing of this meditation; in order that nothing in Scripture should be urged on the authority of Scripture itself, but that whatever the conclusion of independent investigation should declare to be true, should, in an unadorned style, with common proofs and with a simple argument, be briefly enforced by the cogency of reason, and plainly expounded in the light of truth. It was their wish also, that I should not disdain to meet such simple and almost foolish objections as occur to me.

This task I have long refused to undertake. And, reflecting on the matter, I have tried on many grounds to excuse myself; for the more they wanted this work to be adaptable to practical use, the more was what they enjoined on me difficult of execution. Overcome at last, however, both by the modest importunity of their entreaties and by the not contemptible sincerity of their zeal; and reluctant as I was because of the difficulty of my task and the weakness of my talent, I entered upon the work they asked for. But it is with pleasure inspired by their affection that, so far as I was able, I have prosecuted this work within the limits they set.

From Sidney Norton Deane, trans., *St. Anselm. Proslogium; Monologium; an Appendix in Behalf of the Fool by Gaunilon; and Cur Deus Homo*, repr. ed. (La Salle, Ill.: Open Court, 1948), pp. 35–45.

I was led to this undertaking in the hope that whatever I might accomplish would soon be overwhelmed with contempt, as by men disgusted with some worthless thing. For I know that in this book I have not so much satisfied those who entreated me, as put an end to the entreaties that followed me so urgently. Yet, somehow it fell out, contrary to my hope, that not only the brethren mentioned above, but several others, by making copies for their own use, condemned this writing to long remembrance. And, after frequent consideration, I have not been able to find that I have made in it any statement which is inconsistent with the writings of the Catholic Fathers, or especially with those of St. Augustine. Wherefore, if it shall appear to any man that I have offered in this work any thought that is either too novel or discordant with the truth, I ask him not to denounce me at once as one who boldly seizes upon new ideas, or as a maintainer of falsehood; but let him first read diligently Augustine's books on the Trinity, and then judge my treatise in the light of those.

In stating that the supreme Trinity may be said to consist of three substances, I have followed the Greeks, who acknowledge three substances in one Essence, in the same faith wherein we acknowledge three persons in one Substance. For they designate by the word *substance* that attribute of God which we designate by the word *person*.

Whatever I have said on that point, however, is put in the mouth of one debating and investigating in solitary reflection, questions to which he had given no attention before. And this method I knew to be in accordance with the wish of those whose request I was striving to fulfil. But it is my prayer and earnest entreaty, that if any shall wish to copy this work, he shall be careful to place this preface at the beginning of the book, before the body of the meditation itself. For I believe that one will be much helped in understanding the matter of this book, if he has taken note of the intention, and the method according to which it is discussed. It is my opinion, too, that one who has first seen this preface will not pronounce a rash judgment, if he shall find offered here any thought that is contrary to his own belief.

CHAPTER I.

There is a being which is best, and greatest, and highest of all existing beings.

IF any man, either from ignorance or unbelief, has no knowledge of the existence of one Nature which is the highest of all existing beings, which is also sufficient to itself in its eternal blessedness, and which confers upon and effects in all other beings, through its omnipotent goodness, the very fact of their existence, and the fact that in any way their existence is good; and if he has no knowledge of many other things, which we necessarily believe regarding God and his creatures, he still believes that he can at least convince himself of these truths in great part, even if his mental powers are very ordinary, by the force of reason alone.

And, although he could do this in many ways, I shall adopt one which I consider easiest for such a man. For, since all desire to enjoy only those things which they suppose to be good, it is natural that this man should, at some time, turn his mind's eye to the examination of that cause by which these things are good, which he does not desire, except as he judges them to be good. So that, as reason leads the way and follows up these considerations, he advances rationally to those truths of which, without reason, he has no knowledge. And if, in this discussion, I use any argument which no greater authority adduces, I wish it to be received in this way: although, on the grounds that I shall see fit to adopt, the conclusion is reached as if necessarily, yet it is not, for this reason, said to be absolutely necessary, but merely that it can appear so for the time being.

It is easy, then, for one to say to himself: Since there are goods so innumerable, whose great diversity we experience by the bodily senses, and discern by our mental faculties, must we not believe that there is some one thing, through which all goods whatever are good? Or are they good, one through one thing, and another through another? To be sure, it is most certain and clear, for all who are willing to see, that whatsoever things are said to possess any attribute in such a way that in mutual comparison they may be said to possess it in greater, or less, or equal degree, are said to possess it by virtue of some fact, which is not understood to be one thing in one case and another in another, but to be the same in different cases, whether it is regarded as existing in these cases in equal or unequal degree. For, whatsoever things are said to be *just*, when compared one with another, whether equally, or more, or less, cannot be understood as just, except through the quality of *justness*, which is not one thing in one instance, and another in another.

Since it is certain, then, that all goods, if mutually compared, would prove either equally or unequally good, necessarily they are all good by virtue of something which is conceived of as the same in different goods, although sometimes they seem to be called good, the one by virtue of one thing, the other by virtue of another. For, apparently it is by virtue of one quality, that a horse is called *good*, because he is strong, and by virtue of another, that he is called *good*, because he is swift. For, though he seems to be called good by virtue of his strength, and good by virtue of his swiftness, yet swiftness and strength do not appear to be the same thing.

But if a horse, because he is strong and swift, is therefore good, how is it that a strong, swift robber is bad? Rather, then, just as a strong, swift robber is bad, because he is harmful, so a strong, swift horse is good, because he is useful. And, indeed, nothing is ordinarily regarded as good, except either for some utility—as, for instance, safety is called good, and those things which promote safety—or for some honorable character—as, for instance, beauty is reckoned to be good, and what promotes beauty.

But, since the reasoning which we have observed is in no wise refutable, necessarily, again, all things, whether useful or honorable, if they are truly good, are good through that same being through which all goods exist, whatever that being is. But who can doubt this very being, through which all goods exist, to be a great good? This must be, then, a good through itself, since every other good is through it.

It follows, therefore, that all other goods are good through another being than that which they themselves are, and this being alone is good through itself. Hence, this alone is supremely good, which is alone good through itself. For it is supreme, in that it so surpasses other beings, that it is neither equalled nor excelled. But that which is supremely good is also supremely great. There is, therefore, some one being which is supremely good, and supremely great, that is, the highest of all existing beings.

CHAPTER II.

The same subject continued.

BUT, just as it has been proved that there is a being that is supremely good, since all goods are good through a single being, which is good through itself; so it is necessarily inferred that there is something supremely great, which is great through itself. But I do not mean physically great, as a material object is great, but that which, the greater it is, is the better or the more worthy,—wisdom, for instance. And since there can be nothing supremely great except what is supremely good, there must be a being that is greatest and best, i.e., the highest of all existing beings.

CHAPTER III.

There is a certain Nature through which whatever is exists, and which exists through itself, and is the highest of all existing beings.

THEREFORE, not only are all good things such through something that is one and the same, and all great things such through something that is one and the same; but whatever is, apparently exists through something that is one and the same. For, everything that is, exists either through something, or through nothing. But nothing exists through nothing. For it is altogether inconceivable that anything should not exist by virtue of something.

Whatever is, then, does not exist except through something. Since this is true, either there is one being, or there are more than one, through which all things that are exist. But if there are more than one, either these are themselves to be referred to some one being, through which they exist, or they exist separately, each through itself, or they exist mutually through one another.

But, if these beings exist through one being, then all things do not exist through more than one, but rather through that one being through which these exist.

If, however, these exist separately, each through itself, there is, at any rate, some power or property of existing through self (*existendi per se*), by which they are able to exist each through itself. But, there can be no doubt that, in that case, they exist through this very power, which is one, and through which they are able to exist, each through itself. More truly, then, do all things exist through this very being, which is one, than through these, which are more than one, which, without this one, cannot exist.

But that these beings exist mutually through one another, no reason can admit; since it is an irrational conception that anything should exist through a being on which it confers existence. For not even beings of a relative nature exist thus mutually, the one through the other. For, though the terms *master* and *servant* are used with mutual reference, and the men thus designated are mentioned as having mutual relations, yet they do not at all exist mutually, the one through the other, since these relations exist through the subjects to which they are referred.

Therefore, since truth altogether excludes the supposition that there are more beings than one, through which all things exist, that being, through which all exist, must be one. Since, then, all things that are exist through this one being, doubtless this one being exists through itself. Whatever things there are else, then, exist through something other than themselves, and this alone through itself. But whatever exists through another is less than that, through which all things are, and which alone exists through itself. Therefore, that which exists through itself exists in the greatest degree of all things.

There is, then, some one being which alone exists in the greatest and the highest degree of all. But that which is greatest of all, and through which exists whatever is good or great, and, in short, whatever has any existence—that must be supremely good, and supremely great, and the highest of all existing beings.

CHAPTER IV.
The same subject continued.

FURTHERMORE, if one observes the nature of things he perceives, whether he will or no, that not all are embraced in a single degree of dignity; but that certain among them are distinguished by inequality of degree. For, he who doubts that the horse is superior in its nature to wood, and man more excellent than the horse, assuredly does not deserve the name of man. Therefore, although it cannot be denied that some natures are superior to others, nevertheless reason convinces us that some nature is so preëminent among these, that it has no superior. For, if the distinction of degrees is infinite, so that there is among them no degree, than which no higher can be found, our course of reasoning reaches this conclusion: that the multitude of natures themselves is not limited by any bounds. But only an absurdly foolish man can fail to regard such a conclusion as absurdly foolish. There is, then, necessarily some nature which is so superior to some nature or natures, that there is none in comparison with which it is ranked as inferior.

Now, this nature which is such, either is single, or there are more natures than one of this sort, and they are of equal degree.

But, if they are more than one and equal, since they cannot be equal through any diverse causes, but only through some cause which is one and the same, that one cause, through which they are equally so great, either is itself what they are, that is, the very essence of these natures; or else it is another than what they are.

But if it is nothing else than their very essence itself, just as they have not more than one essence, but a single essence, so they have not more than one nature, but a single nature. For I here understand *nature* as identical with *essence*.

If, however, that through which these natures are so great is another than that which they are, then, certainly, they are less than that through which they are so great. For, whatever is great through something else is less than that through which it is great. Therefore, they are not so great that there is nothing else greater than they.

But if, neither through what they are nor through anything other than themselves, can there be more such natures than one, than which nothing else shall be more excellent, then in no wise can there be more than one nature of this kind. We conclude, then, that there is some nature which is one and single, and which is so superior to others that it is inferior to none. But that which is such is the greatest and best of all existing beings. Hence, there is a certain nature which is the highest of all existing beings. This, however, it cannot be, unless it is what it is through itself, and all existing beings are what they are through it.

For since, as our reasoning showed us not long since, that which exists through itself, and through which all other things exist, is the highest of all existing beings; either conversely, that which is the highest exists through itself, and all others through it; or, there will be more than one supreme being. But it is manifest that there cannot be more than one supreme being. There is, therefore, a certain Nature, or Substance, or Essence, which is through itself good and great, and through itself is what it is; and through which exists whatever is truly good, or great, or has any existence at all; and which is the supreme good being, the supreme great being, being or subsisting as supreme, that is, the highest of all existing beings.

PROSLOGIUM
ON THE EXISTENCE OF GOD

Preface

AFTER I had published, at the solicitous entreaties of certain brethren, a brief work [the *Monologium*] as an example of meditation on the grounds of faith, in the person of one who investigates, in a course of silent reasoning with himself, matters of which he is ignorant; considering that this book was knit together by the linking of many arguments, I began to ask myself whether there might be found a single argument which would require no other for its proof than itself alone; and alone would suffice to demonstrate that God truly exists. . . .

CHAPTER I.

Exhortation of the mind to the contemplation of God.—It casts aside cares, and excludes all thoughts save that of God, that it may seek Him. Man was created to see God. Man by sin lost the blessedness for which he was made, and found the misery for which he was not made. He did not keep his good when he could keep it easily. Without God it is ill with us. Our labors and attempts are in vain without God. Man cannot seek God, unless God himself teaches him; nor find him, unless he reveals himself. God created man in his image, that he might be mindful of him, think of him, and love him. The believer does not seek to understand, that he may believe, but he believes that he may understand: for unless he believed he would not understand.

UP now, slight man! flee, for a little while, thy occupations; hide thyself, for a time, from thy disturbing thoughts. Cast aside, now, thy burdensome cares, and put away thy toilsome business. Yield room for some little time to God; and

From Sidney Norton Deane, trans., *St. Anselm. Proslogium; Monologium; an Appendix in Behalf of the Fool by Gaunilon; and Cur Deus Homo*, repr. ed. (La Salle, Ill.: Open Court, 1948), pp. 1, 3–11, 22.

rest for a little time in him. Enter the inner chamber of thy mind; shut out all thoughts save that of God, and such as can aid thee in seeking him; close thy door and seek him. Speak now, my whole heart! speak now to God, saying, I seek thy face; thy face, Lord, will I seek (Psalms 27:8). And come thou now, O Lord my God, teach my heart where and how it may seek thee, where and how it may find thee.

Lord, if thou art not here, where shall I seek thee, being absent? But if thou art everywhere, why do I not see thee present? Truly thou dwellest in unapproachable light. But where is unapproachable light, or how shall I come to it? Or who shall lead me to that light and into it, that I may see thee in it? Again, by what marks, under what form, shall I seek thee? I have never seen thee, O Lord, my God; I do not know thy form. What, O most high Lord, shall this man do, an exile far from thee? What shall thy servant do, anxious in his love of thee, and cast out afar from thy face? He pants to see thee, and thy face is too far from him. He longs to come to thee, and thy dwelling-place is inaccessible. He is eager to find thee, and knows not thy place. He desires to seek thee, and does not know thy face. Lord, thou art my God, and thou art my Lord, and never have I seen thee. It is thou that hast made me, and hast made me anew, and hast bestowed upon me all the blessings I enjoy; and not yet do I know thee. Finally, I was created to see thee, and not yet have I done that for which I was made.

O wretched lot of man, when he hath lost that for which he was made! O hard and terrible fate! Alas, what has he lost, and what has he found? What has departed, and what remains? He has lost the blessedness for which he was made, and has found the misery for which he was not made. That has departed without which nothing is happy, and that remains which, in itself, is only miserable. Man once did eat the bread of angels, for which he hungers now; he eateth now the bread of sorrows, of which he knew not then. Alas! for the mourning of all mankind, for the universal lamentation of the sons of Hades! He choked with satiety, we sigh with hunger. He abounded, we beg. He possessed in happiness, and miserably forsook his possession; we suffer want in unhappiness, and feel a miserable longing, and alas! we remain empty.

Why did he not keep for us, when he could so easily, that whose lack we should feel so heavily? Why did he shut us away from the light, and cover us over with darkness? With what purpose did he rob us of life, and inflict death upon us? Wretches that we are, whence have we been driven out; whither are we driven on? Whence hurled? Whither consigned to ruin? From a native country into exile, from the vision of God into our present blindness, from the joy of immortality into the bitterness and horror of death. Miserable exchange of how great a good, for how great an evil! Heavy loss, heavy grief heavy all our fate!

But alas! wretched that I am, one of the sons of Eve, far removed from God! What have I undertaken? What have I accomplished? Whither was I striving? How far have I come? To what did I aspire? Amid what thoughts am I sighing? I sought blessings, and lo! confusion. I strove toward God, and I stumbled on myself. I sought calm in privacy, and I found tribulation and grief, in my inmost thoughts. I wished to smile in the joy of my mind, and I am compelled to frown by the sorrow of my heart. Gladness was hoped for, and lo! a source of frequent sighs!

And thou too, O Lord, how long? How long, O Lord, dost thou forget us; how long dost thou turn thy face from us? When wilt thou look upon us, and hear us? When wilt thou enlighten our eyes, and show us thy face? When wilt thou restore thyself to us? Look upon us, Lord; hear us, enlighten us, reveal thyself to us. Restore thyself to us, that it may be well with us,—thyself, without whom it is so ill with us. Pity our toilings and strivings toward thee, since we can do nothing without thee. Thou dost invite us; do thou help us. I beseech thee, O Lord, that I may not lose hope in sighs, but may breathe anew in hope. Lord, my heart is made bitter by its desolation; sweeten thou it, I beseech thee, with thy consolation. Lord, in hunger I began to seek thee; I beseech thee that I may not cease to hunger for thee. In hunger I have come to thee; let me not go unfed. I have come in poverty to the Rich, in misery to the Compassionate; let me not return empty and despised. And, if, before I eat, I sigh, grant, even after sighs, that which I may eat. Lord, I am bowed down and can only look downward; raise me up that I may look upward. My iniquities have gone over my head; they overwhelm me; and, like a heavy load, they weigh me down. Free me from them; unburden me, that the pit of iniquities may not close over me.

Be it mine to look up to thy light, even from afar, even from the depths. Teach me to seek thee, and reveal thyself to me, when I seek thee, for I cannot seek thee, except thou teach me, nor find thee, except thou reveal thyself. Let me seek thee in longing, let me long for thee in seeking; let me find thee in love, and love thee in finding. Lord, I acknowledge and I thank thee that thou hast created me in this thine image, in order that I may be mindful of thee, may conceive of thee, and love thee; but that image has been so consumed and wasted away by vices, and obscured by the smoke of wrong-doing, that it cannot achieve that for which it was made, except thou renew it, and create it anew. I do not endeavor, O Lord, to penetrate thy sublimity, for in no wise do I compare my understanding with that; but I long to understand in some degree thy truth, which my heart believes and loves. For I do not seek to understand that I may believe, but I believe in order to understand. For this also I believe,—that unless I believed, I should not understand.

CHAPTER II.

Truly there is a God, although the fool hath said in his heart, There is no God.

AND so, Lord, do thou, who dost give understanding to faith, give me, so far as thou knowest it to be profitable, to understand that thou art as we believe; and that thou art that which we believe. And, indeed, we believe that thou art a being than which nothing greater can be conceived. Or is there no such nature, since the fool hath said in his heart, there is no God? (Psalms 14:1). But, at any rate, this very fool, when he hears of this being of which I speak—a being than which nothing greater can be conceived—understands what he hears, and what he understands is in his understanding; although he does not understand it to exist.

For, it is one thing for an object to be in the understanding, and another to understand that the object exists. When a painter first conceives of what he will afterwards perform, he has it in his understanding, but he does not yet understand it to be, because he has not yet performed it. But after he has made the painting, he both has it in his understanding, and he understands that it exists, because he has made it.

Hence, even the fool is convinced that something exists in the understanding, at least, than which nothing greater can be conceived. For, when he hears of this, he understands it. And whatever is understood, exists in the understanding. And assuredly that, than which nothing greater can be conceived, cannot exist in the understanding alone. For, suppose it exists in the understanding alone: then it can be conceived to exist in reality; which is greater.

Therefore, if that, than which nothing greater can be conceived, exists in the understanding alone, the very being, than which nothing greater can be conceived, is one, than which a greater can be conceived. But obviously this is impossible. Hence, there is no doubt that there exists a being, than which nothing greater can be conceived, and it exists both in the understanding and in reality.

CHAPTER III.

God cannot be conceived not to exist—God is that, than which nothing greater can be conceived.—That which can be conceived not to exist is not God.

AND it assuredly exists so truly, that it cannot be conceived not to exist. For, it is possible to conceive of a being which cannot be conceived not to exist; and this is greater than one which can be conceived not to exist. Hence, if that, than which nothing greater can be conceived, can be conceived not to exist, it is not that, than which nothing greater can be conceived. But this is an irreconcilable contradiction. There is, then, so truly a being that which nothing greater can

And, indeed, whatever else there is, except thee alone, can be conceived not to be conceived to exist, that it cannot even be conceived not to exist; and this being thou art, O Lord, our God.

So truly, therefore, dost thou exist, O Lord, my God, that thou canst not be conceived not to exist; and rightly. For, if a mind could conceive of a being better than thee, the creature would rise above the Creator; and this is most absurd. exist. To thee alone, therefore, it belongs to exist more truly than all other beings, and hence in a higher degree than all others. For, whatever else exists does not exist so truly, and hence in a less degree it belongs to it to exist. Why, then, has the fool said in his heart, there is no God (Psalms 14:1), since it is so evident, to a rational mind, that thou dost exist in the highest degree of all? Why, except that he is dull and a fool?

CHAPTER IV.

How the fool has said in his heart what cannot be conceived.—A thing may be conceived in two ways: (1) when the word signifying it is conceived; (2) when the thing itself is understood. As far as the word goes, God can be conceived not to exist; in reality he cannot.

BUT how has the fool said in his heart what he could not conceive; or how is it that he could not conceive what he said in his heart? since it is the same to say in the heart, and to conceive.

But, if really, nay, since really, he both conceived, because he said in his heart; and did not say in his heart, because he could not conceive; there is more than one way in which a thing is said in the heart or conceived. For, in one sense, an object is conceived, when the word signifying it is conceived; and in another, when the very entity, which the object is, is understood.

In the former sense, then, God can be conceived not to exist; but in the latter, not at all. For no one who understands what fire and water are can conceive fire to be water, in accordance with the nature of the facts themselves, although this is possible according to the words. So, then, no one who understands what God is can conceive that God does not exist; although he says these words in his heart, either without any or with some foreign, signification. For, God is that than which a greater cannot be conceived. And he who thoroughly understands this, assuredly understands that this being so truly exists, that not even in concept can it be non-existent. Therefore, he who understands that God so exists, cannot conceive that he does not exist.

I thank thee, gracious Lord, I thank thee; because what I formerly believed by thy bounty, I now so understand by thine illumination, that if I were unwilling to believe that thou dost exist, I should not be able not to understand this to be true.

CHAPTER V.

God is whatever it is better to be than not to be; and he, as the only self-existent being, creates all things from nothing.

WHAT art thou, then, Lord God, than whom nothing greater can be conceived? But what art thou, except that which, as the highest of all beings, alone exists through itself, and creates all other things from nothing? For, whatever is not this is less than a thing which can be conceived of. But this cannot be conceived of thee. What good, therefore, does the supreme Good lack, through which every good is? Therefore, thou art just, truthful, blessed, and whatever it is better to be than not to be. For it is better to be just than not just; better to be blessed than not blessed.

.   .   .

CHAPTER XV.

He is greater than can be conceived.

THEREFORE, O Lord, thou art not only that than which a greater cannot be conceived, but thou art a being greater than can be conceived. For, since it can be conceived that there is such a being, if thou art not this very being, a greater than thou can be conceived. But this is impossible.

.   .   .

APPENDIX:
IN BEHALF OF THE FOOL

AN ANSWER TO THE ARGUMENT OF ANSELM IN THE
PROSLOGIUM BY GAUNILON, A MONK OF MARMOUTIER

1. IF one doubts or denies the existence of a being of such a nature that nothing greater than it can be conceived, he receives this answer:

The existence of this being is proved, in the first place, by the fact that he himself, in his doubt or denial regarding this being, already has it in his understanding; for in hearing it spoken of he understands what is spoken of. It is proved, therefore, by the fact that what he understands must exist not only in his understanding, but in reality also.

And the proof of this is as follows.—It is a greater thing to exist both in the understanding and in reality than to be in the understanding alone. And if this being is in the understanding alone, whatever has even in the past existed in reality will be greater than this being. And so that which was greater than all beings will be less than some being, and will not be greater than all: which is a manifest contradiction.

And hence, that which is greater than all, already proved to be in the understanding, must exist not only in the understanding, but also in reality: for otherwise it will not be greater than all other things.

2. The fool might make this reply:

This being is said to be in my understanding already, only because I understand what is said. Now could it not with equal justice be said that I have in my

From Sidney Norton Deane, trans., *St. Anselm. Proslogium; Monologium; an Appendix in Behalf of the Fool by Gaunilon; and Cur Deus Homo*, repr. ed. (La Salle, Ill.: Open Court, 1948), pp. 145–70.

understanding all manner of unreal objects, having absolutely no existence in themselves, because I understand these things if one speaks of them, whatever they may be?

Unless indeed it is shown that this being is of such a character that it cannot be held in concept like all unreal objects, or objects whose existence is uncertain: and hence I am not able to conceive of it when I hear of it, or to hold it in concept; but I must understand it and have it in my understanding; because, it seems, I cannot conceive of it in any other way than by understanding it, that is, by comprehending in my knowledge its existence in reality.

But if this is the case, in the first place there will be no distinction between what has precedence in time—namely, the having of an object in the understanding—and what is subsequent in time—namely, the understanding that an object exists; as in the example of the picture, which exists first in the mind of the painter, and afterwards in his work.

Moreover, the following assertion can hardly be accepted: that this being, when it is spoken of and heard of, cannot be conceived not to exist in the way in which even God can be conceived not to exist. For if this is impossible, what was the object of this argument against one who doubts or denies the existence of such a being?

Finally, that this being so exists that it cannot be perceived by an understanding convinced of its own indubitable existence, unless this being is afterwards conceived of—this should be proved to me by an indisputable argument, but not by that which you have advanced: namely, that what I understand, when I hear it, already is in my understanding. For thus in my understanding, as I still think, could be all sorts of things whose existence is uncertain, or which do not exist at all, if some one whose words I should understand mentioned them. And so much the more if I should be deceived, as often happens, and believe in them: though I do not yet believe in the being whose existence you would prove.

3. Hence, your example of the painter who already has in his understanding what he is to paint cannot agree with this argument. For the picture, before it is made, is contained in the artificer's art itself; and any such thing, existing in the art of an artificer, is nothing but a part of his understanding itself. A joiner, St. Augustine says, when he is about to make a box in fact, first has it in his art. The box which is made in fact is not life; but the box which exists in his art is life. For the artificer's soul lives, in which all these things are, before they are produced. Why, then, are these things life in the living soul of the artificer, unless because they are nothing else than the knowledge or understanding of the soul itself?

With the exception, however, of those facts which are known to pertain to the mental nature, whatever, on being heard and thought out by the understanding, is perceived to be real, undoubtedly that real object is one thing, and the understanding itself, by which the object is grasped, is another. Hence, even if it were true that there is a being than which a greater is inconceivable: yet to this being, when heard of and understood, the not yet created picture in the mind of the painter is not analogous.

4. Let us notice also the point touched on above, with regard to this being which is greater than all which can be conceived, and which, it is said, can be none other than God himself. I, so far as actual knowledge of the object, either from its specific or general character, is concerned, am as little able to conceive of this being when I hear of it, or to have it in my understanding, as I am to conceive of or understand God himself: whom, indeed, for this very reason I can conceive not to exist. For I do not know that reality itself which God is, nor can I form a conjecture of that reality from some other like reality. For you yourself assert that that reality is such that there can be nothing else like it.

For, suppose that I should hear something of a man absolutely unknown to me, of whose very existence I was unaware. Through that special or general knowledge by which I know what man is, or what men are, I could conceive of him also, according to the reality itself, which man is. And yet it would be possible, if the person who told me of him deceived me, that the man himself, of whom I conceived, did not exist; since that reality according to which I conceived of him, though a no less indisputable fact, was not that man, but any man.

Hence, I am not able, in the way in which I should have this unreal being in concept or in understanding, to have that being of which you speak in concept or in understanding, when I hear the word God or the words, *a being greater than all other beings*. For I can conceive of the man according to a fact that is real and familiar to me: but of God, or a being greater than all others, I could not conceive at all, except merely according to the word. And an object can hardly or never be conceived according to the word alone.

For when it is so conceived, it is not so much the word itself (which is, indeed, a real thing—that is, the sound of the letters and syllables) as the signification of the word, when heard, that is conceived. But it is not conceived as by one who knows what is generally signified by the word; by whom, that is, it is conceived according to a reality and in true conception alone. It is conceived as by a man who does not know the object, and conceives of it only in accordance with the movement of his mind produced by hearing the word, the mind attempting to image for itself the signification of the word that is heard. And it would be surprising if in the reality of fact it could ever attain to this.

Thus, it appears, and in no other way, this being is also in my understanding, when I hear and understand a person who says that there is a being greater than all conceivable beings. So much for the assertion that this supreme nature already is in my understanding.

5. But that this being must exist, not only in the understanding but also in reality, is thus proved to me:

If it did not so exist, whatever exists in reality would be greater than it. And so the being which has been already proved to exist in my understanding, will not be greater than all other beings.

I still answer: if it should be said that a being which cannot be even conceived in terms of any fact, is in the understanding, I do not deny that this being is, accordingly, in my understanding. But since through this fact it can in no wise attain to real existence also, I do not yet concede to it that existence at all, until some certain proof of it shall be given.

For he who says that this being exists, because otherwise the being which is greater than all will not be greater than all, does not attend strictly enough to what he is saying. For I do not yet say, no, I even deny or doubt that this being is greater than any real object. Nor do I concede to it any other existence than this (if it should be called existence) which it has when the mind, according to a word merely heard, tries to form the image of an object absolutely unknown to it.

How, then, is the veritable existence of that being proved to me from the assumption, by hypothesis, that it is greater than all other beings? For I should still deny this, or doubt your demonstration of it, to this extent, that I should not admit that this being is in my understanding and concept even in the way in which many objects whose real existence is uncertain and doubtful, are in my understanding and concept. For it should be proved first that this being itself really exists somewhere; and then, from the fact that it is greater than all, we shall not hesitate to infer that it also subsists in itself.

6. For example: it is said that somewhere in the ocean is an island, which, because of the difficulty, or rather the impossibility, of discovering what does not exist, is called the lost island. And they say that this island has an inestimable wealth of all manner of riches and delicacies in greater abundance than is told of the Islands of the Blest; and that having no owner or inhabitant, it is more excellent than all other countries, which are inhabited by mankind, in the abundance with which it is stored.

Now if some one should tell me that there is such an island, I should easily understand his words, in which there is no difficulty. But suppose that he went on to say, as if by a logical inference: "You can no longer doubt that this island which is more excellent than all lands exists somewhere, since you have no doubt that it is in your understanding. And since it is more excellent not to be in the understanding alone, but to exist both in the understanding and in reality, for this reason it must exist. For if it does not exist, any land which really exists will be more excellent than it; and so the island already understood by you to be more excellent will not be more excellent."

If a man should try to prove to me by such reasoning that this island truly exists, and that its existence should no longer be doubted, either I should believe that he was jesting, or I know not which I ought to regard as the greater fool: myself, supposing that I should allow this proof; or him, if he should suppose that he had established with any certainty the existence of this island. For he ought to show first that the hypothetical excellence of this island exists as a real and indubitable fact, and in no wise as any unreal object, or one whose existence is uncertain, in my understanding.

7. This, in the mean time, is the answer the fool could make to the arguments urged against him. When he is assured in the first place that this being is so great that its non-existence is not even conceivable, and that this in turn is proved on no other ground than the fact that otherwise it will not be greater than all things, the fool may make the same answer, and say:

When did I say that any such being exists in reality, that is, a being greater than all others?—that on this ground it should be proved to me that it also exists in reality to such a degree that it cannot even be conceived not to exist? Whereas in the first place it should be in some way proved that a nature which is higher, that is, greater and better, than all other natures, exists; in order that from this we may then be able to prove all attributes which necessarily the being that is greater and better than all possesses.

Moreover, it is said that the non-existence of this being is inconceivable. It might better be said, perhaps, that its non-existence, or the possibility of its non-existence, is unintelligible. For according to the true meaning of the word, unreal objects are unintelligible. Yet their existence is conceivable in the way in which the fool conceived of the non-existence of God. I am most certainly aware of my own existence; but I know, nevertheless, that my non-existence is possible. As to that supreme being, moreover, which God is, I understand without any doubt both his existence, and the impossibility of his non-existence. Whether, however, so long as I am most positively aware of my existence, I can conceive of my non-existence, I am not sure. But if I can, why can I not conceive of the non-existence of whatever else I know with the same certainty? If, however, I cannot, God will not be the only being of which it can be said, it is impossible to conceive of his non-existence.

8. The other parts of this book are argued with such truth, such brilliancy, such grandeur; and are so replete with usefulness, so fragrant with a certain perfume of devout and holy feeling, that though there are matters in the beginning which, however rightly sensed, are weakly presented, the rest of the work should not be rejected on this account. The rather ought these earlier matters to be reasoned more cogently, and the whole to be received with great respect and honor.

IN REPLY TO GAUNILON'S ANSWER IN BEHALF OF THE FOOL

IT was a fool against whom the argument of my Proslogium was directed. Seeing, however, that the author of these objections is by no means a fool, and is a Catholic, speaking in behalf of the fool, I think it sufficient that I answer the Catholic.

CHAPTER I.

A general refutation of Gaunilon's argument. It is shown that a being than which a greater cannot be conceived exists in reality.

YOU say—whosoever you may be, who say that a fool is capable of making these statements—that a being than which a greater cannot be conceived is not in the understanding in any other sense than that in which a being that is altogether inconceivable in terms of reality, is in the understanding. You say that the inference that this being exists in reality, from the fact that it is in the understanding, is no more just than the inference that a lost island most certainly exists, from the fact that when it is described the hearer does not doubt that it is in his understanding.

But I say: if a being than which a greater is inconceivable is not understood or conceived, and is not in the understanding or in concept, certainly either God is not a being than which a greater is inconceivable, or else he is not understood or conceived, and is not in the understanding or in concept. But I call on your faith and conscience to attest that this is most false. Hence, that than which a greater cannot be conceived is truly understood and conceived, and is in the understanding and in concept. Therefore either the grounds on which you try to controvert me are not true, or else the inference which you think to base logically on those grounds is not justified.

But you hold, moreover, that supposing that a being than which a greater cannot be conceived is understood, it does not follow that this being is in the understanding; nor, if it is in the understanding, does it therefore exist in reality.

In answer to this, I maintain positively: if that being can be even conceived to be, it must exist in reality. For that than which a greater is inconceivable cannot be conceived except as without beginning. But whatever can be conceived to exist, and does not exist, can be conceived to exist through a beginning. Hence what can be conceived to exist, but does not exist, is not the being than which a greater cannot be conceived. Therefore, if such a being can be conceived to exist, necessarily it does exist.

Furthermore: if it can be conceived at all, it must exist. For no one who denies or doubts the existence of a being than which a greater is inconceivable, denies or doubts that if it did exist, its non-existence, either in reality or in the understanding, would be impossible. For otherwise it would not be a being than which a greater cannot be conceived. But as to whatever can be conceived, but does not exist—if there were such a being, its non-existence, either in reality or in the understanding, would be possible. Therefore if a being than which a greater is inconceivable can be even conceived, it cannot be non-existent.

But let us suppose that it does not exist, even if it can be conceived. Whatever can be conceived, but does not exist, if it existed, would not be a being than which a greater is inconceivable. If, then, there were a being a greater than which is inconceivable, it would not be a being than which a greater is inconceivable: which is most absurd. Hence, it is false to deny that a being than which a greater cannot be conceived exists, if it can be even conceived; much the more, therefore, if it can be understood or can be in the understanding.

Moreover, I will venture to make this assertion: without doubt, whatever at any place or at any time does not exist—even if it does exist at some place or at some time—can be conceived to exist nowhere and never, as at some place and at some time it does not exist. For what did not exist yesterday, and exists to-day, as it is understood not to have existed yesterday, so it can be apprehended by the intelligence that it never exists. And what is not here, and is elsewhere, can be conceived to be nowhere, just as it is not here. So with regard to an object of which the individual parts do not exist at the very places or times: all its parts and therefore its very whole can be conceived to exist nowhere or never.

For, although time is said to exist always, and the world everywhere, yet time does not as a whole exist always, nor the world as a whole everywhere. And as individual parts of time do not exist when others exist, so they can be conceived never to exist. And so it can be apprehended by the intelligence that individual parts of the world exist nowhere, as they do not exist where other parts exist. Moreover, what is composed of parts can be dissolved in concept, and be non-existent. Therefore, whatever at any place or at any time does not exist as a whole, even if it is existent, can be conceived not to exist.

But that than which a greater cannot be conceived, if it exists, cannot be conceived not to exist. Otherwise, it is not a being than which a greater cannot be conceived: which is inconsistent. By no means, then, does it at any place or at any time fail to exist as a whole: but it exists as a whole everywhere and always.

Do you believe that this being can in some way be conceived or understood, or that the being with regard to which these things are understood can be in concept or in the understanding? For if it cannot, these things cannot be understood with reference to it. But if you say that it is not understood and that it is not in the understanding, because it is not thoroughly understood; you should say that a man who cannot face the direct rays of the sun does not see the light of day, which is none other than the sunlight. Assuredly a being than which a greater cannot be conceived exists, and is in the understanding, at least to this extent—that these statements regarding it are understood.

CHAPTER II.

The argument is continued. It is shown that a being than which a greater is inconceivable can be conceived, and also, in so far, exists.

I HAVE said, then, in the argument which you dispute, that when the fool hears mentioned a being than which a greater is inconceivable, he understands what he hears. Certainly a man who does not understand when a familiar language is spoken, has no understanding at all, or a very dull one. Moreover, I have said that if this being is understood, it is in the understanding. Is that in no understanding which has been proved necessarily to exist in the reality of fact?

But you will say that although it is in the understanding, it does not follow that it is understood. But observe that the fact of its being understood does necessitate its being in the understanding. For as what is conceived, is conceived by conception, and what is conceived by conception, as it is conceived, so is in conception; so what is understood, is understood by understanding, and what is understood by understanding, as it is understood, so is in the understanding. What can be more clear than this?

After this, I have said that if it is even in the understanding alone, it can be conceived also to exist in reality, which is greater. If, then, it is in the understanding alone, obviously the very being than which a greater cannot be conceived is one than which a greater can be conceived. What is more logical? For if it exists even in the understanding alone, can it not be conceived also to exist in reality? And if it can be so conceived, does not he who conceives of this conceive of a thing greater than that being, if it exists in the understanding alone? What more consistent inference, then, can be made than this: that if a being than which a greater cannot be conceived is in the understanding alone, it is not that than which a greater cannot be conceived?

But, assuredly, in no understanding is a being than which a greater is conceivable a being than which a greater is inconceivable. Does it not follow, then, that if a being than which a greater cannot be conceived is in any understanding, it does not exist in the understanding alone? For if it is in the understanding alone, it is a being than which a greater can be conceived, which is inconsistent with the hypothesis.

CHAPTER III.

A criticism of Gaunilon's example, in which he tries to show that in this way the real existence of a lost island might be inferred from the fact of its being conceived.

BUT, you say, it is as if one should suppose an island in the ocean, which surpasses all lands in its fertility, and which, because of the difficulty, or rather the impossibility, of discovering what does not exist, is called a lost island; and should say that there can be no doubt that this island truly exists in reality, for this reason, that one who hears it described easily understands what he hears.

Now I promise confidently that if any man shall devise anything existing either in reality or in concept alone (except that than which a greater cannot be conceived) to which he can adapt the sequence of my reasoning, I will discover that thing, and will give him his lost island, not to be lost again.

But it now appears that this being than which a greater is inconceivable cannot be conceived not to be, because it exists on so assured a ground of truth; for otherwise it would not exist at all.

Hence, if any one says that he conceives this being not to exist, I say that at the time when he conceives of this either he conceives of a being than which a greater is inconceivable, or he does not conceive at all. If he does not conceive, he does not conceive of the non-existence of that of which he does not conceive. But if he does conceive, he certainly conceives of a being which cannot be even conceived not to exist. For if it could be conceived not to exist, it could be conceived to have a beginning and an end. But this is impossible.

He, then, who conceives of this being conceives of a being which cannot be even conceived not to exist; but he who conceives of this being does not conceive that it does not exist; else he conceives what is inconceivable. The non-existence, then, of that than which a greater cannot be conceived is inconceivable.

CHAPTER IV.

The difference between the possibility of conceiving of non-existence, and understanding non-existence.

YOU say, moreover, that whereas I assert that this supreme being cannot be *conceived* not to exist, it might better be said that its non-existence, or even the possibility of its non-existence, cannot be *understood.*

But it was more proper to say, it cannot be conceived. For if I had said that the object itself cannot be understood not to exist, possibly you yourself, who say that in accordance with the true meaning of the term what is unreal cannot be understood, would offer the objection that nothing which is can be understood not to be, for the non-existence of what exists is unreal: hence God would not be the only being of which it could be said, it is impossible to understand its non-existence. For thus one of those beings which most certainly exist can be understood not to exist in the same way in which certain other real objects can be understood not to exist.

But this objection, assuredly, cannot be urged against the term *conception*, if one considers the matter well. For although no objects which exist can be understood not to exist, yet all objects, except that which exists in the highest degree, can be conceived not to exist. For all those objects, and those alone, can be conceived not to exist, which have a beginning or end or composition of parts: also, as I have already said, whatever at any place or at any time does not exist as a whole.

That being alone, on the other hand, cannot be conceived not to exist, in which any conception discovers neither beginning nor end nor composition of parts, and which any conception finds always and everywhere as a whole.

Be assured, then, that you can conceive of your own non-existence, although you are most certain that you exist. I am surprised that you should have admitted that you are ignorant of this. For we conceive of the non-existence of many objects which we know to exist, and of the existence of many which we know not to exist; not by forming the opinion that they so exist, but by imagining that they exist as we conceive of them.

And indeed, we can conceive of the non-existence of an object, although we know it to exist, because at the same time we can conceive of the former and know the latter. And we cannot conceive of the nonexistence of an object, so long as we know it to exist, because we cannot conceive at the same time of existence and non-existence.

If, then, one will thus distinguish these two senses of this statement, he will understand that nothing, so long as it is known to exist, can be conceived not to exist; and that whatever exists, except that being than which a greater cannot be conceived, can be conceived not to exist, even when it is known to exist.

So, then, of God alone it can be said that it is impossible to conceive of his non-existence; and yet many objects, so long as they exist, in one sense cannot be conceived not to exist. But in what sense God is to be conceived not to exist, I think has been shown clearly enough in my book.

CHAPTER V.

A particular discussion of certain statements of Gaunilon's. In the first place, he misquoted the argument which he undertook to refute.

THE nature of the other objections which you, in behalf of the fool, urge against me it is easy, even for a man of small wisdom, to detect; and I had therefore thought it unnecessary to show this. But since I hear that some readers of these objections think they have some weight against me, I will discuss them briefly.

In the first place, you often repeat that I assert that what is greater than all other beings is in the understanding; and if it is in the understanding, it exists also in reality, for otherwise the being which is greater than all would not be greater than all.

Nowhere in all my writings is such a demonstration found. For the real existence of a being which is said to be *greater than all other beings* cannot be demonstrated in the same way with the real existence of one that is said to be *a being than which a greater cannot be conceived.*

If it should be said that a being than which a greater cannot be conceived has no real existence, or that it is possible that it does not exist, or even that it can be conceived not to exist, such an assertion can be easily refuted. For the non-existence of what does not exist is possible, and that whose non-existence is possible can be conceived not to exist. But whatever can be conceived not to exist, if it exists, is not a being than which a greater cannot be conceived; but if it does not exist, it would not, even if it existed, be a being than which a greater cannot be conceived. But it cannot be said that a being than which a greater is inconceivable, if it exists, is not a being than which a greater is inconceivable; or that if it existed, it would not be a being than which a greater is inconceivable.

It is evident, then, that neither is it non-existent, nor is it possible that it does not exist, nor can it be conceived not to exist. For otherwise, if it exists, it is not that which it is said to be in the hypothesis; and if it existed, it would not be what it is said to be in the hypothesis.

But this, it appears, cannot be so easily proved of a being which is said to be *greater than all other beings.* For it is not so evident that what can be conceived not to exist is not greater than all existing beings, as it is evident that it is not a being than which a greater cannot be conceived. Nor is it so indubitable that if a being greater than all other beings exists, it is no other than the being than which a greater cannot be conceived; or that if it were such a being, some other might not be this being in like manner; as it is certain with regard to a being which is hypothetically posited as one than which a greater cannot be conceived.

For consider: if one should say that there is a being greater than all other beings, and that this being can nevertheless be conceived not to exist; and that a being greater than this, although it does not exist, can be conceived to exist: can it be so clearly inferred in this case that this being is therefore not a being greater than all other existing beings, as it would be most positively affirmed in the other case, that the being under discussion is not, therefore, a being than which a greater cannot be conceived?

For the former conclusion requires another premise than the predication, *greater than all other beings.* In my argument, on the other hand, there is no need of any other than this very prediction, *a being than which a greater cannot be conceived.*

If the same proof cannot be applied when the being in question is predicated to be greater than all others, which can be applied when it is predicated to be a being than which a greater cannot be conceived, you have unjustly censured me for saying what I did not say; since such a predication differs so greatly from that which I actually made. If, on the other hand, the other argument is valid, you ought not to blame me so for having said what can be proved.

Whether this can be proved, however, he will easily decide who recognises that this being than which a greater cannot be conceived is demonstrable. For by no means can this being than which a greater cannot be conceived be understood as any other than that which alone is greater than all. Hence, just as that than which a greater cannot be conceived is understood, and is in the understanding, and for that reason is asserted to exist in the reality of fact: so what is said to be greater than all other things is understood and is in the understanding, and therefore it is necessarily inferred that it exists in reality.

You see, then, with how much justice you have compared me with your fool, who, on the sole ground that he understands what is described to him, would affirm that a lost island exists.

CHAPTER VI.

A discussion of Gaunilon's argument in his second chapter: that any unreal beings can be understood in the same way, and would, to that extent, exist.

ANOTHER of your objections is that any unreal beings, or beings whose existence is uncertain, can be understood and be in the understanding in the same way with that being which I discussed. I am surprised that you should have conceived this objection, for I was attempting to prove what was still uncertain, and contented myself at first with showing that this being is understood in any way, and is in the understanding. It was my intention to consider, on these grounds, whether this being is in the understanding alone, like an unreal object, or whether it also exists in fact, as a real being. For if unreal objects, or objects whose existence is uncertain, in this way are understood and are in the understanding, because, when they are spoken of, the hearer understands what the speaker means, there is no reason why that being of which I spoke should not be understood and be in the understanding.

How, moreover, can these two statements of yours be reconciled: (1) the assertion that if a man should speak of any unreal objects, whatever they might be, you would understand, and (2) the assertion that on hearing of that being which does exist, and not in that way in which even unreal objects are held in concept, you would not say that you conceive of it or have it in concept; since, as you say, you cannot conceive of it in any other way than by understanding it, that is, by comprehending in your knowledge its real existence?

How, I ask, can these two things be reconciled: that unreal objects are understood, and that understanding an object is comprehending in knowledge its real existence? The contradiction does not concern me: do you see to it. But if unreal objects are also in some sort understood, and your definition is applicable, not to every understanding, but to a certain sort of understanding, I ought not to be blamed for saying that a being than which a greater cannot be conceived is understood and is in the understanding, even before I reached the certain conclusion that this being exists in reality.

CHAPTER VII.

In answer to another objection: that the supremely great being may be conceived not to exist, just as by the fool God is conceived not to exist.

AGAIN, you say that it can probably never be believed that this being, when it is spoken of and heard of, cannot be conceived not to exist in the same way in which even God may be conceived not to exist.

Such an objection could be answered by those who have attained but little skill in disputation and argument. For is it compatible with reason for a man to deny the existence of what he understands, because it is said to be that being whose existence he denies because he does not understand it? Or, if at some times its existence is denied, because only to a certain extent is it understood, and that which is not at all understood is the same to him: is not what is still undetermined more easily proved of a being which exists in some understanding than of one which exists is no understanding?

Hence it cannot be credible that any man denies the existence of a being than which a greater cannot be conceived, which, when he hears of it, he understands in a certain degree: it is incredible, I say, that any man denies the existence of this being because he denies the existence of God, the sensory perception of whom he in no wise conceives of.

Or if the existence of another object, because it is not at all understood, is denied, yet is not the existence of what is understood in some degree more easily proved than the existence of an object which is in no wise understood?

Not irrationally, then, has the hypothesis of a being a greater than which cannot be conceived been employed in controverting the fool, for the proof of the existence of God: since in some degree he would understand such a being, but in no wise could he understand God.

CHAPTER VIII.

*The example of the picture, treated in Gaunilon's third chapter, is examined.—
From what source a notion may be formed of the supremely great being, of which
Gaunilon inquired in his fourth chapter.*

MOREOVER, your so careful demonstration that the being than which a
greater cannot be conceived is not analogous to the not yet executed picture in
the understanding of the painter, is quite unnecessary. It was not for this purpose
that I suggested the preconceived picture. I had no thought of asserting that the
being which I was discussing is of such a nature; but I wished to show that what is
not understood to exist can be in the understanding.

Again, you say that when you hear of a being than which a greater is inconceivable, you cannot conceive of it in terms of any real object known to you
either specifically or generally, nor have it in your understanding. For, you say,
you neither know such a being in itself, nor can you form an idea of it from
anything like it.

But obviously this is not true. For everything that is less good, in so far as it
is good, is like the greater good. It is therefore evident to any rational mind, that
by ascending from the lesser good to the greater, we can form a considerable
notion of a being than which a greater is inconceivable.

For instance, who (even if he does not believe that what he conceives of
exists in reality) supposing that there is some good which has a beginning and an
end, does not conceive that a good is much better, which, if it begins, does not
cease to be? And that as the second good is better than the first, so that good
which has neither beginning nor end, though it is ever passing from the past
through the present to the future, is better than the second? And that far better
than this is a being—whether any being of such a nature exists or not—which in
no wise requires change or motion, nor is compelled to undergo change or
motion?

Is this inconceivable, or is some being greater than this conceivable? Or is
not this to form a notion from objects than which a greater is conceivable, of the
being than which a greater cannot be conceived? There is, then, a means of
forming a notion of a being than which a greater is inconceivable.

So easily, then, can the fool who does not accept sacred authority be refuted, if he denies that a notion may be formed from other objects of a being than
which a greater is inconceivable. But if any Catholic would deny this, let him
remember that the invisible things of God, from the creation of the world, are
clearly seen, being understood by the things that are made, even his eternal
power and Godhead. (Romans 1:20.)

CHAPTER IX.

The possibility of understanding and conceiving of the supremely great being. The argument advanced against the fool is confirmed.

BUT even if it were true that a being than which a greater is inconceivable cannot be conceived or understood; yet it would not be untrue that a being than which a greater cannot be conceived is conceivable and intelligible. There is nothing to prevent one's saying *ineffable*, although what is said to be ineffable cannot be spoken of. *Inconceivable* is conceivable, although that to which the word *inconceivable* can be applied is not conceivable. So, when one says, *that than which nothing greater is conceivable*, undoubtedly what is heard is conceivable and intelligible, although that being itself, than which a greater is inconceivable, cannot be conceived or understood.

Or, though there is a man so foolish as to say that there is no being than which a greater is inconceivable, he will not be so shameless as to say that he cannot understand or conceive of what he says. Or, if such a man is found, not only ought his words to be rejected, but he himself should be contemned.

Whoever, then, denies the existence of a being than which a greater cannot be conceived, at least understands and conceives of the denial which he makes. But this denial he cannot understand or conceive of without its component terms; and a term of this statement is *a being than which a greater cannot be conceived.* Whoever, then, makes this denial, understands and conceives of that than which a greater is inconceivable.

Moreover, it is evident that in the same way it is possible to conceive of and understand a being whose non-existence is impossible; but he who conceives of this conceives of a greater being than one whose non-existence is possible. Hence, when a being than which a greater is inconceivable is conceived, if it is a being whose non-existence is possible that is conceived, it is not a being than which a greater cannot be conceived. But an object cannot be at once conceived and not conceived. Hence he who conceives of a being than which a greater is inconceivable, does not conceive of that whose non-existence is possible, but of that whose non-existence is impossible. Therefore, what he conceives of must exist; for anything whose non-existence is possible, is not that of which he conceives.

CHAPTER X.

The certainty of the foregoing argument.—The conclusion of the book.

I BELIEVE, that I have shown by an argument which is not weak, but sufficiently cogent, that in my former book I proved the real existence of a being than which a greater cannot be conceived; and I believe that this argument cannot be invalidated by the validity of any objection. For so great force does the signification of this reasoning contain in itself, that this being which is the subject of discussion, is of necessity, from the very fact that it is understood or conceived, proved also to exist in reality, and to be whatever we should believe of the divine substance.

For we attribute to the divine substance anything of which it can be conceived that it is better to be than not to be that thing. For example: it is better to be eternal than not eternal; good, than not good; nay, goodness itself, than not goodness itself. But it cannot be that anything of this nature is not a property of the being than which a greater is inconceivable. Hence, the being than which a greater is inconceivable must be whatever should be attributed to the divine essence.

I thank you for your kindness both in your blame and in your praise for my book. For since you have commended so generously those parts of it which seem to you worthy of acceptance, it is quite evident that you have criticised in no unkind spirit those parts of it which seemed to you weak.

᠊᠊᠊ 9 ᠊᠊᠊
THOMAS AQUINAS
(1225–1274)

Undoubtedly in the work of Thomas Aquinas one sees the high point in the achievements of Medieval scholasticism. He has been called "the prince of the schoolmen." Although the date is not absolutely certain, scholars believe Thomas was born in January of A.D. 1225 in the castle of Roccasecca, near Aquino, Italy. When he was six years old his father, the Count of Aquino, placed Thomas in the monastery of Monte Cassino. There he was educated under the supervision of his uncle, the abbot. Thomas was an excellent student with a keen mind. Later his studies at the newly established University of Naples led him to become a Dominican (the Order of Preachers). His family attempted to dissuade him from this goal, but he arrived in Paris in the summer of 1245 to study under Albertus Magnus. In 1248 he followed Magnus to Cologne and there continued his education for four years.

Thomas was a physically large man with a very quiet disposition. Although for a time he was known as the "dumb ox," yet his unusual mental capacities were recognized by his teachers. He began teaching before he reached his thirtieth birthday, and for the rest of his life teaching and writing were his main occupations. Thomas taught at the Dominican convent of St. James for three years. Then from 1259 to 1268 he lectured at the Papal Curia in Italy. He also spent some years in Spain, though he was back in Paris by 1269. In 1272 Thomas was given the task of founding a new school in Naples known as a House of Studies. He regarded his vocation as that of a scholar and a teacher. Throughout all his years of teaching he had a gift for writing. His literary output was enormous.

When Thomas was thirty-four years of age he began work on a manual of Christian doctrine intended for the use of Christian missionaries who were attempting to work with the Muslims in Spain. Known as the *Summa Contra Gentiles*, this classic statement of Christian doctrine was completed in 1264. Though the debates sometimes seem endless, most reputable scholars have recognized that the *Summa Contra Gentiles* was in fact a manual of apologetics written for missionaries who had to face a highly intellectual culture in the Muslim world.

His most famous work, known correctly by the title *Summa Theologiae*, was begun when Thomas was forty years old. In 1268 after three years of work he completed the first of the three parts. He had already begun work on the second part when he was recalled to Paris in 1269. He had finished the second part apparently by 1292 when he began his new work in Naples.

On the feast of St. Nicholas, 1273, Thomas is said to have fallen into a trance, in which he was granted a glimpse of heaven. It is reported that he later confessed that all of his writings now appeared to him to be like so much chaff. Nevertheless he continued his writing, completing the treatise on the Incarnation and apparently finishing more than half of his book on the Sacraments. His work was interrupted, however, when Pope Gregory called the Ecumenical Council of Lyons in an effort to restore the unity in the church between East and West.

In these last years Thomas had grown noticeably weaker. While on his journey to Lyons, he began to realize that he could go on no farther, and he was carried on a mule to the Cistercian Abbey of Fossanuova. Even on his deathbed he spent hour after hour answering his friend's questions on theology and about the Bible. His discussion just prior to his death is said to have been concerning the Song of Songs. He died at the age of forty-nine on March 7, 1274—not far from the castle of Roccasecca, where he was born.

His great achievement is not so much in his originality and creativity in theology. Rather, his enormous influence comes from his ability to summarize the accepted teachings of the church.

Thus his writings became the standard affirmation of the Christian doctrines of the church.

Aquinas achieved a synthesis between Christian theology and Aristotelian philosophy. He related reason and faith in such a way that it made a persuasive impact on the intellectual world. The new translations of Aristotle's works had influenced all of Western Europe. Aquinas made it possible for those who were strongly influenced by Aristotle's views to remain Christians without sacrificing philosophical consistency.

Aquinas clearly rejected the realism of Plato. For Aquinas, as for Aristotle, knowledge is based on what the senses perceive. Aquinas recognized, however, that Christian doctrine could not be limited to what can be known only by reason. Faith is also a road to truth. God has revealed many things that can be understood and known only by faith (by feeling and will). Since God created the human mind, and since He created the world, and, further, since He has revealed truth that is to be known by faith, *reason* and *faith* must not be in conflict unless God is Himself a contradiction. This is inappropriate even to think. Thus, for Aquinas, knowledge reached by reason cannot contradict truth given by revelation and understood through faith.

Aquinas rejected the idea that God's existence can be known only by faith. Certainly God is known by faith, but He can also be known by reason that will be in harmony with all truth known by faith. This "Thomistic" method of relating reason and faith is the source of a major apologetic method that has continued even into the current scene. The essays reprinted in this chapter illustrate this basic methodology. In Book I, chapter x, of the *Summa Contra Gentiles* the reader should recognize many of the arguments that have been used in earlier essays reprinted in this book. One should especially notice that Aquinas is referring to the ontological arguments for God used by Anselm and Augustine. He quite clearly rejects not only the arguments themselves but also the underlying assumptions regarding the relationship between faith and reason. Aquinas is very clear as to why he rejects these arguments (see Book I, chap. xi). He not only criticizes the approach of Anselm and Augustine but he offers his own methodology based on his conclusions about faith and reason expressed in the first portion of the reading reprinted in this chapter. In Question II of the *Summa*

Theologiae Anselm's view is again criticized (see Article 1), and Aquinas offers his classic defense of the evidentialist apologetic in Article 3.

BIBLIOGRAPHY

Aquinas, Thomas. *Basic Writings.* Edited and annotated, with an introduction, by Anton C. Pegis. New York: Random, 1945.
Bonnette, Dennis. *Aquinas' Proofs for God's Existence.* The Hague: Nijhoff, 1972.
Copleston, Fredrick Charles. *Aquinas.* London: Search, 1955.
Grenet, Paul. *Thomism: An Introduction.* Translated by James F. Ross. New York: Harper & Row, 1967.

THE SUMMA CONTRA GENTILES

BOOK I.

CHAPTER III.

In what way it is possible to make known the divine truth

SINCE, however, not every truth is to be made known in the same way, *and it is the part of an educated man to seek for conviction in each subject, only so far as the nature of the subject allows,*[1] as the Philosopher most rightly observes as quoted by Boethius,[2] it is necessary to show first of all in what way it is possible to make known the aforesaid truth.

Now in those things which we hold about God there is truth in two ways. For certain things that are true about God wholly surpass the capability of human reason, for instance that God is three and one: while there are certain things to which even natural reason can attain, for instance that God is, that God is one, and others like these, which even the philosophers proved demonstratively of God, being guided by the light of natural reason.

That certain divine truths wholly surpass the capability of human reason, is most clearly evident. For since the principle of all the knowledge which the reason acquires about a thing, is the understanding of that thing's essence, because according to the Philosopher's teaching[3] the principle of a demonstration is *what a thing is*, it follows that our knowledge about a thing will be in proportion to our understanding of its essence. Wherefore, if the human intellect com-

---

From English Dominican Fathers, trans., *The Summa Contra Gentiles of Saint Thomas Aquinas: First Book* (London: Burns Oates and Washbourne, 1924), pp. 4–33.

[1]*Ethic.* iii. 4.
[2]*De Trin.* ii.
[3]2 *Anal. Post.* iii. 9.

prehends the essence of a particular thing, for instance a stone or a triangle, no truth about that thing will surpass the capability of human reason. But this does not happen to us in relation to God, because the human intellect is incapable by its natural power of attaining to the comprehension of His essence: since our intellect's knowledge, according to the mode of the present life, originates from the senses: so that things which are not objects of sense cannot be comprehended by the human intellect, except in so far as knowledge of them is gathered from sensibles. Now sensibles cannot lead our intellect to see in them what God is, because they are effects unequal to the power of their cause. And yet our intellect is led by sensibles to the divine knowledge so as to know about God that He is, and other such truths, which need to be ascribed to the first principle. Accordingly some divine truths are attainable by human reason, while others altogether surpass the power of human reason.

Again. The same is easy to see from the degrees of intellects. For if one of two men perceives a thing with his intellect with greater subtlety, the one whose intellect is of a higher degree understands many things which the other is altogether unable to grasp; as instanced in a yokel who is utterly incapable of grasping the subtleties of philosophy. Now the angelic intellect surpasses the human intellect more than the intellect of the cleverest philosopher surpasses that of the most uncultured. For an angel knows God through a more excellent effect than does man, for as much as the angel's essence, through which he is led to know God by natural knowledge, is more excellent than sensible things, even than the soul itself, by which the human intellect mounts to the knowledge of God. And the divine intellect surpasses the angelic intellect much more than the angelic surpasses the human. For the divine intellect by its capacity equals the divine essence, wherefore God perfectly understands of Himself what He is, and He knows all things that can be understood about Him: whereas the angel knows not what God is by his natural knowledge, because the angel's essence, by which he is led to the knowledge of God, is an effect unequal to the power of its cause. Consequently an angel is unable by his natural knowledge to grasp all that God understands about Himself: nor again is human reason capable of grasping all that an angel understands by his natural power. Accordingly just as a man would show himself to be a most insane fool if he declared the assertions of a philosopher to be false because he was unable to understand them, so, and much more, a man would be exceedingly foolish, were he to suspect of falsehood the things revealed by God through the ministry of His angels, because they cannot be the object of reason's investigations. . . .

With this the saying of the Philosopher is in accord (2*Metaph.*)[4] where he

---

[4]D. 1*a*. 1, 2. In future references D. stands for the Didot edition of Aristotle's and Plato's works.

says that *our intellect in relation to those primary things which are most evident in nature is like the eye of a bat in relation to the sun.*

To this truth Holy Writ also bears witness. For it is written (Job 11:7): *Peradventure thou wilt comprehend the steps of God and wilt find out the Almighty perfectly?* and (36:26): *Behold God is great, exceeding our knowledge,* and (1 Cor. 13:9): *We know in part.*

Therefore all that is said about God, though it cannot be investigated by reason, must not be forthwith rejected as false, as the Manicheans and many unbelievers have thought.[5]

CHAPTER IV.

That the truth about divine things which is attainable by reason is fittingly proposed to man as an object of belief

WHILE then the truth of the intelligible things of God is twofold, one to which the inquiry of reason can attain, the other which surpasses the whole range of human reason, both are fittingly proposed by God to man as an object of belief. We must first show this with regard to that truth which is attainable by the inquiry of reason, lest it appears to some, that since it can be attained by reason, it was useless to make it an object of faith by supernatural inspiration. Now three disadvantages would result if this truth were left solely to the inquiry of reason. One is that few men would have knowledge of God: because very many are hindered from gathering the fruit of diligent inquiry, which is the discovery of truth, for three reasons. Some indeed on account of an indisposition of temperament, by reason of which many are naturally indisposed to knowledge: so that no efforts of theirs would enable them to reach to the attainment of the highest degree of human knowledge, which consists in knowing God. Some are hindered by the needs of household affairs. For there must needs be among men some that devote themselves to the conduct of temporal affairs, who would be unable to devote so much time to the leisure of contemplative research as to reach the summit of human inquiry, namely the knowledge of God. And some are hindered by laziness. For in order to acquire the knowledge of God in those things which reason is able to investigate, it is necessary to have a previous knowledge of many things: since almost the entire consideration of philosophy is directed to the knowledge of God: for which reason metaphysics, which is about divine things, is the last of the parts of philosophy to be studied. Wherefore it is not possible to arrive at the inquiry about the aforesaid truth except after a most laborious study: and few are willing to take upon themselves this labour for the love of a knowledge, the natural desire for which has nevertheless been instilled into the mind of man by God.

---

[5]S. Aug., *De utilit. credendi* i. 2; *Retract.* xiv. 1.

The second disadvantage is that those who would arrive at the discovery of the aforesaid truth would scarcely succeed in doing so after a long time. First, because this truth is so profound, that it is only after long practice that the human intellect is enabled to grasp it by means of reason. Secondly, because many things are required beforehand, as stated above. Thirdly, because at the time of youth, the mind, when tossed about by the various movements of the passions, is not fit for the knowledge of so sublime a truth, *whereas calm gives prudence and knowledge*, as stated in *7 Phys.*[6] Hence mankind would remain in the deepest darkness of ignorance, if the path of reason were the only available way to the knowledge of God: because the knowledge of God which especially makes men perfect and good, would be acquired only by the few, and by these only after a long time.

The third disadvantage is that much falsehood is mingled with the investigations of human reason, on account of the weakness of our intellect in forming its judgments, and by reason of the admixture of phantasms. Consequently many would remain in doubt about those things even which are most truly demonstrated, through ignoring the force of the demonstration: especially when they perceive that different things are taught by the various men who are called wise. Moreover among the many demonstrated truths, there is sometimes a mixture of falsehood that is not demonstrated, but assumed for some probable or sophistical reason which at times is mistaken for a demonstration. Therefore it was necessary that definite certainty and pure truth about divine things should be offered to man by the way of faith.

Accordingly the divine clemency has made this salutary commandment, that even some things which reason is able to investigate must be held by faith: so that all may share in the knowledge of God easily, and without doubt or error.

Hence it is written (Eph. 4:17–18): That *henceforward you walk not as also the Gentiles walk in the vanity of their mind, having their understanding darkened:* and (Isa. 54:13): *All thy children shall be taught of the Lord.*

·   ·   ·

CHAPTER VI.

That it is not a mark of levity to assent to the things that are of faith, although they are above reason

NOW those who believe this truth, of *which reason affords a proof,*[7] believe not lightly, as though *following foolish*[8] *fables* (2 Pet. 1:16). For divine Wisdom

---

[6]iii. 7.
[7]S. Greg. the Great: *Hom. in Ev.* ii. 26.
[8]Vulg., *cunningly devised (doctas.* S. Thomas read *indoctas.).*

Himself, Who knows all things most fully, deigned to reveal to man *the secrets of God's wisdom* [Job 11:6]: and by suitable arguments proves His presence, and the truth of His doctrine and inspiration, by performing works surpassing the capability of the whole of nature, namely, the wondrous healing of the sick, the raising of the dead to life, a marvellous control over the heavenly bodies, and what excites yet more wonder, the inspiration of human minds, so that unlettered and simple persons are filled with the Holy Ghost, and in one instant are endowed with the most sublime wisdom and eloquence. And after considering these arguments, convinced by the strength of the proof, and not by the force of arms, nor by the promise of delights, but—and this is the greatest marvel of all—amidst the tyranny of persecutions, a countless crowd of not only simple but also of the wisest men, embraced the Christian faith, which inculcates things surpassing all human understanding, curbs the pleasures of the flesh, and teaches contempt of all worldly things. That the minds of mortal beings should assent to such things, is both the greatest of miracles, and the evident work of divine inspiration, seeing that they despise visible things and desire only those that are invisible. And that this happened not suddenly nor by chance, but by the disposition of God, is shown by the fact that God foretold that He would do so by the manifold oracles of the prophets, whose books we hold in veneration as bearing witness to our faith. This particular kind of proof is alluded to in the words of Hebrews 2:3–4: *Which,* namely the salvation of mankind, *having begun to be declared by the Lord, was confirmed with us by them that heard Him, God also bearing witness by signs and wonders, and divers*[9] . . . *distributions of the Holy Ghost.*

Now such a wondrous conversion of the world to the Christian faith is a most indubitable proof that such signs did take place, so that there is no need to repeat them, seeing that there is evidence of them in their result. For it would be the most wondrous sign of all if without any wondrous signs the world were persuaded by simple and lowly men to believe things so arduous, to accomplish things so difficult, and to hope for things so sublime. Although God ceases not even in our time to work miracles through His saints in confirmation of the faith.

On the other hand those who introduced the errors of the sects proceeded in contrary fashion, as instanced by Mohammed, who enticed peoples with the promise of carnal pleasures, to the desire of which the concupiscence of the flesh instigates. He also delivered commandments in keeping with his promises, by giving the reins to carnal pleasure, wherein it is easy for carnal men to obey: and the lessons of truth which he inculcated were only such as can be easily known to any man of average wisdom by his natural powers: yea rather the truths which he taught were mingled by him with many fables and most false doctrines. Nor did

---

[9]Vulg., *divers miracles and distributions* . . .

he add any signs of supernatural agency, which alone are a fitting witness to divine inspiration, since a visible work that can be from God alone, proves the teacher of truth to be invisibly inspired: but he asserted that he was sent in the power of arms, a sign that is not lacking even to robbers and tyrants. Again, those who believed in him from the outset were not wise men practised in things divine and human, but beastlike men who dwelt in the wilds, utterly ignorant of all divine teaching; and it was by a multitude of such men and the force of arms that he compelled others to submit to his law.

Lastly, no divine oracles of prophets in a previous age bore witness to him; rather did he corrupt almost all the teaching of the Old and New Testaments by a narrative replete with fables, as one may see by a perusal of his law. Hence by a cunning device, he did not commit the reading of the Old and New Testament Books to his followers, lest he should thereby be convicted of falsehood. Thus it is evident that those who believe his words believe lightly.

CHAPTER VII.

That the truth of reason is not in opposition to the truth of the Christian faith

NOW though the aforesaid truth of the Christian faith surpasses the ability of human reason, nevertheless those things which are naturally instilled in human reason cannot be opposed to this truth. For it is clear that those things which are implanted in reason by nature, are most true, so much so that it is impossible to think them to be false. Nor is it lawful to deem false that which is held by faith, since it is so evidently confirmed by God. Seeing then that the false alone is opposed to the true, as evidently appears if we examine their definitions, it is impossible for the aforesaid truth of faith to be contrary to those principles which reason knows naturally.

Again. The same thing which the disciple's mind receives from its teacher is contained in the knowledge of the teacher, unless he teach insincerely, which it were wicked to say of God. Now the knowledge of naturally known principles is instilled into us by God, since God Himself is the author of our nature. Therefore the divine Wisdom also contains these principles. Consequently whatever is contrary to these principles, is contrary to the divine Wisdom; wherefore it cannot be from God. Therefore those things which are received by faith from divine revelation cannot be contrary to our natural knowledge. . . .

This is confirmed also by the authority of Augustine who says (*Gen. ad lit.* ii):[10] *That which truth shall make known can nowise be in opposition to the holy books whether of the Old or of the New Testament.*

From this we may evidently conclude that whatever arguments are alleged

---

[10]Ch. xviii.

against the teachings of faith, they do not rightly proceed from the first self-evident principles instilled by nature. Wherefore they lack the force of demonstration, and are either probable or sophistical arguments, and consequently it is possible to solve them.

CHAPTER VIII.

In what relation human reason stands to the truth of faith

IT would also seem well to observe that sensible things from which human reason derives the source of its knowledge, retain a certain trace of likeness to God, but so imperfect that it proves altogether inadequate to manifest the substance itself of God. For effects resemble their causes according to their own mode, since like action proceeds from like agent; and yet the effect does not always reach to a perfect likeness to the agent. Accordingly human reason is adapted to the knowledge of the truth of faith, which can be known in the highest degree only by those who see the divine substance, in so far as it is able to put together certain probable arguments in support thereof, which nevertheless are insufficient to enable us to understand the aforesaid truth as though it were demonstrated to us or understood by us in itself. And yet however weak these arguments may be, it is useful for the human mind to be practised therein, so long as it does not pride itself on having comprehended or demonstrated: since although our view of the sublimest things is limited and weak, it is most pleasant to be able to catch but a glimpse of them. . . .

CHAPTER IX.

Of the order and mode of procedure in this work

ACCORDINGLY, from what we have been saying it is evident that the intention of the wise man must be directed to the twofold truth of divine things and to the refutation of contrary errors: and that the research of reason is able to reach to one of these, while the other surpasses every effort of reason. And I speak of a twofold truth of divine things, not on the part of God Himself Who is Truth one and simple, but on the part of our knowledge, the relation of which to the knowledge of divine things varies.

Wherefore in order to deduce the first kind of truth we must proceed by demonstrative arguments whereby we can convince our adversaries. But since such arguments are not available in support of the second kind of truth, our intention must be not to convince our opponent by our arguments, but to solve the arguments which he brings against the truth, because, as shown above,[11]

---

[11]Ch. vii.

natural reason cannot be opposed to the truth of faith. In a special way may the opponent of this kind of truth be convinced by the authority of Scripture confirmed by God with miracles: since we believe not what is above human reason save because God has revealed it. In support, however, of this kind of truth, certain probable arguments must be adduced for the practice and help of the faithful, but not for the conviction of our opponents, because the very insufficiency of these arguments would rather confirm them in their error, if they thought that we assented to the truth of faith on account of such weak reasonings.

With the intention then of proceeding in the manner laid down, we shall first of all endeavour to declare that truth which is the object of faith's confession and of reason's researches, by adducing arguments both demonstrative and probable, some of which we have gathered from the writings of the philosophers and of holy men, so as thereby to confirm the truth and convince our opponents. After this, so as to proceed from the more to the less manifest, we shall with God's help proceed to declare that truth which surpasses reason, by refuting the arguments of our opponents, and by setting forth the truth of faith by means of probable arguments and authority.[12]

. . . Of those things which we need to consider about God in Himself, we must give the first place (this being the necessary foundation of the whole of this work), to the question of demonstrating that there is a God: for unless this be established, all questions about divine things are out of court.

CHAPTER X.

Of the opinion of those who aver that it cannot be demonstrated that there is a God, since this is self-evident

POSSIBLY it will seem to some that it is useless to endeavour to show that there is a God: they say that it is self-evident that God is, so that it is impossible to think the contrary, and thus it cannot be demonstrated that there is a God. The reasons for this view are as follow. Those things are said to be self-evident which are known as soon as the terms are known: thus as soon as it is known what is a whole, and what is a part, it is known that the whole is greater than its part. Now such is the statement *God is.* For by this word *God* we understand a thing a greater than which cannot be thought of: this is what a man conceives in his mind when he hears and understands this word *God*: so that God must already be at least in his mind. Nor can he be in the mind alone, for that which is both in the mind and in reality is greater than that which is in the mind only. And the very signification of the word shows that nothing is greater than God. Wherefore

---

[12]Bk. IV.

it follows that it is self-evident that God is, since it is made clear from the very signification of the word.

Again. It is possible to think that there is a thing which cannot be thought not to exist: and such a thing is evidently greater than that which can be thought not to exist. Therefore if God can be thought not to exist, it follows that something can be thought greater than God: and this is contrary to the signification of the term. Therefore it remains that it is self-evident that God is.

Further. Those propositions are most evident in which the selfsame thing is predicated of itself, for instance: *Man is man;* or wherein the predicate is included in the definition of the subject, for instance: *Man is an animal.* Now, . . . in God alone do we find that His being is His essence, as though the same were the answer to the question, *What is He?* as to the question, *Is He?* Accordingly when we say, *God is,* the predicate is either identified with the subject, or at least is included in the definition of the subject. And thus it will be self-evident that God is.

Moreover. Things that are known naturally are self-evident, for it is not by a process of research that they become evident. Now it is naturally known that God is, since man's desire tends naturally to God as his last end. . . . Therefore it is self-evident that God is.

Again. That whereby all things are known must needs be self-evident. Now such is God. For just as the light of the sun is the principle of all visual perception, so the divine light is the principle of all intellectual knowledge, because it is therein that first and foremost intellectual light is to be found. Therefore it must needs be self-evident that God is.

On account of these and like arguments some are of opinion that it is so self-evident that God is, that it is impossible for the mind to think the contrary.

CHAPTER XI.

Refutation of the foregoing opinion and solution of the aforesaid arguments

THE foregoing opinion arose from their being accustomed from the beginning to hear and call upon the name of God. Now custom, especially if it date from our childhood, acquires the force of nature, the result being that the mind holds those things with which it was imbued from childhood as firmly as though they were self-evident. It is also a result of failing to distinguish between what is self-evident simply, and that which is self-evident to us. For it is simply self-evident that God is, because the selfsame thing which God is, is His existence. But since we are unable to conceive mentally the selfsame thing which is God, that thing remains unknown in regard to us. Thus it is self-evident simply that every whole is greater than its part, but to one who fails to conceive mentally the meaning of a whole, it must needs be unknown. Hence it is that those things which are most evident of all are to the intellect what the sun is to the eye of an owl, as stated in *Metaph.* ii.[13]

Nor does it follow, as the first argument alleged, that as soon as the meaning of the word God is understood, it is known that God is. First, because it is not known to all, even to those who grant that there is a God, that God is that thing than which no greater can be thought of, since many of the ancients asserted that this world is God. Nor can any such conclusion be gathered from the significations which Damascene[14] assigns to this word God. Secondly because, granted that everyone understands this word God to signify something than which a greater cannot be thought of, it does not follow that something than which a greater cannot be thought of exists in reality. For we must needs allege a thing in the same way as we allege the signification of its name. Now from the fact that we conceive mentally that which the word God is intended to convey, it does not follow that God is otherwise than in the mind. Wherefore neither will it follow that the thing than which a greater cannot be thought of is otherwise than in the mind. And thence it does not follow that there exists in reality something than which a greater cannot be thought of. Hence this is no argument against those who assert that there is no God, since whatever be granted to exist, whether in reality or in the mind, there is nothing to prevent a person from thinking of something greater, unless he grants that there is in reality something than which a greater cannot be thought of.

Again it does not follow, as the second argument pretended, that if it is possible to think that God is not, it is possible to think of something greater than God. For that it be possible to think that He is not, is not on account of the imperfection of His being or the uncertainty thereof, since in itself His being is supremely manifest, but is the result of the weakness of our mind which is able to see Him, not in Himself but in His effects, so that it is led by reasoning to know that He is.

Wherefore the third argument also is solved. For just as it is self-evident to us that a whole is greater than its part, so is it most evident to those who see the very essence of God that God exists, since His essence is His existence. But because we are unable to see His essence, we come to know His existence not in Himself but in His effects.

The solution to the fourth argument is also clear. For man knows God naturally in the same way as he desires Him naturally. Now man desires Him naturally in so far as he naturally desires happiness, which is a likeness of the divine goodness. Hence it does not follow that God considered in Himself is

---

[13]D. 1*a*. 1, 2.
[14]*De Fid. Orth.* i. 9.

naturally known to man, but that His likeness is. Wherefore man must needs come by reasoning to know God in the likenesses to Him which he discovers in God's effects.

It is also easy to reply to the fifth argument. For God is that in which all things are known, not so that other things be unknown except He be known, as happens in self-evident principles, but because all knowledge is caused in us by His outpouring.

CHAPTER XII.

Of the opinion of those who say that the existence of God cannot be proved, and that it is held by faith alone

THE position that we have taken is also assailed by the opinion of certain others, whereby the efforts of those who endeavour to prove that there is a God would again be rendered futile. For they say that it is impossible by means of the reason to discover that God exists, and that this knowledge is acquired solely by means of faith and revelation.

In making this assertion some were moved by the weakness of the arguments which certain people employed to prove the existence of God.

Possibly, however, this error might falsely seek support from the statements of certain philosophers, who show that in God essence and existence are the same, namely that which answers to the question, *What is He?* and that which answers to the question, *Is He?* Now it is impossible by the process of reason to acquire the knowledge of what God is. Wherefore seemingly neither is it possible to prove by reason whether God is.

Again. If, as required by the system of the Philosopher,[15] in order to prove whether a thing is we must take as principle the signification of its name, and since according to the Philosopher (4 *Metaph.*)[16] *the signification of a name is its definition*: there will remain no means of proving the existence of God, seeing that we lack knowledge of the divine essence or quiddity.

Again. If the principles of demonstration become known to us originally through the senses, as is proved in the *Posterior Analytics*,[17] those things which transcend all sense and sensible objects are seemingly indemonstrable. Now such is the existence of God. Therefore it cannot be demonstrated.

The falseness of this opinion is shown to us first by the art of demonstration, which teaches us to conclude causes from effects. Secondly, by the order itself of sciences: for if no substance above sensible substance can be an object of science,

---

[15]2*Poster.* ix. i.
[16]D. 3. iii. 4.
[17]l.xviii.

there will be no science above Physics, as stated in 4 *Metaph.*[18] Thirdly, by the efforts of the philosophers who have endeavoured to prove the existence of God. Fourthly, by the apostolic truth which asserts (Rom. 1:20) that the *invisible things of God are clearly seen, being understood by the things that are made.*

Nor should we be moved by the consideration that in God essence and existence are the same, as the first argument contended. For this is to be understood of the existence by which God subsists in Himself, of which we are ignorant as to what kind of a thing it is, even as we are ignorant of His essence. But it is not to be understood of that existence which is signified by the composition of the mind. For in this way it is possible to prove the existence of God, when our mind is led by demonstrative arguments to form a proposition stating that God is.

Moreover. In those arguments whereby we prove the existence of God, it is not necessary that the divine essence or quiddity be employed as the middle term, as the second argument supposed: but instead of the quiddity we take His effects as middle term, as is the case in *a posteriori* reasoning: and from these effects we take the signification of this word *God.* For all the divine names are taken either from the remoteness of God's effects from Himself, or from some relationship between God and His effects.

It is also evident from the fact that, although God transcends all sensibles and senses, His effects from which we take the proof that God exists, are sensible objects. Hence our knowledge, even of things which transcend the senses, originates from the senses.

CHAPTER XIII.

Arguments in proof of God's existence

HAVING shown then that it is not futile to endeavour to prove the existence of God, we may proceed to set forth the reasons whereby both philosophers and Catholic doctors have proved that there is a God. In the first place we shall give the arguments by which Aristotle sets out to prove God's existence: and he aims at proving this from the point of view of movement, in two ways.

The *first way* is as follows.[19] Whatever is in motion is moved by another: and it is clear to the sense that something, the sun for instance, is in motion. Therefore it is set in motion by something else moving it. Now that which moves it is itself either moved or not. If it be not moved, then the point is proved that we must needs postulate an immovable mover: and this we call God. If, however, it be moved, it is moved by another mover. Either, therefore, we must proceed to

---

[18]D. 3. vii. 9.
[19]7 *Phys.* i.

infinity, or we must come to an immovable mover. But it is not possible to proceed to infinity. Therefore it is necessary to postulate an immovable mover.

This argument contains two propositions that need to be proved: namely that *whatever is in motion is moved by another*, and that *it is not possible to proceed to infinity in movers and things moved*.

The first of these is proved by the Philosopher in *three ways*. *First*, thus. If a thing moves itself, it must needs have the principle of its movement in itself, else it would clearly be moved by another. Again it must be *moved primarily*, that is, it must be moved by reason of itself and not by reason of its part, as an animal is moved by the movement of its foot, for in the latter way not the whole but the part would be moved by itself, and one part by another. Again it must be divisible and have parts, since whatever is moved is divisible, as is proved in 6 *Phys.*[20]

These things being supposed, he argues as follows. That which is stated to be moved by itself is moved primarily. Therefore if one of its parts is at rest, it follows that the whole is at rest. For if, while one part is at rest, another of its parts were in motion, the whole itself would not be moved primarily, but its part which is in motion while another is at rest. Now nothing that is at rest while another is at rest, is moved by itself: for that which is at rest as a result of another thing being at rest must needs be in motion as a result of the other's motion, and hence it is not moved by itself. Hence that which was stated to be moved by itself, is not moved by itself. Therefore whatever is in motion must needs be moved by another.

Nor is this argument traversed by the statement that might be made, that supposing a thing moves itself, it is impossible for a part thereof to be at rest, or again by the statement that to be at rest or in motion does not belong to a part except accidentally, as Avicenna quibbles.[21] Because the force of the argument lies in this, that if a thing moves itself primarily and of itself, not by reason of its parts, it follows that its being moved does not depend on some thing; whereas with a divisible thing, being moved, like being, depends on its parts, so that it cannot move itself primarily and of itself. Therefore the truth of the conclusion drawn does not require that we suppose as an absolute truth that a part of that which moves itself is at rest, but that this conditional statement be true that *if a part were at rest*, the whole would be at rest. Which statement can be true even if the antecedent be false, even as this conditional proposition is true: *If a man is an ass he is irrational.*

Secondly,[22] he proves it by induction, thus. A thing is not moved by itself if

[20]Ch. iv.
[21]2 *Suffic.* i.
[22]8 *Phys.* iv.

it is moved accidentally, since its motion is occasioned by the motion of something else. Nor again if it is moved by force, as is manifest. Nor if it is moved by its nature like those things whose movement proceeds from themselves, such as animals, which clearly are moved by their souls. Nor if it is moved by nature, as heavy and light things are, since these are moved by their generating cause and by that which removes the obstacle to their movement. Now whatsoever things are in motion are moved either *per se* or accidentally; and if *per se*, either by force or by nature: and if the latter, either by something in them, as in the case of animals, or not by something in them, as in the case of heavy and light bodies. Therefore whatever is in motion is moved by another.

Thirdly,[23] he proves his point thus. Nothing is at the same time in act and in potentiality in respect of the same thing. Now whatever is in motion, as such, is in potentiality, because motion is *the act of that which is in potentiality, as such*.[24] Whereas whatever moves, as such, is in act, for nothing acts except in so far as it is in act. Therefore nothing is both mover and moved in respect of the same movement. Hence nothing moves itself.

We must observe, however, that Plato,[25] who asserted that every mover is moved, employed the term *movement* in a more general sense than Aristotle. For Aristotle took movement in its strict sense, for the act of a thing that is in potentially as such, in which sense it applies only to divisible things and bodies, as is proved in 6 *Phys.*[26] Whereas according to Plato that which moves itself is not a body; for he took movement for any operation, so that to understand or to think is a kind of movement, to which manner of speaking Aristotle alludes in 3 *De Anima*.[27] In this sense, then, he said that the first mover moves itself, in as much as it understands, desires and loves itself. This, in a certain respect, is not in contradiction with the arguments of Aristotle; for it makes no difference whether with Plato we come to a first mover that moves itself, or with Aristotle to something first which is altogether immovable.

He proves the other proposition, namely that *it is impossible to proceed to infinity in movers and things moved*, by three arguments.

The *first*[28] of these is as follows. If one were to proceed to infinity in movers and things moved, all this infinite number of things would necessarily be bodies, since whatever is moved is divisible and corporeal, as is proved in 6 *Phys.*[29] Now

[23]8 *Phys. v. 8.*
[24]3 *Phys. i. 6.*
[25]*Phaedrus* § xxiv. (D.).
[26]*L.c.*
[27]Ch. vii.
[28]7 *Phys., l.c.*
[29]*L.c.*

every body that moves through being moved is moved at the same time as it moves. Therefore all this infinite number of things are moved at the same time as one of them is moved. But one of them, since it is finite, is moved in a finite time. Therefore all this infinite number of things are moved in a finite time. But this is impossible. Therefore it is impossible to proceed to infinity in movers and things moved.

That it is impossible for the aforesaid infinite number of things to be moved in a finite time, he proves thus.[30] Mover and moved must needs be simultaneous; and he proves this by induction from each species of movement. But bodies cannot be simultaneous except by continuity or contact. Wherefore since all the aforesaid movers and things moved are bodies, as proved, they must needs be as one movable thing through their continuity or contact. And thus one infinite thing would be moved in a finite time, which is shown to be impossible in 6 *Phys.*[31]

The *second argument*[32] in proof of the same statement is as follows. In an ordinate series of movers and things moved, where namely throughout the series one is moved by the other, we must needs find that if the first mover be taken away or cease to move, none of the others will move or be moved: because the first is the cause of movement in all the others. Now if an ordinate series of movers and things moved proceed to infinity, there will be no first mover, but all will be intermediate movers as it were. Therefore it will be impossible for any of them to be moved: and thus nothing in the world will be moved.

The *third argument*[33] amounts to the same, except that it proceeds in the reverse order, namely by beginning from above: and it is as follows. That which moves instrumentally, cannot move unless there be something that moves principally. But if we proceed to infinity in movers and things moved, they will all be like instrumental movers, because they will be alleged to be moved movers, and there will be nothing by way of principal mover. Therefore nothing will be moved.

We have thus clearly proved both statements which were supposed in the first process of demonstration whereby Aristotle proved the existence of a *first immovable mover.*

The *second*[34] *way* is as follows. If every mover is moved, this statement is true either in itself or accidentally. If accidentally, it follows that it is not neces-

---

[30]*Phys.* i. ii.
[31]Ch. vii.
[32]8 *Phys.* v.
[33]*Ibid.*
[34]*Ibid.*

sary: for that which is accidentally true is not necessary. Therefore it is a contingent proposition that no mover is moved. But if a mover be not moved, it does not move, as the opponent asserts. Therefore it is contingent that nothing is moved, since, if nothing moves, nothing is moved. Now Aristotle holds this to be impossible,[35] namely, that at any time there be no movement. Therefore the first proposition was not contingent, because a false impossibility does not follow from a false contingency. And therefore this proposition, *Every mover is moved by another*, was not accidentally true.

Again, if any two things are found accidentally united in a certain subject, and one of them is to be found without the other, it is probable that the latter can be found without the former: thus if *white* and *musical* are found in Socrates, and *musical* without *white* is found in Plato, it is probable that it is possible to find *white* without *musical* in some subject. Accordingly if mover and moved be united together in some subject accidentally, and it be found that a certain thing is moved without its being a mover, it is probable that a mover is to be found that is not moved. Nor can one urge against this the case of two things one of which depends on the other; because those in question are united not *per se* but accidentally. If, however, the aforesaid proposition is true in itself, again there follows something impossible or unfitting. For the mover must needs be moved either by the same kind of movement or by another kind. If by the same kind, it follows that whatever causes alteration must itself be altered, and furthermore that the healer must be healed, that the teacher must be taught, and in respect of the same science. But this is impossible: for the teacher must needs have science, while the learner must needs not have it, and thus the same will be both possessed and not possessed by the same, which is impossible. And if it be moved by another kind of movement, so that, to wit, that which causes alteration be moved in respect of place, and that which moves in respect of place be increased, and so on, it will follow that we cannot go on indefinitely, since the genera and species of movement are finite in number. And thus there will be some first mover that is not moved by another. Unless, perchance, someone say that a recurrence takes place, in this way, that when all the genera and species of movement have been exhausted, a return must be made to the first; for instance, if that which moves in respect of place be altered, and that which causes alteration be increased, then again that which is increased be moved in respect of place. But the consequence of this will be the same as before; namely, that which moves by one kind of movement is itself moved by the same kind, not immediately indeed but mediately. It remains therefore that *we must needs postulate some first mover that is not moved by anything outside itself.*

Since however, given that there is a first mover that is not moved by any-thing outside itself, it does not follow that it is absolutely immovable, Aristotle proceeds further, saying that this may happen in two ways. First, so that this first mover is absolutely immovable. And if this be granted, our point is established, namely that there is a first immovable mover. Secondly, that this first mover is moved by itself. And this seems probable: because what is of itself is always prior to what is of another: wherefore also in things moved, it is logical that what is moved first is moved by itself and not by another.

But, if this be granted, the same consequence follows.[36] For it cannot be said that the whole of that which moves itself is moved by its whole self, because then the absurd consequences mentioned above would follow, namely that a person might teach and be taught at the same time, and in like manner as to other kinds of movement; and again that a thing would be at the same time in act and in potentiality, since a mover, as such, is in act, while that which is moved is in potentiality. It remains, therefore, that one part thereof is mover only, and the other part moved. And thus we have the same conclusion as before, namely that there is something that moves and is itself immovable.

And it cannot be said that both parts are moved, so that one is moved by the other; nor that one part moves both itself and the other; nor that the whole moves a part; nor that part moves the whole, since the above absurdities would follow, namely that something would both move and be moved by the same kind of movement, and that it would be at the same time in potentiality and in act, and moreover that the whole would move itself not primarily but by reason of its part. It remains, therefore, that in that which moves itself, one part must be immova-ble, and must move the other part.

Since, however, in those things among us which move themselves, namely animals, the part which moves, namely the soul, though immovable of itself, is nevertheless moved accidentally, he goes on to show that in the first mover, the part which moves is not moved neither of itself nor accidentally.[37]

For in those things which among us move themselves, namely animals, since they are corruptible, the part which moves is moved accidentally. Now those corruptible things which move themselves must needs be reducible to some first self-mover that is everlasting. Therefore that which moves itself must have a mover, which is moved neither of itself nor accidentally.

It is clear that, in accordance with his hypothesis, some self-mover must be everlasting. For if, as he supposes, movement is everlasting, the production of these self-movers that are subject to generation and corruption must be everlast-

---

[36] *Phys.*, *l.c.*
[37] *Phys.* vi.

ing. But no one of these self-movers, since it does not always exist, can be the cause of this everlastingness. Nor can all of them together, both because they would be infinite, and because they do not exist all together. It follows therefore that there must be an everlasting self-mover, that causes the everlastingness of generation in these lower self-movers. And thus its mover is not moved, neither of itself nor accidentally. Again, we observe that in self-movers some begin to be moved anew on account of some movement whereby the animal is not moved by itself, for instance by the digestion of food or a change in the atmosphere: by which movement the mover that moves itself is moved accidentally. Whence we may gather that no self-mover, whose mover is moved *per se* or accidentally, is always moved. But the first self-mover is always in motion, else movement could not be everlasting, since every other movement is caused by the movement of the first self-mover. It follows therefore that the first self-mover is moved by a mover who is not moved, neither *per se* nor accidentally.

Nor is this argument rebutted by the fact that the movers of the lower spheres cause an everlasting movement, and yet are said to be moved accidentally. For they are said to be moved accidentally not by reason of themselves, but by reason of the things subject to their motion, which follow the motion of the higher sphere.

Since, however, God is not part of a self-mover, Aristotle goes on in his *Metaphysics*[38] to trace from this motor that is part of a self-mover, another mover altogether separate, which is God. For since every self-mover is moved through its appetite, it follows that the motor that is part of a self-mover, moves on account of the appetite for some appetible object. And this object is above the motor in moving, because the appetent is a moved mover, whereas the appetible is a mover altogether unmoved. Therefore *there must needs be a first mover separate and altogether immovable*, and this is God.

Now two things would seem to weaken the above arguments. The *first* of these is that they proceed from the supposition of the eternity of movement, and among Catholics this is supposed to be false. To this we reply that the most effective way to prove God's existence is from the supposition of the eternity of the world, which being supposed, it seems less manifest that God exists. For if the world and movement had a beginning, it is clear that we must suppose some cause to have produced the world and movement, because whatever becomes anew must take its origin from some cause of its becoming, since nothing evolves itself from potentiality to act, or from non-being to being.

The *second* is that the aforesaid arguments suppose that the first moved

---

[38]D. 11. vii.

thing, namely the heavenly body, has its motive principle in itself, whence it follows that it is animated: and by many this is not granted.

To this we reply that if the first mover is not supposed to have its motive principle in itself, it follows that it is immediately moved by something altogether . immovable. Hence also Aristotle draws this conclusion with an alternative, namely that either we must come at once to a first mover immovable and separate, or to a self-mover from which again we come to a first mover immovable and separate.[39]

The Philosopher proceeds in a *different way* in 2 *Metaph.* to show that it is impossible to proceed to infinity in efficient causes, and that we must come to one first cause, and this we call God. This is how he proceeds. In all efficient causes following in order, the first is the cause of the intermediate cause, and the intermediate is the cause of the ultimate, whether the intermediate be one or several. Now if the cause be removed, that which it causes is removed. Therefore if we remove the first the intermediate cannot be a cause. But if we go on to infinity in efficient causes, no cause will be first. Therefore all the others which are intermediate will be removed. Now this is clearly false. Therefore we must suppose *the existence of a first efficient cause:* and this is God.

Another reason can be drawn from the words of Aristotle. For in 2 *Metaph.*[40] he shows that those things which excel as true excel as beings: and in 4 *Metaph.*[41] he shows that there is something supremely true, from the fact that we see that of two false things one is falser than the other, wherefore it follows that one also is truer than the other. Now this is by reason of approximation to that which is simply and supremely true. Wherefore we may further conclude that *there is something that is supremely being.* And this we call God.

Another argument in support of this conclusion is adduced by Damascene[42] from the government of things: and the same reasoning is indicated by the Commentator in 2 *Phys.*[43] It runs as follows. It is impossible for contrary and discordant things to accord in one order always or frequently except by someone's governance, whereby each and all are made to tend to a definite end. Now we see that in the world things of different natures accord in one order, not seldom and fortuitously, but always or for the most part. Therefore it follows that there is *someone by whose providence the world is governed.* And this we call God.

·   ·   ·

---

[39]8 *Phys.* v. 12.
[40]D. 1*a*. i. 5.
[41]D. 3. iv. 27, 28.
[42]*De Fide Orth.* i. 3.
[43]Text 75.

THE SUMMA THEOLOGIAE

QUESTION II.

THE EXISTENCE OF GOD

BECAUSE the chief aim of sacred doctrine is to teach the knowledge of God, not only as He is in Himself, but also as He is the beginning of things and their last end, and especially of rational creatures, as is clear from what has been already said, therefore, in our endeavour to expound this science, we shall treat: (1) Of God; (2) Of the rational creature's advance towards God: (3) of Christ, Who as man, is our way to God.

In treating of God there will be a threefold division:

For we shall consider (1) whatever concerns the Divine Essence. (2) Whatever concerns the distinctions of Persons. (3) Whatever concerns the procession of creatures from Him.

Concerning the Divine Essence, we must consider:

(1) Whether God exists? (2) The manner of His existence or, rather, what is *not* the manner of His existence. (3) Whatever concerns His operations—namely, His knowledge, will, power.

Concerning the first, there are three points of inquiry:

(1) Whether the proposition 'God exists' is self-evident? (2) Whether it is demonstrable? (3) Whether God exists?

From Fathers of the English Dominican Providence, trans., *The "Summa Theologica". Part I., QQ. I–XXVI.*, 2d and rev. ed. (London: Burns Oates & Washbourne, 1920), pp. 19–27.

FIRST ARTICLE

Whether the existence of God is self-evident?

WE *proceed thus to the First Article:*
Objection 1. It seems that the existence of God is self-evident. Now those things are said to be self-evident to us the knowledge of which is naturally implanted in us, as we can see in regard to first principles. But as Damascene says,[1] *the knowledge of God is naturally implanted in all.* Therefore the existence of God is self-evident.

Obj. 2. Further, those things are said to be self-evident which are known as soon as the terms are known, which the Philosopher[2] says is true of the first principles of demonstration. Thus, when the nature of a whole and of a part is known, it is at once recognized that every whole is greater than its part. But as soon as the signification of the word 'God' is understood, it is at once seen that God exists. For by this word is signified that thing than which nothing greater can be conceived. But that which exists actually and mentally is greater than that which exists only mentally. Therefore, since as soon as the word 'God' is understood it exists mentally, it also follows that it exists actually. Therefore the proposition 'God exists' is self-evident.

Obj. 3. Further, the existence of truth is self-evident. For whoever denies the existence of truth grants that truth does not exist: and, if truth does not exist, then the proposition 'Truth does not exist' is true: and if there is anything true, there must be truth. But God is truth itself: *"I am the way, the truth, and the life"* (John 14:6). Therefore 'God exists' is self-evident.

On the contrary, No one can mentally admit the opposite of what is self-evident; as the Philosopher[3] states concerning the first principles of demonstration. But the opposite of the proposition 'God is' can be mentally admitted: *The fool said in his heart, There is no God* (Ps. 53:1). Therefore, that God exists is not self-evident.

I answer that, A thing can be self-evident in either of two ways; on the one hand, self-evident in itself, though not to us; on the other, self-evident in itself, and to us. A proposition is self-evident because the predicate is included in the essence of the subject, as 'Man is an animal,' for animal is contained in the essence of man. If, therefore, the essence of the predicate and subject be known to all, the proposition will be self-evident to all; as is clear with regard to the first

---

[1]*De Fid. Orth.* i. I. 3.
[2]*I Poster.* iii.
[3]*Metaph.* iv., lect. vi.

principles of demonstration, the terms of which are common things that no one is ignorant of, such as being and non-being, whole and part, and suchlike. If, however, there are some to whom the essence of the predicate and subject is unknown, the proposition will be self-evident in itself, but not to those who do not know the meaning of the predicate and subject of the proposition. Therefore, it happens, as Boethius says (*Hebdom.*, *the title of which is: 'Whether all that is, is good'*), 'that there are some mental concepts self-evident only to the learned, as that incorporeal substances are not in space.' Therefore I say that this proposition, 'God exists,' of itself is self-evident, for the predicate is the same as the subject; because God is His own existence as will be hereafter shown.[4] Now because we do not know the essence of God, the proposition is not self-evident to us; but needs to be demonstrated by things that are more known to us, though less known in their nature—namely, by effects.

Reply Obj. 1. To know that God exists in a general and confused way is implanted in us by nature, inasmuch as God is man's beatitude. For man naturally desires happiness, and what is naturally desired by man must be naturally known to him. This, however, is not to know absolutely that God exists; just as to know that someone is approaching is not the same as to know that Peter is approaching, even though it is Peter who is approaching; for many there are who imagine that man's perfect good which is happiness, consists in riches, and others in pleasures, and others in something else.

Reply Obj. 2. Perhaps not everyone who hears this word 'God' understands it to signify something than which nothing greater can be thought, seeing that some have believed God to be a body. Yet, granted that everyone understands that by this word 'God' is signified something than which nothing greater can be thought, nevertheless, it does not therefore follow that he understands that what the word signifies exists actually, but only that it exists mentally. Nor can it be argued that it actually exists, unless it be admitted that there actually exists something than which nothing greater can be thought; and this precisely is not admitted by those who hold that God does not exist.

Reply Obj. 3. The existence of truth in general is self-evident, but the existence of a Primal Truth is not self-evident to us.

SECOND ARTICLE

Whether it can be demonstrated that God exists?

WE *proceed thus to the Second Article:*

Objection 1. It seems that the existence of God cannot be demonstrated. For it is an article of faith that God exists. But what is of faith cannot be demon-

---

[4]Q. III., A. 4.

strated, because a demonstration produces scientific knowledge; whereas faith is of the unseen (Heb. 11:1). Therefore it cannot be demonstrated that God exists.

Obj. 2. Further, the essence is the middle term of demonstration. But we cannot know in what God's essence consists, but solely in what it does not consist; as Damascene says (*De Fid. Orth.* i. 4.). Therefore we cannot demonstrate that God exists.

Obj. 3. Further, if the existence of God were demonstrated, this could only be from His effects. But His effects are not proportionate to Him, since He is infinite and His effects are finite; and between the finite and infinite there is no proportion. Therefore, since a cause cannot be demonstrated by an effect not proportionate to it, it seems that the existence of God cannot be demonstrated.

On the contrary, The Apostle says: *"The invisible things of Him are clearly seen, being understood by the things that are made"* (Rom. 1:20). But this would not be unless the existence of God could be demonstrated through the things that are made; for the first thing we must know of anything is, whether it exists.

I answer that, Demonstration can be made in two ways: One is through the cause, and is called *a priori*, and this is to argue from what is prior absolutely. The other is through the effect, and is called a demonstration *a posteriori*; this is to argue from what is prior relatively only to us. When an effect is better known to us than its cause, from the effect we proceed to the knowledge of the cause. And from every effect the existence of its proper cause can be demonstrated, so long as its effects are better known to us; because since every effect depends upon its cause, if the effect exists, the cause must pre-exist. Hence the existence of God, in so far as it is not self-evident to us, can be demonstrated from those of His effects which are known to us.

Reply Obj. 1. The existence of God and other like truths about God, which can be known by natural reason, are not articles of faith, but are preambles to the articles; for faith presupposes natural knowledge, even as grace presupposes nature, and perfection supposes something that can be perfected. Nevertheless, there is nothing to prevent a man, who cannot grasp a proof, accepting, as a matter of faith, something which in itself is capable of being scientifically known and demonstrated.

Reply Obj. 2. When the existence of a cause is demonstrated from an effect, this effect takes the place of the definition of the cause in proof of the cause's existence. This is especially the case in regard to God, because, in order to prove the existence of anything, it is necessary to accept as a middle term the meaning of the word, and not its essence, for the question of its essence follows on the question of its existence. Now the names given to God are derived from His effects; consequently, in demonstrating the existence of God from His effects, we may take for the middle term the meaning of the word 'God.'

Reply Obj. 3. From effects not proportionate to the cause no perfect knowledge of that cause can be obtained. Yet from every effect the existence of the cause can be clearly demonstrated, and so we can demonstrate the existence of God from His effects; though from them we cannot perfectly know God as He is in His essence.

THIRD ARTICLE
Whether God exists?

WE *proceed thus to the Third Article:*
Objection 1. It seems that God does not exist; because if one of two contraries be infinite, the other would be altogether destroyed. But the word 'God' means that He is infinite goodness. If, therefore, God existed, there would be no evil discoverable; but there is evil in the world. Therefore God does not exist.

Obj. 2. Further, it is superfluous to suppose that what can be accounted for by a few principles has been produced by many. But it seems that everything we see in the world can be accounted for by other principles, supposing God did not exist. For all natural things can be reduced to one principle, which is nature; and all voluntary things can be reduced to one principle, which is human reason, or will. Therefore there is no need to suppose God's existence.

On the contrary, It is said in the person of god: "*I am Who am*" (Exod. 3:14).

I answer that, The existence of God can be proved in five ways.

The first and more manifest way is the argument from motion. It is certain, and evident to our senses, that in the world some things are in motion. Now whatever is in motion is put in motion by another, for nothing can be in motion except it is in potentiality to that towards which it is in motion; whereas a thing moves inasmuch as it is in act. For motion is nothing else than the reduction of something from potentiality to actuality. But nothing can be reduced from potentiality to actuality, except by something in a state of actuality. Thus that which is actually hot, as fire, makes wood, which is potentially hot, to be actually hot, and thereby moves and changes it. Now it is not possible that the same thing should be at once in actuality and potentiality in the same respect, but only in different respects. For what is actually hot cannot simultaneously be potentially hot; but it is simultaneously potentially cold. It is therefore impossible that in the same respect and in the same way a thing should be both mover and moved, *i.e.,* that it should move itself. Therefore, whatever is in motion must be put in motion by another. If that by which it is put in motion be itself put in motion, then this also must needs be put in motion by another, and that by another again. But this cannot go on to infinity, because then there would be no first mover, and consequently, no other mover; seeing that subsequent movers move only inasmuch as they are put in motion by the first mover; as the staff moves only because it is put in motion by the hand. Therefore it is necessary to arrive at a first mover, put in motion by no other; and this everyone understands to be God.

The second way is from the nature of the efficient cause. In the world of sense we find there is an order of efficient causes. There is no case known (neither is it, indeed, possible) in which a thing is found to be the efficient cause of itself; for so it would be prior to itself, which is impossible. Now in efficient causes it is not possible to go on to infinity, because in all efficient causes following in order, the first is the cause of the intermediate cause, and the intermediate is the cause of the ultimate cause, whether the intermediate cause be several, or one only. Now to take away the cause is to take away the effect. Therefore, if there be no first cause among efficient causes, there will be no ultimate, nor any intermediate cause. But if in efficient causes it is possible to go on to infinity, there will be no first efficient cause, neither will there be an ultimate effect, nor any intermediate efficient causes; all of which is plainly false. Therefore it is necessary to admit a first efficient cause, to which everyone gives the name of God.

The third way is taken from possibility and necessity, and runs thus. We find in nature things that are possible to be and not to be, since they are found to be generated, and to corrupt, and consequently, they are possible to be and not to be. But it is impossible for these always to exist, for that which is possible not to be at some time is not. Therefore, if everything is possible not to be, then at one time there could have been nothing in existence. Now if this were true, even now there would be nothing in existence, because that which does not exist only begins to exist by something already existing. Therefore, if at one time nothing was in existence, it would have been impossible for anything to have begun to exist; and thus even now nothing would be in existence—which is absurd. Therefore, not all things are merely possible, but there must exist something the existence of which is necessary. But every necessary thing either has its necessity caused by another, or not. Now it is impossible to go on to infinity in necessary things which have their necessity caused by another, as has been already proved in regard to efficient causes. Therefore we cannot but postulate the existence of some being having of itself its own necessity, and not receiving it from another, but rather causing in others their necessity. This all men speak of as God.

The fourth way is taken from the gradation to be found in things. Among beings there are some more and some less good, true, noble, and the like. But 'more' and 'less' are predicated of different things, according as they resemble in their different ways something which is the maximum, as a thing is said to be hotter according as it more nearly resembles that which is hottest; so that there is something which is truest, something best, something noblest, and, consequently, something which is uttermost being; for those things that are greatest in truth are greatest in being, as it is written in *Metaph.* ii. Now the maximum in any genus is the cause of all in that genus; as fire, which is the maximum of heat, is the cause of all hot things. Therefore there must also be something which is to all beings the cause of their being, goodness, and every other perfection; and this we call God.

The fifth way is taken from the governance of the world. We see that things which lack intelligence, such as natural bodies, act for an end, and this is evident from their acting always, or nearly always, in the same way, so as to obtain the best result. Hence it is plain that not fortuitously, but designedly, do they achieve their end. Now whatever lacks intelligence cannot move towards an end, unless it be directed by some being endowed with knowledge and intelligence; as the arrow is shot to its mark by the archer. Therefore some intelligent being exists by whom all natural things are directed to their end; and this being we call God.

Reply Obj. 1. As Augustine says: *Since God is the highest good, He would not allow any evil to exist in His works, unless His omnipotence and goodness were such as to bring good even out of evil.* [5] This is part of the infinite goodness of God, that He should allow evil to exist, and out of it produce good.

Reply Obj. 2. Since nature works for a determinate end under the direction of a higher agent, whatever is done by nature must needs be traced back to God, as to its first cause. So also whatever is done voluntarily must also be traced back to some higher cause other than human reason or will, since these can change and fail; for all things that are changeable and capable of defect must be traced back to an immovable and self-necessary first principle, as was shown in the body of the *Article.*

---

[5] *Enchir.* xi.

⋙ 10 ⋘

JOHN CALVIN
(1509–1564)

During the Middle Ages, the Roman Catholic Church had developed a series of theological and practical emphases that were not a part of the apostolic, New Testament church. For example, the doctrine that the pope was the successor of Peter had been so fully established that the pope was considered the universal head of the church as the personal representative of Christ on the earth. Boniface VIII had declared on November 18, 1302, that if a person were not in communion with the pope, he could not be saved.

In addition to that, Mary had been given the title "Mother of God." Perhaps at first this title was only a strong affirmation of the reality of the Incarnation but it soon developed into a doctrinal affirmation implying that Mary participated in the plan of the redemption. The allegorical method of biblical interpretation had become widespread. The sacramental system had been expanded. The sacrament of penance had become the most important one and was particularly tied to the sale of indulgences (a system that supposedly allowed people to purchase forgiveness from the church).

For the Protestant Reformers the primary issues were both theological and practical. Reformation theology was built on the belief that the Word of God had created the church and that the written Scripture was the accurate and permanent location of the prior existing Word of God. The true gospel had been preached. From that preaching the church had been formed. Scripture is the written account of that revealed gospel. It is the Word of God that nourishes, feeds, and sustains the church, they said.

On July 27, 1509, at Noyon, in northern France, Jean Cauvin (better known as John Calvin) was born. His father Gerard was highly esteemed by most of the nobility in the district and had become the financial secretary to the resident bishop. Calvin was a diligent student and received a very liberal education. His father hoped that he would become a priest. However, it was obvious that the legal profession was a more certain road to wealth, and his father later encouraged him strongly to study law. Calvin, in obedience to his father's wishes, did pursue legal studies, but by the providence of God finally took a different direction in his life.

Apparently Calvin was a devoted Catholic. He seems to have been strongly attached both emotionally and intellectually to the papal system. Nevertheless in his own words God produced a "sudden conversion" in his mind. Having discovered true godliness, Calvin was "immediately inflammed with so intense a desire to make progress" in his true godliness that he began to concentrate almost exclusively on his theological studies.

Scholars are uncertain of the exact date of his conversion but it seems likely that it was before 1533. The persecution that began In 1536, before he was twenty-seven years of age, he published his *Institutes of the Christian Religion*. It was revised and enlarged several times. Undoubtedly it is the single most significant exposition of Protestant theology in the sixteenth century.

Although he was now famous, Calvin did not yet have a definite vocational goal. Giving himself to further studies, he traveled to Italy and later returned to France. However, the war between Charles V and Francis forced him to move to Geneva. There he became associated with Farel, and he began daily Bible studies for the people. Serious controversy broke out between the city council and Calvin. He was forced to leave, but later returned to Geneva and tried to establish a new church order.

For more than fifteen years Calvin struggled to get the principles for which he stood accepted in Geneva. The moral and theological battles were endless. By 1555 Calvin had won a majority of support on the city council. Geneva had now become Calvin's city. In fact many saw it as the very center of Protestant life and thought. The Geneva Academy was founded in 1559 to train future ministers from all over Europe. In 1564 Calvin died of a combination of various diseases. He seems to have known that his death was near, because in April of that year he dictated his last will and testament.

In the excerpt reprinted below from Calvin's *Institutes* one can see his classic statement that has molded Reformed apologetic systems. In contemporary terms this would be called a "presuppositional" apologetic. There is no denial that good and sufficient evidence is available to support the authenticity of the biblical revelation. However, the emphasis of Calvin's apologetic method is on the work of the Holy Spirit. It is called "presuppositional" because the method depends entirely on the original assumption that God has revealed Himself through the Holy Scripture. The viewpoint expressed here has been elaborated and carefully defined with precision by many contemporary apologists in the Reformed tradition.

BIBLIOGRAPHY

McNeill, John T. *The History and Character of Calvinism.* London: Oxford University Press, 1954.
Parker, T. H. L. *John Calvin: A Biography.* Philadelphia: Westminster, 1975.
Walker, Williston. *John Calvin: The Organizer of Reformed Protestantism (1509–1564).* New York: Putnam, 1906.
Warfield, Benjamin Breckinridge. *Calvin and Calvinism.* New York: Oxford University Press, 1931.

INSTITUTES
OF
THE CHRISTIAN RELIGION

BOOK FIRST.
OF THE KNOWLEDGE OF GOD THE
CREATOR

CHAPTER I.

The knowledge of God and of ourselves mutually connected.—Nature of the connection.

1. OUR wisdom, in so far as it ought to be deemed true and solid wisdom, consists almost entirely of two parts: the knowledge of God and of ourselves. But as these are connected together by many ties, it is not easy to determine which of the two precedes, and gives birth to the other. For, in the first place, no man can survey himself without forthwith turning his thoughts towards the God in whom he lives and moves; because it is perfectly obvious, that the endowments which we possess cannot possibly be from ourselves; nay, that our very being is nothing else than subsistence in God alone. In the second place, those blessings which unceasingly distil to us from heaven, are like streams conducting us to the fountain. Here, again, the infinitude of good which resides in God becomes more apparent from our poverty. In particular, the miserable ruin into which the revolt of the first man has plunged us, compels us to turn our eyes upwards; not only that while hungry and famishing we may thence ask what we want, but being aroused by fear may learn humility. For as there exists in man something like a world of misery, and ever since we were stript of the divine attire our naked

From John Calvin, *Institutes of the Christian Religion*, trans. Henry Beveridge (Edinburgh: Calvin Translation Society, 1845), 1:47–48, 51, 55–56, 65–68, 72–73, 76–77, 80–81, 83–87, 89–91, 93–109.

shame discloses an immense series of disgraceful properties, every man, being stung by the consciousness of his own unhappiness, in this way necessarily obtains at least some knowledge of God. Thus, our feeling of ignorance, vanity, want, weakness, in short, depravity and corruption, reminds us . . . that in the Lord, and none but He, dwell the true light of wisdom, solid virtue, exuberant goodness. We are accordingly urged by our own evil things to consider the good things of God; and, indeed, we cannot aspire to Him in earnest until we have begun to be displeased with ourselves. For what man is not disposed to rest in himself? Who, in fact, does not thus rest, so long as he is unknown to himself; that is, so long as he is contented with his own endowments, and unconscious or unmindful of his misery? Every person, therefore, on coming to the knowledge of himself, is not only urged to seek God, but is also led as by the hand to find him.

. . .

CHAPTER II.

What it is to know God.—Tendency of this knowledge.

1. BY the knowledge of God, I understand that by which we not only conceive that there is some God, but also apprehend what it is for our interest, and conducive to his glory, what, in short, it is befitting to know concerning him. For, properly speaking, we cannot say that God is known where there is no religion or piety. I am not now referring to that species of knowledge by which men, in themselves lost and under curse, apprehend God as a Redeemer in Christ the Mediator. I speak only of that simple and primitive knowledge, to which the mere course of nature would have conducted us, had Adam stood upright. For although no man will now, in the present ruin of the human race, perceive God to be either a father, or the author of salvation, or propitious in any respect, until Christ interpose to make our peace; still it is one thing to perceive that God our Maker supports us by his power, rules us by his providence, fosters us by his goodness, and visits us with all kinds of blessings, and another thing to embrace the grace of reconciliation offered to us in Christ. Since, then, the Lord first appears, as well in the creation of the world as in the general doctrine of Scripture, simply as a Creator, and afterwards as a Redeemer in Christ,—a twofold knowledge of him hence arises: of these the former is now to be considered. . . .

CHAPTER III.

The knowledge of God naturally implanted in the human mind.

1. THAT there exists in the human mind, and indeed by natural instinct, some sense of Deity, we hold to be beyond dispute, since God himself, to prevent any man from pretending ignorance, has endued all men with some idea of his Godhead, the memory of which he constantly renews and occasionally enlarges, that all to a man, being aware that there is a God, and that he is their Maker, may be condemned by their own conscience when they neither worship him nor consecrate their lives to his service. Certainly, if there is any quarter where it may be supposed that God is unknown, the most likely for such an instance to exist is among the dullest tribes farthest removed from civilisation. But, as a heathen tells us,[1] there is no nation so barbarous, no race so brutish, as not to be imbued with the conviction that there is a God. Even those who, in other respects, seem to differ least from the lower animals, constantly retain some sense of religion; so thoroughly has this common conviction possessed the mind, so firmly is it stamped on the breasts of all men. Since, then, there never has been, from the very first, any quarter of the globe, any city, any household even, without religion, this amounts to a tacit confession, that a sense of Deity is inscribed on every heart. Nay, even idolatry is ample evidence of this fact. For we know how reluctant man is to lower himself, in order to set other creatures above him. Therefore, when he chooses to worship wood and stone rather than be thought to have no God, it is evident how very strong this impression of a Deity must be; since it is more difficult to obliterate it from the mind of man, than to break down the feelings of his nature,—these certainly being broken down, when, in opposition to his natural haughtiness, he spontaneously humbles himself before the meanest object as an act of reverence to God.

.   .   .

CHAPTER V.

The knowledge of God conspicuous in the creation and continual government of the world.

1. SINCE the perfection of blessedness consists in the knowledge of God, he has been pleased, in order that none might be excluded from the means of

---

[1] "Intelligi necesse est deos, quoniam insitas eorum vel potius innatas cognitiones habemus.—Quae nobis natura informationem deorum ipsorum dedit, eadem insculpsit in

obtaining felicity, not only to deposit in our minds that seed of religion of which
we have already spoken, but so to manifest his perfections in the whole structure
of the universe, and daily place himself in our view, that we cannot open our
eyes without being compelled to behold him. His essence, indeed, is incomprehensible, utterly transcending all human thought; but on each of his
works his glory is engraven in characters so bright, so distinct, and so illustrious,
that none, however dull and illiterate, can plead ignorance as their excuse.
Hence, with perfect truth, the Psalmist exclaims, "He covereth himself with light
as with a garment" (Ps. 104:2); as if he had said, that God for the first time was
arrayed in visible attire when, in the creation of the world, he displayed those
glorious banners, on which, to whatever side we turn, we behold his perfections
visibly portrayed. In the same place, the Psalmist aptly compares the expanded
heavens to his royal tent, and says, "He layeth the beams of his chambers in the
waters, maketh the clouds his chariot, and walketh upon the wings of the wind,"
sending forth the winds and lightnings as his swift messengers. And because the
glory of his power and wisdom is more refulgent in the firmament, it is frequently
designated as his palace. And, first, wherever you turn your eyes, there is no
portion of the world, however minute, that does not exhibit at least some sparks
of beauty; while it is impossible to contemplate the vast and beautiful fabric as it
extends around, without being overwhelmed by the immense weight of glory.
Hence, the author of the Epistle to the Hebrews elegantly describes the visible
worlds as images of the invisible (Heb. 11:3), the elegant structure of the world
serving us as a kind of mirror, in which we may behold God, though otherwise
invisible. For the same reason, the Psalmist attributes language to celestial objects, a language which all nations understand (Ps. 19:1); the manifestation of the
Godhead being too clear to escape the notice of any people, however obtuse. The
apostle Paul, stating this still more clearly, says, "That which may be known of
God is manifest in them, for God hath showed it unto them. For the invisible
things of him from the creation of the world are clearly seen, being understood by
the things that are made, even his eternal power and Godhead" (Rom. 1:19–20).

2. In attestation of his wondrous wisdom, both the heavens and the earth
present us with innumerable proofs, not only those more recondite proofs which
astronomy, medicine, and all the natural sciences, are designed to illustrate, but
proofs which force themselves on the notice of the most illiterate peasant, who
cannot open his eyes without beholding them. It is true, indeed, that those who
are more or less intimately acquainted with those liberal studies are thereby as-

---

mentibus ut eos aeternos et beatos habemus."—Cic. de Nat. Deor. lib. i. c. 17.—"Itaque
inter omnes omnium gentium summa constat; omnibus enim innatum est, et in animo
quasi insculptum esse deos."—Lib. ii. c. 4. See also Lact. Inst. Div. lib. iii. c. 10.

sisted and enabled to obtain a deeper insight into the secret workings of divine wisdom. No man, however, though he be ignorant of these, is incapacitated for discerning such proofs of creative wisdom as may well cause him to break forth in admiration of the Creator. To investigate the motions of the heavenly bodies, to determine their positions, measure their distances, and ascertain their properties, demands skill, and a more careful examination; and where these are so employed, as the providence of God is thereby more fully unfolded, so it is reasonable to suppose that the mind takes a loftier flight, and obtains brighter views of his glory.[2] Still, none who have the use of their eyes can be ignorant of the divine skill manifested so conspicuously in the endless variety, yet distinct and well-ordered array, of the heavenly host; and, therefore, it is plain that the Lord has furnished every man with abundant proofs of his wisdom. The same is true in regard to the structure of the human frame. To determine the connection of its parts, its symmetry and beauty, with the skill of a Galen,[3] requires singular acuteness; and yet all men acknowledge that the human body bears on its face such proofs of ingenious contrivance as are sufficient to proclaim the admirable wisdom of its Maker.

3. Hence certain of the philosophers[4] have not improperly called man a *microcosm (minature world)*, as being a rare specimen of divine power, wisdom, and goodness, and containing within himself wonders sufficient to occupy our minds, if we are willing so to employ them. Paul, accordingly, after reminding the Athenians that they "might feel after God and find him," immediately adds, that "he is not far from every one of us" (Acts 17:27); every man having within himself undoubted evidence of the heavenly grace by which he lives, and moves, and has his being. But if, in order to apprehend God, it is unnecessary to go farther than ourselves, what excuse can there be for the sloth of any man who will not take the trouble of descending into himself that he may find Him? For the same reason, too, David, after briefly celebrating the wonderful name and glory of God, as everywhere displayed, immediately exclaims, "What is man, that thou art mindful of him?" and again, "Out of the mouths of babes and sucklings thou hast ordained strength" (Ps. 8:2, 4). Thus he declares not only that the human race are a bright mirror of the Creator's works, but that infants hanging on their mothers' breasts have tongues eloquent enough to proclaim his glory without the aid of other orators. Accordingly, he hesitates not to bring them forward as fully instructed to refute the madness of those who, from devilish

---

[2]Augustinus: Astrologia magnum religiosis argumentum, tormentumque curiosis.
[3]Lib. De Usu Partium.
[4]See Aristot. Hist. Anim. lib. i. c. 17; Macrob. in Somn. Scip. lib. ii. c. 12; Boeth. De Definitione.

pride, would fain extinguish the name of God. Hence, too, the passage which Paul quotes from Aratus, "We are his offspring" (Acts 17:28), the excellent gifts with which he has endued us attesting that he is our Father. In the same way, also, from natural instinct, and, as it were, at the dictation of experience, heathen poets call him the father of men. No one, indeed, will voluntarily and willingly devote himself to the service of God unless he has previously tasted his paternal love, and been thereby allured to love and reverence him.

4. But herein appears the shameful ingratitude of men. Though they have in their own persons a factory where innumerable operations of God are carried on, and a magazine stored with teasures of inestimable value—instead of bursting forth in his praise, as they are bound to do, they, on the contrary, are the more inflated and swelled with pride. They feel how wonderfully God is working in them, and their own experience tells them of the vast variety of gifts which they owe to his liberality. Whether they will or not, they cannot but know that these are proofs of his Godhead, and yet they inwardly suppress them. . . . Can anything be more detestable than this madness in man, who, finding God a hundred times both in his body and his soul, makes his excellence in this respect a pretext for denying that there is a God? He will not say that chance has made him differ from the brutes that perish; but, substituting nature as the architect of the universe, he suppresses the name of God. . . .

.   .   .

7. In the second class of God's works, namely, those which are above the ordinary course of nature, the evidence of his perfections are in every respect equally clear. For in conducting the affairs of men, he so arranges the course of his providence, as daily to declare, by the clearest manifestations, that though all are in innumerable ways the partakers of his bounty, the righteous are the special objects of his favour, the wicked and profane the special objects of his severity. It is impossible to doubt his punishment of crimes; while at the same time he, in no unequivocal manner, declares that he is the protector, and even the avenger of innocence, by shedding blessings on the good, helping their necessities, soothing and solacing their griefs, relieving their sufferings, and in all ways providing for their safety. And though he often permits the guilty to exult for a time with impunity, and the innocent to be driven to and fro in adversity, nay, even to be wickedly and iniquitously oppressed, this ought not to produce any uncertainty as to the uniform justice of all his procedure. Nay, an opposite inference should be drawn. When any one crime calls forth visible manifestations of his anger, it must be because he hates all crimes; and, on the other hand, his leaving many

crimes unpunished, only proves that there is a judgment in reserve, when the punishment now delayed shall be inflicted. In like manner, how richly does he supply us with the means of contemplating his mercy, when, as frequently happens, he continues to visit miserable sinners with unwearied kindness, until he subdues their depravity, and woos them back with more than a parent's fondness?

.   .   .

11. Bright, however, as is the manifestation which God gives both of himself and his immortal kingdom in the mirror of his works, so great is our stupidity, so dull are we in regard to these bright manifestations, that we derive no benefit from them. For in regard to the fabric and admirable arrangement of the universe, how few of us are there who, in lifting our eyes to the heavens, or looking abroad on the various regions of the earth, ever think of the Creator? Do we not rather overlook Him, and sluggishly content ourselves with a view of his works? And then in regard to supernatural events, though these are occurring every day, how few are there who ascribe them to the ruling providence of God— how many who imagine that they are casual results produced by the blind evolutions of the wheel of chance? Even when, under the guidance and direction of these events, we are in a manner forced to the contemplation of God (a circumstance which all must occasionally experience), and are thus led to form some impressions of Deity, we immediately fly off to carnal dreams and depraved fictions, and so by our vanity corrupt heavenly truth. This far, indeed, we differ from each other, in that every one appropriates to himself some peculiar error; but we are all alike in this, that we substitute monstrous fictions for the one living and true God—a disease not confined to obtuse and vulgar minds, but affecting the noblest, and those who, in other respects, are singularly acute. How lavishly in this respect have the whole body of philosophers betrayed their stupidity and want of sense? To say nothing of the others whose absurdities are of a still grosser description, how completely does Plato, the soberest and most religious of them all, lose himself in his round globe?[5] What must be the case with the rest, when the leaders, who ought to have set them an example, commit such blunders, and labour under such hallucinations? In like manner, while the government of the world places the doctrine of providence beyond dispute, the practical result is the same as if it were believed that all things were carried hither and thither at the

---

[5]Plato in Timaeos. See also Cic. De Nat. Deorum, lib. i; Plut. De Philos Placitis, lib. i.

caprice of chance; so prone are we to vanity and error. I am still referring to the most distinguished of the philosophers, and not to the common herd, whose madness in profaning the truth of God exceeds all bounds.

12. Hence that immense flood of error with which the whole world is overflowed. Every individual mind being a kind of labyrinth, it is not wonderful, not only that each nation has adopted a variety of fictions, but that almost every man has had his own god. To the darkness of ignorance have been added presumption and wantonness, and hence there is scarcely an individual to be found without some idol or phantom as a substitute for Deity. . . .

14. In vain for us, therefore, does Creation exhibit so many bright lamps lighted up to show forth the glory of its Author. Though they beam upon us from every quarter, they are altogether insufficient of themselves to lead us into the right path. Some sparks, undoubtedly, they do throw out; but these are quenched before they can give forth a brighter effulgence. Wherefore, the apostle, in the very place where he says that the worlds are images of invisible things, adds that it is *by faith* we understand that they were framed by the word of God (Heb. 11:3); thereby intimating that the invisible Godhead is indeed represented by such displays, but that we have no eyes to perceive it until they are enlightened through faith by internal revelation from God. When Paul says that that which may be known of God is manifested by the creation of the world, he does not mean such a manifestation as may be comprehended by the wit of man (Rom. 1:19); on the contrary, he shows that it has no further effect than to render us inexcusable (Acts 17:27). And though he says, elsewhere, that we have not far to seek for God, inasmuch as he dwells within us, he shows, in another passage, to what extent this nearness to God is availing. God, says he, "in times past, suffered all nations to walk in their own ways. Nevertheless, he left not himself without witness, in that he did good, and gave us rain from heaven, and fruitful seasons, filling our hearts with food and gladness" (Acts 14:16, 17). But though God is not left without a witness, while, with numberless varied acts of kindness, he woos men to the knowledge of himself, yet they cease not to follow their own ways, in other words, deadly errors.

.   .   .

CHAPTER VI.

The need of scripture, as a guide and teacher, in coming to God as a creator.

1. THEREFORE, though the effulgence which is presented to every eye, both in the heavens and on the earth, leaves the ingratitude of man without

excuse, since God, in order to bring the whole human race under the same condemnation, holds forth to all, without exception, a mirror of his Deity in his works, another and better help must be given to guide us properly to God as a Creator. Not in vain, therefore, has he added the light of his Word in order that he might make himself known unto salvation, and bestowed the privilege on those whom he was pleased to bring into nearer and more familiar relation to himself. For, seeing how the minds of men were carried to and fro, and found no certain resting-place, he chose the Jews for a peculiar people, and then hedged them in that they might not, like others, go astray. And not in vain does he, by the same means, retain us in his knowledge, since but for this, even those who, in comparison of others, seem to stand strong, would quickly fall away. For as the aged, or those whose sight is defective, when any book, however fair, is set before them, though they perceive that there is something written, are scarcely able to make out two consecutive words, but, when aided by glasses, begin to read distinctly, so Scripture, gathering together the impressions of Deity, which, till then, lay confused in their minds, dissipates the darkness, and shows us the true God clearly. God therefore bestows a gift of singular value, when, for the instruction of the Church, he employs not dumb teachers merely, but opens his own sacred mouth; when he not only proclaims that some God must be worshipped, but at the same time declares that He is the God to whom worship is due; when he not only teaches his elect to have respect to God, but manifests himself as the God to whom this respect should be paid.

The course which God followed towards his Church from the very first, was to supplement these common proofs by the addition of his Word, as a surer and more direct means of discovering himself. And there can be no doubt that it was by this help, Adam, Noah, Abraham, and the other patriarchs, attained to that familiar knowledge which, in a manner, distinguished them from unbelievers. I am not now speaking of the peculiar doctrines of faith by which they were elevated to the hope of eternal blessedness. It was necessary, in passing from death unto life, that they should know God, not only as a Creator, but as a Redeemer also; and both kinds of knowledge they certainly did obtain from the Word. . . .

2. Whether God revealed himself to the fathers by oracles and visions,[6] or, by the instrumentality and ministry of men, suggested what they were to hand down to posterity, there cannot be a doubt that the certainty of what he taught them was firmly engraven on their hearts, so that they felt assured and knew that the things which they learnt came forth from God, who invariably accompanied his word with a sure testimony, infinitely superior to mere opinion. At length, in

---

[6]The French adds, "C'est à dire, temoignages celestes;"—that is to say, messages from heaven.

order that, while doctrine was continually enlarged, its truth might subsist in the world during all ages, it was his pleasure that the same oracles which he had deposited with the fathers should be consigned, as it were, to public records. With this view the law was promulgated, and prophets were afterwards added to be its interpreters. For though the uses of the law were manifold,[7] and the special office assigned to Moses and all the prophets was to teach the method of reconciliation between God and man (whence Paul calls Christ "the end of the law" [Rom. 10:4]); still I repeat that, in addition to the proper doctrine of faith and repentance in which Christ is set forth as a Mediator, the Scriptures employ certain marks and tokens to distinguish the only wise and true God, considered as the Creator and Governor of the world, and thereby guard against his being confounded with the herd of false deities. Therefore, while it becomes man seriously to employ his eyes in considering the works of God, since a place has been assigned him in this most glorious theatre that he may be a spectator of them, his special duty is to give ear to the Word, that he may the better profit.[8] Hence it is not strange that those who are born in darkness become more and more hardened in their stupidity; because the vast majority, instead of confining themselves within due bounds by listening with docility to the Word, exult in their own vanity. If true religion is to beam upon us, our principle must be, that it is necessary to begin with heavenly teaching, and that it is impossible for any man to obtain even the minutest portion of right and sound doctrine without being a disiple of Scripture. Hence the first step in true knowledge is taken, when we reverently embrace the testimony which God has been pleased therein to give of himself. For not only does faith, full and perfect faith, but all correct knowledge of God, originate in obedience. And surely in this respect God has with singular Providence provided for mankind in all ages.

3. For if we reflect how prone the human mind is to lapse into forgetfulness of God, how readily inclined to every kind of error, how bent every now and then on devising new and fictitious religions, it will be easy to understand how necessary it was to make such a depository of doctrine as would secure it from either perishing by the neglect, vanishing away amid the errors, or being corrupted by the presumptuous audacity of men. It being thus manifest that God, foreseeing the inefficiency of his image imprinted on the fair form of the universe, has given the assistance of his Word to all whom he has ever been pleased to instruct effectually, we, too, must pursue this straight path, if we aspire in earnest to a genuine contemplation of God;—we must go, I say, to the Word, where the

---

[7]Book II. c. vii and viii.

[8]Tertullian, Apologet. adv. Gentes: "Quae plenius et impressius tam ipsum quam dispositiones ejus et voluntates adiremus, instrumentum adjecit literaturae," etc.

character of God, drawn from his works, is described accurately and to the life; these works being estimated, not by our depraved judgment, but by the standard of eternal truth. . . .

.   .   .

CHAPTER VII.

The testimony of the Spirit necessary to give full authority to Scripture. The impiety of pretending that the credibility of Scripture depends on the judgment of the church.

1. BEFORE proceeding farther, it seems proper to make some observations on the authority of Scripture, in order that our minds may not only be prepared to receive it with reference, but be divested of all doubt.

When that which professes to be the Word of God is acknowledged to be so, no person, unless devoid of common sense and the feelings of a man, will have the desperate hardihood to refuse credit to the speaker. But since no daily responses are given from heaven, and the Scriptures are the only records in which God has been pleased to consign his truth to perpetual remembrance, the full authority which they ought to possess with the faithful is not recognised, unless they are believed to have come from heaven, as directly as if God had been heard giving utterance to them. . . .

A most pernicious error has very generally prevailed—viz. that Scripture is of importance only in so far as conceded to it by the suffrage of the Church; as if the eternal and inviolable truth of God could depend on the will of men. With great insult to the Holy Spirit, it is asked, Who can assure us that the Scriptures proceeded from God; who guarantee that they have come down safe and unimpaired to our times; who persuade us that *this* book is to be received with reverence, and *that one* expunged from the list, did not the Church regulate all these things with certainty? On the determination of the Church, therefore, it is said, depend both the reverence which is due to Scripture and the books which are to be admitted into the canon. Thus profane men, seeking, under the pretext of the Church, to introduce unbridled tyranny, care not in what absurdities they entangle themselves and others, provided they extort from the simple this one acknowledgment—viz. that there is nothing which the Church cannot do. But what is to become of miserable consciences in quest of some solid assurance of eternal life, if all the promises with regard to it have no better support than man's judgment? On being told so, will they cease to doubt and tremble? On the other hand, to what jeers of the wicked is our faith subjected—into how great suspicion is it brought with all, if believed to have only a precarious authority lent to it by the good-will of men?

2. These ravings are admirably refuted by a single expression of an apostle. Paul testifies that the Church is "built on the foundation of the apostles and prophets" (Eph. 2:20). If the doctrine of the apostles and prophets is the foundation of the Church, the former must have had its certainty before the latter began to exist. Nor is there any room for the cavil, that though the Church derives her first beginning from thence, it still remains doubtful what writings are to be attributed to the apostles and prophets, until her judgment is interposed. For if the Christian Church was founded at first on the writings of the prophets, and the preaching of the apostles, that doctrine, wheresoever it may be found, was certainly ascertained and sanctioned antecedently to the Church, since, but for this, the Church herself never could have existed.[9] Nothing, therefore, can be more absurd than the fiction, that the power of judging Scripture is in the Church, and that on her nod its certainty depends. When the Church receives it, and gives it the stamp of her authority, she does not make that authentic which was otherwise doubtful or controverted, but, acknowledging it as the truth of God, she, as in duty bound, shows her reverence by an unhesitating assent. As to the question, How shall we be persuaded that it came from God without recurring to a decree of the Church? it is just the same as if it were asked, How shall we learn to distinguish light from darkness, white from black, sweet from bitter? Scripture bears upon the face of it as clear evidence of its truth, as white and black do of their colour, sweet and bitter of their taste.

.   .   .

4. It is necessary to attend to what I lately said, that our faith in doctrine is not established until we have a perfect conviction that God is its author. Hence, the highest proof of Scripture is uniformly taken from the character of him whose word it is. The prophets and apostles boast not their own acuteness, or any qualities which win credit to speakers, nor do they dwell on reasons; but they appeal to the sacred name of God, in order that the whole world may be compelled to submission. The next thing to be considered is, how it appears not probable merely, but certain, that the name of God is neither rashly nor cunningly pretended. If, then, we would consult most effectually for our con-

---

[9] The French adds, "Comme le fondement va deuant l'edifice;"—as the foundation goes before the house.

sciences, and save them from being driven about in a whirl of uncertainty, from wavering, and even stumbling at the smallest obstacle, our conviction of the truth of Scripture must be derived from a higher source than human conjectures, judgments, or reasons; namely, the secret testimony of the Spirit. It is true, indeed, that if we choose to proceed in the way of argument, it is easy to establish by evidence of various kinds, that if there is a God in heaven, the Law, the Prophecies, and the Gospel, proceeded from him. Nay, although learned men, and men of the greatest talent, should take the opposite side, summoning and ostentatiously displaying all the powers of their genius in the discussion; if they are not possessed of shameless effrontery, they will be compelled to confess that the Scripture exhibits clear evidence of its being spoken by God, and, consequently, of its containing his heavenly doctrine. We shall see a little farther on, that the volume of sacred Scripture very far surpasses all other writings. Nay, if we look at it with clear eyes and unbiased judgment, it will forthwith present itself with a divine majesty which will subdue our presumptuous opposition, and force us to do it homage.

Still, however, it is preposterous to attempt, by discussion, to rear up a full faith in Scripture. True, were I called to contend with the craftiest despisers of God, I trust, though I am not possessed of the highest ability or eloquence, I should not find it difficult to stop their obstreperous mouths; I could, without much ado, put down the boastings which they mutter in corners, were anything to be gained by refuting their cavils. But although we may maintain the sacred Word of God against gainsayers, it does not follow that we shall forthwith implant the certainty which faith requires in their hearts. Profane men think that religion rests only on opinion, and, therefore, that they may not believe foolishly, or on slight grounds desire and insist to have it proved by reason that Moses and the prophets were divinely inspired. But I answer, that the testimony of the Spirit is superior to reason. For as God alone can properly bear witness to his own words, so these words will not obtain full credit in the hearts of men, until they are sealed by the inward testimony of the Spirit. The same Spirit, therefore, who spoke by the mouth of the prophets, must penetrate our hearts, in order to convince us that they faithfully delivered the message with which they were divinely intrusted. This connection is most aptly expressed by Isaiah in these words, "My Spirit that is upon thee, and my words which I have put in thy mouth, shall not depart out of thy mouth, nor out of the mouth of thy seed, nor out of the mouth of thy seed's seed, saith the Lord, from henceforth and for ever" (Isa. 59:21). Some worthy persons feel disconcerted, because, while the wicked murmur with impunity at the word of God, they have not a clear proof at hand to silence them, forgetting that the Spirit is called an earnest and seal to confirm the faith of the godly, for this very reason, that, until he enlightens their minds, they are tossed to and fro in a sea of doubts.

5. Let it therefore be held as fixed, that those who are inwardly taught by the Holy Spirit acquiesce implicitly in Scripture; that Scripture, carrying its own evidence along with it, deigns not to submit to proofs and arguments, but owes the full conviction with which we ought to receive it to the testimony of the Spirit.[10] Enlightened by him, we no longer believe, either on our own judgment or that of others, that the Scriptures are from God; but, in a way superior to human judgment, feel perfectly assured—as much so as if we beheld the divine image visibly impressed on it—that it came to us, by the instrumentality of men, from the very mouth of God. We ask not for proofs or probabilities on which to rest our judgment, but we subject our intellect and judgment to it as too transcendent for us to estimate. This, however, we do, not in the manner in which some are wont to fasten on an unknown object, which, as soon as known, displeases, but because we have a thorough conviction that, in holding it, we hold unassailable truth; not like miserable men, whose minds are enslaved by superstition, but because we feel a divine energy living and breathing in it—an energy by which we are drawn and animated to obey it, willingly indeed, and knowingly, but more vividly and effectually than could be done by human will or knowledge. Hence, God most justly exclaims by the mouth of Isaiah, "Ye are my witnesses, saith the Lord, and my servant whom I have chosen, that ye may know and believe me, and understand that I am he" (Isa. 43:10).

Such, then, is a conviction which asks not for reasons; such, a knowledge which accords with the highest reason, namely, knowledge in which the mind rests more firmly and securely than in any reasons; such, in fine, the conviction which revelation from heaven alone can produce. I say nothing more than every believer experiences in himself, though my words fall far short of the reality. I do not dwell on this subject at present, because we will return to it again: only let us now understand that the only true faith is that which the Spirit of God seals on our hearts. Nay, the modest and teachable reader will find a sufficient reason in the promise contained in Isaiah, that all the children of the renovated Church "shall be taught of the Lord" (Isa. 54:13). This singular privilege God bestows on his elect only, whom he separates from the rest of mankind. For what is the

---

[10]The French adds, "Car jaçoit qu'en sa propre majesté elle ait assez de quoy estre reuerée, neantmoins elle commence lors à nous vrayement toucher, quand elle est scellée en nos coeurs par le Sainct Esprit."—For though in its own majesty it has enough to command reverence, nevertheless, it then begins truly to touch us when it is sealed in our hearts by the Holy Spirit.

beginning of true doctrine but prompt alacrity to hear the word of God? And God, by the mouth of Moses, thus demands to be heard: "It is not in heaven, that thou shouldst say, Who shall go up for us to heaven, and bring it unto us, that we may hear and do it? But the word is very nigh unto thee, in thy mouth and in thy heart" (Deut. 30:12, 14). God having been pleased to reserve the treasure of intelligence for his children, no wonder that so much ignorance and stupidity is seen in the generality of mankind. In the *generality*, I include even those specially chosen, until they are ingrafted into the body of the Church. Isaiah, moreover, while reminding us that the prophetical doctrine would prove incredible not only to strangers, but also to the Jews, who were desirous to be thought of the household of God, subjoins the reason, when he asks, "To whom hath the arm of the Lord been revealed?" (Isa. 53:1.) If at any time, then, we are troubled at the small number of those who believe, let us, on the other hand, call to mind, that none comprehend the mysteries of God save those to whom it is given.

CHAPTER VIII.

The credibility of Scripture sufficiently proved, in so far as natural reason admits.

1. IN vain were the authority of Scripture fortified by argument, or supported by the consent of the Church, or confirmed by any other helps, if unaccompanied by an assurance higher and stronger than human judgment can give. Till this better foundation has been laid, the authority of Scripture remains in suspense. On the other hand, when recognising its exemption from the common rule, we receive it reverently, and according to its dignity, those proofs which were not so strong as to produce and rivet a full conviction in our minds, become most appropriate helps. For it is wonderful how much we are confirmed in our belief, when we more attentively consider how admirably the system of divine wisdom contained in it is arranged—how perfectly free the doctrine is from everything that savours of earth—how beautifully it harmonises in all its parts—and how rich it is in all the other qualities which give an air of majesty to composition. Our hearts are still more firmly assured when we reflect that our admiration is excited more by the dignity of the matter than by the graces of style. For it was not without an admirable arrangement of Providence, that the sublime mysteries of the kingdom of heaven have for the greater part been delivered with a contemptible meanness of words. Had they been adorned with a more splendid eloquence, the wicked might have cavilled, and alleged that this constituted all their force. But now, when an unpolished simplicity, almost bordering on rudeness, makes a deeper impression than the loftiest flights of oratory, what does it indicate if not that the Holy Scriptures are too mighty in the power of truth to need the rhetorician's art?

Hence there was good ground for the Apostle's declaration, that the faith of the Corinthians was founded not on "the wisdom of men," but on "the power of God" (1 Cor. 2:5),—his speech and preaching among them having been, "not with enticing words of man's wisdom, but in demonstration of the Spirit and of power" (1 Cor. 2:4). For the truth is vindicated in opposition to every doubt, when, unsupported by foreign aid, it has its sole sufficiency in itself. How peculiarly this property belongs to Scripture appears from this, that no human writings, however skilfully composed, are at all capable of affecting us in a similar way. Read Demosthenes or Cicero, read Plato, Aristotle, or any other of that class: you will, I admit, feel wonderfully allured, pleased, moved, enchanted; but turn from them to the reading of the sacred volume, and whether you will or not, it will so affect you, so pierce your heart, so work its way into your very marrow, that, in comparison of the impression so produced, that of orators and philosophers will almost disappear; making it manifest that in the sacred volume there is a truth divine, a something which makes it immeasurably superior to all the gifts and graces attainable by man.

2. I confess, however, that in elegance and beauty, nay, splendour, the style of some of the prophets is not surpassed by the eloquence of heathen writers. By examples of this description, the Holy Spirit was pleased to show that it was not from want of eloquence he in other instances used a rude and homely style. But whether you read David, Isaiah, and others of the same class, whose discourse flows sweet and pleasant; or Amos the herdsman, Jeremiah and Zechariah, whose rougher idiom savours of rusticity; that majesty of the Spirit to which I adverted appears conspicuous in all. I am not unaware, that as Satan often apes God, that lie may by a fallacious resemblance the better insinuate himself into the minds of the simple, so he craftily disseminated the impious errors with which he deceived miserable men in an uncouth and semi-barbarous style, and frequently employed obsolete forms of expression in order to cloak his impostures. None possessed of any moderate share of sense need be told how vain and vile such affectation is. But in regard to the Holy Scriptures, however petulant men may attempt to carp at them, they are replete with sentiments which it is clear that man never could have conceived. Let each of the prophets be examined, and not one will be found who does not rise far higher than human reach. Those who feel their works insipid must be absolutely devoid of taste.

3. As this subject has been treated at large by others, it will be sufficient here merely to touch on its leading points. In addition to the qualities already mentioned, great weight is due to the antiquity of Scripture.[11] Whatever fables Greek writers may retail concerning the Egyptian Theology, no monument of

---

[11]Euseb. Prepar. Evang. lib. ii. c. i.

any religion exists which is not long posterior to the age of Moses. But Moses does not introduce a new Deity. He only sets forth that doctrine concerning the eternal God which the Israelites had received by tradition from their fathers, by whom it had been transmitted, as it were, from hand to hand, during a long series of ages. For what else does he do than lead them back to the covenant which had been made with Abraham? Had he referred to matters of which they had never heard, he never could have succeeded; but their deliverance from the bondage in which they were held must have been a fact of familiar and universal notoriety, the very mention of which must have immediately aroused the attention of all. It is, moreover, probable, that they were intimately acquainted with the whole period of four hundred years. Now, if Moses (who is so much earlier than all other writers) traces the tradition of his doctrine from so remote a period, it is obvious how far the Holy Scriptures must, in point of antiquity, surpass all other writings.

4. Some perhaps may choose to credit the Egyptians in carrying back their antiquity to a period of six thousand years before the world was created. But their garrulity, which even some profane authors have held up to derision, it cannot be necessary for me to refute. Josephus, however, in his work against Appion, produces important passages from very ancient writers, implying that the doctrine delivered in the law was celebrated among all nations from the remotest ages, though it was neither read nor accurately known. And then, in order that the malignant might have no ground for suspicion, and the ungodly no handle for cavil, God has provided, in the most effectual manner, against both dangers. When Moses relates the words which Jacob, under Divine inspiration, uttered concerning his posterity almost three hundred years before, how does he ennoble his own tribe? He stigmatises it with eternal infamy in the person of Levi. "Simeon and Levi," says he, "are brethren; instruments of cruelty are in their habitations. O my soul, come not thou into their secret; unto their assembly mine honour be not thou united" (Gen. 49:5-6). This stigma he certainly might have passed in silence, not only that he might spare his own ancestor, but also save both himself and his whole family from a portion of the disgrace. How can any suspicion attach to him, who, by voluntarily proclaiming, that the first founder of his family was declared detestable by a Divine oracle, neither consults for his own private interest, nor declines to incur obloquy among his tribe, who must have been offended by his statement of the fact? Again, when he relates the wicked murmuring of his brother Aaron, and his sister Miriam (Num. 12:1), shall we say that he spoke his own natural feelings, or that he obeyed the command of the Holy Spirit? Moreover, when invested with supreme authority, why does he not bestow the office of High Priest on his sons, instead of consigning them to the lowest place? I only touch on a few points out of many; but the Law itself con-

tains throughout numerous proofs, which fully vindicate the credibility of Moses, and place it beyond dispute, that he was in truth a messenger sent forth from God.

5. The many striking miracles which Moses relates are so many sanctions of the law delivered, and the doctrine propounded, by him.[12] His being carried up into the mount in a cloud; his remaining there forty days separated from human society; his countenance glistening during the promulgation of the law, as with meridian effulgence; the lightnings which flashed on every side; the voices and thunderings which echoed in the air; the clang of the trumpet blown by no human mouth; his entrance into the tabernacles, while a cloud hid him from the view of the people; the miraculous vindication of his authority, by the fearful destruction of Korah, Dathan, and Abiram, and all their impious faction; the stream instantly gushing forth from the rock when struck with his rod; the manna which rained from heaven at his prayer;—did not God by all these proclaim aloud that he was an undoubted prophet? If any one object that I am taking debatable points for granted, the cavil is easily answered, Moses published all these things in the assembly of the people. How, then, could he possibly impose on the very eyewitnesses of what was done? Is it conceivable that he would have come forward, and, while accusing the people of unbelief, obstinacy, ingratitude, and other crimes, have boasted that his doctrine had been confirmed in their own presence by miracles which they never saw?

6. For it is also worthy of remark, that the miracles which he relates are combined with disagreeable circumstances, which must have provoked opposition from the whole body of the people, if there had been the smallest ground for it. Hence it is obvious that they were induced to assent, merely because they had been previously convinced by their own experience. But because the fact was too clear to leave it free for heathen writers to deny that Moses did perform miracles, the father of lies suggested a calumny, and ascribed them to magic (Exod. 9:11). But with what probability is a charge of magic brought against him, who held it in such abhorrence, that he ordered everyone who should consult soothsayers and magicians to be stoned? (Lev. 20:1–6.) Assuredly, no imposter deals in tricks, without studying to raise his reputation by amazing the common people. But what does Moses do? By crying out, that he and Aaron his brother are nothing (Exod. 16:7), that they merely execute what God has commanded, he clears himself from every approach to suspicion. Again, if the facts are considered in themselves, what kind of incantation could cause manna to rain from heaven every day, and in sufficient quantity to maintain a people, while any one, who gathered

---

[12]Exod. 24:18; 34:29; 19:16; 40:34. Num. 16:24; 20:10; 11:9.

more than the appointed measure, saw his incredulity divinely punished by its turning to worms? To this we may add, that God then suffered his servant to be subjected to so many serious trials, that the ungodly cannot now gain anything by their clamour. When (as often happened) the people proudly and petulantly rose up against him, when individuals conspired, and attempted to overthrow him, how could any impostures have enabled him to elude their rage? The event plainly shows that by these means his doctrine was attested to all succeeding ages.

7. Moreover, it is impossible to deny that he was guided by a prophetic spirit in assigning the first place to the tribe of Judah in the person of Jacob, especially if we take into view the fact itself, as explained by the event. Suppose that Moses was the inventor of the prophecy, still, after he committed it to writing, four hundred years pass away, during which no mention is made of a sceptre in the tribe of Judah. After Saul is anointed, the kingly office seems fixed in the tribe of Benjamin (1 Sam. 11:15; 16:13). When David is anointed by Samuel, what apparent ground is there for the transference? Who could have looked for a king out of the plebeian family of a herdsman? And out of seven brothers, who could have thought that the honour was destined for the youngest? And then by what means did he afterwards come within reach of the throne? Who dare say that his anointing was regulated by human art, or skill, or prudence, and was not rather the fulfilment of a divine prophecy? In like manner, do not the predictions, though obscure, of the admission of the Gentiles into the divine covenant, seeing they were not fulfilled till almost two thousand years after, make it palpable that Moses spoke under divine inspiration? I omit other predictions which so plainly betoken divine revelation, that all men of sound mind must see they were spoken by God. In short, his Song itself (Deut. 32) is a bright mirror in which God is manifestly seen.

8. In the case of the other prophets the evidence is even clearer. I will only select a few examples, for it were too tedious to enumerate the whole. Isaiah, in his own day, when the kingdom of Judah was at peace, and had even some ground to confide in the protection of the Chaldeans, spoke of the destruction of the city and the captivity of the people (Isa. 45:1). Supposing it not to be sufficient evidence of divine inspiration to foretell, many years before, events which, at the time, seemed fabulous, but which ultimately turned out to be true, whence shall it be said that the prophecies which he uttered concerning their return proceeded, if it was not from God? He names Cyrus, by whom the Chaldeans were to be subdued and the people restored to freedom. After the prophet thus spoke, more than a hundred years elapsed before Cyrus was born, that being nearly the period which elapsed between the death of the one and the birth of the other. It was impossible at that time to guess that some Cyrus would arise to make

war on the Babylonians, and after subduing their powerful monarchy, put an end
to the captivity of the children of Israel. Does not this simple, unadorned narrative plainly demonstrate that what Isaiah spoke was not the conjecture of man,
but the undoubted oracle of God? Again, when Jeremiah, a considerable time
before the people were led away, assigned seventy years as the period of captivity,
and fixed their liberation and return, must not his tongue have been guided by
the Spirit of God? What effrontery were it to deny that, by these evidences, the
authority of the prophets is established, the very thing being fulfilled to which
they appeal in support of their credibility! "Behold, the former things are come to
pass, and new things do I declare; before they spring forth I tell you of them" (Isa.
42:9). I say nothing of the agreement between Jeremiah and Ezekiel, who, living
so far apart, and yet prophesying at the same time, harmonise as completely in all
they say as if they had mutually dictated the words to one another. What shall I
say of Daniel? Did not he deliver prophecies embracing a future period of almost
six hundred years, as if he had been writing of past events generally known (Dan.
9, etc.)? If the pious will duly meditate on these things, they will be sufficiently
instructed to silence the cavils of the ungodly. The demonstration is too clear to
be gainsayed.

9. I am aware of what is muttered in corners by certain miscreants, when
they would display their acuteness in assailing divine truth. They ask, how do we
know that Moses and the prophets wrote the books which now bear their names?
Nay, they even dare to question whether there ever was a Moses. Were any one
to question whether there ever was a Plato, or an Aristotle, or a Cicero, would
not the rod or the whip be deemed the fit chastisement of such folly? The law of
Moses has been wonderfully preserved, more by divine providence than by
human care; and though, owing to the negligence of the priests, it lay for a short
time buried,—from the time when it was found by good King Josiah (2 Kings
22:8; 2 Chron. 34:15),—it has continued in the hands of men, and been transmitted in unbroken succession from generation to generation. Nor, indeed, when
Josiah brought it forth, was it as a book unknown or new, but one which had
always been matter of notoriety, and was then in full remembrance. The original
writing had been deposited in the temple, and a copy taken from it had been
deposited in the royal archives (Deut. 17:18–19); the only thing which had occurred was, that the priests had ceased to publish the law itself in due form, and
the people also had neglected the wonted reading of it. I may add, that scarcely
an age passed during which its authority was not confirmed and renewed. Were
the books of Moses unknown to those who had the Psalms of David in their
hands? To sum up the whole in one word, it is certain beyond dispute, that these
writings passed down, if I may so express it, from hand to hand, being transmitted

in an unbroken series from the fathers, who either with their own ears heard them spoken, or learned them from those who had, while the remembrance of them was fresh.

10. An objection taken from the history of the Maccabees (1 Maccab. 1:57–58) to impugn the credibility of Scripture, is, on the contrary, fitted the best possible to confirm it. First, however, let us clear away the gloss which is put upon it: having done so, we shall turn the engine which they erect against us upon themselves. As Antiochus ordered all the books of Scripture to be burnt, it is asked, where did the copies we now have come from? I, in my turn, ask, In what workshop could they have been so quickly fabricated? It is certain that they were in existence the moment the persecution ceased, and that they were acknowledged without dispute by all the pious who had been educated in their doctrine, and were familiarly acquainted with them. Nay, while all the wicked so wantonly insulted the Jews as if they had leagued together for the purpose, not one ever dared to charge them with having introduced spurious books. Whatever, in their opinion, the Jewish religion might be, they acknowledged that Moses was the founder of it. What, then, do these babblers, but betray their snarling petulance in falsely alleging the spuriousness of books whose sacred antiquity is proved by the consent of all history? But not to spend labour in vain in refuting these vile calumnies, let us rather attend to the care which the Lord took to preserve his Word, when against all hope he rescued it from the truculence of a most cruel tyrant as from the midst of the flames—inspiring pious priests and others with such constancy that they hesitated not, though it should have been purchased at the expense of their lives, to transmit this treasure to posterity, and defeating the keenest search of prefects and their satellites.

Who does not recognise it as a signal and miraculous work of God, that those sacred monuments which the ungodly persuaded themselves had utterly perished, immediately returned to resume their former rights, and, indeed, in greater honour? For the Greek translation appeared to disseminate them over the whole world. Nor does it seem so wonderful that God rescued the tables of his covenant from the sanguinary edicts of Antiochus, as that they remained safe and entire amid the manifold disasters by which the Jewish nation was occasionally crushed, devastated, and almost exterminated. The Hebrew language was in no estimation, and almost unknown; and assuredly, had not God provided for religion, it must have utterly perished. For it is obvious from the prophetical writings of that age, how much the Jews, after their return from the captivity, had lost the genuine use of their native tongue. It is of importance to attend to this, because the comparison more clearly establishes the antiquity of the Law and the Prophets. And whom did God employ to preserve the doctrine of salvation contained in the Law and the Prophets, that Christ might manifest it in its own time?

The Jews, the bitterest enemies of Christ; and hence Augustine justly calls them the librarians of the Christian Church, because they supplied us with books of which they themselves had not the use.

11. When we proceed to the New Testament, how solid are the pillars by which its truth is supported! Three evangelists give a narrative in a mean and humble style. The proud often eye this simplicity with disdain, because they attend not to the principal heads of doctrine; for from these they might easily infer that these evangelists treat of heavenly mysteries beyond the capacity of man. Those who have the least particle of candour must be ashamed of their fastidiousness when they read the first chapter of Luke. Even our Saviour's discourses, of which a summary is given by these three evangelists, ought to prevent every one from treating their writings with contempt. John, again, fulminating in majesty, strikes down more powerfully than any thunderbolt the petulance of those who refuse to submit to the obedience of faith. Let all those acute censors, whose highest pleasure it is to banish a reverential regard of Scripture from their own and other men's hearts, come forward; let them read the Gospel of John, and, willing or unwilling, they will find a thousand sentences which will at least arouse them from their sloth; nay, which will burn into their consciences as with a hot iron, and check their derision. The same thing may be said of Peter and Paul, whose writings, though the greater part read them blindfold, exhibit a heavenly majesty, which in a manner binds and rivets every reader. But one circumstance, sufficient of itself to exalt their doctrine above the world, is, that Matthew, who was formerly fixed down to his money-table, Peter and John, who were employed with their little boats, being all rude and illiterate, had never learned in any human school that which they delivered to others. Paul, moreover, who had not only been an avowed but a cruel and bloody foe, being changed into a new man, shows, by the sudden and unhoped-for change, that a heavenly power had compelled him to preach the doctrine which once he destroyed. Let those dogs deny that the Holy Spirit descended upon the apostles, or, if not, let them refuse credit to the history, still the very circumstances proclaim that the Holy Spirit must have been the teacher of those who, formerly contemptible among the people, all of a sudden began to discourse so magnificently of heavenly mysteries.

12. Add, moreover, that, for the best of reasons, the consent of the Church is not without its weight. For it is not to be accounted of no consequence, that, from the first publication of Scripture, so many ages have uniformly concurred in yielding obedience to it, and that, notwithstanding of the many extraordinary attempts which Satan and the whole world have made to oppress and overthrow it, or completely efface it from the memory of men, it has flourished like the palm-tree and continued invincible. Though in old times there was scarcely a

sophist or orator of any note who did not exert his powers against it, their efforts proved unavailing. The powers of the earth armed themselves for its destruction, but all their attempts vanished into smoke. When thus powerfully assailed on every side, how could it have resisted if it had trusted only to human aid? Nay, its divine origin is more completely established by the fact, that when all human wishes were against it, it advanced by its own energy. Add that it was not a single city or a single nation that concurred in receiving and embracing it. Its authority was recognised as far and as wide as the world extends—various nations who had nothing else in common entering for this purpose into a holy league. Moreover, while we ought to attach the greatest weight to the agreement of minds so diversi-fied, and in all other things so much at variance with each other—an agreement which a Divine Providence alone could have produced—it adds no small weight to the whole when we attend to the piety of those who thus agree; not of all of them indeed, but of those in whom as lights God was pleased that his Church should shine.

13. Again, with what confidence does it become us to subscribe to a doc-trine attested and confirmed by the blood of so many saints? They, when once they had embraced it, hesitated not boldly and intrepidly, and even with great alacrity, to meet death in its defence. Being transmitted to us with such an ear-nest, who of us shall not receive it with firm and unshaken conviction? It is therefore no small proof of the authority of Scripture, that it was sealed with the blood of so many witnesses, especially when it is considered that in bearing testi-mony to the faith, they met death not with fanatical enthusiasm (as erring spirits are sometimes wont to do), but with a firm and constant, yet sober godly zeal. There are other reasons, neither few nor feeble, by which the dignity and majesty of the Scriptures may not be only proved to the pious, but also completely vindi-cated against the cavils of slanderers. These, however, cannot of themselves pro-duce a firm faith in Scripture until our heavenly Father manifest his presence in it, and thereby secure implicit reverence for it. Then only, therefore, does Scrip-ture suffice to give a saving knowledge of God when its certainty is founded on the inward persuasion of the Holy Spirit. Still the human testimonies which go to confirm it will not be without effect, if they are used in subordination to that chief and highest proof, as secondary helps to our weakness. But it is foolish to attempt to prove to infidels that the Scripture is the Word of God. This it cannot be known to be, except by faith. Justly, therefore, does Augustine remind us, that every man who would have any understanding in such high matters must pre-viously possess piety and mental peace.

❧ 11 ❧

JOSEPH BUTLER
(1692–1752)

Joseph Butler was born in 1692 at Wantage, Berkshire, in England. He was raised a Presbyterian, intending at one time to become a Presbyterian minister. His interest in philosophy was apparent even at the early age of twenty-one. After reading the Boyle Lectures by Dr. Samuel Clarke (in which Clarke had offered a demonstrative proof of the existence of God), Butler corresponded with Clarke concerning philosophy and theistic proofs.

He later left the Presbyterian church and entered Anglican life. Although in 1715 he began work toward a law degree at Oriel College, Oxford, he eventually studied divinity and was ordained in 1718.

University work was, in his words, "frivolous" and "unintelligible." His disappointment seems to have come from what he considered a self-assured, closed-mindedness among the faculty.

His first major work, *Fifteen Sermons Preached at the Rolls Chapel* (1726), established his ecclesiastical career. He became the Clerk of the Closet to Queen Caroline in 1736. After the queen died, he was appointed bishop of Bristol by George II. Two years later he became the dean of St. Paul's and then became the bishop of Durham in 1750, two years before he died.

While he was associated with Queen Caroline, he published *The Analogy of Religion* (1736). These were the years when the deist controversy was at its height. Many historians see this book as the greatest refutation of deism that was produced in the early eighteenth century. Deism did not challenge the existence of God but rather contended for a revised understanding of God's relationship to the world. Therefore, in the *Analogy* Butler assumes the existence of an intelligent Author of nature. The deists were not agnostics or atheists, but they did challenge Christian ideas about divine revelation. Butler writes to these deists, who believed that religion is known to humans only by reason or by evidence from the senses. He attempts to offer a proof of the Christian understanding of divine revelation based on an appeal to facts and practical reason.

We find a definite order in nature, he suggests, that is parallel to the order we find in divine revelation. Difficulties that we may discover in divine revelation bear a close analogy to similar difficulties that one can discourse in nature. He held that further scientific study may clear up some of the present difficulties in understanding nature, and, similarly, further theological study may clear up present difficulties in divine revelation. Nevertheless, he believed that the common patterns found in both nature and Holy Scripture should serve as evidence of a common Author. If someone believes that God created the world (which is exactly what deists did believe) and recognizes the difficulties in understanding all aspects of nature, then that person could not deny the validity of divine revelation in Holy Scripture simply on the basis of its having features that may be difficult to understand. Especially is this true if the difficulties can be shown to be analogous. Such reasoning, of course, was very effective with deists but would hardly have served to answer similar objections from atheists. Butler was not defending Christianity against atheism, however.

Butler seems to have been writing directly to answer Matthew Tindal the distinguished Fellow from Oxford. Tindal had published *Christianity as old as the Creation: Or, the Gospel, a Republication of the Religion of Nature* (1730), commonly known as "the Deist's Bible."

Butler's argument is that all knowledge is based on probability. In this presupposition he was following the empiricist approach of Newton and Locke. Butler argued that there are three kinds of known matters. Some are matters of speculation. Others are matters of practice. Still others are matters of great consequence. Religion, of course, is placed among those matters of great consequence. Nevertheless, evidence always leads only to the probability of truth. Evidence is never sufficient to guarantee that our conclusions are absolutely true. This does not reduce the confidence that we can have in our religious beliefs, he thought, because all knowledge, including scientific knowledge, is also based on the same kind of evidence. Thus if a person admits the validity of knowledge at all, he can equally admit the strength of the evidence for Christianity.

Butler's *Analogy* is perhaps the classic statement of the "evidential" approach to apologetics. His works were standard textbooks at the two major English universities until about 1870. With the arrival of evolutionary theories, the approach to difficulties in nature radically changed. Not only that, but also attitudes about the possibility of creation by God changed. The new scientific attitude toward the world and its history challenges the relevance of some aspects of Butler's argument. Even so, there is still much of great value to be found in a careful reading of Butler's works.

BIBLIOGRAPHY

Butler, Joseph. *Works*. 2 vols. Edinburgh: James Ballantyne, 1804. To this work is prefixed a life of the author by Dr. Kippis; a preface by Samuel Halifax was also added, giving some account of Butler's character and writings.

———. *The Works of Bishop Butler*. Edited by J. H. Bernard. 2 vols. London: Macmillan, 1900.

———. *The Works of Joseph Butler*. Edited by W. G. Gladstone. 3 vols. Oxford: Clarendon, 1896–97.

Mossner, Ernest C. *Bishop Butler and the Age of Reason: A Study in the History of Thought*. New York: Macmillan, 1936.

Ramsey, Ian T. *Joseph Butler*. London: Dr. William's Trust, 1969.

THE ANALOGY OF RELIGION

CHAPTER VII.

Of the particular Evidence for Christianity

THE presumptions against revelation, and objections against the general scheme of Christianity, and particular things relating to it, being removed, there remains to be considered what positive evidence we have for the truth of it. . . .

Now, in the evidence of Christianity, there seems to be several things of great weight, not reducible to the head, either of miracles, or the completion of prophecy, in the common acceptation of the words. But these two are its direct and fundamental proofs; and those other things, however considerable they are, yet ought never to be urged apart from its direct proofs; but always to be joined with them. Thus the evidence of Christianity will be a long series of things, reaching, as it seems, from the beginning of the world to the present time, of great variety and compass, taking in both the direct, and also the collateral proofs, and making up, all of them together, one argument; the conviction arising from which kind of proof may be compared to what they call *the effect* in architecture or other works of art a result from a great number of things so and so disposed, and taken into one view. I shall therefore, *first,* make some observations relating to miracles, and the appearing completions of prophecy; and consider what analogy suggests, in answer to the objections brought against this evidence. And, *secondly,* I shall endeavour to give some account of the general argument now

From Joseph Butler, *The Analogy of Religion* (New York: Lovell, 1736), pp. 445–50, 453–55, 457–71, 473–84, 486–89, 506–9, 514, 516.

mentioned, consisting both of the direct and collateral evidence, considered as making up one argument: this being the kind of proof, upon which we determine most questions of difficulty concerning common facts, alleged to have happened, or seeming likely to happen; especially questions relating to conduct.

First, I shall make some observations upon the direct proof of Christianity from miracles and prophecy, and upon the objections alleged against it.

I. Now, the following observations, relating to the historical evidence of miracles wrought in attestation of Christianity, appear to be of great weight.

1. The Old Testament affords us the same historical evidence of the miracles of Moses and of the prophets, as of the common civil history of Moses and the kings of Israel; or, as of the affairs of the Jewish nation. And the Gospels and the Acts afford us the same historical evidence of the miracles of Christ and the Apostles, as of the common matters related in them. This, indeed, could not have been affirmed by any reasonable man, if the authors of these books, like many other historians, had appeared to make an entertaining manner of writing their aim; though they had interspersed miracles in their works, at proper distances, and upon proper occasions. These might have animated a dull relation, amused the reader, and engaged his attention. And the same account would naturally have been given of them, as of the speeches and descriptions of such authors; the same account, in a manner, as is to be given, why the poets make use of wonders and prodigies. But the facts, both miraculous and natural, in Scripture, are related in plain unadorned narratives: and both of them appear, in all respects, to stand upon the same footing of historical evidence. Farther: some parts of Scripture, containing an account of miracles fully sufficient to prove the truth of Christianity, are quoted as genuine, from the age in which they are said to be written, down to the present: and no other parts of them, material in the present question, are omitted to be quoted in such manner, as to afford any sort of proof of their not being genuine. And, as common history, when called in question in any instance, may often be greatly confirmed by contemporary or subsequent events more known and acknowledged; and as the common Scripture history, like many others, is thus confirmed; so likewise is the miraculous history of it, not only in particular instances, but in general. For, the establishment of the Jewish and Christian religions, which were events contemporary with the miracles related to be wrought in attestation of both, or subsequent to them, these events are just what we should have expected, upon supposition such miracles were really wrought to attest the truth of those religions. These miracles are a satisfactory account of those events, of which no other satisfactory account can be given, nor any account at all, but what is imaginary merely and invented. It is to be added, that the most obvious, the most easy and direct account of this history, how it came to be written, and to be received in the world as a true history, is,

that it really is so; nor can any other account of it be easy and direct. Now, though an account, not at all obvious, but very far-fetched and indirect, may indeed be, and often is, the true account of a matter; yet, it cannot be admitted on the authority of its being asserted. Mere guess, supposition, and possibility, when opposed to historical evidence, prove nothing, but that historical evidence is not demonstrative.

Now, the just consequences from all this, I think is, that the Scripture history, in general, is to be admitted as an authentic genuine history, till somewhat positive be alleged sufficient to invalidate it. But no man will deny the consequence to be, that it cannot be rejected, or thrown by as of no authority, till it can be proved to be of none; even though the evidence now mentioned for its authority were doubtful. This evidence may be confronted by historical evidence on the other side, if there be any; or general incredibility in the things related, or inconsistence in the general turn of the history, would prove it to be of no authority. But since, upon the face of the matter, upon a first and general view, the appearance is, that it is an authentic history, it cannot be determined to be fictitious without some proof that it is so. And the following observations, in support of these, and coincident with them, will greatly confirm the historical evidence for the truth of Christianity.

2. The Epistles of St. Paul, from the nature of epistolary writing, and moreover, from several of them being written, not to particular persons, but to churches, carry in them evidences of their being genuine, beyond what can be, in a mere historical narrative, left to the world at large. . . .

In them the author declares that he received the gospel in general . . . Christ himself. . . .

And he declares further that he was endued with a power of working miracles, as what was publicly known to this very people; speaks of frequent and great variety of miraculous gifts, as then subsisting in those very churches to which he was writing; which he was reproving for several irregularities, and where he had personal opposers: he mentions these gifts incidentally, in the most easy manner, and without effort; by way of reproof to those who had them, for their indecent use of them; and by way of depreciating them, in comparison of moral virtues. In short, he speaks to these churches, of these miraculous powers, in the manner any one would speak to another of a thing, which was as familiar, and as much known in common to them both, as any thing in the world.[1] And this, as hath been observed by several persons, is surely a very considerable thing.

---

[1]Rom. 15:19. 1 Cor. 12:8–10—28, etc., and chap. 13:1–2, 8. and the whole 14th chap. 2 Cor. 12:12–13. Gal. 3:2, 5.

3. It is an acknowledged historical fact, that Christianity offered itself to the world, and demanded to be received, upon the allegation, that is, as unbelievers would speak, upon the pretence of miracles, publicly wrought to attest the truth of it in such an age; and that it was actually received by great numbers in that very age, and upon the professed belief of the reality of these miracles. And Christianity, including the dispensation of the Old Testament, seems distinguished by this from all other religions. . . .

Upon the whole: As there is large historical evidence, both direct and circumstantial, of miracles wrought in attestation of Christianity, collected by those who have writ upon the subject, it lies upon unbelievers to show, why this evidence is not to be credited. This way of speaking is, I think, just, and what persons who write in defence of religion naturally fall into. Yet in a matter of such unspeakable importance, the proper question is, not whom it lies upon, according to the rules of argument, to maintain or confute objections; but whether there really are any, against this evidence, sufficient in reason, to destroy the credit of it? However, unbelievers seem to take upon them the part of showing that there are.

They allege, that numberless enthusiastic people, in different ages and countries, expose themselves to the same difficulties which the primitive Christians did; and are ready to give up their lives, for the most idle follies imaginable. But it is not very clear, to what purpose this objection is brought. For every one, surely, in every case, must distinguish between opinions and facts. And though testimony is no proof of enthusiastic opinions, or of any opinions at all; yet it is allowed, in all other cases, to be a proof of facts. And a person laying down his life in attestation of facts, or of opinions, is the strongest proof of his believing them. And if the apostles and their contemporaries did believe the facts, in attestation of which they exposed themselves to sufferings and death, this their belief, or rather knowledge, must be a proof of those facts; for they were such as came under the observation of their senses. And though it is not of equal weight, yet it is of weight, that the martyrs of the next age, notwithstanding they were not eye-witnesses of those facts, as were the apostles and their contemporaries, had, however, full opportunity to inform themselves, whether they were true or not, and give equal proof of their believing them to be true.

But enthusiasm, it is said, greatly weakens the evidence of testimony, even for facts, in matters relating to religion; some seem to think, it totally and absolutely destroys the evidence of testimony upon this subject. And, indeed, the powers of enthusiasm, and of diseases, too, which operate in a like manner, are very wonderful, in particular instances. But if great numbers of men, not appearing in any peculiar degree weak, nor under any peculiar suspicion of negligence, affirm that they saw and heard such things plainly with their eyes and their ears, and are admitted to be in earnest; such testimony is evidence of the strongest kind we can have, for any matter of fact. Yet, possibly it may be overcome, strong as it is, by incredibility in the things thus attested, or by contrary testimony. And in an instance where one thought it was so overcome, it might be just to consider, how far such evidence could be accounted for by enthusiasm: for it seems as if no other imaginable account were to be given of it. But till such incredibility be shown, or contrary testimony produced, it cannot surely be expected, that so far-fetched, so indirect and wonderful an account of such testimony, as that of enthusiasm must be; an account so strange, that the generality of mankind can scarce be made to understand what is meant by it; it cannot, I say, be expected, that such account will be admitted of such evidence, when there is this direct, easy, and obvious account of it, that people really saw and heard a thing not incredible, which they affirm sincerely, and with full assurance, they did see and hear. . . .

It is objected farther, that however it has happened, the fact is, that mankind have, in different ages, been strangely deluded with pretences to miracles and wonders. But it is by no means to be admitted, that they have been oftener, or are at all more liable to be deceived by these pretences, than by others.

It is added, that there is a very considerable degree of historical evidence for miracles, which are on all hands, acknowledged to be fabulous. But suppose that there were even the like historical evidence for these, to what there is for those alleged in proof of Christianity, which yet is in nowise allowed, but suppose this; the consequence would not be, that the evidence of the latter is not to be admitted. Nor is there a man in the world who, in common cases, would conclude thus. For what would such a conclusion really amount to but this, that evidence confuted by contrary evidence, or any way overbalanced, destroys the credibility of other evidence, neither confuted, nor overbalanced? To argue, that because there is, if there were, like evidence from testimony, for miracles acknowledged false, as for those in attestation of Christianity, therefore the evidence in the latter case is not to be credited; this is the same as to argue, that if two men of equally good reputation had given evidence in different cases no way connected, and one of them had been convicted of perjury, this confuted the testimony of the other.

.   .   .

And over against all these objections, is to be set the importance of Christianity, as what must have engaged the attention of its first converts, so as to have rendered them less liable to be deceived from carelessness, than they would in common matters; and likewise the strong obligations to veracity, which their religion laid them under: so that the first and most obvious presumption is, that they could not be deceived themselves, nor would deceive others. And this presumption, in this degree, is peculiar to the testimony we have been considering.

In argument, assertions are nothing in themselves, and have an air of positiveness, which sometimes is not very easy: yet they are necessary, and necessary to be repeated, in order to connect a discourse, and distinctly to lay before the view of the reader, what is proposed to be proved, and what is left as proved. Now, the conclusion from the foregoing observations is, I think, beyond all doubt this: that unbelievers must be forced to admit the external evidence for Christianity, that is, the proof of miracles wrought to attest it, to be of real weight and very considerable; though they cannot allow it to be sufficient, to convince them of the reality of those miracles. And as they must, in all reason, admit this, so it seems to me, that upon consideration they would, in fact, admit it; those of them, I mean, who know any thing at all of the matter: in like manner as persons, in many cases, own, they see strong evidence from testimony, for the truth of things, which yet they cannot be convinced are true; cases, suppose, where there is contrary testimony, or things which they think, whether with or without reason, to be credible. But there is no testimony contrary to that which we have been considering, and it has been fully proved, that there is no incredibility in Christianity in general, or in any part of it.

II. As to the evidence for Christianity from prophecy, I shall only make some few general observations, which are suggested by the analogy of nature; that is, by the acknowledged natural rules of judging in common matters concerning evidence of a like kind to this from prophecy.

1. The obscurity or unintelligibleness of one part of a prophecy, does not in any degree, invalidate the proof of foresight, arising from the appearing completion of those other parts which are understood. For the case is evidently the same, as if those parts which are not understood, were lost, or not written at all, or written in an unknown tongue. . . .

For the same reason, though a man should be incapable, for want of learning, or opportunities of inquiry, or from not having turned his studies this way, even so much as to judge, whether particular prophecies have been throughout completely fulfilled yet he may see, in general, that they have been fulfilled to such a degree, as, upon very good ground, to be convinced of foresight more than human in such prophecies, and of such events being intended by them. For the same reason also, though by means of the deficiencies in civil history, and the different accounts of historians, the most learned should not be able to make out to satisfaction, that such parts of the prophetic history have been minutely and throughout fulfilled; yet, a very strong proof of foresight may arise, from that general completion of them which is made out: as much proof of foresight, perhaps, as the Giver of prophecy intended should ever be afforded by such parts of prophecy.

2. A long series of prophecy being applicable to such and such events, is itself a proof, that it was intended of them; as the rules by which we naturally judge and determine, in common cases parallel to this, will show. This observation I make in answer to the common objection against the application of the prophecies, that considering each of them distinctly by itself, it does not at all appear, that they were intended of those particular events to which they are applied by Christians; and therefore it is to be supposed, that, if they meant any thing, they were intended of other events unknown to us, and not of these at all.

Now, there are two kinds of writing, which bear a great resemblance to prophecy, with respect to the matter before us; the mythological and the satirical, where the satire is, to a certain degree, concealed. And a man might be assured, that he understood what an author intended by a fable or parable, related without any application or moral, merely from seeing it to be easily capable of such application, and that such a moral might naturally be deduced from it. And he might be fully assured, that such persons and events were intended in a satirical writing, merely from its being applicable to them. And, agreeably to the last observation, he might be in a good measure satisfied of it, though he were not enough informed in affairs or in the story of such persons, to understand half the satire. For, his satisfaction, that he understood the meaning, the intended meaning, of these writings, would be greater or less, in proportion as he saw the general turn of them to be capable of such application, and in proportion to the number of particular things capable of it. And thus, if a long series of prophecy is applicable to the present state of the church, and to the political situations of the kingdoms of the world, some thousand years after these prophecies were delivered, and a long series of prophecy delivered before the coming of Christ is applicable to him; these things are in themselves a proof, that the prophetic history was intended of him, and of those events; in proportion as the general turn of it is capable of such application, and to the number and variety of particular prophecies capable of it. And, though in all just way of consideration, the appearing completion of prophecies is to be allowed to be thus explanatory of, and to determine their meaning; yet it is to be remembered farther, that the ancient Jews applied the prophecies to a Messiah before his coming, in much the same manner as Christians do now; and that the primitive Christians interpreted the prophecies respecting the state of the church and of the world, in the last ages, in the sense which the event seems to confirm and verify. And from these things it may be made to appear,

3. That the showing, even to a high probability, it that could be, that the prophets thought of some other events, in such and such predictions, and not

those at all which Christians allege to be completions of those predictions; or that such and such prophecies are capable of being applied to other events than those to which Christians apply them—that this would not confute or destroy the force of the argument from prophecy, even with regard to those very instances. For, observe how this matter really is. If one knew such a person to be the sole author of such a book, and was certainly assured, or satisfied to any degree, that one knew the whole of what he intended in it, one should be assured or satisfied to such a degree, that one knew the whole meaning of that book; for the meaning of a book is nothing but the meaning of the author. But if one knew a person to have compiled a book out of memoirs, which he received from another, of vastly superior knowledge in the subject of it, especially if it were a book full of great intricacies and difficulties, it would in nowise follow, that one knew the whole meaning of the book, from knowing the whole meaning of the compiler; for the original memoirs, that is, the author of them, might have, and there would be no degree of presumption, in many cases, against supposing him to have, some farther meaning than the compiler saw. To say, then, that the Scriptures and the things contained in them can have no other or farther meaning, than those persons thought or had, who first recited or wrote them, is evidently saying, that those persons were the original, proper, and sole authors of those books, that is, that they are not inspired; which is absurd, whilst the authority of these books is under examination, that is, till you have determined they are of no divine authority at all. Till this be determined, it must in all reason be supposed, not indeed that they have, for this is taking for granted that they are inspired, but that they may have some farther meaning than what the compilers saw or understood. And, upon this supposition, it is supposable also, that this farther meaning may be fulfilled. Now, events corresponding to prophecies, interpreted in a different meaning from that in which the prophets are supposed to have understood them; this affords, in a manner, the same proof that this different sense was originally intended, as it would have afforded, if the prophets had not understood their predictions in the sense it is supposed they did; because there is no presumption of their sense of them being the whole sense of them. And it has been already shown, that the apparent completions of prophecy must be allowed to be explanatory of its meaning. So that the question is, whether a series of prophecy has been fulfilled, in a natural or proper, that is, in any real, sense of the words of it. For such completion is equally a proof of foresight more than human, whether the prophets are, or are not, supposed to have understood it in a different sense. I say, supposed; for though I think it clear, that the prophets did not understand the full meaning of their predictions, it is another question, how far they thought they did, and in what sense they understood them.

Hence may be seen, to how little purpose those persons busy themselves, who endeavour to prove that the prophetic history is applicable to events of the age in which it was written, or of ages before it. Indeed, to have proved this before there was any appearance of a further completion of it, might have answered some purpose; for it might have prevented the expectation of any such farther completion. Thus, could Porphyry have shown, that some principal parts of the book of Daniel, for instance, the seventh verse of the seventh chapter, which the Christians interpreted of the latter ages, was applicable to events which happened before or about the age of Antiochus Epiphanes; this might have prevented them from expecting any farther completion of it. And unless there was then, as I think there must have been, external evidence concerning that book, more than is come down to us, such a discovery might have been a stumbling-block in the way of Christianity itself; considering the authority which our Saviour has given to the book of Daniel, and how much the general scheme of Christianity presupposes the truth of it. But even this discovery, had there been any such,[2] would be of very little weight with reasonable men now; if this passage, thus applicable to events before the age of Porphyry, appears to be applicable also to events which succeeded the dissolution of the Roman empire. I mention this, not at all as intending to insinuate, that the division of this empire into ten parts, for it was plainly divided into about that number, were, alone, and by itself, of any moment verifying the prophetic history; but only as an example of the thing I am speaking of. And thus, upon the whole, the matter of inquiry evidently must be, as above put, Whether the prophecies are applicable to Christ, and to the present state of the world and of the church; applicable in such a degree, as to imply foresight: not whether they are capable of any other application; though I know no pretence for saying, the general turn of them is capable of any other.

These observations are, I think, just, and the evidence referred to in them, real; though there may be people who will not accept of such imperfect information from Scripture. Some too have not integrity and regard enough to truth, to attend to evidence, which keeps the mind in doubt, perhaps perplexity, and which is much of a different sort from what they expected. And it plainly requires a degree of modesty and fairness, beyond what every one has, for a man to say, not to the world, but to himself, that there is a real appearance of somewhat of great weight in this matter, though he is not able thoroughly to satisfy himself

---

[2]It appears, that Porphyry did nothing worth mentioning in this way. For Jerome on the place says: *Duas posteriores bestias—in uno Macedonum regno ponit.* And as to the ten kings: *Decem reges enamerat, qui, fuerunt soevissimi; ipsosque reges non unius ponit regni, verbi gratia, Macedoniae, Syriae, Asiae, et Egypti; sed de diversis regnis unum efficit regum ordinem.* And in this way of interpretation, any thing may be made of any thing.

about it; but it shall have its influence upon him, in proportion to its appearing reality and weight. . . .

I shall now, *secondly*, endeavour to give some account of the general argument for the truth of Christianity, consisting both of the direct and circumstantial evidence, considered as making up one argument. . . .

The thing asserted, and the truth of which is to be inquired into, is this: that over and above our reason and affections, which God has given us for the information of our judgment and the conduct of our lives, he has also, by external revelation, given us an account of himself and his moral government over the world, implying a future state of rewards and punishments; that is, hath revealed the system of natural religion; for natural religion may be externally revealed by God, as the ignorant may be taught it by mankind, their fellow-creatures—that God, I say, has given us the evidence of revelation, as well as the evidence of reason, to ascertain this moral system; together with an account of a particular dispensation of Providence, which reason could no way have discovered, and a particular institution of religion founded on it, for the recovery of mankind out of their present wretched condition, and raising them to the perfection and final happiness of their nature.

This revelation, whether real or supposed, may be considered as wholly historical. For prophecy is nothing but the history of events before they come to pass: doctrines also are matters of fact: and precepts come under the same notion. And the general design of Scripture, which contains in it this revelation, thus considered as historical, may be said to be, to give us an account of the world, in this one single view, as God's world; by which it appears essentially distinguished from all other books, so far as I have found, except such as are copied from it. It begins with an account of God's creation of the world, in order to ascertain and distinguish from all others, who is the object of our worship, by what he has done; in order to ascertain who he is, concerning whose providence, commands, promises, and threatenings, this sacred book all along treats; the Maker and Proprietor of the world, he whose creatures we are, the God of nature: in order likewise to distinguish him from the idols of the nations, which are either imaginary beings, that is, no beings at all; or else part of that creation, the historical relation of which is here given. And St. John, not improbably with an eye to this Mosaic account of the creation, begins his gospel with an account of our Saviour's pre-existence, and that "all things were made by him, and without him was not any thing made that was made;" agreeably to the doctrine of St. Paul, that "God created all things by Jesus Christ." This being premised, the Scripture, taken together, seems to profess to contain a kind of an abridgment of the history of the world, in the view just now mentioned; that is, a general account of the condition of religion and its professors, during the continuance of that apostacy from God, and state of wickedness, which it every where supposes the world to lie in. . . .

Together with the moral system of the world, the Old Testament contains a chronological account of the beginning of it, and from thence, an unbroken genealogy of mankind for many ages before common history begins; and carried on as much farther, as to make up a continued thread of history, of the length of between three and four thousand years. It contains an account of God's making a covenant with a particular nation, that they should be his people, and he would be their God, in a peculiar sense; of his often interposing miraculously in their affairs; giving them the promise, and, long after, the possession, of a particular country; assuring them of the greatest national prosperity in it, if they would worship him, in opposition to the idols which the rest of the world worshipped, and obey his commands, and threatening them with unexampled punishments, if they disobeyed him, and fell into the general idolatry; insomuch, that this one nation should continue to be the observation and the wonder of all the world. It declares particularly, that "God would scatter them among all people, from one end of the earth unto the other" [Deut. 28:64]; but that "when they should return unto the Lord their God, he would have compassion upon them, and gather them, from all the nations whether he had scattered them" [Deut. 30:2–3]; that "Israel should be saved in the Lord, with an everlasting salvation, and not be ashamed or confounded, world without end" [Isa. 45:17]. And as some of those promises are conditional, others are as absolute as any thing can be expressed, that the time should come, when "the people should be all righteous, and inherit the land for ever" [Isa. 60:21]; that "though God would make a full end of all nations whither he had scattered them, yet would he not make a full end of them" [Jer. 30:11; 46:28]: that "he would bring again the captivity of his people Israel, and plant them upon their land, and they should be no more pulled out of their land" [Amos. 9:15]: that "the seed of Israel should not cease from being a nation forever" [Jer. 31:36]. It foretels, that God would raise them up a particular person, in whom all his promises should finally be fulfilled; the Messiah, who should be, in a high and eminent sense, their anointed Prince and Saviour. This was foretold in such a manner, as raised a general expectation of such a person in the nation, as appears from the New Testament, and is an acknowledged fact; an expectation of his coming at such a particular time, before any one appeared, claiming to be that person, and when there was no ground for such an expectation but from the prophecies; which expectation, therefore, must in all reason be presumed to be explanatory of those prophecies, if there were any doubt about their meaning. It seems moreover to foretel, that this person should be rejected by that nation, to whom he had been so long promised, and though he was so much desired by them [Isa. 8:14–15; 49:5; 53; Mal. 1:10–11; 3]. And it expressly

foretels, that he should be the Saviour of the Gentiles; and even that the completion of the scheme contained in this book, and then begun and in its progress,
should be somewhat so great, that, in comparison with it, the restoration of the
Jews alone would be but of small account: "It is a light thing that thou shouldst
be my servant to raise up the tribes of Jacob, and to restore the preserved of Israel:
I will also give thee for a light to the Gentiles, that thou mayest be for salvation
unto the end of the earth" [Isa. 49:6]. And, "In the last days, the mountain of the
Lord's house shall be established in the top of the mountains, and shall be exalted
above the hills; and all nations shall flow into it. . . . for out of Zion shall go
forth the law, and the word of the Lord from Jerusalem. And he shall judge
among the nations. . . . and the Lord alone shall be exalted in that day, and the
idols he shall utterly abolish" [Isa. 2:2–4, 17–18].[3] The Scripture farther contains
an account, that at the time the Messiah was expected, a person rose up, in this
nation, claiming to be that Messiah, to be the person whom all the prophecies
referred to, and in whom they should centre; that he spent some years in a
continued course of miraculous works, and endued his immediate disciples and
followers with a power of doing the same, as a proof of the truth of that religion
which he commissioned them to publish; that, invested with this authority and
power, they made numerous converts in the remotest countries, and settled and
established his religion in the world; to the end of which, the Scripture professes
to give a prophetic account of the state of this religion amongst mankind.

Let us now suppose a person utterly ignorant of history, to have all this
related to him, out of the Scripture. Or, suppose such a one, having the Scripture put into his hands, to remark these things in it, not knowing but that the
whole, even its civil history, as well as the other parts of it, might be, from
beginning to end, an entire invention; and to ask, What truth was in it, and
whether the revelation here related was real, or a fiction? And, instead of a direct
answer, suppose him, all at once, to be told the following confessed facts; and
then to unite them into one view.

Let him first be told, in how great a degree the profession and establishment
of natural religion, the belief that there is one God to be worshipped, that virtue
is his law, and that mankind shall be rewarded and punished hereafter, as they
obey and disobey it here; in how very great a degree, I say, the profession and
establishment of this moral system in the world, is owing to the revelation,
whether real or supposed, contained in this book; the establishment of this moral
system, even in those countries which do not acknowledge the proper authority of

---

[3]See also Isa. 11; 56:7; Mal. 1:11. To which must be added, the other prophecies of
the like kind, several in the New Testament and very many in the Old, which describe what
shall be the completion of the revealed plan of Providence.

the Scripture. Let him be told also what number of nations do acknowledge its proper authority. Let him then take in the consideration, of what importance religion is to mankind. And upon these things, he might, I think, truly observe, that this supposed revelation obtaining and being received in the world, with all the circumstances and effects of it, considered together as one event, is the most conspicuous and important event in the story of mankind: that a book of this nature, and thus promulged and recommended to our consideration, demands, as if by a voice from heaven, to have its claims most seriously examined into; and that, before such examination, to treat it with any kind of scoffing and ridicule is an offence against natural piety. But it is to be remembered, that how much soever the establishment of natural religion in the world is owing to the Scripture revelation, this does not destroy the proof of religion from reason. . . .

Let such a person as we are speaking of, be, in the next place, informed of the acknowledged antiquity of the first parts of this book; and that its chronology, its account of the time when the earth, and the several parts of it, were first peopled with human creatures, is no way contradicted, but is really confirmed, by the natural and civil history of the world, collected from common historians, from the state of the earth, and from the late invention of arts and sciences. And, as the Scripture contains an unbroken thread of common and civil history, from the creation to the captivity, for between three and four thousand years; let the person we are speaking of be told, in the next place, that this general history, as it is not contradicted, but is confirmed by profane history, as much as there would be reason to expect, upon supposition of its truth; so there is nothing in the whole history itself to give any reasonable ground of suspicion of its not being, in the general, a faithful and literally true genealogy of men, and series of things. . . . There may be incidents in Scripture, which, taken alone in the naked way they are told, may appear strange, especially to persons of other manners, temper, education; but there are also incidents of undoubted truth, in many of most persons' lives, which, in the same circumstances, would appear to the full as strange. There may be mistakes of transcribers, there may be other real or seeming mistakes, not easy to be particularly accounted for; but there are certainly no more things of this kind in the Scripture, than what were to have been expected in books of such antiquity; and nothing, in any wise, sufficient to discredit the general narrative. Now, that a history, claiming to commence from the creation, and extending in one continued series, through so great a length of time, and variety of events, should have such appearances of reality and truth in its whole contexture, is surely a very remarkable circumstance in its favour. And as all this is applicable to the common history of the New Testament, so there is a farther credibility, and a very high one, given to it by profane authors; many of these writing of the same times, and confirming the truth of customs and events, which are incidentally, as well as more purposely mentioned in it. And this credibility of the common Scripture history gives some credibility to its miraculous history: especially as this is interwoven with the common, so as that they imply each other, and both together make up one relation.

Let it then be more particularly observed to this person, that it is an acknowledged matter of fact, which is indeed implied in the foregoing observation, that there was such a nation as the Jews, of the greatest antiquity, whose government and general polity was founded on the law, here related to be given them by Moses as from heaven: that natural religion, though with rites additional, yet no way contrary to it, was their established religion, which cannot be said of the Gentile world; and that their very being, as a nation, depended upon their acknowledgment of one God, the God of the universe. For suppose, in their captivity in Babylon, they had gone over to the religion of their conquerors, there would have remained no bond of union, to keep them a distinct people. And whilst they were under their own kings in their own country, a total apostacy from God would have been the dissolution of their whole government. They, in such a sense, nationally acknowledged and worshipped the Maker of heaven and earth, when the rest of the world were sunk in idolatry, as rendered them, in fact, the peculiar people of God. And this, so remarkable an establishment and preservation of natural religion amongst them, seems to add some peculiar credibility to the historical evidence for the miracles of Moses and the prophets; because these miracles are a full satisfactory account of this event, which plainly wants to be accounted for, and cannot otherwise.

Let this person, supposed wholly ignorant of history, be acquainted farther, that one claiming to be the Messiah, of Jewish extraction, rose up at the time when this nation, from the prophecies above mentioned, expected the Messiah: that he was rejected, as it seemed to have been foretold he should, by the body of the people, under the direction of their rulers: that in the course of a very few years he was believed on, and acknowledged as the promised Messiah, by great numbers among the Gentiles, agreeable to the prophecies of Scripture, yet not upon the evidence of prophecy, but of miracles, of which miracles we also have strong historical evidence; . . . that this religion approving itself to the reason of mankind, and carrying its own evidence with it, so far as reason is a judge of its system, and being no way contrary to reason in those parts of it which require to be believed upon the mere authority of its Author; that this religion, I say, gradually spread and supported itself, for some hundred years, not only without any assistance from temporal power, but under constant discouragements, and often the bitterest persecutions from it, and then became the religion of the world: that in the mean time, the Jewish nation and government were destroyed in a very remarkable manner, and the people carried away captive and dispersed through the most distant countries; in which state of dispersion they have remained fifteen hundred years: and that they remain a numerous people, united amongst themselves, and distinguished from the rest of the world, as they were in the days of Moses, by the profession of his law; and every where looked upon in a manner, which one scarce knows how distinctly to express, but in the words of the prophetic account of it, given so many ages before it came to pass: "Thou shalt become an astonishment, a proverb and a by-word, among all nations whither the Lord shall lead thee" [Deut. 28:37].

And as several of these events seem, in some degree expressly, to have verified the prophetic history already; so likewise, they may be considered farther, as having a peculiar aspect towards the full completion of it; as affording some presumption that the whole of it shall one time or other be fulfilled. Thus, that the Jews have been so wonderfully preserved in their long and wide dispersion; . . . that natural religion came forth from Judea, and spread in the degree it has done over the world, before lost in idolatry; . . . that this great change of religion over the earth was brought about under the profession and acknowledgment, that Jesus was the promised Messiah: things of this kind naturally turn the thoughts of serious men towards the full completion of the prophetic history, concerning the final restoration of that people; concerning the establishment of the everlasting kingdom among them, the kingdom of the Messiah; and the future state of the world, under this sacred government. Such circumstances and events compared with these prophecies, though no completions of them, yet would not, I think, be spoken of as nothing in the argument, by a person upon his first being informed of them. . . .

All these things, and the several particulars contained under them, require to be distinctly and most thoroughly examined into; that the weight of each may be judged of, upon such examination, and such conclusion drawn as results from their united force. But this has not been attempted here. I have gone no farther than to show, that the general imperfect view of them now given, the confessed historical evidence for miracles, and the many obvious appearing completions of prophecy, together with the collateral things here mentioned, and there are several others of the like sort; that all this together, which, being fact, must be acknowledged by unbelievers, amounts to real evidence of somewhat more than human in this matter; evidence much more important than careless men, who have been accustomed only to transient and partial views of it, can imagine; and indeed abundantly sufficient to act upon. And these things, I apprehend, must be acknowledged by unbelievers. For, though they may say, that the historical evidence of miracles, wrought in attestation of Christianity, is not sufficient to convince them that such miracles were really wrought, they cannot deny that there is such historical evidence, it being a known matter of fact that there is. They may say, the conformity between the prophecies and events is by accident; but there are many instances in which such conformity itself cannot be denied. They may say, with regard to such kind of collateral things as those above-mentioned, that any odd accidental events, without meaning, will have a meaning found in them by fanciful people; and that such as are fanciful in any one certain way, will make out a thousand coincidences, which seem to favour their peculiar follies. Men, I say, may talk thus; but no one who is serious, can possibly think these things to be nothing, if he considers the importance of collateral things, and even of lesser circumstances, in the evidence of probability, as distinguished, in nature, from the evidence of demonstration. In many cases, indeed, it seems to require the truest judgment, to determine with exactness the weight of circumstantial evidence; but it is very often altogether as convincing as that which is the most express and direct. . . .

. . . But the truth of our religion, like the truth of common matters, is to be judged of by all the evidence taken together. And unless the whole series of things which may be alleged in this argument, and every particular thing in it, can reasonably be supposed to have been by accident, (for here the stress of the argument for Christianity lies,) then is the truth of it proved. . . .

It is obvious, how much advantage the nature of this evidence gives to those persons who attack Christianity, especially in conversation. For it is easy to show, in a short and lively manner, that such and such things are liable to objection, that this and another thing is of little weight in itself; but impossible to show, in like manner, the united force of the whole argument in one view.

However, *lastly*, as it has been made appear, that there is no presumption against a revelation as miraculous; that the general scheme of Christianity, and the principal parts of it, are conformable to the experienced constitution of things, and the whole perfectly credible; so the account now given of the positive evidence for it, shows that this evidence is such as, from the nature of it, cannot be destroyed, though it should be lessened.

.   .   .

CONCLUSION

. . . LET us then suppose, that the evidence of religion in general, and of Christianity, has been seriously inquired into, by all reasonable men among us. Yet we find many professedly to reject both, upon speculative principles of infidelity. And all of them do not content themselves with a bare neglect of religion, and enjoying their imaginary freedom from its restraints. Some go much beyond this. They deride God's moral government over the world: they renounce his protection, and defy his justice: they ridicule and vilify Christianity, and blaspheme the Author of it; and take all occasions to manifest a scorn and contempt of revelation. This amounts to an active setting themselves against religion; to what may be considered as a positive principle of irreligion; which they cultivate within themselves, and, whether they intend this effect or not, render habitual, as a good man does the contrary principle. And others, who are not chargeable with all this profligateness, yet are in avowed opposition to religion, as if discovered to be groundless. Now admitting, which is the supposition we go upon, that these persons act upon what they think principles of reason, and otherwise they are not to be argued with; it is really inconceivable, that they should imagine they clearly see the whole evidence of it, considered in itself, to be nothing at all; nor do they pretend this. They are far indeed from having a just notion of its evidence; but they would not say its evidence was nothing, if they thought the system of it, with all its circumstances, were credible, like other matters of science or history. So that their manner of treating it must proceed, either from such kind of objections against all religion, as have been answered or obviated in the former part of this treatise; or else from objections and difficulties, supposed more peculiar to Christianity. Thus, they entertain prejudices against the whole notion of a revelation and miraculous interpositions. They find things in Scripture, whether in coincidental passages or in the general scheme of it, which appear to them unreasonable. They take for granted, that if Christianity were true, the light of it must have been more general, and the evidence of it more satisfactory, or rather overbearing; that it must and would have been, in some way, otherwise put and left, than it is. Now, this is not imagining they see the evidence itself to be nothing, or inconsiderable; but quite another thing. It is being fortified against the evidence, in some degree acknowledged, by thinking they see the system of Christianity or somewhat which appears to them necessarily connected with it, to be incredible or false: fortified against that evidence, which might otherwise make great impression upon them. Or, lastly, if any of these persons are, upon the whole, in doubt concerning the truth of Christianity; their behaviour seems owing to their taking for granted, through strange inattention, that such doubting is in a manner the same thing, as being certain against it.

To these persons, and to this state of opinion concerning religion, the foregoing treatise is adapted. For, all the general objections against the moral system of nature having been obviated, it is shown, that there is not any peculiar presumption at all against Christianity, either considered as not discoverable by reason, or as unlike to what is so discovered; nor any worth mentioning, against it as miraculous, if any at all; none certainly, which can render it in the least incredible. . . . And it is so far from being the method of Providence, in other cases, to afford us such overbearing evidence, as some require in proof of Christianity, that, on the contrary, the evidence upon which we are naturally appointed to act, in common matters, throughout a very great part of life, is doubtful in a high degree. And, admitting the fact, that God has afforded to some, no more than doubtful evidence of religion, the same account may be given of it, as of difficulties and temptations with regard to practice. But as it is not impossible, surely, that this alleged doubtfulness may be men's own fault, it deserves their most serious consideration, whether it be not so. However, it is certain, that doubting implies a degree of evidence for that of which we doubt; and that this degree of evidence as really lays us under obligations, as demonstrative evidence.

. . . *Lastly*, It will appear, that blasphemy and profaneness, I mean with regard to Christianity, are absolutely without excuse. For there is no temptation to it, but from the wantonness of vanity or mirth; and these, considering the infinite importance of the subject, are no such temptations as to afford any excuse for it. If this be a just account of things, and yet men can go on to vilify or disregard Christianity, which is to talk and act as if they had a demonstration of its falsehood; there is no reason to think they would alter their behaviour to any purpose though there were a demonstration of its truth.

⤮ 12 ⤮

WILLIAM PALEY
(1743–1805)

According to the register of the cathedral in Peterborough, England, William Paley was baptized as an infant on August 30, 1743. In 1745 he moved to Giggleswick and received his early education at the Giggleswick School, where his father was the headmaster. Paley apparently showed little promise for scholarship. He seems to have been rather inactive even to the point of finding horseback riding to be very difficult. When riding his own pony on his first journey to Cambridge, he demonstrated his awkwardness by falling from the pony's back no fewer than seven times.

He entered Christ's College at Cambridge in November, 1758, and became a resident at the university the following year. Paley was habitually indolent. He was almost always late for everything, and on those days in which he did not have to attend class lectures he would invariably sleep until noon.

Lethargy did not produce idleness, however. Although he was somewhat slow in his reading, he was, on the other hand, incessant about it.

A decided change in Paley's intellectual motivation took place at the beginning of his third year in college. One of his companions in leisure woke him up suddenly at five o'clock one morning to tell Paley that he was a "fool." To be able to do nothing and thus to idle away one's time was justifiable perhaps, he said, but Paley himself had much ability, yet was wasting his opportunities.

"I have had no sleep all night because of these reflections and am now come solemnly to inform you that if you persist in your indolence, I must renounce your society."

Paley later remarked, "I was so struck with the visit and the visitor, that I lay in bed the greater part of the day and formed my plan." He did eventually put his plan into action, and after this period of his life Paley never seemed to relax in his mental activity. Before he was twenty-one years of age he had become a senior "wrangler" at the university and a tutor at a private academy.

Paley left the academy in 1766 to enter the ministry of the church, but he gained little reputation as a preacher. He continued his studies at Christ's College and was ordained as a priest in December, 1767. The next year he was appointed one of the tutors of Christ's College.

His first publication was in 1774, a tract entitled "A Defense of the Considerations on the Propriety of Requiring a Subscription to Articles of Faith." He became the archdeacon of Carlisle on August 5, 1782. From this position he published his three greatest works.

His first large work was *Moral and Political Philosophy*, the substance of which he had delivered in his lecture at Christ's College. Paley had some difficulty in getting it published but finally was able to finance the publication himself. The sale of the book was surprisingly large, and Paley at once became known as an eloquent and profound thinker. His thoughts were not particularly original, but neither was he simply a compiler. He had a gift of effectively stating plain arguments in a way that made them very convincing to people even though he gathered his information from ordinary sources of reference.

Five years later he published *Horae Paulinae*. Many consider this Paley's masterpiece. Nevertheless, his other more popular works have been more widely influential. *The Evidences of Christianity* was published in 1794, followed by his famous *Natural Theology* in 1802. After the publication of his *Evidences of Christianity*, he was rapidly promoted in the church, eventually being offered the valuable rectory of Bishop's Wearmouth. Paley remained at this rectory until his death in 1805.

His mother died in 1796 and his father died three years later. In the summer of 1800 he first felt the attacks of the kidney disorder that finally brought him to his grave.

The impact of Paley's work has often been underestimated. Nineteenth-century exponents of new scientific and philosophical theories often used Paley as the basis for their attacks against Christianity. Paley is the last great apologist to write prior to the rise of the modern critical movements in philosophy and theology. Whatever technical weaknesses his views may have, the sincerity and the strength of his faith and of his arguments have continued to have an impact on Christian people in the Western world. In fact, his argument that a watch proves a watchmaker is perhaps the single most famous illustration for the teleological argument for the existence of God. For many people it continues to be a persuasive argument.

BIBLIOGRAPHY

Paley, William. *Works.* With "Memoirs" by G. W. Meadley. 6 vols. Boston: Joshua Belcher, 1810–27.

————. *Works.* New ed. With a corrected account of the life and writings of the author by Edmund Paley. 7 vols. London: C. and J. Rivington, 1825.

————. *Works.* With a "Memoir" by Rev. Robert Lynam. 2 vols. London: H. Fisher, Son, and P. Jackson, 1828.

————. *Natural Theology: Selections.* Edited, with an introduction by Frederick Ferré. Indianapolis: Bobbs-Merrill, 1963.

————. *A View of the Evidences of Christianity.* With annotations by Richard Whately. Murfreesboro, Tenn.: Dehoff, 1952.

NATURAL THEOLOGY

CHAPTER I

State of the Argument

IN crossing a heath, suppose I pitched my foot against a *stone*, and were asked how the stone came to be there; I might possibly answer, that, for any thing I knew to the contrary, it had lain there for ever: nor would it perhaps be very easy to show the absurdity of this answer. But suppose I had found a *watch* upon the ground, and it should be inquired how the watch happened to be in that place: I should hardly think of the answer which I had before given, that, for any thing I knew, the watch might have always been there. Yet why should not this answer serve for the watch as well as for the stone? why is it not as admissible in the second case, as in the first? For this reason and for no other, viz. that, when we come to inspect the watch, we perceive (what we could not discover in the stone) that its several parts are framed and put together for a purpose, *e.g.* that they are formed and adjusted as to produce motion, and that motion so regulated as to point out the hour of the day; that, if the different parts had been differently shaped from what they are, of a different size from what they are, or placed after any other manner, or in any other order, than that in which they are placed, either no motion at all would have been carried on in the machine, or none which would have answered the use that is now served by it. . . . This mechanism being observed (it requires indeed an examination of the instrument, and

From William Paley, *Natural Theology or Evidences of the Existence and Attributes of the Deity Collected from the Appearances of Nature*, 13th ed. (London: Faulder, 1810).

perhaps some previous knowledge of the subject, to perceive and understand it; but being once, as we have said, observed and understood), the inference, we think, is inevitable, that the watch must have had a maker: that there must have existed, at some time, and at some place or other, an artificer or artificers who formed it for the purpose which we find it actually to answer: who comprehended its construction, and designed its use.

1. Nor would it, I apprehend, weaken the conclusion, that we had never seen a watch made; that we had never known an artist capable of making one; that we were altogether incapable of executing such a piece of workmanship ourselves or of understanding in what manner it was performed; all this being no more than what is true of some exquisite remains of ancient art, of some lost arts, and, to the generality of mankind, of the more curious productions of modern manufacture. Does one man in a million know how oval frames are turned? Ignorance of this kind exalts our opinion of the unseen and unknown artist's skill, if he be unseen and unknown, but raises no doubt in our minds of the existence and agency of such an artist, at some former time, and in some place or other. Nor can I perceive that it varies at all the inference, whether the question arise concerning a human agent, or concerning an agent of a different species, or an agent possessing, in some respects, a different nature.

2. Neither, secondly, would it invalidate our conclusion, that the watch sometimes went wrong, or that it seldom went exactly right. The purpose of the machinery, the design, and the designer, might be evident, and in the case supposed would be evident, in whatever way we accounted for the irregularity of the movement, or whether we could account for it or not. It is not necessary that a machine be perfect, in order to show with what design it was made: still less necessary, where the only question is, whether it were made with any design at all.

3. Nor, thirdly, would it bring any uncertainty into the argument, if there were a few parts of the watch, concerning which we could not discover, or had not yet discovered, in what manner they conduced to the general effect; or even some parts, concerning which we could not ascertain, whether they conduced to that effect in any manner whatever. For, as to the first branch of the case; if by the loss, or disorder, or decay of the parts in question, the movement of the watch were found in fact to be stopped, or disturbed, or retarded, no doubt would remain in our minds as to the utility or intention of these parts, although we should be unable to investigate the manner according to which, or the connexion by which, the ultimate effect depended upon their action or assistance: and the more complex is the machine, the more likely is this obscurity to arise. Then, as to the second thing supposed, namely, that there were parts which might be spared, without prejudice to the movement of the watch, and that we had proved

this by experiment,—these superfluous parts, even if we were completely assured that they were such, would not vacate the reasoning which we had instituted concerning other parts. The indication of contrivance remained, with respect to them, nearly as it was before.

4. Nor, fourthly, would any man in his senses think the existence of the watch, with its various machinery, accounted for, by being told that it was one out of possible combinations of material forms; that whatever he had found in the place where he found the watch, must have contained some internal configuration or other; and that this configuration might be the structure now exhibited, viz. of the works of a watch, as well as a different structure.

5. Nor, fifthly, would it yield his inquiry more satisfaction to be answered, that there existed in things a principle of order, which had disposed the parts of the watch into their present form and situation. He never knew a watch made by the principle of order; nor can he even form to himself an idea of what is meant by a principle of order, distinct from the intelligence of the watch-maker.

6. Sixthly, he would be surprised to hear that the mechanism of the watch was no proof of contrivance, only a motive to induce the mind to think so:

7. And not less surprised to be informed, that the watch in his hand was nothing more than the result of the laws of *metallic* nature. It is a perversion of language to assign any law, as the efficient, operative cause of any thing. A law presupposes an agent; for it is only the mode, according to which an agent proceeds: it implies a power; for it is the order, according to which that power acts. Without this agent, without this power, which are both distinct from itself, the *law* does nothing; is nothing. The expression, "the law of metallic nature," may sound strange and harsh to a philosophic ear; but it seems quite as justfiable as some others which are more familiar to him, such as "the law of vegetable nature," "the law of animal nature," or indeed as "the law of nature" in general, when assigned as the cause of phenomena, in exclusion of agency and power; or when it is substituted into the place of these.

8. Neither, lastly, would our observer be driven out of his conclusion, or from his confidence in its truth, by being told that he knew nothing at all about the matter. He knows enough for his argument: he knows the utility of the end: he knows the subserviency and adaptation of the means to the end. These points being known, his ignorance of other points, his doubts concerning other points, affect not the certainty of his reasoning. The consciousness of knowing little, need not beget a distrust of that which he does know.

CHAPTER II

State of the Argument Continued

SUPPOSE, in the next place, that the person who found the watch, should, after some time, discover, that, in addition to all the properties which he had hitherto observed in it, it possessed the unexpected property of producing, in the course of its movement, another watch like itself (the thing is conceivable); that it contained within it a mechanism, a system of parts, a mould for instance, or a complex adjustment of lathes, files, and other tools, evidently and separately calculated for this purpose; let us inquire, what effect ought such a discovery to have upon his former conclusion.

1. The first effect would be to increase his admiration of the contrivance, and his conviction of the consummate skill of the contriver. Whether he regarded the object of the contrivance, the distinct apparatus, the intricate, yet in many parts intelligible mechanism, by which it was carried on, he would perceive, in this new observation, nothing but an additional reason for doing what he had already done,—for referring the construction of the watch to design, and to supreme art. . . .

2. He would reflect, that though the watch before him were, *in some sense*, the maker of the watch, which was fabricated in the course of its movements, yet it was in a very different sense from that, in which a carpenter, for instance, is the maker of a chair; the author of its contrivance, the cause of the relation of its parts to their use. With respect to these, the first watch was no cause at all to the second: in no such sense as this was it the author of the constitution and order, either of the parts which the new watch contained, or of the parts by the aid and instrumentality of which it was produced. We might possibly say, but with great latitude of expression, that a stream of water ground corn: but no latitude of expression would allow us to say, no stretch of conjecture could lead us to think, that the stream of water built the mill, though it were too ancient for us to know who the builder was. What the stream of water does in the affair, is neither more nor less than this; by the application of an unintelligent impulse to a mechanism previously arranged, arranged independently of it, and arranged by intelligence, an effect is produced, viz. the corn is ground. But the effect results from the arrangement. The force of the stream cannot be said to be the cause or author of the effect, still less of the arrangement. Understanding and plan in the formation of the mill were not the less necessary, for any share which the water has in grinding the corn: yet is this share the same, as that which the watch would have contributed to the production of the new watch, upon the supposition assumed in the last section. Therefore,

3. Though it be now no longer probable, that the individual watch, which our observer had found, was made immediately by the hand of an artificer, yet doth not this alteration in anywise affect the inference, that an artificer had been originally employed and concerned in the production. The argument from design remains as it was. . . . There cannot be design without a designer; contrivance without a contriver; order without choice; arrangement, without any thing capable of arranging; subserviency and relation to a purpose, without that which could

intend a purpose; means suitable to an end, and executing their office, in accomplishing that end, without the end ever having been contemplated, or the means accommodated to it. Arrangement, disposition of parts, subserviency of means to an end, relation of instruments to a use, imply the presence of intelligence and mind. . . .

4. Nor is any thing gained by running the difficulty farther back, *i.e.* by supposing the watch before us to have been produced from another watch, that from a former, and so on indefinitely. Our going back ever so far, brings us no nearer to the least degree of satisfaction upon the subject. Contrivance is still unaccounted for. . . . A chain, composed of an infinite number of links, can no more support itself, than a chain composed of a finite number of links. And of this we are assured (though we never *can* have tried the experiment), because, by increasing the number of links, from ten for instance to a hundred, from a hundred to a thousand, etc. we make not the smallest approach, we observe not the smallest tendency, towards self-support. There is no difference in this respect (yet there may be a great difference in several respects) between a chain . . . that is finite and one that is infinite. This very much resembles the case before us. The machine which we are inspecting, demonstrates, by its construction, contrivance and design. Contrivance must have had a contriver; design, a designer; whether the machine immediately proceeded from another machine or not. That circumstance alters not the case. That other machine may, in like manner, have proceeded from a former machine: nor does that alter the case; contrivance must have had a contriver. That former one from one preceding it: no alteration still; a contriver is still necessary. No tendency is perceived, no approach towards a diminution of this necessity. It is the same with any and every succession of these machines; a succession of ten, of a hundred, of a thousand; with one series, as with another; a series which is finite, as with a series which is infinite. In whatever other respects they may differ, in this they do not. In all equally, contrivance and design are unaccounted for.

The question is not simply, How came the first watch into existence? which question, it may be pretended, is done away by supposing the series of watches thus produced from one another to have been infinite, and consequently to have had no such *first*, for which it was necessary to provide a cause. This, perhaps, would have been nearly the state of the question, if nothing had been before us but an unorganised, unmechanised substance, without mark or indication of contrivance. It might be difficult to show that such substance could not have existed from eternity, either in succession (if it were possible, which I think it is not, for unorganised bodies to spring from one another), or by individual perpetuity. But that is not the question now. To suppose it to be so, is to suppose that it made no difference whether we had found a watch or a stone. As it is, the metaphysics of that question have no place; for, in the watch which we are examining, are seen contrivance, design; an end, a purpose; means for the end, adaptation to the purpose. And the question which irresistibly presses upon our thoughts, is, whence this contrivance and design? The thing required is the intending mind, the adapting hand, the intelligence by which that hand was directed. . . .

5. Our observer would farther also reflect, that the maker of the watch before him, was, in truth and reality, the maker of every watch produced from it; there being no difference (except that the latter manifests a more exquisite skill) between the making of another watch with his own hands, by the mediation of files, lathes, chisels, etc. and the disposing, fixing, and inserting of these instruments, or of others equivalent to them, in the body of the watch already made in such a manner, as to form a new watch in the course of the movements which he had given to the old one. It is only working by one set of tools, instead of another.

The conclusion of which the *first* examination of the watch, of its works, construction, and movement, suggested, was, that it must have had, for the cause and author of that construction, an artificer, who understood its mechanism, and designed its use. This conclusion is invincible. A *second* examination presents us with a new discovery. The watch is found, in the course of its movement, to produce another watch, similar to itself; and not only so, but we perceive in it a system or organisation, separately calculated for that purpose. What effect would this discovery have, or ought it to have, upon our former inference? What, as hath already been said, but to increase, beyond measure, our admiration of the skill, which had been employed in the formation of such a machine? Or shall it, instead of this, all at once turn us round to an opposite conclusion, viz. that no art or skill whatever has been concerned in the business, although all other evidences of art and skill remain as they were, and this last and supreme piece of art be now added to the rest; Can this be maintained without absurdity? Yet this is atheism.

CHAPTER III
Application of the Argument

THIS is atheism: for every indication of contrivance, every manifestation of design, which existed in the watch, exists in the works of nature; with the difference, on the side of nature, of being greater and more, and that in a degree which exceeds all computation. I mean that the contrivances of nature surpass the contrivances of art, in the complexity, subtility, and curiosity of the mechanism: and still more, if possible, do they go beyond them in number and variety; yet, in a multitude of cases, are not less evidently mechanical, not less evidently contrivances, not less evidently accommodated to their end, or suited to their office, than are the most perfect productions of human ingenuity.

I know no better method of introducing so large a subject than that of comparing a single thing with a single thing: an eye, for example, with a telescope. As far as the examination of the instrument goes, there is precisely the same proof that the eye was made for vision, as there is that the telescope was made for assisting it. They are made upon the same principles; both being adjusted to the laws by which the transmission and refraction of rays of light are regulated. I speak not of the origin of the laws themselves; but such laws being fixed, the construction, in both cases, is adapted to them. . . .

. . . The lenses of the telescope, and the humours of the eye, bear a complete resemblance to one another, in their figure, their position, and in their power over the rays of light, viz. in bringing each pencil to a point at the right distance from the lens; namely, in the eye, at the exact place where the membrane is spread to receive it. How is it possible, under circumstances of such close affinity, and under the operation of equal evidence, to exclude contrivance from the one; yet to acknowledge the proof of contrivance having been employed, as the plainest and clearest of all propositions, in the other?

The resemblance between the two cases is still more accurate, and obtains in more points than we have yet represented, or than we are, on the first view of the subject, aware of. In dioptric telescopes, there is an imperfection of this nature. Pencils of light, in passing through glass lenses, are separated into different colours, thereby tinging the object, especially the edges of it, as if it were viewed through a prism. To correct this inconvenience, had been long a desideratum in the art. At last it came into the mind of a sagacious optician, to inquire how this matter was managed in the eye; in which, there was exactly the same difficulty to contend with, as in the telescope. His observation taught him, that, in the eye, the evil was cured by combining lenses composed of different substances, *i.e.* of substances which possessed different refracting powers. Our artist borrowed thence his hint; and produced a correction of the defect by imitating, in glasses made from different materials, the effects of the different humours through which the rays of light pass before they reach the bottom of the eye. Could this be in the eye without purpose, which suggested to the optician the only effectual means of attaining that purpose?

But farther; there are other points, not so much perhaps of strict resemblance between the two, as of superiority of the eye over the telescope; yet of a superiority which, being founded in the laws that regulate both, may furnish topics of fair and just comparison. . . .

. . .And forasmuch as this organ would have to operate under different circumstances, with strong degrees of light, and with weak degrees, upon near objects, and upon remote ones, and these differences demanded, according to the laws by which the transmission of light is regulated, a corresponding diversity of structure: that the aperture, for example, through which the light passes, should be larger or less; the lenses rounder or flatter, or that their distance from the tablet, upon which the picture is delineated, should be shortened or lengthened: this, I say, being the case and the difficulty, to which the eye was to be adapted, we find its several parts capable of being occasionally changed, and a most artificial apparatus provided to produce that change. This is far beyond the common regulator of a watch, which requires the touch of a foreign hand to set it: but it is not altogether unlike Harrison's contrivance for making a watch regulate itself, by inserting within it a machinery, which, by the artful use of the different expansion of metals, preserves the equability of the motion under all the various temperatures of heat and cold in which the instrument may happen to be placed. The ingenuity of this last contrivance has been justly praised. Shall, therefore, a structure which differs from it chiefly by surpassing it, be accounted no contrivance at all? or, if it be a contrivance, that it is without a contriver!

.　　.　　.

CHAPTER V

Application of the Argument Continued

EVERY observation which was made in our first chapter, concerning the watch, may be repeated with strict propriety, concerning the eye; concerning animals; concerning plants; concerning, indeed, all the organised parts of the works of nature. As,

1. When we are inquiring simply after the *existence* of an intelligent Creator, imperfection, inaccuracy, liability to disorder, occasional irregularities, may subsist in a considerable degree, without inducing any doubt into the question: just as a watch may frequently go wrong, seldom perhaps exactly right, may be faulty in some parts, defective in some, without the smallest ground of suspicion from thence arising that it was not a watch; not made; or not made for the purpose ascribed to it. . . . So likewise it is in the works of nature. Irregularities and imperfections are of little or no weight in the consideration, when that consideration relates simply to the existence of a Creator. When the argument respects his attributes, they are of weight; but are then to be taken in conjunction (the attention is not to rest upon them, but they are to be taken in conjunction) with the unexceptionable evidences which we possess, of skill, power, and benevolence, displayed in other instances: which evidences may, in strength, number,

and variety, be such, and may so overpower apparent blemishes, as to induce us, upon the most reasonable ground, to believe, that these last ought to be referred to some cause, though we be ignorant of it, other than defect of knowledge or of benevolence in the author.

2. There may be also parts of plants and animals, as there were supposed to be of the watch, of which, in some instances, the operation, in others, the use, is unknown. . . . Instances of the former kind, namely, in which we cannot explain the operation, may be numerous; for they will be so in proportion to our ignorance. They will be more or fewer to different persons, and in different stages of science. Every improvement of knowledge diminishes their number. . . . Instances of the second kind, namely, where the part appears to be totally useless, I believe to be extremely rare; compared with the number of those, of which the use is evident, they are beneath any assignable proportion; and, perhaps, have never been submitted to a trial and examination sufficiently accurate, long enough continued, or often enough repeated. No accounts which I have seen, are satisfactory. . . . But . . . these superfluous parts do not negative the reasoning which we instituted concerning those parts which are useful, and of which we know the use; the indication of contrivance, with respect to them, remains as it was before.

3. One atheistic way of replying to our observations upon the works of nature, and to the proofs of a Deity which we think that we perceive in them, is to tell us, that all which we see must necessarily have had some form, and that it might as well be its present form as any other. Let us now apply this answer to the eye, as we did before to the watch. Something or other must have occupied that place in the animal's head: must have filled up, we will say, that socket: we will say also, that it must have been of that sort of substance which we call animal substance, as flesh, bone, membrane, cartilage, etc. But that it should have been an *eye*, knowing as we do what an eye comprehends,—viz. that it should have consisted, first, of a series of transparent lenses (very different, by-the-bye, even in their substance, from the opaque materials of which the rest of the body is in general at least, composed; and with which the whole of its surface, this single portion of it excepted, is covered): secondly, of a black cloth or canvass (the only membrane of the body which is black) spread out behind these lenses, so as to receive the image formed by pencils of light transmitted through them; and placed at the precise geometrical distance at which, and at which alone, a distinct image could be formed, namely, at the concourse of the refracted rays: thirdly, of a large nerve communicating between this membrane and the brain; without which, the action of light upon the membrane, however modified by the organ, would be lost to the purposes of sensation:—that this fortunate conformation of parts should have been the lot, not of one individual out of many thousand

individuals, like the great prize in a lottery, or like some singularity in nature, but the happy chance of a whole species; nor of one species out of many thousand species, with which we are acquainted, but of by far the greatest number of all that exist; and that under varieties, not casual or capricious, but bearing marks of being suited to their respective exigencies:—that all this should have taken place, merely because something must have occupied those points in every animal's forehead;—or, that all this should be thought to be accounted for, by the short answer, "that whatever was there, must have had some form or other," is too absurd to be made more so by any augmentation. . . . Nor does it mend the answer to add, with respect to the singularity of the conformation, that, after the event, it is no longer to be computed what the chances were against it. This is always to be computed, when the question is, whether a useful or imitative conformation be the produce of chance, or not: I desire no greater certainty in reasoning, than that by which chance is excluded from the present disposition of the natural world. Universal experience is against it. What does chance ever do for us? In the human body, for instance, chance, *i.e.*, the operation of causes without design, may produce a wen, a wart, a mole, a pimple, but never an eye. Amongst inanimate substances, a clod, a pebble, a liquid drop might be; but never was a watch, a telescope, an organized body of any kind, answering a valuable purpose by a complicated mechanism, the effect of chance. In no assignable instance hath such a thing existed without intention somewhere.

4. There is another answer which has the same effect as the resolving of things into chance; which answer would persuade us to believe, that the eye, the animal to which it belongs, every other animal, every plant, indeed every organized body which we see, are only so many out of the possible varieties and combinations of being, which the lapse of infinite ages has brought into existence; that the present world is the relict of that variety; millions of other bodily forms and other species having perished, being by the defect of their constitution incapable of preservation, or of continuance by generation. Now there is no foundation whatever for this conjecture in any thing which we observe in the works of nature; no such experiments are going on at present; no such energy operates, as that which is here supposed, and which should be constantly pushing into existence new varieties of beings. Nor are there any appearances to support an opinion, that every possible combination of vegetable or animal structure has formerly been tried. Multitudes of conformations, both of vegetables and animals, may be conceived capable of existence and succession, which yet do not exist. Perhaps almost as many forms of plants might have been found in the fields, as figures of plants can be delineated upon paper. A countless variety of animals might have existed, which do not exist. Upon the supposition here stated, we should see unicorns and mermaids, sylphs and centaurs, the fancies of

painters, and the fables of poets, realised by examples. Or, if it be alleged that these may transgress the limits of possible life and propagation, we might, at least, have nations of human beings without nails upon their fingers, with more or fewer fingers and toes than ten, some with one eye, others with one ear, with one nostril, or without the sense of smelling at all. All these, and a thousand other imaginable varieties, might live and propagate. We may modify any one species many different ways, all consistent with life, and with the actions necessary to preservation, although affording different degrees of conveniency and enjoyment to the animal. And if we carry these modifications through the different species which are known to subsist, their number would be incalculable. No reason can be given why, if these deperdits ever existed, they have now disappeared. Yet, if all possible existences have been tried, they must have formed part of the catalogue.

But, moreover, the division of organised substances into animals and vegetables, and the distribution and sub-distribution of each into genera and species, which distribution is not an arbitrary act of the mind, but founded in the order which prevails in external nature, appear to me to contradict the supposition of the present world being the remains of an indefinite variety of existences; of a variety which rejects all plan. The hypothesis teaches, that every possible variety of being hath, at one time or other, found its way into existence (by what cause or in what manner is not said), and that those which were badly formed, perished; but how or why those which survived should be cast, as we see that plants and animals are cast, into regular classes, the hypothesis does not explain; or rather the hypothesis is inconsistent with this phenomenon.

The hypothesis, indeed, is hardly deserving of the consideration which we have given to it. What should we think of a man who, because we had never ourselves seen watches, telescopes, stocking-mills, steam-engines, etc. made, knew not how they were made, or could prove by testimony when they were made, or by whom,—would have us believe that these machines, instead of deriving their curious structures from the thought and design of their inventors and contrivers, in truth derive them from no other origin than this; viz. that a mass of metals and other materials having run when melted into all possible figures, and combined themselves in all possible forms, and shapes, and proportions, these things which we see, are what were left from the accident, as best worth preserving; and, as such, are become the remaining stock of a magazine, which, at one time or other, has by this means, contained every mechanism, useful, and useless, convenient and inconvenient, into which such like materials could be thrown? I cannot distinguish the hypothesis as applied to the works of nature, from this solution which no one would accept, as applied to a collection of machines.

5. To the marks of contrivance discoverable in animal bodies, and to the argument deduced from them, in proof of design, and of a designing Creator, this turn is sometimes attempted to be given, namely, that the parts were not intended for the use, but that the use arose out of the parts. This distinction is intelligible. A cabinet-maker rubs his mahogany with fish-skin; yet it would be too much to assert that the skin of the dog-fish was made rough and granulated on purpose for the polishing of wood, and the use of cabinet-makers. Therefore the distinction is intelligible. But I think that there is very little place for it in the works of nature. When roundly and generally affirmed of them, as it hath sometimes been, it amounts to such another stretch of assertion, as it would be to say, that all the implements of the cabinet-maker's work-shop, as well as his fish-skin, were substances accidentally configurated, which he had picked up, and converted to his use; that his adzes, saws, planes, and gimlets, were not made, as we suppose, to hew, cut, smooth, shape out, or bore wood with; but that, these things being made, no matter with what design, or whether with any, the cabinet-maker perceived that they were applicable to his purpose, and turned them to account.

But, again. So far as this solution is attempted to be applied to those parts of animals the action of which does not depend upon the will of the animal, it is fraught with still more evident absurdity. It is possible to believe that the eye was formed without any regard to vision; that it was the animal itself which found out, that, though formed with no such intention, it would serve to see with: and that the use of the eye, as an organ of sight, resulted from this discovery, and the animal's application of it? The same question may be asked of the ear; the same of all the senses. . . .

. . . If we apply the solution to the human body, for instance, it forms itself into questions, upon which no reasonable mind can doubt; such as, whether the teeth were made expressly for the mastication of food, the feet for walking, the hands for holding? or whether, these things being as they are, being in fact in the animal's possession, his own ingenuity taught him that they were convertible to these purposes, though no such purposes were contemplated in their formation?

.   .   .

Lastly; the solution fails entirely when applied to plants. The parts of plants answer their uses, without any concurrence from the will or choice of the plant.

6. Others have chosen to refer every thing to a *principle of order* in nature. A principle of order is the word: but what is meant by a principle of order, as different from an intelligent Creator, has not been explained either by definition or example: and, without such explanation, it should seem to be a mere substitu-

tion of words for reasons, names for causes. Order itself is only the adaptation of means to an end: the principle of order therefore can only signify the mind and intention which so adapts them. Or, were it capable of being explained in any other sense, is there any experience, any analogy, to sustain it? Was a watch ever produced by a principle of order? and why might not a watch be so produced, as well as an eye?

Farthermore, a principle of order, acting blindly and without choice, is neg-atived, by the observation, that order is not universal; which it would be, if it 'issued from a constant and necessary principle; nor indiscriminate, which it would be, if it issued from an unintelligent principle. Where order is wanted, there we find it: where order is not wanted, *i.e.* where, if it prevailed, it would be useless, there we do not find it. In the structure of the eye (for we adhere to our example), in the figure and position of its several parts, the most exact order is maintained. In the forms of rocks and mountains, in the lines which bound the coasts of continents and islands, in the shape of bays and promontories, no order whatever is perceived, because it would have been superfluous. No useful pur-pose would have arisen from moulding rocks and mountains into regular solids, bounding the channel of the ocean by geometrical curves; or from the map of the world, resembling a table of diagrams in Euclid's Elements, or Simpson's Conic Sections.

7. Lastly; the confidence which we place in our observations upon the works of nature, in the marks which we discover of contrivance, choice, and design; and in our reasoning upon the proofs afforded us; ought not to be shaken, as it is sometimes attempted to be done, by bringing forward to our view our own igno-rance, or rather the general imperfection of our knowledge of nature. Nor, in many cases, ought this consideration to affect us, even when it respects some parts of the subject immediately under our notice. True fortitude of understand-ing consists in not suffering what we know, to be disturbed by what we do not know. If we perceive a useful end, and means adapted to that end, we perceive enough for our conclusion. If these things be clear, no matter what is obscure. The argument is finished. . . .

CHAPTER VI

The Argument Cumulative

WERE there no example in the world, of contrivance, except that of the *eye*, it would be alone sufficient to support the conclusion which we draw from it, as to the necessity of an intelligent Creator. It could never be got rid of; because it could not be accounted for by any other supposition, which did not contradict all the principles we possess of knowledge; the principles, according to which, things do, as often as they can be brought to the test of experience, turn out to be true or false. Its coats and humours, constructed, as the lenses of a telescope are constructed, for the refraction of rays of light to a point, which forms the proper action of the organ; the provision in its muscular tendons for turning its pupil to the object, similar to that which is given to the telescope by screws, and upon which power of direction in the eye, the exercise of its office as an optical instrument depends; the farther provision for its defence, for its constant lubricity and moisture, which we see in its socket and its lids, in its gland for the secretion of the matter of tears, its outlet or communication with the nose for carrying off the liquid after the eye is washed with it; these provisions compose altogether an apparatus, a system of parts, a preparation of means, so manifest in their design, so exquisite in their contrivance, so successful in their issue, so precious, and so infinitely beneficial in their use, as, in my opinion, to bear down all doubt that can be raised upon the subject. And what I wish, under the title of the present chapter, to observe is, that if other parts of nature were inaccessible to our inquiries, or even if other parts of nature presented nothing to our examination but disorder and confusion, the validity of this example would remain the same. If there were but one watch in the world, it would not be less certain that it had a maker. If we had never in our lives seen any but one single kind of hydraulic machine, yet, if of that one kind we understood the mechanism and use, we should be as perfectly assured that it proceeded from the hand, and thought, and skill of a workman, as if we visited a museum of the arts, and saw collected there twenty different kinds of machines for drawing water, or a thousand different kinds for other purposes. Of this point, each machine is a proof, independently of all the rest. So it is with the evidences of a Divine agency. The proof is not a conclusion which lies at the end of a chain of reasoning, of which chain each instance of contrivance is only a link, and of which, if one link fail, the whole falls; but it is an argument separately supplied by every separate example. An error in stating an example, affects only that example. The argument is cumulative, in the fullest sense of that term. The eye proves it without the ear; the ear without the eye. The proof in each example is complete; for when the design of the part, and the conduciveness of its structure to that design is shown, the mind may set itself at rest; no future consideration can detract any thing from the force of the example.

A VIEW OF THE EVIDENCES OF CHRISTIANITY

PART 3

CHAPTER VIII

The Conclusion

IN religion, as in every other subject of human reasoning, much depends upon the *order* in which we dispose our inquiries. A man who takes up a system of divinity with a previous opinion that either every part must be true, or the whole false, approaches the discussion with great disadvantage. No other system, which is founded upon moral evidence, would bear to be treated in the same manner. Nevertheless, in a certain degree, we are all introduced to our religious studies under this prejudication. And it cannot be avoided. The weakness of the human judgment in the early part of youth, yet its extreme susceptibility of impression, renders it necessary to furnish it with some opinions, and with some principles, or other. Or indeed, without much express care, or much endeavour for this purpose, the tendency of the mind of man to assimilate itself to the habits of thinking and speaking which prevail around him, produces the same effect. That indifferency and suspense, that waiting and equilibrium of the judgment, which some require in religious matters, and which some would wish to be aimed at in the conduct of education, are impossible to be preserved. They are not given to the condition of human life.

It is a consequence of this situation that the doctrines of religion come to us before the proofs; and come to us with that mixture of explications and inferences

---

From William Paley, A *View of the Evidences of Christianity*, 15th ed. in 2 vols. (Edinburgh: Adam Black, 1811), 2:371–73, 375–96.

from which no public creed is, or can be, free. And the effect which too frequently follows, from Christianity being presented to the understanding in this form, is, that when any articles, which appear as parts of it, contradict the apprehension of the persons to whom it is proposed, men of rash and confident tempers hastily and indiscriminately reject the whole. But is this to do justice, either to themselves, or to the religion? The rational way of treating a subject of such acknowledged importance is to attend, in the first place, to the general and substantial truth of its principles, and to that alone. When we once feel a foundation; when we once perceive a ground of credibility in its history, we shall proceed with safety to inquire into the interpretation of its records, and into the doctrines which have been deduced from them. Nor will it either endanger our faith, or diminish or alter our motives for obedience, if we should discover that these conclusions are formed with very different degrees of probability, and possess very different degrees of importance.

.   .   .

It hath been my care, in the preceding work, to preserve the separation between evidences and doctrines as inviolable as I could; to remove from the primary question all considerations which have been unnecessarily joined with it; and to offer a defence to Christianity, which every Christian might read, without seeing the tenets in which he had been brought up attacked or decried: and it always afforded a satisfaction to my mind to observe that this was practicable; that few or none of our many controversies with one another affect or relate to the proofs of our religion; that the rent never descends to the foundation.

The truth of Christianity depends upon its leading facts, and upon them alone. Now of these we have evidence which ought to satisfy us, at least until it appear that mankind have ever been deceived by the same. We have some uncontested and incontestable points, to which the history of the human species hath nothing similar to offer. A Jewish peasant changed the religion of the world, and that, without force, without power, without support; without one natural source or circumstance of attraction, influence, or success. Such a thing hath not happened in any other instance. The companions of this Person, after he himself had been put to death for his attempt, asserted his supernatural character, founded upon his supernatural operations; and, in testimony of the truth of their assertions, *i.e.* in consequence of their own belief of that truth, and in order to communicate the knowledge of it to others, voluntarily entered upon lives of toil and hardship, and, with a full experience of their danger, committed themselves to the last extremities of persecution. This hath not a parallel. More particularly, a very few days after this Person had been publickly executed, and in the very city in which he was buried, these his companions declared with one voice that his body was restored to life; that they had seen him, handled him, eat with him, conversed with him; and, in pursuance of their persuasion of the truth of what they told, preached his religion, with this strange fact as the foundation of it, in the face of those who had killed him, who were armed with the power of the country, and necessarily and naturally disposed to treat his followers as they had treated himself; and having done this upon the spot where the event took place, carried the intelligence of it abroad, in despite of difficulties and opposition, and where the nature of their errand gave them nothing to expect but derision, insult, and outrage.—This is without example. These three facts, I think, are certain, and would have been nearly so, if the Gospels had never been written. The Christian story, as to these points, hath never varied. No other hath been set up against it. Every letter, every discourse, every controversy, amongst the followers of the religion; every book written by them, from the age of its commencement to the present time, in every part of the world in which it hath been professed, and with every sect into which it hath been divided (and we have letters and discourses written by contemporaries, by witnesses of the transaction, by persons themselves bearing a share in it, and other writings following that age in regular succession), *concur* in representing these facts in this manner. A religion, which now possesses the greatest part of the civilized world, 'unquestionably sprang up at Jerusalem at this time. Some account must be given of its origin; some cause assigned for its rise. All the accounts of this origin, all the explications of this cause, whether taken from the writings of the early followers of the religion (in which, and in which perhaps alone, it could be expected that they should be distinctly unfolded), or from occasional notices in other writings of that or the adjoining age, either 'expressly allege the facts above stated as the means by which the religion was set up, or advert to its commencement in a manner which agrees with the supposition of these facts being true, and which testifies their operation and effects.

These propositions alone lay a foundation for our faith; for they prove the existence of a transaction, which cannot even in its most *general* parts be accounted for, upon any reasonable supposition, except that of the truth of the mission. But the particulars, the *detail* of the miracles or miraculous pretences (for such there necessarily must have been), upon which this unexampled transaction rested, and *for* which these men acted and suffered as they did act and suffer, it is undoubtedly of great importance to us to know. We *have* this detail from the fountain-head, from the persons themselves; in accounts written by eyewitnesses of the scene, by contemporaries and companions of those who were so; not in one book, but four, each containing enough for the verification of the religion, all agreeing in the fundamental parts of the history. We have the authenticity of these books, established, by more and stronger proofs than belong to almost any other ancient book whatever, and by proofs which widely distinguish them from any others claiming a similar authority to theirs. If there were any good reason for doubt concerning the names to which these books are ascribed (which there is not, for they were never ascribed to any other, and we have evidence not long after their publication of their bearing the names which they now bear), their antiquity, of which there is no question, their reputation and authority amongst the early disciples of the religion, of which there is as little, form a valid proof that they must, in the main at least, have agreed with what the first teachers of the religion delivered.

When we open these ancient volumes, we discover in them marks of truth, whether we consider each in itself, or collate them with one another. The writers certainly knew something of what they were writing about, for they manifest an acquaintance with local circumstances, with the history and usages of the times, which could only belong to an inhabitant of that country, living in that age. In every narrative we perceive simplicity and undesignedness; the air and the language of reality. When we compare the different narratives together, we find them so varying as to repel all suspicion of confederacy; so agreeing under this variety, as to show that the accounts had one real transaction for their common foundation; often attributing different actions and discourses, to the person whose history, or rather memoirs of whose history, they profess to relate, yet actions and discourses so similar, as very much to bespeak the same character; which is a coincidence, that, in such writers as they were, could only be the consequence of their writing from fact, and not from imagination.

These four narratives are confined to the history of the Founder of the religion, and end with his ministry. Since, however, it is certain that the affair went on, we cannot help being anxious to know *how* it proceeded. This intelligence hath come down to us in a work purporting to be written by a person himself connected with the business during the first stages of its progress, taking up the story where the former histories had left it, carrying on the narrative, oftentimes with great particularity, and throughout with the appearance of good sense,[1] information, and candour; stating all along the origin, and the only probable origin, of effects which unquestionably were produced, together with the natural consequences of situations which unquestionably did exist; and *confirmed*, in the

---

[1]See Peter's speech upon curing the cripple (Acts 3:18.), the council of the apostles (Acts 15), Paul's discourse at Athens (Acts 17:22.), before Agrippa (Acts 26). I notice these passages, both as fraught with good sense, and as free from the smallest tincture of enthusiasm.

substance at least of the account, by the strongest possible accession of testimony which a history can receive, *original letters*, written by the person who is the principal subject of the history, written upon the business to which the history relates, and during the period, or soon after the period, which the history comprises. No man can say that this altogether is not a body of strong historical evidence.

When we reflect that some of those from whom the books proceeded, are related to have themselves wrought miracles, to have been the subject of miracles, or of supernatural assistance in propagating the religion, we may perhaps be led to think, that more credit, or a different kind of credit, is due to these accounts, than what can be claimed by merely human testimony. But this is an argument which cannot be addressed to sceptics or unbelievers. A man must be a Christian before he can receive it. The inspiration of the historical Scriptures, the nature, degree, and extent of that inspiration, are questions undoubtedly of serious discussion; but they are questions amongst Christians themselves, and not between them and others. The doctrine itself is by no means necessary to the belief of Christianity, which must, in the first instance at least, depend upon the ordinary maxims of historical credibility.[2]

In viewing the detail of miracles recorded in these books, we find every supposition negatived, by which they can be resolved into fraud or delusion. They were not secret, nor momentary, nor tentative, nor ambiguous; nor performed under the sanction of authority, with the spectators on their side, or in the affirmance of tenets and practices already established. We find also the evidence alleged for them, and which evidence was by great numbers received, different from that upon which other miraculous accounts rest. It was contemporary, it was published upon the spot, it continued; it involved interests and questions of the greatest magnitude; it contradicted the most fixed persuasions and prejudices of the persons to whom it was addressed; it required from those who accepted it, not a simple, indolent assent, but a change, from thenceforward, of principles and conduct, a submission to consequences the most serious and the most deterring, to loss and danger, to insult, outrage, and persecution. How such a story should be false, or, if false, how, under such circumstances, it should make its way, I think impossible to be explained; yet such the Christian story was, such were the circumstances under which it came forth, and in opposition to such difficulties did it prevail.

An event so connected with the religion, and with the fortunes, of the Jewish people, as one of their race, one born amongst them, establishing his authori-

---

[2]See Powell's Discourses, disc. xv. p. 245.

ty and his law throughout a great portion of the civilized world, it was perhaps to be expected, should be noticed in the prophetic writings of that nation; especially when this Person, together with his own mission, caused also to be acknowledged the divine original of their institution, and by those who before had altogether rejected it. Accordingly, we perceive in these writings, various intimations *concurring* in the person and history of Jesus, in a manner, and in a degree, in which passages taken from these books could not be made to concur in any person arbitrarily assumed, or in any person, except him who has been the Author of great changes in the affairs and opinions of mankind. Of some of these predictions the weight depends a good deal upon the concurrence. Others possess great separate strength: one in particular does this in an eminent degree. It is an entire description, manifestly directed to one character and to one scene of things: it is extant in a writing, or collection of writings, declaredly prophetic; and it applies to Christ's character, and to the circumstances of his life and death, with considerable precision, and in a way which no diversity of interpretation hath, in my opinion, been able to confound. That the advent of Christ, and the consequences of it, should not have been more distinctly revealed in the Jewish sacred books, is, I think, in some measure accounted for by the consideration, that for the Jews to have foreseen the fall of their institution, and that it was to merge at length into a more perfect and comprehensive dispensation, would have cooled too much, and relaxed, their zeal for it, and their adherence to it, upon which zeal and adherence the preservation in the world of any remains, for many ages, of religious truth might in a great measure depend.

Of what a revelation discloses to mankind, one, and only one, question can properly be asked, Was it of importance to mankind to know, or to be better assured of? In this question, when we turn our thoughts to the great Christian doctrine of the resurrection of the dead, and of a future judgment, no doubt can possibly be entertained. He who gives me riches or honours, does nothing; he who even gives me health, does little, in comparison with that which lays before me just grounds for expecting a restoration to life, and a day of account and retribution; which thing Christianity hath done for millions.

Other articles of the Christian faith, although of infinite importance when placed beside any other topic of human inquiry, are only the adjuncts and circumstances of this. They are, however, such as appear worthy of the original to which we ascribe them. The morality of the religion, whether taken from the precepts or the example of its Founder, or from the lessons of its primitive teachers, derived, as it should seem, from what had been inculcated by their Master, is, in all its parts, wise and pure; neither adapted to vulgar prejudices, nor flattering popular notions, nor excusing established practices, but calculated, in the matter of its instruction, truly to promote human happiness, and, in the form in which it was conveyed, to produce impression and effect; a morality, which, let it have proceeded from any person whatever, would have been satisfactory evidence of his good sense and integrity, of the soundness of his understanding and the probity of his designs; a morality, in every view of it, much more perfect than could have been expected from the natural circumstances and character of the person who delivered it; a morality in a word, which is, and hath been, most beneficial to mankind.

Upon the greatest, therefore, of all possible occasions, and for a purpose of inestimable value, it pleased the Deity to vouchsafe a miraculous attestation. Having done this for the institution, when this alone could fix its authority, or give to it a beginning, he committed its future progress to the natural means of human communication, and to the influence of those causes by which human conduct and human affairs are governed. The seed, being sown, was left to vegetate; the leaven, being inserted, was left to ferment; and both according to the laws of nature: laws, nevertheless, disposed and controlled by that Providence which conducts the affairs of the universe, though by an influence inscrutable, and generally undistinguishable by us. And in this, Christianity is analogous to most other provisions for happiness. The provision is made; and, being made, is left to act according to laws, which, forming a part of a more general system, regulate this particular subject, in common with many others.

Let the constant recurrence to our observation of contrivance, design, and wisdom in the works of nature, once fix upon our minds the belief of a God, and after that all is easy. In the councils of a being possessed of the power and disposition which the Creator of the universe must possess, it is not improbable that there should be a future state: it is not improbable that we should be acquainted with it. A future state rectifies every thing; because, if moral agents be made, in the last event, happy or miserable, according to their conduct in the station and under the circumstances in which they are placed, it seems not very material by the operation of what causes, according to what rules, or even, if you please to call it so, by what chance or caprice, these stations are assigned, or these circumstances determined. This hypothesis, therefore, solves all that objection to the divine care and goodness, which the promiscuous distribution of good and evil (I do not mean in the doubtful advantages of riches and grandeur, but in the unquestionably important distinctions of health and sickness, strength and infirmity, bodily ease and pain, mental alacrity and depression) is apt on so many occasions to create. This one truth changes the nature of things; gives order to confusion; makes the moral world of a piece with the natural.

Nevertheless, a higher degree of assurance than that to which it is possible to advance this, or any argument drawn from the light of nature, was necessary, especially to overcome the shock which the imagination and the senses receive from the effects and the appearances of death; and the obstruction which thence arises to the expectation of either a continued or a future existence. This difficulty, although of a nature, no doubt, to act very forcibly, will be found, I think, upon reflection, to reside more in our habits of apprehension, than in the subject; and that the giving way to it, when we have any reasonable grounds for the contrary, is rather an indulging of the imagination, than any thing else. Abstractedly considered, that is, considered without relation to the difference which habit, and merely habit, produces in our faculties and modes of apprehension, I do not see any thing more in the resurrection of a dead man, than in the conception of a child; except it be this, that the one comes into his world with a system of prior consciousness about him, which the other does not: and no person will say, that he knows enough of either subject to perceive, that this circumstance makes such a difference in the two cases, that the one should be easy, and the other impossible; the one natural, the other not so. To the first man, the succession of the species would be as incomprehensible, as the resurrection of the dead is to us.

Thought is different from motion, perception from impact: the individuality of a mind is hardly consistent with the divisibility of an extended substance; or its volition, that is, its power of originating motion, with the inertness which cleaves to every portion of matter which our observation or our experiments can reach. These distinctions lead us to an *immaterial* principle: at least, they do this; they so negative the mechanical properties of matter, in the constitution of a sentient, still more of a rational, being, that no argument, drawn from these properties, can be of any great weight in opposition to other reasons, when the question respects the changes of which such a nature is capable, or the manner in which these changes are effected. Whatever thought be, or whatever it depend upon, the regular experience of *sleep* makes one thing concerning it certain, that it can be completely suspended, and completely restored.

If any one find it too great a strain upon his thoughts to admit the notion of a substance strictly immaterial, that is, from which extension and solidity are excluded, he can find no difficulty in allowing, that a particle as small as a particle of light, minuter than all conceivable dimensions, may just as easily be the depositary, the organ, and the vehicle of consciousness, as the congeries of animal substance which forms a human body, or the human brain; that being so, it may transfer a proper identity to whatever shall hereafter be united to it; may be safe amidst the destruction of its integuments; may connect the natural with the spiritual, the corruptible with the glorified body. If it be said, that the mode and means of all this is imperceptible by our senses, it is only what is true of the most important agencies and operations. The great powers of nature are all invisible. Gravitation, electricity, magnetism, though constantly present, and constantly exerting their influence; though within us, near us, and about us; though diffused throughout all space, overspreading the surface, or penetrating the contexture, of all bodies with which we are acquainted, depend upon substances and actions which are totally concealed from our senses. The Supreme Intelligence is so himself.

But whether these or any other attempts to satisfy the imagination, bear any resemblance to the truth, or whether the imagination, which, as I have said before, is the mere slave of habit, *can* be satisfied or not; when a future state, and the revelation of a future state, is not only perfectly consistent with the attributes of the Being who governs the universe; but when it is more; when it alone removes the appearances of contrariety which attend the operations of his will towards creatures capable of comparative merit and demerit, of reward and punishment; when a strong body of historical evidence, confirmed by many internal tokens of truth and authenticity, gives us just reason to believe that such a revelation hath actually been made; we ought to set our minds at rest with the assurance, that in the resources of Creative Wisdom, expedients cannot be wanted to carry into effect what the Deity hath purposed: that either a new and mighty influence will descend upon the human world to resuscitate extinguished consciousness; or that, amidst the other wonderful contrivances with which the universe abounds, and by some of which we see animal life, in many instances, assuming improved forms of existence, acquiring new organs, new perceptions, and new sources of enjoyment, provision is also made, though by methods secret to us (as all the great processes of nature are), for conducting the objects of God's moral government, through the necessary changes of their frame, to those final distinctions of happiness and misery, which he hath declared to be reserved for obedience and transgression, for virtue and vice, for the use and the neglect, the right and the wrong employment, of the faculties and opportunities with which He hath been pleased, severally, to entrust, and to try us.

THE REST
OF THE STORY:
A BIBLIOGRAPHICAL
ESSAY ON APOLOGETIC
WRITING IN THE
NINETEENTH AND
TWENTIETH CENTURIES

PREFACE

The rational defense of biblical Christianity, of course, did not end in 1800. The eighteen decades since then have seen apologetic writings increase numerically in unprecedented ways. Gradually, the academic discipline of Christian apologetics has come into its own, and the subject has gained independent status.

Apologetics, in the broad sense, is what all theologians use when they commend their views to those unbelievers who might listen to them. The format is often defensive because apologetic work frequently arises in response to attacks by skeptics and critics upon the reasonableness of the Christian faith.

The fact of the matter is, however, that most modern apologetic work is read by (and, to be honest, is written for) those who are already Christians. There is nothing illegitimate about this. Quite to the contrary, true believers are the ones who are confronted with the intellectual attacks as well as the personal prejudice against the biblical world view. Biblical doctrines and the

New Testament way of life are challenged in the marketplaces as well as in the universities of our world. Christian people often need help in sorting out the issues and in grasping the implications of biblical faith with special regard for the "secular objections" to it.

APOLOGETIC METHODS

In this final chapter I want to outline the developments that have taken place in this field in the nineteenth and twentieth centuries. The primary, though not the exclusive, interest will be to focus on apologetic writings within the traditions of Protestant orthodoxy. The apologetic works of Roman Catholic theologians have often followed the pattern set forth in the writings of Thomas Aquinas. This method has been called Thomism. On the other hand, Protestants have not come to a general methodological agreement.

Obviously Augustine, Calvin, and Luther have had a formative influence on Protestant thinking, but modern apologetic methods have varied widely. Those who follow Augustine in finding the ultimate test for divine revelation in the laws of logic are usually classified as *rationalists*. Those who, like Joseph Butler, test revelation by examining its compatibility with nature or experience are properly designated *empiricists*. *Fideists* believe, as did John Calvin, that ultimately faith has to be self-validating to each individual and that revelation can be tested only by this faith, which is produced directly and exclusively by the Holy Spirit. On the other hand, *evidentialists* follow William Paley in making a direct appeal to various evidences (historical and scientific) as a means of verifying divine revelation even to the skeptic.

It is not an entirely unjustified simplification to combine fideism and rationalism under the rubric of *presuppositionalism* and to combine empiricism with *evidentialism*. Thus today many write as if evidentialism vs. presuppositionalism is the essence of the modern debate about apologetic methodology. I am not at all satisfied, however, with this "us and them" approach, nor do I think that these two categories are ultimately sufficient to describe the current situation even among evangelicals. Nevertheless these terms do in a general way point toward Thomistic or Augustinian methods, and in a brief survey such as this, oversimplifications are perhaps inevitable.

From the earliest days of Christianity, the apologists shifted their emphasis as the grounds of the attacks and objections against the faith shifted. When pagan persecution focused on charges that Christians were cannibals (since they spoke of eating the body of Christ), the apologists replied to such charges. When in the seventeenth century irreligion began to spread as a result of the radical changes that came with the new cosmology and with the cultural shifts flowing out of the late Renaissance, apologetic literature took up those challenges and offered definitive answers in light of the then-current questions.

Apologetic studies prior to 1800 were essentially topical, not systematic. However, under the influence of Friedrich Schleiermacher (1768–1834) the various departments of theology began to be self-consciously organized. K. H. Sack was the first to suggest a scientifically organized Christian apologetic (*Christian Apologetics* [Hamburg, 1829; 2d ed., 1841]). Since then the presses have produced a seemingly endless stream of "scientific" systems of apologetical works. These works are difficult to classify, for they differ in scope, in method, and even in their conception of the task. They often differ radically on what it is that they are trying to offer a defense of; that is, they differ in their conception of God and of the religious faith that they claim to be defending. But as an independent discipline within the field of theological studies, capable of and demanding separate treatment, Christian apologetics came into its own during the nineteenth century.

NINETEENTH-CENTURY APOLOGETICS

Several nineteenth-century German scholars produced historical surveys of apologetic works. H. E. Tzschirmer published *Geschichte der Apologetik* in 1805. In 1846 G. H. van Senden offered a two-volume *Geschichte der Apologetik*. From a Roman Catholic perspective K. Werner published his five-volume *Geschichte der apologetischen und polemischen Literatur* between 1861 and 1867.

Not only did interest in the history of apologetics rise in the nineteenth century but so did interest in systematic apologetic literature. Some of the key titles include W. H. Hetherington, *Apologetics of the Christian Faith* (1867); J.H.A. Ebrard, *Apologetics, or The Scientific Vindication of Christianity*, 2 vols. (1886–87); G. F. Wright, *Logic of Christian Evidence* (1884); L. F. Stearns *The*

Evidence of Christian Experience (1891) (considered by B. B. Warfield to be "the best book on the subject"); P. Schanz, *Christian Apology* (1894) (Roman Catholic); A. B. Bruce, *Apologetics, or Christianity Defensively Stated* (1892); W. Devivier, *Christian Apologetics*, 2 vols. (1903); A. Harnack, *What is Christianity?* (1902); and, of course, the Boyle and the Bampton lectures, taken collectively, form a double set of apologetic works. The Boyle lectures are a yearly lecture series to defend Christianity against unbelief. They were provided for in the will of Robert Boyle, a British physicist, who died in 1691. John Bampton, an English clergyman, gave his name to a distinguished lectureship at Oxford University. Since 1895 the Bampton Lectures have been given every other year.

F. R. Beattie began a three-volume work entitled *Apologetics, or The Rational Vindication of Christianity* in 1903, but apparently he never completed the second and third volumes. The first volume, *Fundamental Apologetics*, was widely read in conservative Presbyterian circles.

EARLY TWENTIETH-CENTURY APOLOGETICS

James Orr, a Scottish theologian, was well known for his apologetic studies at the beginning of the twentieth century. He taught church history from 1891 to 1901 at the United Presbyterian theological college in Scotland. He became the professor of apologetics and theology at the college of the United Free Church in Glasgow from 1901 until his death in 1913. Orr was widely respected on both sides of the Atlantic for his defense of historic evangelical Christianity in a day of rising liberalism. His most important apologetic work, *A Christian View of God and the World* (1893), is actually the publication of his Kerr lectures. (The Kerr lectureship was founded by the United Presbyterian Synod meeting in Edinburgh through monies from Miss Joan Kerr's will. James Orr was the first lecturer.) Even at this early period in his career he clearly opposed the Ritschlian view. (Albrecht Ritschl of Goettingen (1822–89) denied the orthodox teaching concerning the penal suffering of Christ and taught that Christ's work was primarily one of moral persuasion.) Orr restated his opposition to Ritschl's view more than once in subsequent publications. His *Resurrection of Jesus* (1905) and *The Problem of the Old Testament* (1906) stand out as classic statements defending evangelical views.

During the early twentieth century, the Fundamentalist-Modernist controversy dominated American church life, and many of the books published could be seen in an apologetic context. Much of the work, however, was popular in style, and very few titles survived to be reprinted in later years. One that did was J. Gresham Machen's *Christianity and Liberalism* (1923). Machen also published *The Virgin Birth of Christ* (1930), a study on the Virgin Birth that has never been superseded. *The Fundamentals*, the series of booklets published between 1909 and 1915, were clearly apologetic in intent though no single methodology was adopted by the contributors.

The only outstanding apologist in the early twentieth century among Southern Baptists was E. Y. Mullins. His *Why Is Christianity True?* (1905) and *The Axioms of Religion* (1908) were widely read by Baptists, though it cannot be said that their impact spread much beyond his own denomination. Mullins stresses the Christian experience, particularly the conversion experience, as the ultimate test of divine truth. This subjective empiricism is most clearly elaborated in his major work, *The Christian Religion in Its Doctrinal Expression* (1920).

MID-TWENTIETH-CENTURY APOLOGETICS

One of the leaders in the postwar intellectual awakening among American Evangelicals was E. J. Carnell. Having taught at Gordon College and Divinity School in Massachusetts beginning in 1945, he moved in 1948 to Fuller Theological Seminary in California and remained there for nineteen years. Probably, his *Introduction to Christian Apologetics* (1948) has been the single most influential apologetic textbook of the third quarter of the twentieth century. Carnell's verification procedure, self-designated as the method of systematic consistency, has been widely adopted, and his treatment of biblical criticism, modern science, miracles, and the problem of evil remain bench marks of evangelical discussions of these issues. Carnell has been called a *combinationalist* because of the presence of both rationalistic and empiricist elements in his methodology. Clearly, however, if the categories are broadly taken as being the exclusive alternatives, Carnell is surely Augustinian rather than Thomistic. In his later writings, Carnell seems to have broadened his views beyond his strictly rationalistic stance in *Apologetics*. Carnell's *Philosophy of the Christian Re-*

ligion (1952) and *Christian Commitment* (1957) develop his apologetic interests significantly. See also his *Case for Orthodox Theology* (1959) for an example of his mature apologetic method in action.

Within the academic evangelical community, Gordon Clark, for many years professor of philosophy at Butler University in Indiana, has been one of the most influential apologists of the modern era. Clearly supporting Augustinian rationalism, Clark has maintained that no world view is capable of absolute proof and that empirical evidence does not qualify as truth or knowledge at all. Everyone must ultimately choose a set of axioms from which to interpret life, and those axioms, drawn from authentic Christianity, bring the maximum coherence to the minds given to humans by divine creation. Clark's lifelong task, then, has been to elaborate the internal inconsistencies of non-Christian viewpoints and to commend Christianity (in its Augustinian-Calvinistic form) as being the view that produces the most rational and coherent view of all facts and experiences. His *Christian View of Men and Things* (1952) is the classic statement of his view. He elaborates the view (consistently) in *Karl Barth's Theological Method* (1963), *Historiography* (1971), and *The Philosophy of Science and Belief in God* (1972). Clark's systematic evaluation of the history of philosophy is found in *Thales to Dewey* (1957). Some think his most important work is *Religion, Reason, and Revelation* (1961). Nevertheless, the best introduction to his methodology and to the debates that have centered around it is *The Philosophy of Gordon Clark* (1968) edited by Ronald Nash.

Bernard Ramm is another widely read theologian among Protestant Evangelicals who has given special attention to biblical apologetics. His article "Apologetics, Biblical" in ISBE (Rev., 1979) summarizes both Old and New Testament materials. Ramm's earlier publications include *The Pattern of Religious Authority* (1957) and *Special Revelation and the Word of God* (1961).

His *Protestant Christian Evidences* (1953) was widely read, but it represented only one element in his overall understanding of proper apologetic method. Ramm's systematic statement of method came in *The God Who Makes a Difference* (1972), later retitled *A Christian Appeal to Reason*. From the rational or logical standpoint, Ramm roots everything in human choice, but this is not a purely arbitrary or even a fully autonomous choice. The inner witness of the Holy Spirit is a persuasive work of God in our lives, and thus our choice is guided. As Christians, we confirm this inner testimony by discovering the many adequate evidences from nature and history that point to the rightness of our choice. Then finally we build a philosophical world view (Ramm calls this a "synoptic vision") that ties everything together and fills in the gaps, so that we achieve a coherent view of life, including religion, science, philosophy, etc.

Other relevant works by Ramm include *The Christian View of Science and Scriptures* (1954) and *Types of Apologetic Systems* (1953), revised in 1961 and published as *Varieties of Christian Apologetics*.

Among the strongly Calvinistic Dutch Reformed apologists of the twentieth century, perhaps no one has been more widely read in America than Cornelius Van Til of the Westminster Theological Seminary in Philadelphia. Abraham Kuyper, the Dutch Calvinist theologian, educator, and political leader in Amsterdam, had so strongly opposed apologetics (by which he meant the defense of the faith against the attacks of unbelievers) that Reformed scholars had virtually abandoned all efforts in that direction. Indeed it seemed to many that Christianity was struggling to hold on to less and less territory. Van Til, however, took a new approach that not only sought to take the offensive rather than merely defend the faith but it also denied the unbeliever the right to possess any territory at all. For Van Til there was no common ground between believers and unbelievers.

The best introduction both to Van Til's thought and to the methodological debates that his presuppositional fideism has spawned is the volume edited by E. R. Geehan, *Jerusalem and Athens: Critical Discussions on the Philosophy and Apologetics of Cornelius Van Til* (1971; the paperback edition of 1974 has an updated bibliography). According to Van Til, the triune God of the Old and New Testaments is the final reference point for all predication. This must be presupposed. To argue from some other starting point, even if the argument concludes by affirming the reality of the biblical God, is to allow fallen humanity to be the reference point and is therefore non-Christian. Van Til's key books include *The Defense of the Faith* (1955; 2d ed. rev. 1963) and *A Christian Theory of Knowledge* (1969). However, much of his writing is found in the form of class syllabi, such as: *Christian Apolo-*

getics (1935, 1939, 1950, 1953); *Christian Theistic Evidences* (1947); *The New Evangelicalism* (1960); and *Christianity in Conflict*, 3 vols. (1962).

C. S. Lewis of Oxford University published a series of popular and semipopular books that have had an enormous apologetic value. *Mere Christianity* (1952) and *Miracles* (1947) were clearly written with apologetic intent, but in many ways his more popular books—*The Screwtape Letters* (1942), *The Chronicles of Narnia* (1950–56), and his science fiction trilogy (*Out of the Silent Planet* [1938], *Perelandra* [1943], and *That Hideous Strength* [1945]) have done more to make Christianity psychologically understandable to a culture dominated by naturalistic humanism than have any of the formal apologetic treatises of the professional theologians.

Anglicans such as Austin Farrer, *Finite and Infinite* (1943), and E. L. Mascall—*He Who Is* (1943), *Christian Theology and Natural Science* (1943), and *The Secularization of Christianity* (1965)—have been strong supporters of Thomism. On the other hand, Alan Richardson's *Christian Apologetics* (1947) and his *History: Sacred and Profane* (1964) support a modified Augustinian methodology.

THE LAST THIRD OF THE TWENTIETH CENTURY

The most important restatement of the Augustinian or presuppositionalist methodology in a publication of clear apologetic intent in the 1970s was Carl F. H. Henry's major work *God, Revelation, and Authority*. The first four volumes were published between 1976 and 1979. A fifth volume appeared in 1982, and the final volume in 1983. This set constitutes the most comprehensive modern presentation of the case for, and the implications of, the Augustinian view of religious knowledge and authority. Henry's first volume *The God Who Speaks and Shows: Preliminary Considerations*, contains an extended discussion of apologetic method (see especially chapters 12–24). It becomes clear that apologetic method and theological method are for Henry the same. To know theology well one must know apologetics well. Theology is, of course, broader than apologetics, but relevant theology cannot be adequately done if apologetics is ignored.

Surely the most widely read popular apologist of the 1970s was Francis Schaeffer of L'Abri, Switzerland. His Christian critique of culture was not only readable in style but it also literally penetrated the evangelical student community, giving them a handle (superficial though it was) on the nature of the problem that they felt but did not understand. *Escape From Reason* (1968) served as the primer and *The God Who Is There* (1968) became the text-manual. Schaeffer is a presuppositionalist apologist, though his method has been modified by the practical experience of evangelistic dialogue with students trained in European universities. His book *How Should We Then Live?* (1976) was accompanied by a series of ten half-hour films that document the loss of biblical norms in modern culture.

Schaeffer's primary emphasis seems to be that the implicit denial of the laws of logic (concerning contradiction and the excluded middle) that has increasingly characterized modern culture since Hegel has made the presentation of the gospel unintelligible to modern people. (The understanding of the gospel clearly depends on our ability to distinguish between truth and error both intellectually and morally.) Our modern inability to make the distinction between truth and error or between right and wrong has led culturally and personally to a severe relativism in which truth has been lost. This "loss of truth" has produced intellectual and moral despair that can be resolved only by the acceptance of a total biblical world view. Key works by Schaeffer include *He Is There and He Is Not Silent* (1972); *Death in the City* (1969); *The Church at the End of the Twentieth Century* (1970); *Genesis in Space and Time* (1972); and *A Christian Manifesto* (1982).

Conservative evidentialists have also published widely in recent years. Popular-style presentations of Christian evidences have come from Josh McDowell of Campus Crusade. His *Evidence That Demands a Verdict* (1972) put compilations of factual evidences supporting biblical authenticity in the hands of thousands of Christian students to strengthen their ability to survive the pressures of hostile university environments.

Clark Pinnock has also produced evidentialist arguments in a philosophically sophisticated context in *Set Forth Your Case* (1967) and *Reason Enough* (1980). Pinnock has always tried to build an evidentialist case from a wide base, but he has become less dogmatic in his more recent works.

Evidentialist John Warwick Montgomery argues that the Resurrection of Jesus is a historical event so persuasively documented that only "a recalcitrant will" can deny its truth. The historical context of this event, moreover, demands that one recognize the validity of the claims of Christ and submit to the full authority of infallible Scripture. His book *The Shape of the Past* (1968) sets forth his foundational argument, and this was restated in *Where Is History Going?* (1969) and in *History and Christianity* (1971). Montgomery's *Suicide of Christian Theology* (1970) is a collection of essays illustrating the use of an empirical theological method rigorously applied to a variety of issues.

Henry Morris's *Many Infallible Proofs* (1974) is a textbook of Christian evidences covering many lines of evidence often overlooked by other writers. Morris is also well known for his many books on science and Christian faith.

The most serious systematic theology to be produced by an evangelical evidentialist in the 1960s was James Oliver Buswell's *Systematic Theology of the Christian Religion*. The first volume (1962) begins with an introduction that sets forth the empirical approach clearly and persuasively. It is instructive to read Buswell's discussion of self-evident truths and presuppositions in light of the positions taken by the Augustinian presuppositionalists. Buswell, of Wheaton College, Wheaton, Illinois, has been a key figure in the contemporary apologetics debate because he not only discusses the questions of method but also develops a full theological statement of evangelical doctrines from a position that many presuppositionalists have claimed is "non-Christian."

Norman Geisler's *Christian Apologetics* (1976) is the most comprehensive apologetics textbook to appear in recent years. Gordon Lewis has also produced a well-balanced assessment of the contemporary situation in his *Testing Christianity's Truth Claims* (1976). These two books together provide the most accessible introduction to the variety of apologetic methods available to conservative evangelical theological students to date. Geisler writes from a Thomistic perspective in many ways, whereas Lewis is more Augustinian, though both writers have a great appreciation for Carnell.

This survey of nineteenth- and twentieth-century apologetic writings is painfully brief. It omits far more than it includes. (The *Subject Guide to Books in Print 1981–1982* lists over one hundred titles under "Apologetics," not counting those in relevant cross references.) A student who masters the works mentioned above, however, will certainly be introduced to the key recent apologetic literature as far as Protestant Orthodoxy is concerned. For those with broader interests, the one indispensible reference work is by Avery Dulles, entitled A *History of Apologetics* (1971). Dulles gives only slight attention to American Evangelicals, but his survey of Protestant and Catholic apologists is otherwise quite comprehensive. The volume provides an excellent working bibliography for a person wanting to begin research in the field.

CONCLUSION

By way of conclusion, I want to make several comments that may also be considered as suggestions for the future direction of apologetic work. First of all, we must not discount the debates about methodology simply because they seem to be sources of division among Christians who are in so many other ways in fundamental agreement. We should, however, seek to alleviate this division by rigorous self-criticism, by in-depth cultural analysis, and by penetrating exegetical analyses of relevant biblical passages.

How do the apostolic preachers in Acts present the gospel? Do they vary their method as they face new audiences? How do the gospel writers try to persuade readers to believe in Christ? Are these methods available to us?

What cultural factors influence the beliefs of those to whom we preach the gospel? How does the Holy Spirit testify of Christ to people immersed in scientific naturalism and humanistic philosophy? Does Christian testimony play a part in the Spirit's work and if so what part? What exactly is the nature of a cultural influence and how does it affect a person's reason or values? What part does a general cultural analysis play in witnessing to individual sinners?

To what extent are we influenced by our own cultural context and by our denominational traditions? Did we come to know Christ according to the methodology by which we do our apologetics? Are there general principles that are true in all valid cases of true conversion? Are all people persuadable, and if so, how? and if not, why not?

Christians need to define (and if it seems appropriate, distinguish between) apologetics and theology—not that the two should be practiced separately, but that they should not be thought of as synonyms. No good theology can ignore philosophical implications, nor can philosophy ignore theological considerations.

Contradictory viewpoints, ideas, values, or systems of thought cannot eternally coexist in reality. Either there is a God or there is not, and if God *is*, then that God is either the biblical God or else some other god. If there is a God, then we either can or cannot know that God *is*. If we can know (and we in fact do know some things; cf. Rom. 1:18–20), then it must be possible to know *how* we can know, and it seems likely that we could also discover *why* not everyone agrees on these matters.

To explain *why* these logical disjunctions and logical implications are (or at least seem to be) necessary is a task of the Christian *philosopher*. To tell us *how* Christian truth should be presented most effectively is the task of the Christian *apologist*. To describe *what* Christian truth is, is certainly the task of the Christian *theologian*. And these three are one.